# Shake Well
# Before Use

## TOM ISAACS

Published by Cure Parkinsons Press
with the Free Thinking Consultancy - www.freethinking.tv

First published 2007
Isbn: 978-0-9557730-0-6 hardback

A catalogue record for this book is available from the British Library

Printed in Great Britain by Biddles Ltd. 24 Rollesby Road,
Hardwick Industrial Estate, King's Lynn, Norfolk PE30 4LS

Text and cover design by Two Associates

# Shake Well Before Use
## TOM ISAACS

# ACKNOWLEDGEMENTS

Special thanks to the following for inspiring me
to keep writing and to 'get it finished':

Lyndsey

Jane Isaacs

Caroline and Chris Boxall

Mark and Rebecca Isaacs

Helen Matthews – "Q"

Jacqueline Burns

David Hutchinson

Nick Spicer

Janet Ward

Tony Hawks

Sally Thomas

Shally Hunt

Matt Morgan

Paul Sussman

Harvey Cammell

James Habershon

Peter Tummons

Like me, the illustrator, Janet Ward has Parkinson's. Her maps and drawings are a testimony to the art that is so often found in Parkinson's. The illustrations are dedicated to the memory of Janet's husband, Gerry Ward, who was such a huge support to an extraordinary lady.

FOR HELP WITH THE BOOK:

Tony Andrews, Clare Balding, Catherine Best, Sharon and Pete Blanchard, Gina and John Bonham, Richard and Judy Catlow, Tiffany and Steven Crosby, Mike and Jenny Dicken, David Eldridge, Suzie Flowers, Michael J Fox, Peter and Mrs Hayward, Lee Holden, KT Hurley, David Jones, Lizzie Kremer, Vanessa Lawrence, Professor Andrew Lees, Mark Lucas, Carolyn Lycett, Fiona MacD-Smith, Candi 'Gula' Mair, Caroline Morrow, Nick Nelson, Sir Richard and Lady Nichols, Theresa Samworth, Becky Warren.

DEDICATION:

IN MEMORY OF DAD

"GEOFF"

# FOREWORD

## BY SIR RICHARD AND LADY SHELAGH NICHOLS

Our first sight of Tom, as we walked towards him on the Millennium Bridge at the end of his epic journey, was of a man in khaki shorts and a white T-shirt with a logo of a little man in red boots, and the word Coastin' emblazoned on it. He had the most enormous grin on his face and was surrounded by people, many of whom had helped him along the way. We had all come to witness the finish of the most amazing challenge for Tom Isaacs. At the time we had no idea that the completion of his walk would bring Tom to the conclusion that he must do all he could to find a cure for Parkinson's, nor that his infectious enthusiasm would affect us, and that we would work so closely with him to that end.

This is a book that, in places, will make you laugh and cry; but above all you will marvel at the courage and determination of a young man who will not be beaten at any cost. If the phrase "mind over matter" ever springs to your lips, think of walking 4,500 miles with Parkinson's and then wonder whether you have chosen the right expression. Not only is this a book about Tom's physical journey, and that in itself is a worthwhile tale, but it is also about his mental journey in coming to terms with Parkinson's. The way he lives his life today will show that he has fought that battle and won.

Those of you reading this who have Parkinson's disease will find that this book is a message of real hope for the future. Tom's undoubted commitment and tenacity in completing the task he set himself is now fully harnessed to finding a cure. The Cure Parkinson's Trust is funding exciting research which will, we have no doubt, eventually lead to a cure for this degenerative neurological condition.

We have pleasure in commending the story of *Coastin'* to young and old alike. We are proud to know Tom Isaacs and hope that many readers will be inspired by the sheer single-minded determination exhibited in this book.

*Sir Richard Nichols is a co-founder and Chairman of the Cure Parkinson's Trust and is an ex-Lord Mayor of London. Lady Shelagh Nichols was the High Sheriff of Hertfordshire in 2004/2005. Both work tirelessly and enthusiastically with the Cure Parkinson's Trust in pursuit of its goal.*

BY PROFESSOR ANDREW LEES,
CONSULTANT NEUROLOGIST TO TOM ISAACS

I have been a neurological coastguard for Tom Isaacs for more than a decade. The waters he is navigating are foreign to me despite years of reading and a long apprenticeship but I have tried to alert him to the presence of treacherous undersea rocks and creeks known to be teeming with crocodiles. What little advice I have felt able to give him has come from hard learned gardening tips, avuncular anecdote and limited erudite evidence. There are things an arm chair cartographer can never quite understand about Parkinson's.

Six years ago Tom was said to be walking around the coast of Britain without a fridge but with a monkey on his back called Parkinson. When he finally re-appeared he told me he had set up an organisation called *The Movers and Shakers* whose mission was to work for a cure for Parkinson's. He also informed me that he had succeeded in walking all the folds of Britain's labyrinthine coastline and that he had raised a considerable amount of money for research.

Tom told me he would write a book about his year out and here it is. *Shake Well Before Use* is much more than a pathography about young onset Parkinson's. It has much to tell us about Britain and its people, the differences between urban and rural living, the beauty and ugliness of our coast, the deep humanity and reptilian insensitivity of its folk, the tragedy of loss and the regional differences in landscape, accent and manners. Its lucid and subtle style brought back memories of Theroux and school-day reminiscences of JB Priestley's *An English Voyage*. There are fine descriptions of the wilder parts of our coastline; Cape Wrath and Conway Mountain proved to him that he was able to find deep fulfilment.

Tom Isaacs' book differs from other travel writing in that it describes the experience of walking round Britain from the perspective of someone with an outwardly visible physical handicap. *Shake Well Before Use* can be considered a field study rather than a laboratory experiment in the enclosed cage of a physician's consulting room but it is no less illuminating. The capriciousness, permanent imbalance and chaos wrought by the malady is present every step of the way but there is never self pity only wry amusement at his own physical shortcomings or an occasional episode of blind panic.

Parkinson's disease is a condition which, when you want to be at your best you are at your worst – the reverse chameleon effect as Tom calls it. The conflicts all patients have between trying to be normal and coming clean are also beautifully described. His knack in bending the vernacular to resonate with the shaking palsy reflected in the title of his book and his ability to see the funny side of his many mishaps sets this book apart from previous personal accounts of living with a chronic neurological disorder.

There are perceptive observations of Parkinsonian euphoria, the kinetic melody of the open road, the spectacular benefit of a cat nap and the pernicious effect of intercurrent illness or stress. The reaction of those strangers he meets on his peregrination also provide us with insight into what it is like to have to deal with an ignorant outside world. Most people Tom encountered were sympathetic and generous but through misunderstanding or callousness there were some responses which must have been hard to deal with.

Coastin' round Britain was a momentous milestone for Tom. During his year out he realised that even the brute of Parkinson could be channelled to enable him to achieve very important personal goals. It led to him becoming a talisman and a spokesman and his heroic achievement proved to the world that far from being a death sentence Parkinson's disease can be beaten by the human spirit. When Tom approached a road block or difficult stretch he frequently found himself humming *Fog on the Tyne*. As I followed in his footsteps through his book I found myself singing out loud *Five Hundred Miles* by The Proclaimers. *Shake Well Before Use* has provided me with a new pair of eyes to scan the horizon as I help to guide Tom's boat safely into port. I wish it the success and wide readership it unquestionably deserves.

*Prof Andrew Lees, M.D., FRCP (U.K.) is a Director of the Reta Lila Weston Institute of Neurological Studies at the University College London, and Professor of Neurology at the National Hospital for Neurology and Neurosurgery, Queen Square, London. He is a former President of the Movement Disorder Society and is a member of the Cure Parkinson's Trust's Scientific Advisory Team.*

# Contents

# PROLOGUE

## 4ᵀᴴ NOVEMBER 1996

"I shouldn't be here," I thought to myself. Standing at the threshold of the neurology department waiting room, I felt a sudden sense of dread about crossing an invisible line. The area was open-plan and there was no particular moment when I was "in" or "out" of the room; but I had stopped at a point where my presence was not yet felt by those seated within it. I scanned the scene. The bright colours of the furniture and wall posters did nothing to lift a thick cloud of sadness, which hung over the people gathered there. I felt strangely claustrophobic; hemmed in by the immensity of the room and a strong sense of foreboding. I shook it off. It was nothing. I always felt like this in hospitals. It amazed me how buildings with such high ceilings and such space could be so airless. The Hammersmith Hospital was no exception.

I took a deep breath and moved forward. I realised that, at 27 years old, I was the youngest person there by a good forty years. I made for a remote outpost of the room, trying to put as much distance as I could between me and "them", not just in the physical sense, but also in my head. It was no use. Each time one of the patients was called into a consulting room, everyone, including me, looked up to see the spectacle. All the patients had their own set of difficulties in making the 25-yard journey. The effort was immense for all, except those in wheelchairs. Some shook so badly the whole room seemed to reverberate. Others were stuck rigid and unable to move at all; they seemed so brittle that they might snap in two at any moment. Worst of all, though, were those at the other extreme: those who couldn't stop moving. Their perpetual limb convulsions and contorted writhing was shockingly compelling. I found myself staring. Over the years, whatever neurological demons had been preying on these people had taken their toll. It was as if they had looked through odd-shaped mirrors at a fairground and assumed the same distorted shapes as their reflections. The room was heavy with melancholy born out of resignation to a life less wonderful than it once was. It dawned on me that no one really wanted to be there. It was a cheerless pilgrimage; a biannual expedition to measure the extent of symptom degeneration. The mood was contagious. I felt bleak. My furtive glances around the room had not been a constructive use of time. I picked up a book from the table in front of me. I read the front cover; *My Little Pig*. This would be an infinitely better use of my time. I escaped to a world of little red pigs and talking tractors for a while. Better that, I thought, than to worry about the likelihood of my having developed an illness that had anything to do with the people in this room.

I was called in to the consulting room, and underwent several co-ordination tests. I felt I must have passed them all with flying colours. Recently, the tremors in my right hand which had so been plaguing me had not been nearly so bad. Ever since I had been taking the pink pills that Dr Evans (a consultant neurologist) had given me, there had been no problem. Whatever it was, I was cured of it now. But when I had gone back to see Dr Evans to tell him the good news, he had not looked pleased for me at all. Instead, he had referred me on to see "an expert in this particular field".

"Did Dr Evans tell you what these pills were?" asked my new consultant.

"No," I replied, somewhat concerned at his intonation. It sounded to me as though he rather wished Dr Evans had told me what the pills were.

Since finishing *My Little Pig*, my mood had been far more upbeat. Clearly, I was in a very different boat to all the other people in the waiting room. After all, no one else in the waiting room could have sailed through those co-ordination tests with the ease that I had. Whatever the diagnosis was, I could cope with it. It couldn't be all that bad, could it?

"You have something which falls within the parameters of Parkinson's disease," my consultant said.

The words stabbed deep; right to my core, filling me instantly with a silent, cold dread. My worst fears had become reality. I was aware that he was still talking, but I was not hearing him. At that moment, my world was no bigger than myself. Nothing else outside would penetrate it for the time being. It was a defence mechanism; a suit of armour protecting me until I had analysed what had just been said. My mind raced: "Did he say Parkinson's disease? Yes he did. He said that I was suffering something that fell within the parameters of Parkinson's disease. Parkinson's disease. That means I've got Parkinson's disease. I've got Parkinson's disease."

I did not for a second question the diagnosis. Even though my symptoms were negligible, somewhere deep within me I had sensed this was something serious.

"Parkinson's disease. I wonder what that is?"

I tuned back in to what the consultant was saying. "You can live a very long time with Parkinson's."

I retreated again to my world. OK. So I was not going to die. This was good.

It was strange how I could be so matter-of-fact about this particular issue. I did not, after all, know that Parkinson's was not terminal.

"So what would be the repercussions of having Parkinson's?" I wondered. I attempted to listen to what the consultant was saying, but it was no good. The word "Parkinson's" reverberated over and over again in my head, almost like Big Ben's hourly chime; and it was filling me with a cold stark dread of what the future held. Now he was spewing out words that meant nothing to me anyway: "basal ganglia", "substantia nigra", and then he went on to inform me that it was actually my "cogwheel rigidity" which really confirmed the diagnosis. "Damn the cogwheel rigidity," I thought.

I nodded my head, pretending that I had been listening and understood. The whole thing seemed absurd. Here was I, feeling as well as I ever had, being told that I was showing serious signs of cogwheel rigidity. What was wrong with having cogwheel rigidity? It had to be better than having a floppy cogwheel. I wondered sadly whether a canister of WD40 might do the trick – it had certainly helped with all the rigid cogwheels I had previously encountered.

"Your Parkinson's is of the shaky variety. If you are going to contract Parkinson's, it is better to have the shaky variety, rather than the more rigid type."

I felt annoyed now. Annoyed and confused. If I did not have the rigid type, why was my cogwheel showing signs of rigidity? I couldn't face finding out.

"It is better to have no bloody type at all," I blurted out, instantly regretting it.

"This I am afraid is true." The consultant's response was kindly put and we looked at each other. There was true compassion in his eyes, which provided me with a measure of the severity of the situation. His look gave me the answer. This was bad. Having set up another appointment in a few weeks, I got up to leave. I held out my arm to the consultant and, for a moment, my hand hovered motionless in mid-air, before it started to twitch randomly, as if wanting to confirm the diagnosis on its own. The consultant and I stared at the quivering hand for a second, before he made a grab for it in an attempt to minimise any distress it might be causing me.

I shook the consultant's hand warmly as if to say, "Thank you for diagnosing me with Parkinson's disease." I have no idea why I felt so grateful. I suppose I also wanted him to think that I was OK; that he need not feel bad about giving me the news. It must have been a tough thing to do. Cheerfully

I left the room, and once out of sight of the consultant, I felt my shoulders slump. Waiting outside the room was a man in a wheelchair. He was one of the more badly affected people from the main waiting room. He had absolutely no control over his body and it twisted and skewed with no pattern or uniformity. His facial expression was distorted and bordered on the grotesque. He looked thin, gaunt, frightening. His tongue was out of his mouth and stretched to its limit. It writhed about agonisingly like an injured snake. A trail of saliva left the corner of his mouth and dribbled onto the sleeve of his jumper. There seemed to be little dignity left in his life. The body in which he resided had been sufficiently warped and contorted to render him totally reliant on others for every function.

How long would it be before I too would be like this? Decades? Years? Months? It was a terrifying thought. Earlier I had felt so very different towards all the other patients in the waiting room. But half an hour had become forty years. I looked on this small collection of people now with different eyes and felt ashamed of my earlier lack of understanding of their plight. Mentally I had spurned them; dismissed them as strangers. Now I felt as if I knew them. After all, I was one of them now. I had no concept of my state of shock when I left the hospital and I genuinely thought I was in control when I rang my parents. They both answered the phone together.

"They say I've got Parkinson's disease," I told them.

There was a pause and I imagined them both trying to process the information in silent horror. I tried to think up something a bit less dramatic to say in an attempt to dampen the effect of the news.

"It's OK, I've got the shaky variety, which is better than the rigid strand of the condition." I was trying to seem both knowledgeable and in control. I was neither, and my parents knew it.

"So what do we do next?" It was a typically stoical response from Mum. By using the word "we" she was immediately showing me I was not alone and the rest of the question was already searching for a resolution to the problem.

I did not have an answer to the question. What was next? I had not asked the consultant, and if he had told me, I hadn't heard. In fact, all I had really wanted to do while I was in his room was to get out of it. So I resorted to my last defence: "Start working in a cocktail bar, I suppose."

Dad laughed. "Stupid boy," he said, "I don't think you'll have to resort to shaking cocktails just yet." I was pleased he got my feeble joke, but there was something in his laugh that was unnatural. Both my parents were putting on a brave face for me. They wanted to come up to London to take me out for a meal, but I would not let them. I needed time and space alone to work this one through for myself.

I walked a lot of the way home; forcing myself to look on the bright side; trying to convince myself that at least "Parkinson's" sounded like a good British sort of illness. It was not after all an Alzheimer's, a Crohn's or a Creutzfeldt–Jakob. It did not sound too painful either, unlike other possibles such as multiple sclerosis, typhoid, or deep vein thrombosis with an acute pulmonary embolism. At least I had a disease that sounded palatable.

But I was clutching at straws; hoping that the symptoms of my condition were as innocuous as its name. The only thing that felt positive on that day was that I did not have something from which I was going to die. Also, Parkinson's, or PD as it was referred to, seemed to be an illness which a lot of people had and it was therefore likely to be well treated. These were just streaks of grey in the darkness that lay ahead.

At the time, I was living in a basement flat in Pimlico which my friend and fellow chartered surveyor Davey Ads (David Adams) owned and also occupied. It was here I sat in quiet contemplation, not really knowing what to do with myself. The day had washed my spirit clean of any kind of emotion. I felt detached; as if I was standing back and analysing my own life dispassionately. It was not a very constructive thing to do at that precise moment, but then I had little grasp of anything much that day. My trance-like actions since the diagnosis seemed to be pre-ordained by some higher authority. I did not make any conscious decisions. I just operated on autopilot. I could make no sense of it. I had not even started my life yet. I had not found my niche or my purpose. So far, all I had accumulated was a sense of fun, and a sound knowledge of rental values of offices in the West End of London. If my useful life was, to all intents and purposes, now over, how could I underpin the rest of my days based on the pride of knowing that air-conditioned offices in Wigmore Street could be rented for as little as £25 per square foot? Granted, my skills as a chartered surveyor extended further than this, but would I ever get to use them as my friends and colleagues would? And while they would all progress to untold success and fortune; while they all got married and started families; I would be forever betrothed to a degenerative neurological disorder and find myself on a fast track to obsolescence. I felt suddenly suffocated by my demons. Parkinson's was the stuff of nightmares, except that when I woke up from this strange and distant reverie, the reality of my situation would be even worse. Everything I had done to date suddenly seemed to be worthless. It all counted for nothing.

Yesterday I had potential. Today everything felt useless.

Yesterday I had the best of my life ahead of me. Today that prospect seemed to have gone.

I went to the kitchen and opened the door of the fridge in the hope that something within it would fill the gaping void in my stomach. I realised as I scanned the contents that I was not hungry. It had been a mistake. The gaping void that I felt in the pit of my stomach was more a reflection of my feelings about my future. Instead, I chose a carton of grapefruit juice. My hand twitched into life and moved towards the carton. As I lifted the container it wobbled slightly in my hand, a further confirmation of my diagnosis. There seemed to be constant reminders everywhere. I looked at the one-litre container. I would not have been surprised to see the words "You have Parkinson's" on it. Four words on the carton of grapefruit juice seemed to be vying for my attention: "Shake well before use". The words seemed to trigger something within me; making me want to withdraw to a time and place where such a phrase was not steeped in irony. I didn't want to be associated with this word "shake". Shaking had nothing to do with me or my life. I wanted to ignore it; shut it out. I wanted it to be yesterday again.

The clatter of something or someone falling down the steps outside jolted me into the present. I went to the door to investigate.

I found him in a crumpled, tangled heap; all briefcase, plastic bag and suit.

"Ads?" I said, concerned.

"Hello," he gurgled. At least somebody has had a good day, I thought.

After a while, he gathered himself up and bundled through the front door as if he was two people trying to get through at the same time.

"I've had a…bsholutely… terrible time." His eyes moved slowly as if he was trying to familiarise himself with his own flat. He made a lunge for his post, which was sitting on the dining table, and started inspecting the letter fronts, searching for clues to who had sent them. Realising that he was unable to focus, he pushed them away in disgust.

"I should have been home hours ago." His words were fumbled and slurred. "But my glarsh wouldn't empty. Shumbuddy kept filling it up. I had to go to the Dozer Street Wine Bar and then getta taxshi home."

Use of the words "Dover Street Wine Bar" was a measure of Davey Ads' level of inebriation. He only went to the "DSWB" when he was on a real bender. He opened up his plastic bag and pulled out a half-eaten doner kebab. Another sign. He was not going to feel good in the morning. But then, nor would I. As Davey Ads munched contentedly on his supper, he caught me reflecting on my day, and something clicked in his mind. "How wosh your trip to th'ospital?" he asked.

"Not great."

"Do they know what it is?"

"Yes. It's Parkinson's disease."

There was a silence while my words sank in. The combination of alcohol and shock gave him a look of total befuddlement. In fact, so ludicrous was his expression, as he battled to get a grip on himself, that he saw me smirk. Davey Ads then did something that I really was not expecting. He laughed. It was one of his deep gurgling guffaws. The absurdity of the situation set me off laughing too. I doubted whether anyone had been laughed at before, having imparted such news. The hysterics subsided. He staggered over towards me and gave me a drunken hug, overwhelming my senses with the stench of kebab and putrid toxins accumulated from his night out.

It is difficult to explain how anyone could laugh at my diagnosis and for it to be the right thing to do. Of course, it was easier to deal with in the knowledge that he was off his trolley, but his cackling had cheered me up. It had released me from a detached, almost zombie-like state. It was typical of Davey Ads to manage to cheer me up no matter what the circumstances. This had been by far his biggest test.

Lying in bed that night, I had one more positive thought to cling to. Whatever happened, I knew my family and friends would not fail me. I would not have to go through this alone. Despite his response this evening, I knew that Davey Ads would be devastated by my diagnosis. It was better that he didn't show it. I needed the people around me to ignore Parkinson's. Maybe then, I could do the same. I made a conscious decision that for the time being, I would close it out of my mind. I would tell a few people who ought to know, but other than that, I would carry on. For the time being, at least, I would hide behind a mental barricade where I could continue pretending I was indestructible. But the state of mind was a brittle one and I wondered how long it would take for it to be snapped in two. I had no idea what lay ahead...

FROM SYDNEY TO WHY ME?
DECEMBER 1996

CHAPTER 1

Harvey Cammell is my oldest friend. As he was half camel, half human, I called him "Mule". I have other extremely close friends, but Mule is the one who has been there all the time; the one who has seen the whole thing unfurl. At the end of 1996, we went to Australia on a tightly packed, three-week lads' extravaganza. The time off work had assumed another, perhaps more important role than merely a "holiday". I used the prospect of space away from it all as a dumping ground for any anxieties I was having about my diagnosis.

"I'll think about that in Australia," I kept saying to myself. I could put off any meaningful decisions about my life until then. I would talk it through with Mule... at some stage.

I knew Sydney at New Year would be difficult to beat. There is an intense feel-good factor about the place. It is bright and warm. Everyone is on holiday. Happiness prevails. After qualifying as a chartered surveyor three years before I had lived in Australia for about nine months and I was keen to show my old friend why I raved about the place so much.

Mule is tall, swarthy, slightly aloof, well built and sickeningly charming; perhaps even debonair. He also has the capacity to make people laugh – not so much uproarious, pit of the stomach laughter; just quietly, constantly entertaining people so that they come away feeling happy that they have met him. As a team, Mule and I were sustaining our incredible run of luck with members of the opposite sex. There was a lot of talk back home about it. We had acquired a bit of a reputation and we were not happy about it. Through the years, we had always been a most unlikely double act – Mule at 6 foot 5 inches and me at 5 foot 7 – but it had worked wonders. When trying to pick up girls, we had experienced an extraordinary success rate. We dovetailed our quick-fire gags and self-deprecating humour superbly and as a team our record was unblemished. Through 15 years of working together "picking up" we had managed to attract the interest and attention of precisely zero girls.

In recent months, though, matters had got even worse. Now, we were failing to attract girls even on our own. It was known as being "in a Gobi". I blame him for our lack of success. He had been responsible for the first in a long list of shambolic encounters with girls.

Julie Waugh was the name of my first girlfriend. She was a stunner. It had been my intention to "act cool" in her company, but my 12-year-old heart raced every time I was with her. It was difficult to be "cool" however, when, on our first date, we were kicked out of the cinema for not being 14, or even looking it. On our second date, Julie had brought her best friend, Sam, and I took Mule. He tried a little too hard in his attempts to make an impression.

"Where's all the sex and glory then?" were his first words. The girls were not impressed and the double date never really recovered. Mule never saw Julie's best friend again and Julie dumped me two weeks later, leaving my poor heart shattered.

I blamed him, and still do.

Ever since then, the extent of our ineptitude as a pulling double-act had defied all reasonable bounds of probability. A new approach was needed and, after years of planning, a brilliant, but simple new girl-pulling strategy would be unveiled and tested in Australia – we would pretend not to know each other. Experience had shown us that there had to be infinitely more chance of finding an oasis in our bewildered "Gobi" wanderings by avoiding teamwork at all costs.

I have known Mule since I was four. On that first day at school in 1972, I had been told I would be starting with two others: a Simon Fox and a Harvey Cammell. I was very excited to be starting with two different animals. I had wondered what a "Harvey camel" would look like, and was disappointed to find that it was just a tall, fuzzy-haired boy. I had been expecting something else entirely. I didn't know that this "Cammell" was going to play such a large part in my life and that a "Fox," albeit a different one, called "Michael J.", would too.

The first time I really encountered Mule, however, was in the heat of schoolboy battle. He was ruthless. Taking no account of the fact that I was smaller and five days younger than him, he ripped my defences apart. I was actually concerned that he might even inflict irreparable damage on me.

But he made a schoolboy error. On the very point of a resounding triumph, he disappeared to the toilet when within three moves of victory and a place in round two of the school's under-seven chess tournament. During this time, I made an enlightening discovery. The big pieces at the back could move in all different directions and not just forwards. Mrs Williams, the teacher, told me. By the time Mule returned, my queen had magically leapt over everything and had his knight in checkmate. Neither of us really had a clue how to play chess, but I was pretty certain Mule couldn't cope without his "horsey". He knew he was finished. We shook hands. We were little gentlemen at York House School.

On the plane over to Australia, Mule accused me of cheating, 22 years after the event. I forced a look of astonishment onto my face and retaliated. "You just bottled it, Cammell. You didn't have the killer instinct."

From previous travelling experiences, I had quite a few friends in Australia and as a result, as soon as we landed at Sydney Airport, we were able to launch into the holiday immediately. We hit the ground running, and as the new boys in town it was not long before we were greatly enjoying more attention than usual, and certainly more than we deserved.

We had been invited on a "party boat" which pottered around Sydney harbour on New Year's Eve before jostling for position to watch the fireworks at midnight. Mule and I had performed a cursory inspection of the dance floor below deck, but were now sitting out on the top deck, which was open to the elements, and were watching as people filed on board.

"Have you noticed there seem to be an awful lot of single girls boarding this boat?" I remarked.

"Are there? I hadn't noticed," responded Harvey in a highly pitched squeak. The competition was on again. It was an extension of the under-seven chess match. Who would get out of the Gobi first?

Mule stood up, seemed to limber up for a second, pretending he was some great Italian gigolo, and pulled a pair of huge 1970s mirrored sunglasses out of his top pocket. He looked over to me, shrugged as if to say, "I can't help it, I'm just a red-blooded male," and swaggered off towards a group of blonde bombshells. His comic timing was always good. Having taken three paces, he stopped, removed his glasses, turned through ninety degrees and went to join a group of lads who were talking about rugby.

I didn't see him for a couple of hours after that, by which time I had started chatting to a pretty Australian girl called Claire. I was anxious to show my friend that while he had been talking sport, I had been making progress out of the desert. I found him on the dance floor, now wearing his shades again and putting on the gigolo act. Two girls were draped all over him and laughing hysterically at something he had just said, and another was trying to lasso him with a pink feather boa.

Checkmate.

At midnight, the boat came to a standstill and we stood on deck to watch the most spectacular fireworks display I had ever seen. They cracked and sparkled up above and lit up the opera house, harbour bridge and the magnificent Sydney skyline. I suddenly felt the urge to sing out loud, and fuelled by booze and the excitement of the occasion I began bellowing out Puccini's "Nessun Dorma" in what I considered to be a voice so like Luciano Pavarotti as to be uncanny. People started joining in. They were laughing. I looked around me. Happy times. Mule was in his pink feather boa. I was in my element. Nobody knew I had Parkinson's. Even I had forgotten. Every now and then, I popped a few pills into my mouth, completely disregarding doctor's orders. "Live for the moment," I told myself as another few were washed down with a can of Toohey's Red beer. The pills were certainly doing their job tonight and I felt completely normal; blissfully free of both mental and physical burdens that had been haunting me recently.

The party went on at someone's house. Some of the revellers went elsewhere. Claire was one of them, but I was having too good a time to worry about that. Mule and I found ourselves among people who were mostly strangers, in a living room which was decked out like an old 1970s dance floor. The Bee Gees were thumping out from a futuristic-looking CD player. We ventured further into the room to find a full-height window, which seemed to hang over Sydney harbour looking south. The view was spectacular, and despite an urge to perform Travolta-like moves on the dance floor, all I did was stand and gape. The concave angles of the opera house and the huge arch of the harbour bridge were illuminated dramatically against the night sky. It was fantastic to be here in Sydney again feeling good, feeling like my old self, despite my health concerns, which had formed the backdrop of everything recently.

I focused in on the foreground and the reflection of the party in the window. I felt a wave of euphoria course through me. Perhaps there really was no need to worry. I felt confident, relaxed and in complete control – the combination of which I had not felt for some time. As if in confirmation of these thoughts, a pretty blonde girl sidled up to me and took my hand.

"Come on. Dance!" she teased.

I loved this place. I always felt better here. It was partly the weather, partly the culture, partly the quality of life, but mostly it was the only place I knew where pretty blonde girls asked you to dance.

Ever since winning a packet of Tooty Frooties in a dance contest for the most outrageous routine at the age of nine, I had felt comfortable on a dance floor. Parkinson's had already begun to take that away from me, but not tonight. I closed my eyes and let the music take control of my movements. It felt fantastic. When I opened my eyes again the blonde girl had moved in closer to me so that we were nearly touching. She was smiling at me and I began to smile back.

My flirting was dramatically interrupted by a loud crash from behind me. I turned to find Mule and some Ozzy Sheila collapsed under their own weight while trying to limbo under a feather boa. I wanted this party to last forever.

∗ ∗ ∗

I grinned with satisfaction as I walked back over the harbour bridge from north Sydney at 10 a.m. the next morning. Jauntily, I slung off my jacket, put a finger through the loop and draped it over my shoulder. The jacket rattled as I did so; a reminder of the small pot of pink pills which had allowed me to enjoy the previous night so much. I reached inside the pocket and when I pulled out the pills I found that there was also a piece of paper in my hand. It was a phone number and the name Claire. I had forgotten about her. I laughed out loud before putting the number in my wallet for safe keeping. I then inspected the bottle of pink pills: "One to be taken three times a daily", the label read. The prescription had been ignored completely but there had not been any adverse effects so far. Still perhaps I ought to stop taking them now.

The top three buttons of my shirt were open. The cool breeze which brushed past me on the exposed expanse of bridge was invigorating. It was one of those pre-hangover moments when every sensation you experience seems to be exaggerated tenfold. Today, my emotional barometer was firmly fixed in the "fantastic" position. I swaggered towards Circular Quay under the absurd misapprehension that every girl I passed was checking me out. I would have been thoroughly obnoxious company for anyone that morning. On my own though, I was harmless, and it just felt great to be experiencing self-belief again after recent events.

Last night my ego had been given a turbo boost. Mule and I had cleaned up. We were party gods. We had started the holiday teetering on the brink of the Gobi desert's flaming cliffs of singledom, but in Sydney, Australia, on New Year's Eve, the rains had finally come. By the end of the evening Mule and I had been offered so many passes out of the desert it was almost embarrassing. I wondered, briefly, where Mule was. I smiled at the mental image of him spread-eagled on the floor under the feather boa.

As I waited at the bus stop in George Street, my thoughts turned to my diagnosis again and what the future held. I felt surprisingly relaxed about it. If last night was anything to go by, I had "no worries". I could handle it. Everything was as it had always been. The only difference was some pink pills. And as I climbed onto the bus I thought it did seem as simple as that. I could "just take the pills" and everything would be fine.

Unlike some of the buses in Sydney, the one I caught towards Glebe Point Road was not "Express", nor was it air-conditioned. Once inside, the stale dehydrating air changed my mood almost instantly. There were no seats. I suddenly felt tired. I had only had a couple of hours' sleep and the effort of remaining standing for the 15-minute journey suddenly seemed enormous. It was too hot. A bead of sweat dripped from my head as I clung on to the overhead rail. Ten minutes later, the hand holding the rail felt uncomfortable, so I replaced it with the other. As I did so the hand no longer supporting me twitched quite violently. It waved at me in mid-air, defiantly, and I thrust it deep into my trouser pocket as if it were an embarrassing child's toy. The airlessness of the bus became rather oppressive. The hand in my pocket started to pulsate again, only more furiously this time so that my whole arm started gyrating. Conscious that I might look like a pervert, I brought the hand up to the rail again so that I was now clinging on, using both hands.

It was no use. My body was in freefall. I sensed that people were beginning to become aware of the strange chap who, despite the relative stability of the bus, seemed to have lost control of his right arm. This had never happened before, but then I had never taken so many drugs in such a short space of time. It appeared I was now suffering the consequences. I released hold of the rail to wipe the sweat from my head. In doing so, my hand flapped almost playfully; as if it was not a part of me. Of its own accord my right hand was waving at everyone on the bus. All eyes were now homing in on my developing situation. Try as I might to hide the offending body part from view, it kept letting me down. People were wondering why I was waving at them. This was a nightmarish new world, a place where I had no control.

I felt like a seaside attraction – a sort of X-rated glove puppet show – Punch and Judy stripped nude on a bus. Everyone looked on solemnly. My body had finally been overtaken by the monstrous secret that had germinated unknown, even to me, for many years. Now it revealed itself in its rawest and most conspicuous guise. My inner self lay exposed; laid bare in front of strangers.

I needed more drugs. There was nowhere to hide. The trembling was getting worse still …

I received a tap on my shoulder. "Do you want my seat?" asked the elderly lady. She was at least 70. There was a look of pity in her eyes.

"No thank you," I replied with an air of surprise and as if the strange physical manifestations of my condition were the most natural thing in the world. The lady sat down again, and a few seconds later the bus stopped. I got off. I knew that it wasn't my stop. I just had to get off the bus.

Beyond the words "Do you want my seat?" was a world which I knew nothing about; a world which I wanted to know nothing about. My life seemed to have pivoted on an old lady's simple and kind question.

Lying in the bath 20 minutes later, I recognised this fact. My life had changed irretrievably. Living in denial was no longer feasible with the conspicuousness of physical symptoms I had just displayed. I was not ready for this. I had not yet nearly come to terms with the diagnosis. This lesson had been too sharp; the fall too precipitous. In an hour I had experienced complete metamorphosis. I was 27 years old and someone had pressed the fast-forward button on my life.

Two words entered my head: "why" and "me". They were only words; individually so small and innocuous. But for the first time in my life, the words seemed dangerously close together. I did not want the words to meet today, so I dismissed them from my head. That was for another day.

*"I am still determined to be cheerful and happy,*
*in whatever situation I may be;*
*for I have also learned from experience*
*that the greater part of our happiness*
*or misery depends upon our dispositions,*
*and not upon our circumstances."*
MARTHA WASHINGTON 1731-1802

CHAPTER 2

The sun was streaming through a gap in the curtains, and instinctively my arm came up to shield my eyes. My hand felt warm on my forehead, and yet it was inanimate; a dead weight. It was as if it did not belong to me at all. The "night shakes" were becoming more frequent, two and a half years after diagnosis. The only way to stop them was to lie on my right hand, which was worse affected than my left. As waking consciousness and blood circulation restored ownership of the numb hand to me, I awaited the inevitable visit of something that threatened to take control not just of my hand but of the whole of me. Every day now I was fighting a battle against Mr Parkinson for custody of my body.

But this morning I did feel different. Something had changed and I couldn't decide what it was. I suspected it was the latest in a long line of evil tricks Parkinson's was going to throw at me. I analysed the symptoms. They were strange, to say the least. It couldn't be dementia; that only affected a small proportion of people with Parkinson's and it was far too soon for that to be a possibility. No, it looked as if I would just have to accept that, this morning, I had woken up feeling fantastic. There did not seem to be any rhyme or reason to it, but at that moment I felt cleansed of disease and cleansed of toxic medication. It was a rare thing now for brain and body to communicate without outside interference, but when they did it felt wonderful. On the emotional side, this euphoria was a major departure from the script in the Parkinson's guidebook. After shock, horror, anger and denial was supposed to come isolation, not jubilation. But surely my improved mental state was just a reaction to the lack of PD symptoms I was experiencing.

Neither would last long. Soon he would come – this dark, malevolent force sent daily to kidnap my body. The labels on my medication spelt out the exact requirements for temporary recovery of my hijacked self. I didn't need to read them any more. I knew what they said. They were reminders from Mr Parkinson; his ransom note: "Take the pills or your body gets it."

I flexed my fingers as if I was stretching them prior to playing a musical instrument. Usually, the movement would have been sufficient for me to have the confidence to play a one-fingered, stilted version of "Chopsticks" on the tinny synthesizer someone had once given me. But this morning, I would have felt comfortable sitting at a grand piano with my hands flowing over the ivories; my body intuitively accentuating the movement of my hands and at the same time conveying all the subtle changes in the mood of the music I was playing. And if anyone had been watching, they would not have known I had Parkinson's. Instead, they would have been completely beguiled by my passionate rendition of "Chopsticks".

The "Chopsticks" tune in my head was abruptly replaced by a noise more akin to Motorhead. The pneumatic drills on the Vauxhall Bridge Road had started up again and seemed to make my London flat shudder. I realised it was the drilling that had woken me up in the first place. Slowly, I started to put together the pieces of last night's dream, in which I had been watching two men drilling the road outside:

"'Ere Barry, this drill's not working."

"None of 'em work Jim. Power cut."

I stood at the side of the road and watched as Barry and Jim disappeared to have a cup of tea, leaving their tools behind them. I clambered in to the cordoned-off area and quietly looked at one of the drills. I picked it up and positioned the drill bit in the road where I had seen them digging. As I held the device it began to resonate in unison with the tremor in my hands. The action made a crack in the tarmac, the road splintered and then, with no time seeming to pass at all, I found myself in a cavernous hole. I looked at my hands. They were still shaking, but for once it did not seem to matter.

"Do you want a job?" asked the foreman.

I couldn't remember much more of the dream. Only that everything else in it was positive and that I had ended up in Africa deriving immense satisfaction from boring holes for water in drought-affected areas with no electricity. I smiled to myself. What an epic dream. And it had instigated a new mind-set. The idea that I could make something positive out of what had so far been an all-consuming negative in my life had to be worthy of further analysis. I tried to think of other more likely uses for my shaking in the commercial world. There did not seem to be many, so I ruminated further on drilling. Maybe I could go to the Middle East and drill for oil, earn millions, become the "Sheikh of Shakes".

I realised that it was in fact the mental state in which I had awoken this morning that was different. Earlier I had confused my feeling fantastic with a reaction to a better-than-normal physical state. But having remembered the dream, I realised the big mistake I had been making. Prior to this morning, my mood had been dictated by the state of my Parkinson's at any given time. It had not dawned on me until now to turn this around and attempt to influence my state of health through a positive mental attitude.

I had started to shake a little now and I stared at the array of brightly coloured pills on my bedside table. There was an assortment of them these days: Entacapone, Madopar, Mirapexin, Amantadine and Zelapar. The list sounded to me a bit like a dessert menu in an Italian restaurant. I now took twenty pills a day. If I took my morning dose, the shaking would stop in forty minutes. But then the purity of this moment would be gone. I decided to ignore them for the time being. I would get up and see what happened. I just wanted to be the "old me" for a while, not a pharmaceutically engineered version. Besides, I wanted to test my theory: to see if the sunny disposition with which I had woken up could continue, despite my fast-approaching entry to the Kingdom of Shakes. The best description of Parkinson's I have heard was thought up by friend and neuroscientist Mike Hurley. He said the best way to explain the condition is to imagine that you are a car. Your brain is the engine and your arms and legs are the wheels. Normally you drive the car using the relatively simple controls (pedals and steering wheel), and using these you are able to get from A to B. But in Parkinson's disease it is as if the accelerator cable has snapped. The engine is still running and everything else works, but the driver cannot make the car move. This would be a severe case. For most people with Parkinson's, movement is possible, but it is very slow and can be similar to having poor clutch control and bunny-hopping forward in a series of jerky movements. Although the patient is trying to move, he or she finds it hard to get started. And once someone with Parkinson's does get started it can actually be equally difficult to stop.

Of course, with a car, you can go to the local mechanic to get things fixed. With Parkinson's you nip to the chemist to get your medication.

Unfortunately the medication only provides a temporary fix to the problems. Living with Parkinson's becomes a never-ending battle to maintain your own personal accelerator cable and brake pads. In medical terms Parkinson's is caused by a deficit of dopamine, which is a chemical messenger in the brain that controls movement. The gold-standard treatment for the condition is replacement of the dopamine with l-dopa. But this has side effects after continued use. It was time to get up and see whether I could cope with any of the day's activities without pills. For the next twenty minutes, I battled with contact lenses and razor blades. Bathrooms, kitchens - and auction rooms - are places of grave danger for people with pronounced tremor. Once I had reduced the bathroom to a place that looked as if it had witnessed the Texas Chainsaw Massacre, I decided that I really ought to take some medication. Yet despite the fact that I had both skinned myself alive and poked both eyes until they were swollen and bloodshot, I still felt chirpy. Before Parkinson's I had always been quite outgoing, but since being diagnosed, I had bottled everything up. In the same way that the symptoms of the illness crept menacingly onward, a less tangible process had been quietly throttling my previously cheerful demeanour without my even noticing.

I thought about the first year after diagnosis. That had been the worst. Ever since the kind lady offered me a seat on the bus in Sydney, my perception of the future had been grim. It was all being taken away from me. I was still ambitious, wanted to go on nice holidays, wanted to be in control. I was in my late twenties with an old person's disease. From a world of sport, parties and exotic travel, I was leapfrogging to infirmity, long TV sessions and disabled car badges. During this time there was nothing specific that was affecting my day-to-day life. It was more the cumulative effect of my changing perception of what I thought my body could achieve. The truth was that I was now trapped inside a body that was now ageing at an alarming rate and was often incapable of responding to the demands put on it. Neither body nor mind would adapt to the other's capabilities. In my darkest moments, I had been convinced that any hopes for love, marriage and everlasting happiness were gone forever. Who would want someone with a degenerative neurological problem that made them tremble uncontrollably? In those early days of Parkinson's, I had tended to do this. In my head, I had made out that it was worse than it actually was. I had been living in the tragedy of my perceived future. My self-confidence took a dive. Everyone else's life around me seemed solid, like granite. Mine had suddenly seemed fragile, like crumbly sandstone. But I was determined that the dream I'd just woken from would be a turning point for me. I had to believe that I could make something positive out of the Sheikh of Shakes. Otherwise what else was there?

Having taken a dose of pills, I knew my shakes would get worse first, before they disappeared completely. I went to the kitchen and fumbled with a new carton of juice. The lid was a bit fiddly, and by the time I managed to get it off, most of its contents were on the floor. Having got to that point, however, I was determined to fill my glass. It was then that I noticed those four words on the carton again: "Shake well before use".

Amidst the kitchen devastation, I laughed. I laughed not because the instruction was a superfluous requirement in my case, but because at last I felt able to laugh. On the day of diagnosis, my reaction to these four words had been very different. When I shook as much as I was now, there was only one thing I could do that was constructive. I marched back into the bathroom, delivered some toothpaste to my brush and thrust it into my mouth. The extra high-frequency resonance of my hand gave a thorough clean of both gums and teeth of which my dentist would have been proud.

Over the course of the next few months, I began to see a way forward and a new life strategy unveiled itself to me. Once again it was time to peel back some of the protective layers; only this time I would do it on my own terms. Storing things up for too long had never been my thing anyway. There had been a moment many years ago when my sister Caroline triumphantly revealed an Easter egg she had been hoarding for about eight months. We had sneaked away together to feast our eyes and bellies on the booty. Carefully, she pulled back the wrapping. Our expectant faces turned to ones of dismay. The egg was coated in a rancid-looking fluffy blue fungus which seemed to be expanding as we looked on. It was a lesson well learned. I would not go rotten inside. I had seen people like the Easter egg, festering within their shells. I was in danger of a similar fate. Self-pity, bitterness and introspection were all characteristics to which it would be easy to surrender and end up a poor reflection of my once cheery self. In an attempt to stave off such a fate, I would go public and reveal my illness to everyone. I would fight it now. The question was, how?

CHAPTER 3

I tried not to take the London Underground to work in the mornings even though it was just three stops from Pimlico to Oxford Circus. I much preferred sitting high up on the red double-decker bus which passed within a hundred yards of my flat and dropped me at the same distance from my office in Cavendish Square. I always tried to get the front seat on the top of the Number 88. From here I could get a different perspective of London, and being above everyone else made me feel as if I was disconnected from all the rest of humanity who were scurrying to work beneath me.

Also, the twenty or thirty minutes on the bus gave me valuable thinking time. Thinking time seemed like a scarce resource these days, and yet it would not be long before I would be starting a completely new lifestyle when "thinking time" would be practically the only thing I had. For the umpteenth time I began to wonder whether the physical challenge on which I was about to embark was the right thing to do. So far, there had been surprisingly few obstacles. I reminisced about the time when the idea was first hatched – in a geography lesson when I was 14.

We were supposed to write a project on islands. Everyone else had been given exciting exotic islands - there was Madagascar, New Zealand, Japan and Jamaica. All of these were allocated to boys whose names were before mine on the register. I waited with bated breath as the teacher neared my name on the list.

"Hamilton… Papua New Guinea; Isaacs…Great Britain; Krais…Western Samoa," came the booming voice of the geography master.

"Great," I grumbled to myself. "Britain," I added cynically.

It was such a shame. I had been so looking forward to researching some mysterious-sounding island far away and examining its coastal features. But instead I had been asked to undertake an investigation into an island whose most prominent coastal features were, I imagined, the beer bellies of overweight men in string vests and knotted handkerchiefs.

I was distraught. However I started to trace round the map of Britain in my atlas and pretty soon became fascinated by the way the coastline wiggled in and out randomly. Sometimes it was smooth; sometimes it was heavily indented. I could also tell from the map that there was a huge difference in the make-up of the coastal scenery. From sandy bays to mighty chalk cliffs, shingle-strewn beaches to drowned river valleys, as far as I could make out, the variety of coastal features on the map of Britain was more diverse than anywhere else in the world. How did it get that way? What did it all look like?

"I'm going to walk around the coastline of Britain one day," I announced to Hamilton, who was sitting next to me.

"I'll come with you," came the response, "but we'll get eaten alive by midges in Scotland. How about walking round my island?"

We looked at each other as we both mulled over the prospect of walking around Papua New Guinea. As the realisation dawned that being eaten alive by midges might be preferable to the Papua New Guinean alternative, we both agreed that perhaps Britain would be a safer bet.

It seemed extraordinary that now, some nineteen years later, my life had somehow returned to that particular daydream. Perhaps that project on Britain's coastal features would now stand me in good stead. It was odd how my life always seemed to turn out OK when I came back to the things which I was most familiar with. When I had first started researching Parkinson's, the subject of neurology seemed like a different language; it seemed so remote from my world. I tried to immerse myself in a large medical dictionary that someone had given me in the hope that I could find some clue, some vital piece of information that linked the person I was with Parkinson's. From my medical dictionary deliberations, it quickly became apparent that I was never going to make it as a neurosurgeon; even if I did eventually learn the language, the shaky hands might also be a bit of a barrier to progress. But what could I do? I felt helpless. I wanted to take Parkinson's on; compete with it; fight it; anything other than just wait for it to gradually take hold.

Next to the medical dictionary on the bookshelf was an atlas. I pulled it out and started flicking. I looked at the map of Britain, remembered the geography lesson; and I started to think.

I wasn't sure at what stage the concept of walking round Britain's coastline graduated from "daft notion" to something that might actually happen, but an important milestone in that process was when I sought my parents' views on the matter.

I was standing in the middle of their living room. Dad was half-asleep in his reclining Parker Knoll chair – which reverted to an upright position pretty hastily when I announced my plan:

"How on earth are you going to do that?" (Mum did not like the idea.)

"You're mad." (Dad liked the idea but wanted to know more.)

"You must get permission from your neurologist." (Mum still didn't like the idea and would be worried sick, but if I was sensible, then, well, maybe.)

"Do you realise how far that is?" (Dad didn't have a clue how far it was, but wanted to know.)

"What an amazing idea." (Mum's sense of adventure was getting the better of her.)

"It would be quite an achievement." (Dad would be proud if I did it.)

"Can I come for some of it?" (I had my parents' support to walk around the coastline of Britain.)

Looking back on these times now, from the front of the bus, made me realise that actually the transition from chartered surveyor with PD to long-distance walker had, surprisingly, been a silky-smooth process thus far.

The process was set to continue in the same vein. I had roped in a prolific marketing man who was silky smooth both by name and by nature.

"It works at every level. It's good for you, it's good for Parkinson's, it's good for people with Parkinson's." Tommy Silk's enthusiasm was infectious.

I had met Tommy at a stag weekend in Cambridge a year previously. Having found out he was in sports marketing, I had asked him about the potential for publicity and sponsorship of my walking around the coastline. It was not so much what he said, but the energy and enthusiasm with which he said it that bowled me over. He pulled out a business card and said, "I would really love to help you with this," and paused in the delivery of his card and looked me in the eye to show me that he meant it. He made me think that the whole thing might be possible.

Tommy Silk's name is apt. He has a silky-smooth voice and a silky-smooth demeanour. He is capable of delivering the super-slick sales patter and yet, beneath the chat, there is a man of sincerity, substance and incredible generosity. It was Silky Smooth who helped to get the whole project moving, setting me up with a business plan and a small team of people to think up branding, logos and ideas for sponsorship and publicity. He asked for nothing in return. Silky taught me to "think big". "Always make out you're bigger than you actually are," he said. And this is what we set about doing, only he was far better at it.

"You've got Muhammad Ali coming over to walk with you!" the editor of the Health section of the Daily Mail exclaimed incredulously.

I looked at Silky across the meeting table in disbelief. "You've gone too far this time, Silky," I thought to myself. I wondered what on earth he was going to say next. But Silky was up to the challenge, and smoothly he delivered the most sublime of responses. I could only marvel at his impudence. "Yes, we're in touch with his people, but we're not entirely sure whether he will be fit enough to keep up with Tom."

He had overstepped the mark. He grinned cheekily in admission of his over-exuberance. There was a tense moment of silence. Then the editor laughed. Tommy Silk had won her over. She agreed to run a full page on the story before I started the walk. This gave us the credibility we needed. We could now approach corporate sponsors after the Christmas break. Perfect timing for an April 11th start date.

Slowly the marketing was coming together. We opted to call the walk Coastin', which, combined with a logo of a little man in big red boots on all our marketing and promotional literature, made for a positive and jaunty message conveying a sense of progress; progress around the coastline and progress towards a cure.

We secured patrons to give the walk an aura of credibility. Two leading scientists in the field of Parkinson's; three business people: my boss, the director general of the Ordnance Survey and the chairman of Next plc, who had PD himself; and two celebrities: Elizabeth Hurley and Michael Palin. They all agreed to lend their names in support of Coastin'. Most of them would do an awful lot more than merely lend their names.

Through a combination of personal, business and pharmaceutical company contacts, and after countless presentations of what I was intending to do, we succeeded in selling eleven of the sixteen legs into which Coastin' had been split. This meant there was already an attractive £55,000 promised to the Parkinson's Disease Society, before I had even taken a step.

Although the commercial and philanthropic side of Coastin' was going well, the practical and logistical elements of the event were a distinct worry. Three years before, I had undertaken a walk from John O'Groats to Land's End, a walk of some 1,200 miles. This gave me knowledge of what I would need but it also made me blasé. Planning the route, where to stay, what to take, moving luggage, communications, clothing, food, maps and so on; all needed organising and, in the end, my previous experience amounted to nothing and just made me more disorganised.

Mum and I spent hours and hours working through over one hundred 1/50,000 scale Ordnance Survey maps in an attempt to draw a suitable route which would take me exactly one year, with one day off per week, and ensured that I would finish each day in a place with some sort of food and shelter for the night. (See rules of the walk in appendix).

It was a triumph when we finally finished this exercise, but when I tallied the mileages up it came to 4,500 miles. I was rather shocked by this, and was even more so when I established that this was the equivalent distance of walking from London to Bombay, from Cape Town to Cairo, Hong Kong to Hamburg or Bognor to Bermuda.

One of my many reasons and inspirations for the walk was the comedian, Tony Hawks, who, for a £100 bet, had hitch-hiked around Ireland with a fridge. This journey had sown the seed in my head, spurring me on to do something out of the ordinary; something that no one had done before.

A handful of people had walked around the coastline of Britain before, so I thought I needed the "fridge factor". I tried to think up some sort of burden that would set me apart from the rest and allow me to raise a significant amount of money. I did not want to copy Tony Hawks, but I had grown rather attached to the idea of carting around something that was white, unwieldy and had a top compartment with the ability to freeze. And then it dawned on me.

I didn't need a fridge. I was the fridge! I was white, unwieldy and my "top compartment" – my Parkinson's-affected brain – had the potential to "freeze" me instantly; it might literally stop me in my tracks and render me motionless like a block of ice.

In the final run-up to Coastin', it became clear that Silky Smooth, the team and I had created a bit of a monster with which we could no longer cope. Silky did not have sufficient spare time. Despite the fact that we had already generated significant funds, credibility and media presence, I was becoming deeply concerned that there was no one suitable to run the administrative, PR and marketing side of Coastin' while I was away walking. It struck me that without such a person, the project would probably lose its impetus and by the time I reached the wilds of Scotland, it might well fizzle out altogether.

Just as I was beginning to think this problem was becoming insurmountable, I had two incredible strokes of good fortune. First, I managed to get a meeting with David Jones, an extraordinary man who had been suffering with Parkinson's for many years, but had kept it a secret. This is an amazing feat in itself, but given that he was chief executive of Next plc and had steered them to being the biggest retail success story of the 1980s is verging on supernatural.

"You're a complete nutter," he said when I told him what I was about to do. It was not a good start.

I had a long sales patter ready, courtesy of Silky Smooth, to try to get him and Next to support me. But David Jones noticed a piece of paper next to me entitled "wish list".

"What's on your wish list?" he asked kindly, sparing me what would have been a cringeworthy effort at putting forward a business case for sponsoring me.

I was a little embarrassed by his direct approach, as my wish list was rather long. It included clothes, corporate sponsorship, 200 T-shirts, access to other people in Next, and a request that he might be a patron of the walk – and that he might walk with me at some stage.

He insisted that I read the whole list and then said, "That's fine."

"What?"

"That's fine," he repeated. He was grinning. "In fact let's make it 500 T-shirts and I'll give you £20,000 personally for you to get some administrative and PR support or whatever you need it for."

After we had talked Parkinson's for half an hour, I got up to leave and shook him warmly by the hand. He had single-handedly turned Coastin' around for me.

"I don't know what to say, except thank you."

"Well, we Parkies have got to stick together." I was halfway out of the door when I heard his voice behind me again, "I still think you're a nutter though."

The second good thing that happened was Helen Matthews. She had been at university with my old schoolfriend, Mule. She had formerly been PR manager at Legoland and was now looking for a part-time project. I was naïve when it came to the media and her skills were just what we needed.

I had met Helen a few times, but had never really had a conversation with her. When we met for a chat, I knew instantly we were going to get on. I noticed she was sympathetic to the cause, and yet displayed no sympathy towards me. Perfect. I would not be able to tolerate anyone who treated me with kid gloves.

I couldn't believe my luck. Here was someone who was not only reliable and efficient, but also kind, and harboured an evil sense of humour. It quickly became clear how capable she really was. Within days she had magically assumed control of everything and she remained in charge for the entire year; supremely effective and totally indispensable. I might have been driving Coastin', but Helen was the engine, and she was turbo-charged and fuel-injected.

With Helen on board, I began to think that perhaps Coastin' might achieve all that I hoped it would achieve. The framework was in place. I felt proud and satisfied with what I had achieved. But now, as I sat thinking on the bus, my thoughts came full circle and back to the present. It suddenly dawned on me – the awful truth. Now I had to walk the bloody thing.

I had reached Oxford Circus and, leaping off the bus, I marched off towards Cavendish Square. As I did so I felt my right foot curving inwards slightly and I started to limp. This was not good.

London

Dagenham

Corringham

Tilbury

Southend on-sea
15th April

River Thames

Millennium Bridge
11th April

Isle of Dogs

W — E
N
S

Coastin

CHAPTER 4

There was no better place to start my walk around the coastline of Britain than the Millennium Bridge in London. Here was a bridge which, despite its name, was in fact only completed in 2001. When it was finally opened to the public, it was found to oscillate so much that it had to be closed again for modifications.

"They're kindred spirits, that bridge and Isaacs," one of my friends had remarked, "late and wobbly!"

Certainly, I did feel some affinity with the "wobbly bridge" and hoped that if five million quid could be spent stopping a bridge from wobbling, then maybe a similar amount invested would assist scientists in the rectification of wobbly people.

The night before the start of the walk was spent in the Moathouse Hotel in Drury Lane. The hotel isn't far from the "wobbly bridge", and Moathouse had generously donated accommodation on my travels wherever they had a hotel.

For most of the evening, I was locked to my computer trying to finish off final letters to sponsors, and thank you letters to people who had helped so much in the preparation of my send-off the following day. But I didn't finish the work. Seven years into the illness and there were now times when there was nothing to do except to surrender to the Parkinson's after the medication wore off. If I didn't surrender every action, every movement required enormous mental effort. The harder I tried to do anything, however simple the task, the worse the tremor got and the less likely I was to succeed in doing it, whether it was doing up the top button of my trousers, replacing the money in my wallet or putting a key in a lock.

On the night before Coastin' began, I plummeted fast from being in a state of control over my limb movements to having no control whatsoever. I had continued working on the computer, heedless of impending incapacitation, until without warning my body's power of co-ordination went into reverse. And as so often, it was while I was in the throes of performing the most innocuous of tasks that my sudden helplessness catapulted me into a state of incalculable fury. This particular night it was clicking the "save" icon on my computer. This simple tap on the mouse was transformed from a subconscious act of minor importance to a Herculean labour that represented the very meaning of life. All my powers of concentration were devoted to this one act. The frustration built. My fingers and hands simply would not do what they were told. The cursed cursor flew randomly around the screen like a demented bluebottle. I had to complete this one task before I could relax.

I gave up, lay on the bed and surrendered possession of my body to the shaking demons. My anger dissipated and gave way to sleep.

I awoke at 5 a.m. Four and a half hours' sleep. Great. For the next two hours I lay awake in bed wondering how I had come to be in this position. Eight years ago, my life had been going so well. The odds had been stacked in my favour for the rest of my days to be full, happy and free from major complications. It was a rubber-stamp exercise. But here, now, I had woken up in a situation where I had committed myself to walking 4,500 miles with a movement disorder which by its very nature would affect every step I took. This was madness. I was digging my own pit.

Walking down to the bridge from the Moathouse Hotel in Drury Lane, I felt utterly exhausted. So much preparation. So much time spent organising. So little sleep. This was it though. I couldn't pull out now. I dared not think of the distance. But in the back of my mind, 4,500 miles loomed large and daunting. The scale of the undertaking had never been real until today. Now, suddenly, the reality was all-consuming. I was actually going to do this. (For the rules of the walk, the logistics and other information – see appendix)

On reaching the bridge, I found it awash with supporters. Oddly I found that the presence of lots of people calmed my nerves. They had all come. I was not doing this alone. I had already received tremendous backing for the venture from family, friends, sponsors and the Parkinson's Disease Society. But now they were all here, in person, in one place. All the strands had come together and were now focused on this one event.

It was a fantastic day. Not a cloud in the sky. We had for some time been seeking a celebrity or two to come and wave me off. It was last-minute stuff, but Faye Tozer from the recently split pop group STEPS had agreed to attend, as had Bear Grylls, the youngest person at the time to climb Everest.

I was so pleased they had come, but I was embarrassed that they had both arrived before me. The press were there, predictably snapping away at Faye and leaving Bear alone. I went over and shook him by his paw. Both he and Faye, just by their presence, had assured us a good PR start for Coastin'.

Being interviewed and filmed while friends looked on was strange. "Come on Tom. Smile!" But all they got back was a fixed grimace. It's difficult enough to relax your facial muscles with Parkinson's without 15 lenses trained on you.

There was a sickly sinking feeling inside me as I took the first tentative steps. They seemed so momentous that it felt suddenly as though I was walking a tightrope. Wobbling, I set off from the ex-wobbling bridge and made my way down onto the south bank of the Thames. A great cheer came from on top of the bridge, as twelve of us strode off. We turned and waved and then continued on our way. I wondered how I would feel the next time I saw the Millennium Bridge. It disappeared out of sight. I was on my way. Blimey.

I reckoned I had an elite squad to walk the first six miles with me. The "Day One Dozen" consisted of a photographer, a Parkinson's fundraiser par excellence, a PR specialist, an acupuncturist, an osteopath, a small child in a pushchair for "aaah" value, two parents, a flatmate, a chef and, in case we got lost, two travel agents and the director general of the Ordnance Survey.

A couple of hundred yards later, we stopped. One of our party "suggested" that we pause for sustenance at Hay's Galleria. "But I still have over 4,499 miles to go!" I protested.

"I'm cold and hungry," came the response. There was no argument to this. When Mr Beef wants food, all else is of secondary concern. Mr Beef is a man who loves his food. Nowadays he is slightly more cautious though, ever since I introduced him to someone as "my flatmate" and later the person told me that he had not heard the "l" in the word. Thinking this incredibly funny, I decided to tell Mr Beef the story. When he subsequently commenced a strict dietary regime, I felt terribly guilty.

It should be said that "guilt" is something which is usually a superfluous emotion with Mr Beef. I may call him "Mr Beef", but he calls me "Mr Shaky Hands Man". Our friendship is founded on a long-standing game of verbal abuse which this book should give me the opportunity of finally winning. It will be disappointing when it's over. Honesty in its rawest form is refreshing: Mr Beef has not altered his way with me because I contracted Parkinson's.

James Habershon (Mr Beef) has been a friend for many years. Mr Beef is big: big of heart, big in intellect, big on charisma and big in physique. He would be equally at home in a stag weekend beach sumo wrestling ring as in the Mastermind chair. Sadly for him, but to the benefit of the rest of us, he suffers minor addictions to sport, food, trivia, alcohol, armchairs, spending money and possessing absurdly strong views about totally unimportant issues. Such vices are, of course, everyday hazards of being a twenty-first-century male. Beef performs them all with great panache. An afternoon spent in Mr Beef's company watching some sporting activity on the television, the outcome of which will dictate whether or not he will undertake his weekly shop at Fortnum and Mason or Super Budget Groceries is surprisingly life enriching.

Waiting for Beef to dispatch a hamburger less than half a mile into my 4,500 mile journey was not enriching my life; it was trying my patience. A newspaper cutting from the morning's *Times* was thrust in front of me and I was instantly and predictably appeased. My head swelled up like a giant pumpkin. In the article, the journalist's first observation had been that "The Pope, Muhammad Ali and Tom Isaacs have Parkinson's." To be mentioned in the same sentence as such exalted company would have been sufficient to project many people's levels of self-importance into the stratosphere. I was no exception. Of course, it would have been infinitely preferable to be likened to arguably two of the best-known individuals on the planet for some other reason, but I'll take what I can get. After all, I have a lot of other things, besides Parkinson's, in common with God's representative on earth and perhaps the most dynamic sportsman of our time. The second letter to all our names is the same… for instance… except for Muhammad Ali.

When we set off at last after the unscheduled stop, I had a very swift reality check. Despite some small progress, I was certainly not Coastin'. To begin with, I was still four days away from the point at which I joined the coast proper and secondly, and more notably, just north of Deptford I started to limp.

I had not spoken to anyone, apart from a friend in Australia, of my gravest concern about this whole venture: my ability to walk. Now there was no hiding it. Here I was, not quite a thousandth of the way through a year of walking and only able to propel myself at any speed by punting myself forward with a walking pole. There was a tacit understanding between all the people with me that day that my state of gait was a taboo subject. The first day was not the time to register any such concerns. The mood was buoyant and there was absolutely no desire on anyone's part to voice an analysis of the long-term repercussions facing a long-distance walker who couldn't walk.

I caught a couple of the party glancing anxiously in my direction. I knew what they were thinking, but I too wanted to avoid the issue. I was tired. It had been a gruelling couple of months. The limping would pass when I had got some sleep; when my body became accustomed to walking. It had to.

There was relief all round when the Cutty Sark came into view. No one was more relieved than I. And hey, only 364 days left and 4,494 miles; it didn't sound nearly so bad now.

Staying with a friend who lived on the Isle of Dogs on the first night of this adventure seemed odd. Everything to do with my former life was so close; only a taxi ride away, and yet in reality I was now closer to Bombay than my flat in Pimlico.

Waking up on Day Two, my mind was still heavy with doubts. "What have I done?"

Fortunately I was still on a high from yesterday's triumphant departure and this enabled me to laugh at the absurd predicament in which I had put myself. But my inward chuckling was spiked with a sense of slight hysteria. Catastrophe at not being able to even reach the sea on a walk called Coastin' was by no means inconceivable. The first six miles had seen me limping. Would these be my easiest miles? I got out of bed to move out from underneath the cloud of uncertainty which was rapidly forming above my head.

"What am I doing?" I said to my friend Shazzer as we walked off the Isle of Dogs.

Shazzer looked at me and smiled. "You're doing what you do – taking on a challenge; doing something positive."

I could rely on Shazzer for words of encouragement. It was typically thoughtful of her to have taken the day off on the second day of my walk, knowing that it would be a day when I would need support and further reassurance. Shazzer is a close friend, a couple of years younger than me and one of those people whom everyone likes. We share a love of travel and adventure which was largely a product of our travels together through New Zealand, Australia and South-East Asia between 1993 and 1995.

She had been present when my first symptoms appeared. At the time we were in Sumatra. Our life savings had been all but spent and it was nearly time to come home. It was March 1995 and we had reached Tuk-Tuk, a little island in the middle of Lake Toba. It was a wonderful spot and as I sat in the shade sipping a cinnamon-infused iced coffee and writing a postcard, how could I have known that what happened next would be the beginning? It was an innocuous little occurrence. All that happened was that I couldn't finish the postcard. I experienced a slight spasm in my right hand. It was nothing much. I would finish it later on and when I got home I would just have that hand checked out – perhaps it was a trapped nerve or something.

"Do you remember when I couldn't finish that postcard? That was over seven years ago. I couldn't even finish a postcard then. What hope have I got of finishing a 4,500-mile walk?"

Shazzer smiled sympathetically. "Ahh, but you finished the postcard in the end; the same way that you'll finish this thing, in the end."

I regretted using the postcard analogy. Finishing the postcard and the next twelve months of hard walking was not a comparison that gave me much confidence.

"Do you really think I'll make it all the way round?"

"Of course you'll do it." Shazzer was unequivocal and it was what I needed to hear.

I don't know what I would have done without Shazzer on Day Two, plodding in full hiking gear through the vast industrial sprawl of East London and drawing many an amused stare as we did so. The Dagenham Ford motor plant was even less attractive than it sounds, and on the roads, huge juggernauts thundered past us, hurling up great swirls of dust which caked our skin and lungs. It was a total pollution experience.

To cheer ourselves up as we walked, we reminisced about other places we had walked together which were slightly more conducive to the whole experience. It was difficult to draw any comparisons between the Patagonian wilderness, Canada's Rockies, New Zealand's fiordland and the A13 to Rainham. By the time we reached our destination, with me limping again, we both concluded that it would be almost impossible to find a less pleasurable place to walk.

For the next two days I struggled on. Choice of route was often difficult. I tended to opt for the noise and fumes of juggernauts and heavy industry but on occasion was forced into languishing through the pungently scented landfill sites and sewerage works that adorned the area. Just before Tilbury I narrowly avoided plunging into a cesspit, in an attempt to follow a footpath which appeared to be continuous on the map.

Despite only covering small mileages, I could already feel myself flagging both mentally and physically. I realised that this whole thing was going to be harder than I had ever dreamed.

Canvey Island
Corringham ◀— 22 miles —▶ Southend-on-Sea
15th April

Thames Estuary

CHAPTER 5

A public right of way marked on my map at a place called Fobbing Horse did not seem to exist. I was left with no alternative but to set off on an 8-mile detour which would result in a 22-mile day I was not yet ready for. What is more, it had started to rain, and it became slowly apparent that I had a hole in my boot. I had decided that I would start the walk in an old pair to avoid blisters. As the cold damp seeped into my socks, I used the lack of blisters as my consolation.

There was little consolation in the fact that I would have to return to the horror of the A13. As I waded towards its constant drone through tall, wet, dense grass and several clumps of stinging nettles, I felt my spirits sink. While my feet shrivelled, my legs swelled red with nettle rash. Both itched. There was no enjoyment in this.

I shuffled dejectedly towards a delightful little church midway between Pitsea and South Benfleet, and here I was appalled to see a bright orange mattress, which had been deposited on the pretty lane outside. I looked at this hideous piece of garbage with the contempt that it deserved. It was stained, damp, noxious and probably infested with all manner of vermin. But I then had to wrestle with conflicting emotions, because as I slumped onto it, exhausted, it dawned on me that this wantonly discarded piece of junk offered a relaxation experience which, at that moment, fulfilled my every wish. I took a few minutes to recline and gorged myself on its filthy luxury.

The footpath was supposed to continue along the railway, but once again it petered out and I was forced into a further detour through the centre of South Benfleet. The realisation that on top of everything else my medication had failed me rendered me about as morose as I could get. I knew the consequences of the drugs not working. It would herald a complete system failure. My brain no longer had control of my body and my body was on strike. The progress I was making now was painstakingly slow. I could barely put one foot in front of the other and I was shaking; shaking really badly. I had to stop to rest again.

I had been here many times before, but usually I could rest in the privacy of my own home. It was now the only time I allowed Parkinson's to take my spirit. These are the times when I have felt totally stranded, frighteningly helpless and utterly miserable. Sometimes I wonder whether the shaking will ever stop. It's like waiting for a lifeboat.

I didn't feel like me at all, and I wasn't going to allow this shaking, shuffling monster to walk through South Benfleet, looking like he did. Children coming out of school would mock me. Or, worse still, passers-by might stare at this strange, afflicted visitor and offer me assistance.

So I hid behind a wall, and for half an hour I just sat and shook. I dreaded someone finding me and insisting that they could help. I just wanted to be alone. I was cold and wet, and the time passed incredible slowly. Pneumonia would have been imminent had the shaking not generated sufficient heat to keep my body temperature above teeth-chattering point. It struck me that right here, right now, I was probably more visible than I had ever been in my life.

I could hear voices nearby. Someone was out walking their dog and had stopped to have a chat just the other side of the wall. The rain had started again. My shaking was now attributable to both Parkinson's and lack of body warmth. Yet if I tried to put on another layer, laboured fumblings in my pack would bring attention to my presence. I huddled up, squeezing myself into a tighter ball. The dog-walker would surely see me any second. I dreaded his look of pity. If he saw me, then I would try to avoid his gaze. I would just get up and slope off, shaking and limping. It would be better to be labelled "weirdo" than to suffer the look of pity. Pitiful looks were reserved for ladies in Australia offering me seats on buses. I would avoid these at almost any cost.

The dog suddenly appeared round the corner of the wall. He was a black medium-sized mongrel and he was visibly shocked by my presence. He immediately turned, taking a deep gasp of air as he did so. He was about to raise the alarm with some high-volume barking. But as the momentum of his body took him back towards his owner he then rocked back again as if teetering with indecision. He looked back at me as if in a delayed double-take. We stared at each other for about fifteen seconds before he retreated silently.

He seemed to understand exactly what I was feeling, and he trotted off, leaving me alone. His owner walked past and my presence remained unnoticed.

I was grateful to the dog. I knew what would have happened had he called attention to my trembling form. Fuss. Lots of it. Compounding my misery; prolonging the stress of the situation, which would delay still further the moment when calm would return to my body.

I have always been an optimistic sort of bloke. If things are bad, I can generally look ahead to tomorrow, when they usually improve. Crouched behind that wall, shivering in the rain, soaking, sulking, I could see no way forward. I felt utterly defeated. It was as if all joy had been sapped out of me, leaving me hopeless. At that moment, I thought I couldn't go on. It might have even ended there, with me sitting on the ground just short of South Benfleet. I had not yet even reached the coast. But the shaking subsided and I got up and moved on.

An hour later, I sat down under a tree, exhausted. I started thinking that I might just try to make it up to Newcastle and then stop there. That would be a pretty good effort, and everyone would just have to accept it. But how could I tell all the people who'd worked so hard to help me?

I moved on. I had today to finish first.

I ate supper late and, for the first time, felt alone.

On the way back to the B&B my mother rang. "Hello," she said, "how was Day Five?"

"Fine."

Suffolk
Snape
27th April
Aldeburgh
Felixstowe
Harwich
Tollesbury
19th April
Clacton-on-sea
Maldon
Burnham
Southend-on-sea
Margate

FROM SOUTHEND TO SNAPE
116 MILES
APRIL

CHAPTER 6

Day Six, a brand new day and a fresh start. I was in better spirits. An hour after leaving Southend, I arrived back at the exact same point from where I had started the day. Never at any stage during this time did I believe I was lost, but I had with pinpoint accuracy managed to walk in a perfect circle. You might think this would be nigh on impossible, but my impressive feat was caused by a combination of talking on the telephone instead of map reading, confusing signposts and sheer absentmindedness. What a complete waste of time. What an idiot.

I was infuriated by my stupidity, particularly after the problems of yesterday. It was hard enough doing this walk without making ridiculous errors. I had lost two whole hours. To make matters worse, I was limping again; struggling to find any sort of rhythm. I was trying to goad my brain into communicating important messages to my feet: "Heel, then toe, then heel, then toe"; and instead what my brain was churning out was: "Toe, bit of heel, drag other foot forward, painful blister, tight hamstrings. Toe and heel together, people staring, where's my other leg, tight hamstring, oh I've stopped." If I hadn't been so miserable, it would have been comical. But the low point was over with. Despite severe difficulties on Day Six, they were nothing compared to the misery I had suffered on Day Five. For some time after this I benefited from an improvement in my walking endeavours. Gradually, my stride was becoming more consistent, and the periods of lamely dragging myself forward with my walking pole grew less frequent.

Things were definitely improving. I even started looking at the scenery. That was improving too. The A13 was a thing of the past, and now I was enjoying the immaculate carpets of rape, often extending as far as the eye could see. The tightly packed flowers provided an extraordinary intensity of yellow which, when bathed in a warm spring sun, held my gaze and soothed the concerns from previous days. It was as if finally breaking out of the dusty urbanized sprawl of London had honed all my senses. Slowly the shackles were loosening; the shackles of my illness as well as those of the tension which had gradually been building over the past few months. Now I was walking. Perhaps even Coastin'. Messages sent from brain to legs were being received on a more regular basis and I gathered speed and momentum.

Essex was now looking very good indeed. I had studied the proliferation of river estuaries in this area with a certain amount of frustration in the route-planning stages. The Crouch, the Blackwater, the Colne and the Stour are all estuaries that conspire to obstruct a coastal walker's swift passage into Suffolk. But I was more than happy trundling along their scenic banks and marshy creeks. The River Crouch was negotiated with the help of Dan at the Marina Office near Paglesham Creek who, without the slightest hesitation, offered me a lift in his boat across to Burnham. It transpired that Dan's grandfather had Parkinson's, but Dan would have ferried me over the river whatever the cause. I wondered how many more such generous acts I would experience on my journey. On the television that night there was news of a pioneering neurosurgeon called Steven Gill who had, for the first time ever, demonstrated regeneration of the neurones, the loss of which are associated with Parkinson's. The pilot study on five patients had been conducted in Bristol. A substance called GDNF was the key to this treatment - it was delivered to the centre of the brain via a catheter from the stomach in controlled doses. Good news indeed. Psychologically, it would put a spring in my step even though physically I had about as much spring as a hippopotamus. I needed this GDNF stuff now.

The next morning a friend rang and, laughing, he told me that I could stop walking now. "They have found a cure." To my delight the prospect of not continuing my walk now filled me with horror. On entering Tollesbury that night, I spotted a large sign outside a pub called The Hope Inn. It was a big but homely-looking place with a large chalkboard sign outside. "Man walking around Britain in pub tonight. Come and support."

This was a bit of a blow. Someone else was doing the same thing as me. No doubt he would have come a lot further than I had and would have some fantastic stories, putting my feeble 118 miles to shame. It rankled a bit that this "man" was here in the same place; stealing my thunder. How could he be here doing "my" walk and staying at the same place as me? How unlucky can you get? I walked into a crowded bar looking a bit disgruntled.

"You must be Tom Isaacs. What would you like to drink?"

And suddenly people were slapping me on the shoulder, my rucksack was being hauled off my back and taken upstairs, and within moments I was sandwiched between a bar stool and a pint of something that looked refreshing. The penny finally dropped. This was a hero's welcome. It just had not occurred to me that the notice outside referred to me.

"There is a package that has arrived for you, Mr Isaacs." The words were straight out of a Bond movie, as was the package, which was large and a strange shape. The contents of the package allowed the fantasy to continue.

Inside was a veritable treasure trove of state-of–the-art walking paraphernalia: boots, mobile phone with email, waterproof garments, blister-proof socks and a cap with earphones and a radio housed within its lining. Inside was a little note. "Some walking gadgets for you. Love, Helen at Coastin' HQ." She would from now on be known as "Q."

The names of villages were becoming more satisfying. Passing through Deptford, Rainham and Tilbury was, as you might imagine, significantly less enchanting than Little Wigborough, Fingringhoe and Brightlingsea. On the other hand, Mucking Marshes, just north of Tilbury, is a place name of hugely satisfying quality. As you would also expect though, there is very little satisfaction derived from being there. The improving sequence of names and places culminated abruptly at Clacton. Clacton felt sad. The gentle rural scenes, which had been a consistent feature of the past few days, surrendered to a decaying clutter of drab beach huts. Clacton strings itself half-heartedly along an attractive stretch of the east coast. A little further on, Frinton maintains an air of genteel respectability, but it seemed to be lacking in motivation or enthusiasm. I was pleased to leave Frinton's grassy seafront and stride out to Kirby-le-Soken. More blissful weather and, if all went according to plan, I could reach Suffolk today. Amidst the picturesque inlets of Hamford Water, I noticed something different about my walking. I had a spring in my step. I analysed it. I couldn't believe the change that had come over me in the past week. I now felt comfortable, confident, fit. It dawned on me that I could do it. I had only walked 160 miles but it hit me like a bolt of lightning. The whole thing. I could do it. I was swept up in a sudden surge of glorious euphoria. I could do it and I had not felt as good as this for ages. Parkinson's was not going to stop me completing this walk – perhaps nothing would. I was running late for the ferry from Harwich. With my newfound zest I started to jog. I found I could run quite well and upped the pace, enjoying the challenge. Five miles later I staggered onto the quayside. I was one minute late. It didn't matter. Tourist Information had got it wrong. There was no ferry until summer. This was the first major logistical problem I had encountered and it gave me four options: swim; walk the 45 miles to Felixstowe via Manningtree, Shotley Gate and Ipswich; wait until summer; or cadge a lift from my mother who was in the vicinity.

None of the above seemed satisfactory. The first three were daft and the fourth would be cheating. I had stipulated in my rules that boats and ferries were okay, motor vehicles not.

"Is there no way of getting across?" I asked a man who was painting a jetty. I was trembling after the exertion of the run. "I am on a charity walk for Parkinson's." The man gave me a look as if he was estimating what size suit would fit me. "Come with me," he instructed and set off at speed, not bothering to see if I was following. It was like a relay. I was swiftly passed up Harwich International Port Control Centre's chain of command. Each person I was introduced to was told that I was "on a charity walk for Parkinson's", and each time the word "Parkinson's" was delivered, there was emphasis of voice, expression and body language. They all understood. By the time I was sitting in the control tower with a hot mug of tea with someone who was dressed like Lord Nelson, the entire workforce at Harwich knew I had Parkinson's. Charity walks are taken very seriously at Harwich. It was a bit like a military exercise, but there was underlying warmth to their efficiency. Ten minutes later a pilot boat was transporting me to Felixstowe. I felt triumphant. As with Dan in Burnham, there was no hesitation to the generosity exhibited. The help given was unconditional; a display of pure fellowship which left me glowing. What a fantastic way to reach Suffolk.

The next day, I left Suffolk bound for Channel 5 TV stardom. Open House with Gloria Hunniford was a weekday broadcast and they wanted my story. They arranged for a chauffeur-driven car to pick me up so I travelled to London in style. Despite this, I looked distinctly worse for wear when I arrived at the studios. Concerned that I might look "too well" on the programme I had only taken one set of pills that day. It wasn't my intention to be interviewed in a complete state. What I did want was for them to broadcast a 30-second clip showing the sort of effects from which I was suffering; the full effects of Parkinson's. I was asked to pour some water out of a heavy jug into a plastic cup. The problem is that a heavy jug does not cause me any real difficulty. It is when my limbs have no goal that serious problems arise. It is a "resting tremor". Ask me to hold a golf club and I can grip it and swing it almost as well as I ever could. But tell my hands to hover without any further instruction and I look like I am playing invisible maraccas. So, when I reached for the jug, my arms were wagging like a terrier's tail, but the moment I clamped my hand round the handle, my limbs and entire body became as solid as a British bulldog.

The absurd thing was that for the purposes of this exercise, I wanted hyperactive terrier tails and invisible maraccas. I took control of the situation. I knew what would make me shake. The piece ended up being a magnificent display of me fumbling around with the cup of water, which I succeeded in chucking over half the film crew. I then spent 45 seconds putting on my jumper and getting tangled up like a deranged octopus. I have mixed emotions looking at the tape. It did the job well, but was that really me?

Gloria's sofa would have been comfortable but the lights and cameras made me feel distinctly small and naïve. Ironically, I was so nervous by the time she interviewed me that I was trembling with fear. I suspect viewers were thinking "Those drugs he takes are completely useless."

I arrived back in Suffolk shattered. I am not sure whether it was the fact that I had broken my drug regime for a day, whether I had picked up a virus, or whether I had developed an allergy for large cities. It seemed as if I was starting from scratch and all the positive thoughts I had been exuding in north Essex had disappeared. The weather had changed for the worse too.

In the gathering gloom, there were two good things to focus on. The first was that however hard the walking was at the moment, I would come through it and re-discover the spring in my step which I'd had walking to Harwich. The second was that I was soon to reach my first major milestone: Thorpeness. I have been holidaying in Thorpeness all my life. It is a special place for all the family and I could use it as a base of operations for the next week.

FROM SNAPE TO SNORING
140 MILES
APRIL – MAY

C H A P T E R  7

What a curious sensation it was to be walking from Aldeburgh to Thorpeness. It was a walk I had completed countless times before, and yet this time it seemed so different. I walked from the beach up the steps to the family flat. I had walked the whole way from London to Thorpeness. I quietly reflected on my first real sense of progress around Britain's coastline.

My first-ever holiday had been to Thorpeness. I was nine months old and my health was already cause for concern. My mother was worried by the fact that I was so lethargic all the time. She began touring a largely unsympathetic doctor's circuit, until at last she came across a paediatrician who agreed with her. Something was wrong. He diagnosed coeliac disease: a severe allergy to wheat and other cereals containing gluten. Nowadays, the condition is widely recognised and understood. In 1968, it took a long time for anyone to take my mother or my lack of energy seriously – I was not diagnosed until I was thirteen months old.

The move to a gluten-free diet paid dividends and I rewarded my mother by beginning to bounce. Away from home, people made a fuss about my diet. I never understood why. It was easy. I suppose in a way it was like a religion. My mother had instilled in me the four commandments of no wheat, no barley, no oats and no rye. I knew from experience that if I ever strayed from the gluten-free path, I would, without fail, be suffering a wretched, retching penance three hours later. There is no compromising a coeliac diet. There was no happy medium and this made it far simpler to deal with. I knew no other way; and yet I still received the plaudits for being so restrained. Parents of friends gasped in disbelief and admiration as I would steadfastly refuse all manner of tasty treats.

"He's so good," they would say to my mother, "when all the others were having a Kit Kat, he just politely refused."

It seemed odd to me that not making myself sick should warrant such praise, but I lapped it all up nevertheless.

Coeliac disease had other advantages. I was the only one allowed a packed lunch at school. While everyone else struggled with revolting-looking stews, I would tuck into tasty-looking gluten-free sandwiches, crisps and large bars of Galaxy chocolate.

Despite being slightly different (so often the scourge of playground Britain), I was reasonably popular at school. But then that was hardly surprising. Dad had an Aston Martin.

I had no idea that an Aston Martin was anything special until one day at the bus stop, the school bully, while holding me by the throat against a wall, asked me what car my dad drove. He was so shocked by my response that he decided to spare my life and to see if it was true.

"What does your dad do?" asked the bully.

I wasn't sure about this one and went home that evening to find out. I had not understood the word "solicitor" and Dad must have had difficulty explaining to me, because what I came away with was the word "policeman"; he was involved with the law, after all. The following day Dad did his stuff beautifully and dropped me off at the bus stop in the Aston Martin. Swelling with pride, more because I got out of the front seat than because it was an Aston Martin, I joined the queue.

Bully was visibly impressed. "What does your dad do?" came the question again.

"He's a policeman," I replied.

"How come he's got no uniform then?" Oh dear. This was not one I was prepared for. Once again, I consulted my solicitor on the subject and he gave me an answer.

"My dad is not in uniform because he is a plain-clothes policeman," I announced at the bus stop the next day.

Bully considered this at length, assimilating the pieces of the jigsaw in his head: plain-clothes policeman, Aston Martin.

"Is your dad James Bond?"

My dad was James Bond. How proud can a little boy be?

\* \* \*

Many people are deterred from visiting Suffolk's coast by the predominance of shingle beaches and the grey-brown sea water. Those who dig a little deeper beneath the surface of the Heritage Coastline will uncover many of its untapped treasures: glorious sunrises, abundant and diverse birdlife, wonderfully crooked architecture and totally uncrooked and friendly people. Above all else, however, Suffolk by the sea is pervaded with a sense of constant change, whether it is the seasons, the wind direction, or the texture and form of the endless banks of shingle which are piled high on the shore with each incoming tide.

Having rounded the Ness, I started enjoying the tranquillity of Minsmere Nature Reserve, despite being on the receiving end of some unfriendly stares from the copious bird-watchers. I have long thought these "twitchers" are a completely different species of human being to long-distance walkers because they do not seem to understand why I walk, and I certainly cannot fathom why anyone would want to "twitch".

Of course, twitching, albeit a different kind, was something I did rather a lot of. I can usually tell when my medication is about to kick out because it starts with a twitch in one of my hands. That's when I realise I am on the brink of the helter-skelter down to "The Land of Shake"; a place to be avoided at all costs.

The genteel village of Walberswick and the Victorian splendour of Southwold reminded me that it was not just the physical character of the East Anglian coast that was changeable. Beyond Southwold was remote and quiet until I marched through Kessingland, and soon after, Lowestoft, whose soul is still firmly rooted in the sea. Perhaps I would feel something similar at the end of the walk. I did not feel the same about Great Yarmouth and beyond, which has some of the less pleasant features of a tourist mecca.

The caravans, chalets and cheap tat-selling stalls continued for another 20 miles or so and I felt that Caister-on-Sea would be considerably improved if it suffered the same fate as Dunwich and became Caister-under-Sea.

I was surprised when a signpost welcomed me to California. By virtue of what I was doing, I felt like an honorary latter-day Beach Boy and I scoured the immediate vicinity to see if these really were "the cutest girls in the land". The best I could say is that the jury was out on that one! As if in punishment for my impure thoughts, I felt the familiar twitch in my right hand and so changed the Beach Boy tune in my head to "Good, good, good,

good vibrations".

I limped on beyond Winterton and eventually sat in some dunes on a deserted beach gazing at about fifteen seals basking in the sun. They looked fat and lazy, like beer-swilling lads collapsed on an Ibizan beach.

There was absolutely no connection between this thought and the arrival of another of my closest friends, Will Cook. It was he who at his wedding famously uttered the words: "I do solemnly declare, that I, Will Cook..." but it is rumoured that he has not once set foot in a kitchen since.

Will arrived with his family for the weekend in appalling weather. They were understandably unenthusiastic about joining me on a beach walk from Sea Palling to Cromer, which I later likened to spending several hours standing in a carwash with a built-in sandblaster.

Having reached Cromer, I had supper with the Cooks that night. There was a time when Will and I would have sunk a few beers after such an occasion, but my beer-drinking days were all but over. In fact, the only alcohol which did not affect me adversely any more was gin and vodka. Strangely, it had been indirectly through vodka and Will that I was on this walk at all.

After dinner we reminisced about the time we both went to one of his university mates' stag weekend. The Saturday had been going quite smoothly for me until the afternoon. It was while we were playing football that it had started going wrong. I had completely bamboozled the opposition defence with a mazy run into the penalty area. The unintentional twist of my body due to Parkinson's sent three of the opposition the wrong way and I had been left with a clear strike at goal. It would have been a goal worthy of Maradona. It would have gone down as the greatest goal ever scored in lads' five-a-side history. But although my body stood in front of the goal, my brain had been sold the dummy, the same as everyone else. So instead of hoofing the ball into the top right-hand corner, I just stood there like a lemon until I was tackled by the goalkeeper.

"And that evening was the first time I met Silky Smooth," I said to Will.

"So was it that weekend you decided to walk the coastline of Britain?"

"Yes," I replied and recounted the story to him.

*I was sitting next to Tommy Silk in the Indian restaurant. "What do you do?" I asked him.*

*"Sports marketing."*

It sounded interesting and I wondered if I should tell him about my dream of walking around the coastline of Britain. I took the plunge.

Tommy Silk bowled me over with his enthusiasm for the idea. The conversation spiralled upwards in a series of ever more ambitious marketing ideas. His drive and excitement was infectious and fuelled mine. But it was all just a pipe dream really.

"Go on Tommy, get it down you. It will do you good!" We were interrupted.

The lads were certainly encouraging, perhaps even well intentioned, but the presumption that my fourth vodka Red Bull would do me "good" was not strictly accurate. In fact it was flawed in every respect. I knew this before I arched back over-dramatically in my chair and threw the contents of the glass into my mouth. With the departure of the drink there was a cheer. I inspected the glass. All the liquid had gone, as had the last remnants of my common sense.

The rules of the drinking game were barbaric, especially when applied to me. If you were caught with your hands in your lap, you had to down one of the vicious cocktails in the centre of the table. Everyone was completely oblivious to the fact that clasping my hands in my lap was practically the only way I could curb the dreadful writhing motion with which my arms were suddenly afflicted. What is more, the more I drank, the worse it would get.

I had taken a double dose of pills this evening in order to ensure I was not displaying any shakes or muscle stiffness. Ironically, instead of the tremor and rigidity making any movement difficult, a new symptom, which was a side effect of the medication, put me in a state of continuous but involuntary movement. These spasms were random and sometimes quite violent. It is called dyskinesia. I called it "the discos".

The lads would have given me a special dispensation in the game had I wanted it, but that was the very thing I didn't want. I didn't want special anything. I just wanted to be one of the boys for the night; to play a daft drinking game the same as I had always done on all the other stag nights I'd been to. One of my biggest fears with Parkinson's was that others might feel I had taken a turn for the worse. I imagined the conversation:

"How's Tom?"

"Well, we don't see him much any more. His Parkinson's is quite bad now. Poor chap. He was such a sociable person."

I had resolved that I would do my utmost to ensure that people did not use the word "was" in connection with my name and character. It was my goal instead to ensure that people spoke in terms of what "Tom is" and what "Tom will be". The merest hint of pity made me feel quite sick.

But sometimes I took this resolve to extremes. The drinking game was a case in point. And yet I continued regardless. I knew I would be caught lap-handed time and time again. I knew vodka Red Bulls would send me into a "disco inferno"; a "boogie wonderland".

Eight vodka Red Bulls ensured that I was no longer self-conscious enough to keep my arms in my lap. Instead, my arms whirled randomly around and above me. At times my right hand jerked so violently that I found myself having to apologise to my new friend Tommy Silk for unwittingly punching him hard several times.

By the time we left the restaurant, I had lost control. I was very drunk and was trying to convince everyone I was a helicopter.

At the nightclub, I apparently looked like John Travolta on speed: legs pumping, hips gyrating and arms flailing. I was not trying to dance. I was actually attempting to get to the bar. If I had been wearing a white suit and flares, it is quite probable that the dance floor would have cleared for a solo performance. It was Will and another friend, Sean, who had picked up the pieces after "the night of the vodka Red Bulls".

"Tommy, if you want a lift home with Sean and me, you'll need to be ready in an hour." It was Will's voice through the bedroom door.

"It must be morning," I thought hazily. There was a pause.

"How are you feeling?" he continued.

"Great!" I said with a conviction I did not feel. I heard Will's footsteps disappear down the corridor. "Never again. Never ever again!" I shouted after him. I had woken up with the mother of all hangovers and had all the mobility of a Tin Man. For the first time, I felt as if I had absolutely no control over any part of myself. I hoped the medication I had just taken would solve that.

I stared at my hands as they flapped wildly. They were enjoying themselves, taunting me with their treacherous behaviour. I smiled at them. As long as I was not trying to do something with them, they no longer made me angry. Now, they were just ridiculous. They were possessed by the castanets of Satan and he was playing them at a prodigious rate this morning.

I thought about Will checking up on me. He was a good friend. When all of this Parkinson's business had started, he had gone to a library and read up everything he could find about the disease. He had even joined the Parkinson's Disease Society so that he could be kept up to date. In those days most things that were written about the condition had been what he termed "pretty gloomy *and not worth reading". I had not taken his advice, and foolishly visited the Parkinson's Disease Society myself to read up on what the future was likely to have in store for me. After half an hour of reading about my own personal apocalypse, I very nearly decided to leave the third-floor library room by the window. Will and Sean ended up having to wait for me. They bundled me into the back seat where I slouched silently, immersed in my own misery, but every now and then I tuned in to the conversation in the front seat:*

*"Sean," Will said, "if you had been kidnapped by Colombian drug barons and were held captive in a secret hideaway location somewhere in the Amazonian jungle; who from the lads present last night would you choose to rescue you?"*

*It was a standard question and it would be debated for the remainder of the journey. I pondered the question myself, wondering who would eventually be chosen. Once upon a time, I might have made the list. It was strange how knowing that I would no longer be a suitable candidate made me sad. But it was often stupid little things like this which made me realise how much Parkinson's had affected my life. With stealth being a key attribute for selection into the crack team of lads to save Sean, I couldn't really argue my case. Stealth and Parkinson's have nothing in common.*

*Lying in the back of the car, I wondered at what point my life had branched away from those of the two friends who sat in front of me. It had all happened so suddenly. It seemed as if one day we had all been working, playing, travelling and drinking hard, and the next they were both married with children and I had contracted Parkinson's. Sean and Will had been hugely supportive when I was diagnosed – Cooky with his "confront the issue" style and Sean with his conspicuous presence and ability to talk easily about normal topics totally unrelated to Parkinson's. I knew they would both have been first on the list of lads ensuring I got home safely last night.*

*All my friends had been incredible; every one of them. They had provided me with a platform from which to bounce back. As everything stood, I could cope. But the future still loomed large and threatening. How long would it be before every morning would be like this morning; having no control; barely able to move? I was defiant at the moment because I could, when my medication was working properly, pass myself off as someone without PD. It was extremely doubtful that this would continue for much longer though. In ten years it was conceivable that I might be wheelchair bound in a nursing home with people over twice my age.*

*"How about Tommy Silk?" I heard Will say in the front. "There's no one like*

*him for sheer audacity and confidence."*

*I reflected that my own confidence was suffering due to the pressures I was putting on myself in social situations. As anyone would, I always tried to look my best when out and would often just go home if my tremor materialised earlier than anticipated. Even if people knew and accepted my Parkinson's, it was only natural for people to stare at a wayward or trembling limb. Unfortunately, I became acutely aware of this and would catch their eye and see that look; that same look as on the Sydney bus. And when I left parties early, people would say, "He shouldn't be embarrassed. It's only us." But embarrassment had nothing to do with it. It was more that I didn't want others to feel uncomfortable about me or, worse still, to pity me.*

*At least, at the moment, my state of mind was relatively positive. This was good, but it couldn't achieve anything tangible for me. All it did was to make me feel better temporarily; until the next inevitable slide down this game of shakes and ladders.*

*Maybe there were too many intangibles in my life. I needed something solid to fight for. There was only one thing that could resolve all these issues: a cure. Of course, I had no hope of finding that myself even if I had been a bit of a dab hand converting my Bunsen burner at school into a lethal blowtorch.*

*Recently there had been a lot more in the way of positive news reports. And yet most of the people within the Parkinson's community seemed resolutely pessimistic. Whenever I used the word "cure", people would gasp as if I had blasphemed. I couldn't work out why this was.*

*I tuned back in to the kidnapping debate.*

*"I wouldn't have Harvey [Mule]," said Sean. "Sure, he's great at a cocktail party, shaking hands and circulating, but has he got the bottle to shoot a man at point-blank range…"*

*"He hasn't got the killer instinct," I chimed in, remembering the under-seven chess tournament.*

*But Sean's words "shaking hands and circulating" reminded me of something a former boss had said to me shortly after I qualified as a chartered surveyor: "The key to success in property, in fact, in life, young Isaacs, is to shake hands and circulate."*

*It all came to me in a flash: the conversation with Tommy Silk; the recognition that in order to survive, I would have to achieve something tangible; my ex-boss's favourite maxim. Now I had a reason to put it into practice. I could and would do it. I would walk around the coastline of Britain with shaky hands. "Shake hands and circulate: the key to success."*

"And now here I am doing exactly that," I finished my monologue to Will.

"Do you regret it?" he asked.

"It's hard, but whatever happens now, no, I won't regret it. Using Parkinson's as an excuse to do something has to be better than using it as an excuse not to do things."

"Are you enjoying it?" It was typical of Will to be so direct.

"I think that this could be the best thing I will ever do," I said, looking him in the eye. He nodded back. He understood.

Fortunately the wind had died down the following day, but the Cooks had only come to Norfolk for one night. I felt bad about this and also frustrated; I had wanted Will to experience the pleasure of the walk.

"There's plenty of time for that," said Will, waving goodbye, "you've still got over eleven months of walking."

The thought of this made me feel tired, but for the next three nights I would be staying in a village called Great Snoring. It sounded like a place where I might get some rest.

The 45 miles of Norfolk Coastal Path from Cromer to Hunstanton via Blakeney and Burnham Overy Staithe provided some of the best scenery I had yet witnessed, and there was plenty of interest en route, from steam trains and royal beach huts to a wonderful variety of period architecture and magnificent churches, each one of which seemed large enough to house the entire population of Norfolk.

I was joined on this stretch by, amongst others, David, Vivien and Tiggy Culling, whose hospitality I was enjoying at their cottage in Great Snoring. By the time we reached Burnham, David was obviously in some pain with a blister. On further inspection of his foot later that evening we discovered not so much a blister but more a small cave on the sole of his foot. Vivien and Tiggy the dog had fared better and continued with me to Hunstanton, which probably has the distinction of being the only east coast resort where you can watch the sun setting over the sea.

FROM HUNSTANTON
TO HUMBERSIDE
128 MILES
MAY

C H A P T E R  8

"You're a media tart," said Q. She was referring to my undisguised enjoyment of being interviewed by local newspapers and local radio stations. There was something rather satisfying about the fact that my going on a long walk was newsworthy. Having said that, not all the local media seemed to be excited by the story. It was a lottery as to whether the concept of Coastin' captured their imagination. Q continued to be an absolute star. She was the Coastin' co-ordination queen, going miles beyond the call of duty, constantly enthusing and encouraging. She seemed so driven by the whole thing. It was easy for me; I had Parkinson's. My "unshakable" motivation was there for all to see. It was obvious. But where did Q's energy and determination come from? I was extraordinarily lucky that she was working with me on this. She explained how to work the media. "It's important to convey key messages in as short a time as possible." And she had given me three points which I would recite to the newspaper reporters and radio and TV stations, regardless of the questions they asked me:

1. You don't have to be old to get Parkinson's
2. We are genuinely close to a cure
3. I'm raising funds and awareness – you can donate
   on the Coastin' website – www.coastin.co.uk

Inevitably, the reporter's final question would be: "What do you think of this area and the people here?"

Walking into Lincolnshire, I wondered what I would say to the reporters here. My perception of the county was such that I thought a truthful response might well be: "Well, the people are not quite as attractive or as fun as they were in Norfolk, and your county is a little too flat for my liking…" I doubted that this would make me first choice for the front page of the Lincolnshire Echo.

I prefer hills. From the map the coast looked like a featureless desert of arable land. I prepared myself for some endless trudging. This was going to be dull.

But I was wrong. There was actually something incredibly restorative about walking the coastline of Lincolnshire. No real concentration was required. It was simply a case of padding along the sea walls and beaches in a quiet relaxed hypnosis, free from the interruption of corners, inclines and rapidly changing views. There seemed so much more space everywhere. Gradually, I began to feel much stronger, as if I was being drip-fed vitality and stamina.

The horizon was a blur. Just by gaining a few feet in altitude the perspective seemed to increase my range of view disproportionately and another few miles of the county's reliefless map would unfurl before me.

I was enjoying the solitude. At last, some space to walk and think on my own. Not that I didn't like having company. I had just had an extremely pleasant weekend with friends marching the runway-straight roads and paths of the coastline of the Wash, from King's Lynn to Fosdyke Bridge. Due to a lack of accommodation, we had been forced to stay in a "travel motel" on one of the nights. The receptionist was expecting "a man with Parkinson's disease who was walking the coastline of Britain".

"I have set aside the disabled room on the ground floor," she said to the others as if I did not exist.

"Thank you, but that actually won't be necessary," I said, stealing the attention myself. She looked at me with a "but you're disabled" look on her face. How she thought I was going to walk another 4,100 miles, if I couldn't get up a flight of stairs, I'm not entirely sure.

My route was pretty simple from Fosdyke Bridge all the way up to Grimsby. But then, I was in a no-nonsense sort of county. Nothing seemed out of place, or jarred the sense of continuity in Lincolnshire. It didn't pretend to be anything other than precisely what it was. There was an unassuming honesty in its endless farmland and even its tacky seaside resorts.

My sense of progress whilst walking was virtually non-existent. The unchanging view should have made me disillusioned, but instead I found it strangely comforting. In the knowledge that it would be nigh on impossible to take a wrong turn (principally because there weren't any turns), I felt more in control with my walking. In fact, I felt more in control with Coastin' as a whole. It had been a good start, if a little hectic. Now I was into my stride. I had established a rhythm for my new life of walking every day; a pace at which everything seemed to work well. When I looked at maps in the evening, I was amazed how much headway I was making. Walking from fold to fold on the map became a measure of my progress. On one occasion, I walked from the centre fold of a map right to the edge in a single morning. This was intensely satisfying.

Boston seemed like an attractive market town of the south; very East Anglian in flavour, whereas Cleethorpes had a definite sense of the north; it almost felt like Yorkshire. Yet both are in Lincolnshire. It took only four days to walk the 70 miles from one to the other and, in so doing, to cross an invisible north/south divide.

My only experience of Cleethorpes was from the 1970s outdoor game show, It's a Knockout, in which the town regularly competed. An image of enormous absurd costumes bumping into one another and the sound of Eddie Waring's northern drawl and Stuart Hall's infectious laughter were all that I could associate with the place before I went there. Having now been there, I can still only associate these things with the place. I can't remember it at all.

Now I was in the north, I noticed people were more direct: "Why are you carrying that stick?" a young girl asked on the beach just beyond Mablethorpe. I didn't really have a short answer for this.

"It helps me walk," I replied, in a rather unhelpful and vague way. The girl seemed satisfied with my response and went back to her bucket and spade.

"Ewan", my stick, had become indispensable. By the time I reached Cleethorpes, I had covered a distance of 450 miles with him, and whenever I walked anywhere without him, it felt odd. It was not so much that I needed him to help me walk, particularly in gradient-free Lincolnshire, it was more that I now felt bereft without him. He had become an extension of my right arm.

I remembered when I had been more than a little scathing about walking poles. I couldn't see their purpose at all. But I had been forced to eat my words when travelling in Chile, where the bridges across rivers on walking tracks often comprised makeshift log arrangements requiring a not inconsiderable sense of balance. Balance is one of a long list of switches in my brain's circuit board turned to the "off" position with Parkinson's. In Chile I blew a fuse.

Nothing was hurt but my pride when I fell in the river. Everyone else had got across, but I toppled in without the slightest hesitation. The worst of it was that I was unable to scramble up the steep-sided banks, resulting in the final ignominy of my rescue by two German girls. They held out their walking poles and hauled me out with infuriatingly condescending expressions on their faces.

"You must buy zee volking steeks," they said. "Zay vill help you viz your balance."

"But then I wouldn't have had the fun of falling in the river," I replied. Unamused, they had looked at each other perplexed by my "English stupidity".

I bought my first walking poles two years later. The two-year wait was sufficient time to allow me to believe that I made the decision by myself and that no credit for the purchase could be attributed to the German girls. In naming the stick "Ewan" – "you won" – there was however a rather blatant admission of defeat.

Now I felt quite emotionally attached to Ewan; an ally in the face of walking adversity. But Lincolnshire was just not throwing many obstacles at me. Even a farmer trying to throw me off his land became an ultimately rewarding experience.

"Where do you think you're going?" he shouted across at me.

I had been forced inland to Wainfleet All Saints by the estuary of the Steeping River, I was now heading back to the coast as soon as possible and also attempting to find an alternative to slogging up the A52 to Skegness. I found myself on a minor road which would eventually take me to the sea.

The man who apprehended me had been perusing documents, leaning over the bonnet of his Land Rover. I reckoned he was probably in his mid- to late forties. He was not particularly big, just one of those weather-beaten, solid types; the sort that look as though if you hit them, you would come away with a broken hand.

"Just walking to the coast," I replied innocently, but I knew what was coming next.

"You're on private land … you can't come through here."

This was bad news. This would mean five miles retraced and a long main road slog to Skegness instead of a short saunter along the beach.

Having apologised profusely, I said, "Would you mind if I continued on this road, only I am on a charity walk around the coast and I am trying to stick as close to the sea as possible?"

To this, he agreed.

Ten minutes later, I heard the Land Rover behind me again. "What have I done now?" I wondered instinctively. But this time his manner was different:

"How much of the coast are you walking?" he asked.

"Er, all of it," I replied, with an embarrassed smile.

"That's amazing," the farmer said.

"It will be if I make it."

"I would be fascinated to talk to you about it. I did a bit of cycling in Australia a few years back… how about we meet for a drink tonight?"

Later on, he met me at my B&B and we walked to the local hostelry. His name was Mark Caudwell. We had lots to talk about. His "bit of cycling in Australia" turned out to be about 3,000 miles, and we chatted about our respective experiences over there. Having refused to let me pay for drinks or supper, he produced a thick leather-bound book from a bag and handed it over to me.

"From John O'Groats to Land's End – 1,372 miles on foot" it said on the front. Although it was in pristine condition, I carefully pulled open the cover and turned a few pages as if they might crumble to dust.

It was a fabulous book dated 1916, although the walk had actually been undertaken in 1882. Amazingly, it was packed full of old black-and-white photographs of places which were familiar to me, having done the walk myself in 1999. I spent a few minutes poring over it enthusiastically.

"This is amazing," I said.

"You can have it if you want it."

"Oh no, I couldn't."

"I want you to have it," he said, with more conviction this time and looking me in the eyes.

I spluttered meaningless words, and then gave up and just looked stunned. "Thank you," I said quietly, trying to convey the sentiment as profoundly as I felt it. "Do you always treat your trespassers this way?"

He grinned. "No."

It was a strange phenomenon, Coastin'. Although these encounters with people along the way were memorable, they were also dissatisfying in their brevity and they felt inconclusive. I longed to stay a while in some places and to get to know certain people much better. Mark Caudwell was a case in point, but I had to keep going. It was a case of enjoying a moment for exactly what it was; a moment. Both Mark and I were fully aware that we would more than likely never see each other again.

I was on the front page of the Skegness Citizen. Not so much for attempting to walk 4,500 miles with Parkinson's disease. Not even for nearly being thrown off a farmer's land. I was on the front page of the Skegness Citizen for getting my eyes tested at the local optician's. It was to do with a sponsorship deal I had been showing off about for some time. I had done well with my sponsored equipment: my boots, my clothes and even my little palmtop computer were sponsored. But the one I was most proud of was that a contact lens company was sponsoring my eyes.

If you believe the article, the local optician had heard about my walk and also about the problems I had with putting in and taking out contact lenses with shaky hands. He had tracked me down with some advice.

"These continuous wear contact lenses can be worn for up to 30 days without having to take them out…" said the article. I had then apparently said, "These lenses should make a considerable difference to my nomadic lifestyle… they should save me a lot of time and effort." The article went on to talk a little about the walk and then finished with another quote from me: "As long as I keep the sea on my right, I shouldn't get lost, quipped Mr Isaacs."

The most extraordinary thing was, exactly the same thing happened in Scarborough and again in Berwick-on-Tweed, Edinburgh and Banff. In fact every three to four weeks or so for the remainder of the journey, opticians would track me down to extol the virtues of continuous wear contact lenses. Not wanting to upset any of them unduly, I would pretend that I had never heard of the lenses on each occasion.

Of course, the real story was that the manufacturers' PR company were co-ordinating the whole thing by sending out the same press release to local media.

It was harmless enough. Coastin', the contact lens company and the local optician all benefited from publicity. The local newspaper got a story and the public learnt about a good new product. It is only frightening if you apply the concept on a much larger scale. More frightening than anything, though, was the fact that I was apparently still cracking the same joke when I reached Brighton months later. "As long as I keep the sea on my right, I shouldn't get lost, quipped Mr Isaacs."

I was late into Grimsby town centre. As well as the local press at 9 a.m., I had an appointment with the local optician. He had tracked me down. My tardiness did not matter as it happened. The *Grimsby Telegraph* did not turn up. Instead, I received a phone message: "Could you get someone to take a picture of you having your eyes tested and e-mail the photographs over?"

Ah, what it is to be a celebrity. Despite actually feeling rather indignant about this, I did it anyway. Q was right. I am a media tart.

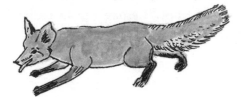

FROM FOXES TO FLEMINGS
14 MILES
MAY

CHAPTER 9

I had no reason to expect a bad day at the office. Walking 14 miles would surely be a piece of cake after yesterday's 22 miles. I marched easily through long grass by the side of a long straight railway line. Oblivious to my presence, a fox, with its head down, no doubt deep in thought on the complexities of Farmer MacDonald's crop rotation system, had trotted to within 20 feet of me. Suddenly aware of our imminent confrontation on the path, its body became rigid as it stared, paralysed with astonishment. Our eyes met. Such was its shock, that it looked as if the poor thing had Parkinson's and inwardly I named him Michael J.

"It's OK, I am not going to hurt you." It was my standard one-liner for wild animals and one that did not break the mould in terms of my chatting-up rate of success for anything. I felt the familiar pang of disappointment when the fox tore away in a blur of legs, ears and bushy tail.

It had been a similar result when I tried to "chat up" the real Michael J. in a letter, trying to persuade him to come and walk with me. "Perhaps you could just come for a few thousand miles," I had joked. I pictured him with the same look on his face as the fox. I received a pleasant response from him though, wishing me luck and praising the venture and the cause. I carried it with me for name-dropping purposes.

I had noticed that pictures of him recently were showing the tell-tale signs of a few years with Parkinson's. I hated the thought that I would inevitably go the same way. In Michael J. Fox I see someone who has the same symptoms in his illness, only at a more advanced stage than me. His high profile is like a crystal ball that I may not wish to see.

Conscious of the bleakness of this train of thought, I turned my attention to the important issue of what the "J." in Michael J. Fox stands for. I rather hoped it was something Beatrix Potteresque. Jeremiah perhaps.

Michael J. Fox had announced to the world that he had Parkinson's disease shortly after my diagnosis. I didn't wish it on him, but this was seriously good news: a celebrity who might champion the cause; inject a bit of interest, pace and glitz to Parkinson's. Before Michael J. Fox, Parkinson's had been an old person's illness, or it affected boxers. Old people got ill and boxers had their heads bashed about. In people's minds, it did not affect the young; not like cancer, HIV or even multiple sclerosis.

For Parkinson's, nothing could come even close to the Michael J. Fox phenomenon. It was probably the most important thing that had happened in Parkinson's since they first found the drug dopamine to treat it.

Fox delivered. Big time. Setting up his own foundation, writing a book entitled *Lucky Man* and raising awareness and millions of dollars in funds throughout the world.

Although I had successfully avoided getting caught up in a melancholic snowball, thinking about Parkinson's did make me feel quite ill with fatigue. The small village of Healing seemed like an appropriate place to rest and I lay down for a power nap in the corner of a large playing field. It did the trick, and when I awoke I suddenly felt excited about reaching the 500-mile mark at the Humber Bridge. One-ninth of the way there.

Beyond the Humber Bridge is a different type of coastline. Although the horizontal nature of Lincolnshire had acted like a slow mental therapy for me, I now felt ready for a few verticals in Yorkshire. Lincolnshire had allowed my mind to wander far from the walk itself, as there was nothing to jolt me back into the here and now. I knew from experience that the more strenuous headland and bay features of the next stretch of coastline would not allow such indulgences and my thoughts would not stray far from the task of walking. Hills would break my rhythm. Map, view and the physical demands on my body would be constantly competing for my attention. I wondered how these extra considerations would affect me, and more particularly, my Parkinson's.

But first the rest of Lincolnshire and Humberside had to be dispensed with, and, judging by the clouds that were now rolling in, I was not going to be allowed to do that with quite the ease that I had hoped for. The remainder of my walk from Grimsby to Habrough was unspeakably awful. The transition from the dry, optimistic young man who left Healing, to a sodden, disgruntled specimen, was startlingly quick.

The path beside the railway line had become overgrown and I was annoyed with myself for not having put gaiters in my daypack. The dampness was quick to pervade my footwear and it seemed almost spitefully cool when compared to the warmth of the day. It spilled over the rims of my boots and coursed through the fabric of my socks as if I had just stepped into a large puddle. It is not just the weather conditions outside that can affect the enjoyment of a day's walk; the weather conditions within my boots also play a large part. Today the conditions within my boots were the worst since records began. I had counted two blisters, a corn (looking as if it might shortly get promoted to a verruca), a dose of athlete's foot, and a burgeoning crop of Portobello mushrooms sprouting between my toes. All seemed to be thriving well at sock saturation point.

Meanwhile outside the heavens opened and I was enveloped in a blanket of rain. Huge clumps of mud defiantly attached themselves to the underside of my boots. For a while I strode out, grim faced, enjoying not the walk but the challenge. It felt like Mission Impossible. I had to prevail. Nothing was going to stop me.

I stopped. I felt a sudden need to munch the rest of my family-sized bar of Galaxy under the shelter of a tree. My sudden lack of commitment to Mission Impossible made me feel rather guilty. But guilt does tend to make chocolate taste so much better.

Scoffing the chocolate brought me joy that was disproportionate to the event. I failed to attain the same level of enthusiasm for the appalling conditions. I was cold and wet. Very wet. I stumbled into a pub and was faced with that uncomfortable feeling when everyone turns to look at you as you walk through the door. As I stood there, with water streaming off every overhanging extremity, the entire pub burst out laughing. It was a fair cop. The facts were plain to see. I was a soft Southerner out walking in appalling conditions and dripping from every extremity. There is simply no dignity in being wet, and although I had reached Habrough, so far my greeting there had not lifted my spirits.

On leaving the pub I looked down at my feet. I longed to peel off my socks, to see what the damage was. I suspected my feet would look magnificently rancid. It's a boy thing.

Having said that, I was discovering that the nation has an all-consuming fascination with feet. Invariably, the first question I was asked was, "How are your feet?" When I responded that they were mildly gangrenous and that I seemed to be growing an extra little toe, everyone screwed up their faces in disgust. Personally, I am only interested in my own feet, but perhaps the realisation of this only came after I had asked about somebody else's.

Back in Habrough, my haphazard meanderings in search of the B&B did not ease my suffering. Asking for directions has always been out of the question. Willingly I have extended many a day's torment by an hour just by stubbornly refusing to ask someone the way. It goes hand in hand with not reading instruction manuals. I can work it out myself. I don't want help – even if I need it. It's another boy thing. These stubborn traits run deep. I can become quite angry with someone if they try to help me while I am struggling with some task, due to Parkies. No matter how long it takes, I must finish whatever it is I have started on my own. I have no problem in asking someone to carry a drink for me or to write something down for me, but if I have started to open a bottle of water when in the midst of a shaking fit, I must complete the task for myself. By crossing a starting line, I have contracted to also cross the finishing line. It is an obstinacy which will probably annoy the hell out of everyone when or if things get worse. But to me, a failure to complete what you have begun is the definition of disability.

I knew the moment I met the Flemings that I would like them. The warmth of their welcome. The cosiness of their house. The effort that went towards making me feel at home.

I am sure when I finally arrived at their doorstep dripping with mud, they would much rather have hosed me down and hung me out on the washing line for a couple of hours prior to letting me into their immaculate Victorian home. And yet if they were thinking this, they certainly did not show it. Having been introduced by Ken Fleming to his wife Régine and two daughters, I was put on the Fleming comfort conveyor belt. Within half an hour of setting foot in The Old Vicarage bed and breakfast, I was dry, content and smiling into a piping hot cup of tea. No small achievement, given that I had shambled into their driveway morose, bedraggled and shivering with both cold and Parkinson's.

April 9, 2002

Tom Isaacs
Coastin'
c/o Parkinson's Disease Society
215 Vauxhall Bridge Road
London SW1V 1EJ

Dear Tom,

I am writing to offer you my support and well wishes for your ambitious plan to raise Parkinson's awareness through your "Coastin'    A walk around the coastline of Britain in aid of Parkinson's Research" tour.  Your story, as a sufferer from Young Onset Parkinson's, is obviously one I can relate to personally.  I am therefore especially thrilled about your plan to walk the coast line of Britain, not only because you are doing so to raise money towards advancement of a cure, but also because you are taking on a personal and physical challenge that is inspirational to all sufferers of Parkinson's.

I understand that the kick off date for the "Coastin'" tour is April 11, 2002. Everyone at the Foundation will have you in their thoughts that day, as you take the first steps of your yearlong journey.  We wish you the absolute best and look forward to updates on your progress.

With kind regards,

Michael J. Fox

FROM HABROUGH
TO MIDDLESBROUGH
187 MILES
MAY - JUNE

CHAPTER 10

I needed to make a rendezvous at the Humber Bridge in two hours and I still had eight miles to go.

I never allow enough time to do things. I had not foreseen that exceptional company and sumptuous food at the Fleming breakfast table would cause me to lose track of time. I had started late. Carefully positioned clumps of stinging nettles on every footpath on my route hampered progress still further. Both of these factors had conspired to leave me concerned about meeting the local press at the Humber Bridge. I would need to run. As I goaded myself to set off jogging, a muffled voice from behind made me jump out of my skin.

"Are you the footpath official?"

The words were startling enough, but when I turned to find the voice had emanated from Star Wars no-gooder, Darth Vader, armed with his latest weapon of mass destruction, I was completely dumbfounded. I stood motionless, transfixed by his appearance. What was he doing here?

I tried to pull myself together but couldn't remember what he had asked me. I decided it would be sensible not to ask him to repeat the question, so I replied, "Er… yes, I think so."

Darth Vader took his protective mask off, unhitched himself from the tentacles of his instrument of doom and laid the contraption on the ground. He actually looked normal enough. His face was weathered, his nose large and his beard grey and a touch unruly; but then after 40 years on the Dark Side, you could forgive him that.

He was looking at me quizzically, but seemed undeterred by my state of complete apoplexy. He started speaking again. "There are just too many nettles for one man."

It all became clear to me. He was exterminating nettles. I felt sorry for him; the Dark Lord, a onetime ruler of the galaxy and potential destroyer of all mankind, was now demoted to a potential destroyer of all nettles in the East Humberside area.

"Yes, there are a lot of them, aren't there?" I lifted the leg of my trousers to prove that I had first-hand knowledge of the subject matter. He looked sadly back at me, as if I had called into question his aptitude for nettle extermination.

"But it looks like you're doing a good job with this path," I added, pretending that I was just completing the previous sentence.

I gazed at the field, through which a tiny path could just be made out amidst row upon row of impenetrable waist-high nettles.

"So are you the footpath official?" he asked again, looking at me out of the corner of his eye. He was now unsure as to my authenticity.

"Er, no, sorry, I am not. I misunderstood you earlier."

He did not seem altogether convinced by this either. In fact, now, I rather got the impression that he thought I was some kind of public footpath spy, hell-bent on proving there was simply no justification in council funds being spent employing Jedi knights to clear the county's footpaths of irksome plant life. Completely ignoring my claims of having nothing to do with footpath officialdom, he proceeded to inform me about the broken gate in the far field, the missing footpath waymarkers between here and Goxhill and how stinging nettles were the scourge of the nation.

I could sense a dangerous amount of time elapsing before I broke free from his monologue. I tried to excuse myself politely. Again he looked crestfallen, but there was nothing I could do. I had a deadline with the Humber Bridge.

We parted and he put his mask back on, ripped at the start lead of his monstrous-looking machine, and as it fired up into action, he once again set about his epic struggle against nettle domination of the world.

The next section of footpath was confusing and I stood scratching my head, not really knowing which bush of nettles to walk through. Just then, a head popped out of the gorse bush behind me.

"Hello again," said Darth Vader, "are you lost?" His great voice rasped behind the gas mask, but still managed to sound gleeful at the prospect of my not knowing my whereabouts.

"Well, not exactly, but I'm trying to get to Goxhill."

A huge arm extended through the gorse bush, and out of a black glove uncurled a seemingly endless finger.

"Just you go through that clump of stingers over there," he pointed. "That will get you back on the right path."

I thanked him and did as he suggested, using Ewan as a machete to clear myself a passage. When I reached the path, he was still there, with his head and arm poked through the bush. His shiny black gloves were waving at me. I waved back. Later, when I was recounting the tale, I made out at this point that "he then returned to the dark side of the gorse."

I didn't get any laughs then either.

I was only ten minutes late for the Humber Bridge, but at least I had the excuse of having walked 500 miles to get there. Quite a few people had turned up and I was excited by the attendance of a man from the local TV network. With a slot on the local news bulletin, I would get my message across to thousands. Coastin' could easily pick up momentum and by the end become national news. Perhaps I would be the saviour of people with Parkinson's across the world. Delusions of grandeur were short-lived when the cameraman announced that his batteries had run out and went home.

Nevertheless, I was quite pleased early next morning to hear a somewhat "cheesy" piece of broadcasting on Hull FM, which had a series of quotes from me on the bridge, intermingled with excerpts from songs such as "These boots were made for walking", "Walk of life" and, yes, I am afraid so, "You'll never walk alone".

Despite this promise of company, I was distinctly alone as I walked out of the city on the joyless A1033. It was ironic that I was walking along a dual carriageway without a pavement in a hurricane when I rang my mother to say that I had made it through Hull in one piece. She had, for some reason, been more worried about my passing through Hull than anywhere else in the country. She seemed greatly relieved that I had slipped through the chic restaurants and bars of the central waterfront area unscathed.

"You've got nothing to worry about now," I said as a violent gust of wind sent me tottering into the road and into the path of a large juggernaut.

"Nothing to worry about at all!" I repeated after the vehicle had thundered past and I had made a mental check that it had not taken any of my limbs with it. Over the next few days, I experienced a very real sense of being in the north. Perhaps it was the accents, perhaps it was the fact that people were a little bit more likely to say "hello" as I walked past, or perhaps it was that I passed through a village called "Thorngumbold".

In Patrington Haven, I stopped at a pub to fill up my water bottle. The landlady started enthusing greatly when she read my Coastin' T-shirt. She followed me out of the pub as I was leaving to inform her husband, who was lounging in the sun.

"He's walking right round the coast of Britain," she told him excitedly.

"Is he?" came an unimpressed response.

"4,500 miles."

"Really?"

"Yes, it's for charity. It's going to take a whole year." There was desperation in her voice.

"Oh."

I glanced back to see her scurrying into the pub again. I felt the man looking at my back as I walked away. The effort of assimilating all this new information was clearly too much for him. It was as if he had been pickled in apathy and told to sit outside until sun-dried. I stole another look. For a moment there was a flicker of something, movement perhaps. But the effort was too great and he retreated, slipping back easily to that place of self-indulgent, wallowing indifference.

I know the place he was in. Mr Beef knows this place. I suspect a lot of people do. It comprises a loop of totally rational thought which always arrives at the same conclusion: "Do nothing."

The more laps of the "do nothing loop" the brain completes in one sitting, the more stimulating the sign for the exit has to be for a change of scenery.

As I reached a bend that would take me out of Patrington Haven and out of sight of the pub for good, the man's inertia finally failed him. Up to this moment, he had failed miserably to give me even a grunt of recognition. Now he heaved his frame out of his chair, and with a ponderous shift in stance, he stood facing me. I looked across at him and he waved.

"Good luck!" he called. The gesture seemed so much more satisfying and important after the wait.

I felt ecstatic to have walked the 27 miles from Hull to Kilnsea in one day. Admittedly, due to medication failure, for at least five of these miles I had been bent double, limping into a fierce headwind. The posture at least allowed me to avoid the pitying eyes of strangers with ease. Admittedly, an exhausting bout of shaking had driven me to spread my waterproofs in a meadow just off the path and curl up in a ball to sleep for an hour before being able to go on. And admittedly, it took me over 13 hours to complete the distance. But despite all of that, I had done it and was elated. Once again I had a sense of being able to complete the entire year's walking. I could go full circle. I knew I could.

My confidence had grown immeasurably since those first tentative days. Confidence was something I had been short on for a while in the early days of Parkinson's. Over the first few years with it I had suffered a series of little episodes which had bruised me. A few girls had turned down my advances and I had been convinced that this had been because of my Parkinson's.

In those early days, I tended to do this. In my head, I would make out that it was worse than it actually was. I was living in the tragedy of my perceived future. Nowadays, I try to live more in the comedy of the present. Even though my health is now worse, the "Parkier" I get, the perkier I seem to become. In fact friends now say I am "obsessively positive" – I can think of worse mental states in which to be.

Back then, I had confided in Mule. "No girl will take me on looking like this…" and I stood there in front of him looking like a vibrating wind-up kangaroo.

He could easily have said, "Pull yourself together, Isaacs, you're pathetic." It would have been a fair description of me at that moment. But he sensed the depths from which the words had come and his reply was one of pinpoint precision, the sort that can only be delivered by someone who really knows you.

"Girls are not as shallow as us men."

At face value, the words were a comfort, but they also struck a deeper chord, a raw nerve perhaps. He had been kind when he had used the expression "us men." He meant me.

And he was right. My concern was not actually about the prospect of the physical deterioration caused by my PD. It was more about my fears of self-loathing through disability. I couldn't adjust to the prospect of being chronically ill. I suppose subconsciously, until now, I had pigeon-holed people into "physically handicapped" and "able-bodied". Two totally separate ways of life with an obvious dividing line. I couldn't see how cross-border relationships would work without pity playing its part.

But of course, these categories only existed in my head. The only time I would ever be "disabled" was when I considered myself to be so. The trick was to concentrate on "abilities" I still possessed. And there were plenty of those. I had not recognised self-doubt – I had interpreted my slight personality change as being an inevitable by-product of the condition. I started thinking that even some of my closest friends didn't understand me and for a while I found it difficult to talk to them. "They don't understand – no one understands."

But actually it was not they who misunderstood. It was me. My fear of the future, the "how much longer will I be able to do this" factor, was driving me ever backwards into becoming someone who might soon be no fun to be with, no longer happy in himself.

It was about this time, no more than a year after diagnosis, that I had the extraordinary "Sheikh of Shakes" dream, which helped shape my perception of how the rest of my life would be lived.

That had been the turning point for me. The belief that I could make something positive out of an all-consuming negative has stood me in good stead ever since. The "Sheikh of Shakes" attitude would provide me with a sense of purpose, and one which was stronger, more determined and more focused than any I had had in my life, even before Parkinson's.

As long as I had purpose, there was the promise of fulfilment, and that surely is all anyone asks for, even if the means of getting there are different.

Quite quickly, I began to take back control of my life. Instead of hiding the fact that I had Parkinson's disease, I forced myself to allow people to see me shaking so that both they and I would be comfortable with it. Before, I had thought it enough to try to convince people that although Tom Isaacs might have changed physically, the person underneath had not. What I had not realised before was that I needed to convince myself first. If I ever thought of myself as "disabled", then it would be through a deterioration of my spirit rather than any physical deterioration. After all, who was more disabled, the apathetic man at the pub or the Parkinson's man walking 4,500 miles around Britain?

So, slowly, I had pulled myself together bit by bit; hoping that positive actions would bring greater self-assurance and self-esteem. One event and one person would do more than anything else to help me back to the prospect of a good life again: Lyndsey.

\* \* \*

Soon after the *Daily Mail* meeting when Silky had said that Muhammad Ali was going to walk with me, he held a party. I was not feeling great that day and did not really want to go. I did not know many of Silky's friends and the prospect of shaking in front of a lot of strangers did not really appeal to me. Deciding that it would be appalling not to turn up after all Silky had done for me, I made a late appearance.

Silky did me proud, introducing me to everyone as a soon-to-be all-conquering hero. I tried to act in a manner appropriate to my billing – I was probably highly obnoxious. But it was surprising how interested people seemed to be in what I was about to undertake.

One person who was showing more interest than anyone was an attractive girl with a Scottish accent. As we chatted, I felt the dyskinesia in my right hand. I jammed the thing in my trouser pocket, which only served to set my arm off into a twisty fit. "Damn this Parkies," I thought to myself. I really didn't want her to see the difficulties I was experiencing.

We were getting on well. We both knew it. I was not sure whether she had noticed my restless right hand and arm. We had a lot in common: travel, walking, sense of humour. There was a twinkle in her eyes; a bit of mischief waiting to be unleashed. "I really quite like you," I thought as she chattered excitedly about when she had lived in New Zealand.

One of her friends came to collect her – they were all off to see a band.

"Do you want to come?" she asked.

"Of course I want to come," I thought, but I knew the dyskinesia was going to get worse and if my medication stopped working completely while we were watching the band, that would be that.

"Sorry, I'm going to see a friend," I lied. We stood staring at each other for a moment. "Do something, Isaacs," I urged myself. "Quick, say something." I willed myself to take control.

"It's been great talking to you," I said. It was a pathetic, half-hearted line to gauge her response. I would probably have left it at that. At that time, with the Parkinson's having advanced so far, I did not feel the confidence to ask anyone out for a date. It would mean I would have to reveal the truth about my having an "old person's disease". And then I would have to deal with the rejection. After all, what sane girl would take on a 33-year-old guy who'd had Parkinson's for nearly six years.

She made it easy for me, scribbling her phone number on a piece of card. "Call me if you want to have another chat some time," she said, and giving me a peck on the cheek, she was gone.

The following evening I hatched my plan of attack. I thought I would play it cool; I didn't want to appear too keen. Perhaps I would ring her in a week or so. Twenty minutes later I picked up the phone and rang her.

We agreed to meet in a cafe in Islington. For once, I was on time. She was late. She had that same cheeky grin and the sparkling eyes. We chatted. Small talk really. For me, everything was just a precursor to the main event. It was something I just wanted to blurt out; to get it out of the way, to clear my conscience. It was so tempting just to come out with it: "I have got Parkinson's disease, so if you want to leave, go now. I will quite understand."

But I managed to hold my course; biding my time until it was appropriate to say something. Until these words were out in the open though, I felt restless and insecure. I needed it over and done with.

I found out she had been a nurse and was now working in recruitment while at the same time doing a part-time degree in Chinese Medicine so that she could become an acupuncturist. She turned the conversation back to me.

"Are you getting sponsored for your walk?" she asked.

"Yes, I am doing it for Parkinson's disease." Here we go.

"Why Parkinson's disease?" came the inevitable response.

"Principally because I have got it myself." I looked her straight in the eyes; searching them for clues. They gave nothing away.

There. I'd said it. It was over. Whatever the outcome, I could relax now.

She nodded and paused to take in the information. I looked away, giving her a bit of space to consider the repercussions of the news just imparted. As I did so, she said very gently, "... that's OK."

Her intonation was easy to interpret. She was not saying, "It doesn't bother me," but she was saying, "It's not going to stop me from getting to know you." I felt instantly at ease.

She asked a few questions about the condition, but an insufficient number to make me think there was an issue. It felt comfortable talking to her about my Parkinson's. She seemed totally at ease and there was no awkwardness whatsoever; her nursing background and open nature gave her a rare and refreshing attitude. Even so, I still found myself playing down how bad it was; as if it was not a big issue in my life and that it was just a problem for everyone else. Walking along the Grand Union canal, after lunch, we found we had a lot more in common: Thai green curries, sense of adventure, a love of travel and the outdoors. As we headed back to Upper Street, my medication started to wear off and I began to limp. We reached a coffee bar before it became too pronounced, but I sensed that she had noticed it.

"Now I also need to tell you about my right leg," I said to her. She gave me a look of sympathetic horror. "It's wooden," I said, smiling.

"Oh my God, is it?" she said, not completely convinced I was telling the truth.

"No," I replied.

"You bastard!" she laughed.

It had been a cracking first date. At the time, I don't think Lyndsey could find any reasonable rationale behind her decision to go out with a man who had suffered from Parkinson's for six years and on top of that would shortly be wandering around the country for a year.

\* \* \*

Walking from Kilnsea down to Spurn Head was a strange thing to do. For starters I didn't need to walk there. My rules were that I needed to see the sea every day. It would have been easy to take a more direct route from Hull to Bridlington. But I was curious about the long finger of land which seemed to be making a brave attempt to reach across to Lincolnshire and seal up the mouth of the Humber.

I started the five-mile walk out to the tip of Spurn Head with the sea on my left. Something was wrong. I was going the wrong way. My body felt like a stubborn dog on a lead wanting to go in the opposite direction. In fact, it felt so peculiar that I crossed over to the western side of the narrow strip of land so that the river was on my right. I found my rhythm again.

I experienced a sort of sick satisfaction on reaching the lighthouse at Spurn Head. There, just a few miles across the Humber, was a spot somewhere between Grimsby and Cleethorpes where I had been walking some five days earlier. "If I had rowed it…" my thought process was interrupted as I stared at the churning cauldron of salt water in front of me. It made me re-word the end of the sentence, "…I would have drowned five days ago."

The coastline is almost dead straight for the 50 or so miles from Spurn Head to Bridlington. The walking continued to be a little bit uninspiring and I was beginning to feel a bit cheated by Yorkshire, which did not seem to be delivering its promise of hills. But slowly, the gentle sloping of the coastline, which had been the norm until now, was replaced by a more dramatic transition between land and sea.

The cliffs on this southern stretch of the Yorkshire coast are some of the fastest disappearing in the country, becoming victims of the North Sea's progress westwards at a rate of six to eight feet each year. The knowledge of this had me stepping gingerly along paths which often seemed to ignore the fact that they were "within range."

Lyndsey had finished her final exams in Chinese Medicine and I was excited about seeing her. She had reached the hotel in Skipsea early and had started walking back along the coast to meet me.

I saw her light blue jacket in the distance when she was about a mile away and waved my hands furiously; but it was too far. When we got so there was about fifty yards between us, it was too much like a Mills and Boon romantic novel for me not to perform like an idiot. Slipping off my rucksack and letting Ewan fall to the ground, I bounded with huge strides and in slow motion towards her with an expression of unbridled rapture on my face.

She laughed as I wrapped her in my arms over-passionately so as to enjoy the full effect of the joke. Once we were in the embrace, the joke was, for me at least, suddenly forgotten and I realised as I stared north at the coast how good it was to have her here and how much I had missed her. We set off back the way she had come.

"Er, haven't you forgotten something?" she said. I stared at her for a moment, wondering what I hadn't done. Then I remembered Ewan and the rucksack fifty yards back down the coast. I ran back to retrieve them.

"What's the hotel like?" I asked.

"It's OK."

Lyndsey was not one to fuss about accommodation. She would be as happy in a tent as in five-star luxury. If Lyndsey said it was "OK", that meant it was downright awful.

"What's wrong with it?"

"It's just not great," she said. "There's no one else staying there. In fact, I'm not sure whether anyone has ever stayed there!"

We arrived at a shabby-looking oversized pub, which had a separate entrance marked "Hotel". I took comfort that the bar seemed to be full, and having checked in, put my head round the door. It was a bit like entering the annual convention of Dangerous Drunken Devil-worshippers Anonymous.

I had never seen such a frightening collection of characters in one place at one time. They were ugly in every sense. Most of them seemed to be bloated with excess and quite angry about it too. The atmosphere in the room

Faye Tozer and Bear Grylls
at the start of Coastin'

Shazzer

Suffolk

'Q' – Helen Matthews

Cley-next-the-Sea Norfolk

The Flemings and Mr Beef in Middlesborough

Cleveland Way

Lyndsey and her parents

Mr Shaky and the Piper

Davey Ads, Sally and
'Winston' the Landrover

Lindisfarne Castle at Sunset

Earlsferry, Fife       Boddam Lighthouse, near Peterhead

Croft at Farr Bay, North Coast

'...dressed like
a snack- sized bar
of Dairy Milk'

'The swirling sandbanks
of the Kyle of Durness'

Fording the
River Naver

Ewan and some stones

Kearvaig beach view

First view of Kearvaig Beach near Cape Wrath

Wild Rover at Achmelvich,
near Lochinver

Stoer Penninsula

Rat infested sleeping quarters
at Carnmore

Elma McPherson

was threatening. There was nothing nice going on in there; all sneers and leers. Had I entered, I suspected there might have been the odd jeer too. Withdrawing quietly, I grimaced to Lyndsey. "Don't go in there. It's not nice."

"What do you mean, 'not nice'?

"The people aren't…very…nice…"

Lyndsey barged past me to go and have a look as I knew she would. She often made fun of what she called my "public school upbringing". She was Glaswegian. She could talk to anyone.

Ten seconds later she scurried back through the door of the bar. "OK," she said in admission that even Glaswegians drew the line somewhere. We beat a hasty retreat to our room.

"I've never seen so many body piercings, tattoos and zips," puffed Lyndsey as she grappled with the key in the lock. "Why would anyone want to do that to themselves?"

"Don't be so judgemental, Lyndsey. Honestly! Maybe they were caught up in some freak sewing machine accident or something."

The bedroom was huge and awful. It didn't matter, we were having a good time.

Deep in the night I was awoken by bloodcurdling shrieking. I shuffled down deeper beneath the covers, trying to shut out thoughts of whatever savage ritual was being staged downstairs. But the shrieking continued. I listened harder and noticed another background noise: a strangely familiar whine of electric guitars and drums building to a crescendo.

I exposed one ear from beneath the sheets. To my relief, I realised that the screaming was just a failed attempt at attaining the necessary vocal range to sing Meatloaf's "Bat out of Hell", karaoke style.

Initially we were relieved that we were not in immediate danger of being the subject of some pagan ritual sacrifice, courtesy of the occupants of the hotel bar. But had we realised that instead we were to be treated to a karaoke version of the entire Bat out of Hell album at 1 a.m., we might have preferred that option.

I was furious. And I like Meatloaf! Satanists or not, there would be stiff words with the management in the morning. Above all else, Lyndsey and I just wanted to be on the road again and out of this place.

"Who do I pay?" I asked a frightened-looking girl on the stairs.

"He's in that room there." She pointed before scurrying up past me as if wanting to be as far away from "that room" as possible.

With some trepidation, I poked my head around the door to "that room" and there "he" was, sitting amidst piles and piles of coins, which he was counting. He looked like an East End gangster-cum-pirate. Even sitting down, he was huge and menacing. I recognised the chaotic sound of Iron Maiden's "666, The Number of the Beast" from a black speaker which was not up to the task it had been set.

All thoughts of complaining about last night's lack of sleep were immediately abandoned, I think they call it cowardice. I would just be content to give the man some money (lots of money, if necessary), and get the hell out of here.

"I've come to settle up," I said as boldly as I could muster.

"Have you?" His response seemed to be laden with malevolent intent, and as he raised his head from counting bits of treasure, he gave me a long slow look as if searching for weaknesses.

"I've heard about you." He paused and smiled. His teeth gleamed white in contrast to everything else in the room, which seemed to be black.

"There will be no charge and I am sorry if the karaoke kept you awake last night. Good luck with the rest of your walk."

The lack of sleep from the previous night meant that I was quite shaky for the first full day's walking with Lyndsey. I had heard my consultant use the term "bat-wing tremor" before. It was a good analogy and ironic that it had been caused by someone singing "Like a bat out of hell". It was also precisely how I felt. When my medication finally kicked in, there was the usual sense of euphoria at being able to move freely again.

"Do you know Bat out of Hell is my favourite album of all time," I said to Lyndsey. I fully expected to be ridiculed mercilessly for this admission, but to my absolute astonishment she replied, "Och yes, it's great. I haven't heard it for years."

"I could sing it for you?" I asked, not quite believing what I was hearing.

"Go on then."

I needed no second bidding and spent the next half-hour regaling with her a rendition of the complete album. For me it was a seminal moment. Here was a girl who not only liked Meatloaf, but was also prepared to listen to me sing. I didn't think a girl like that existed.

She was even interested in my theories on what makes a good Bed and Breakfast. Together we agreed that there were five fundamental criteria:
1. A good, friendly welcome

2. A comfortable, hard bed
3. A hot, powerful shower
4. A hearty breakfast
5. A good, friendly send-off

If our hotel in Skipsea fell some way short on the first four criteria, it redeemed itself sensationally with its performance in category five.

Two days later, we put our new marking system to the test with our B&B in Bridlington.

1. Welcome – 0/10

Having had my ability to read situations completely turned on its head in Skipsea, I was wary of jumping to conclusions with the B&B owners in Bridlington. Nevertheless, when a surly man asked us to pay for our accommodation upfront with barely a single word of welcome, things did not bode well.

2. Bed – 0/10

It was like sleeping on a soft warped sponge, and midway through the night I decided the floor was a better option.

3. Shower – 0/10

Tired and aching after only two hours' sleep, I staggered into the bathroom on the landing. A piping hot shower was the only thing that would revive me this morning. As the incontinent dribble of icy cold water hit my body, I emitted a far more powerful stream of words. I waited for quarter of an hour, during which time the water changed from icy to cool, and I changed from tepid to boiling point.

4. Breakfast – 0/10

Due to (2) and (3), Lyndsey and I arrived for breakfast five minutes later than the time allocated by the B&B.

"I'm afraid you are late. We cannot cook you breakfast."

Decision time. Should I boil over now or try politeness first in an attempt to get some breakfast? I opted for breakfast, and with a conspicuous display of restraint, I revealed the reasons for our lateness.

I felt frustrated by the apology and the paltry breakfast that followed. It seemed like an unsatisfactory trade-off after our experiences. They knew what I was doing. They knew how important our breakfast would be to us. Yet they made no effort whatsoever. It was an extraordinary display of a total lack of hospitality.

5. Send-off – 0/10

There was none. We just left. And it was rotten weather too.

I felt guilty about being so miserable for Lyndsey's final day with me, but fatigue, weather and circumstances had conspired to put me in a filthy temper. The guilt compounded this still further. And then guilt was heaped on guilt, when my mother turned up, having driven all the way from Hertfordshire, to be met by her youngest son scowling thunderously.

Mum saw my cheerlessness as a challenge and at the end of the day's short walk, she whisked me off to a hotel where the floors were less comfortable than the beds.

Apart from coming up to replenish my drugs supply and other essentials, my mother had come to walk. Dad, with his heart problem, couldn't keep up. Besides, he did not love walking like Mum did. Dad needed a golf club in his hand. Mum just loved being out there.

I was a new person the next morning. It is amazing how the world can change overnight. I had gone to sleep sombre, run-down and foul-tempered. I woke up full of bounce and vigour. Mum was relieved – she had been worried that the walk was becoming too much for me.

My mother has been the principal influence in my life. She is the one who has instilled in me the strength to deal with Parkinson's.

I maintain that my Parkinson's disease is worse for her than it is for me. This may seem an odd statement. Mum would be the first to dismiss it as "nonsense". But although she may not have to deal with the physical difficulties of the condition, I suspect that, mentally, it may now be more trying for her than it is for me.

In a sense it's easy for me; I know what it's like to have it. I have accepted it and moved on. But for Mum, there is no hope of acceptance, no pay-off. My brief flirtation with the "why me" syndrome is now a long way behind me. I need never return there. But as a mother, "why him" must be a place that she revisits over and over again. Every time she notices symptoms not seen before – a new body part that shakes or a new level of immobility – she must think, "Why? Why him?"

There is a wonderful saying I once heard that "You are only given what you can deal with." So far as my Parkinson's is concerned, I would probably agree with this. But what I am not very good at dealing with is the paradoxical situation in which my mother and I find ourselves. Mutual worry is a terrible affliction for which there is no cure. I hate the fact that my mother must watch as Parkinson's tightens its grip on me. It feels as if I am inflicting on her some slow mental torture.

My grave concern for her grave concern about me has been gravely concerning for both of us since my diagnosis. It is a totally unpreventable vicious circle. We are both aware of the futility of the situation.

But which is best? I still haven't worked it out. Do I tell Mum when I'm feeling terrible, when I know it will make her miserable for days; in fact, probably a far longer time than I am feeling terrible? Or do I go against her express wishes, putting a strain on her trust by covering up the worst of it? Somewhere between the two, we have struck an unsatisfactory balance. The fact remains that from her perspective I should stop worrying about her and concentrate on myself. For me, the reverse is true.

At breakfast in the hotel, all lingering worries from the previous day were washed away as we were entertained by four elderly ladies who were having fun at the expense of the pregnant waitress.

"Could you walk past a bit more slowly next time, love," one of them remonstrated, "only, you're making one heck of a draught!"

It was difficult not to listen in to the lively discussion between these women, all of whom must have been over 70. I was impressed with their in-depth knowledge of Premiership football, but even more splendid was the ensuing heated debate on the merits of Wembley as a location for the proposed national stadium.

Mum dropped me at the day's start point, Flamborough Head. I was amazed how a change in mood and weather could transform a place from dreary, exposed and lonely to one that was so invigorating and inspiring.

I sat for a while under a sign that pointed to both John O'Groats and Land's End and proclaimed boldly that both were 362 miles away. I did my calculations. For me they would be much further. For me it would be 760 miles before I turned left at John O'Groats. As for my route to Land's End, that would involve walking a further 2,900 miles from here. I found this strangely satisfying, but knew that, had it been raining, the prospect of walking such distances would not seem so appealing.

Someone read my thoughts. Half an hour later, the prospect of walking such distances did not seem so appealing. It was raining.

The rain didn't seem to stop the "twitchers", who were lining the cliffs in their droves to look at the razorbills, kittiwakes and guillemots. My first drugs of the day were starting to kick out, so I avoided people as best I could. My brand of "twitching" is best done alone.

At Filey Brigg (a large rock promontory supposedly built by the devil in an attempt to link us to Europe), I joined the start of the 110-mile Cleveland Way. I would be walking almost exactly half of it as far as Saltburn-on-Sea, where the path turns inland.

As a stretch of coast to walk, the Cleveland Way is a joy. For me, after 600 miles of relatively flat walking, the sharp changes in gradient which are a feature of the track made me more enthusiastic than ever for the walk. In a way, I suppose it was like having driven miles and miles to a funfair and then having a go on the rollercoaster. Going up and down hills gave me repeated adrenalin shots. Each day became more of a battle. I was challenging myself that bit more, pushing back the boundaries, defying Parkinson's.

I would pace myself up hills: counting the steps; only allowing myself a rest after I had counted to a hundred. I could feel the tightness in my calves and quadriceps. It was a good pain. A pain that meant I was getting stronger with every stride. And then there was the reward of reaching the top and feeling the waves of euphoria as endorphins fizzed and sparkled in my head, making me giddy with satisfaction.

This was me in my element. "I'm not Coastin' any more," I enthused to Q on the phone, "I'm Rollercoastin'!"

"Go Tommy!" she encouraged at the other end.

But it was not just the challenge of the Cleveland Way which made me enjoy this stretch so much. From the towering heights of Beast Cliff to the depths of enchanting wooded valleys such as Hayburn Wyke and Boggle Hole; every mile seemed to hold something of interest, something that wrested my attention back to the beauty of the scenery.

The string of fishing villages along this coast are ridiculously picturesque; their tightly packed houses seemed either to cling implausibly to plunging headlands or nestle cosily in sheltered hollows. I suspected Robin Hood's Bay, Runswick Bay and Staithes had all adorned many a cake tin and jigsaw puzzle. I wished I had longer to explore their labyrinthine back streets, footpaths and alleyways. Even the bustling centres of Scarborough and Whitby were far more than just seaside resorts. I felt cheated that I couldn't do them justice.

A lack of time for exploration became the most annoying feature of the walk for me. It was like being given a set of travel guides and only ever being allowed to look at the pictures. I longed to learn a bit more; even just to read the captions.

B&B owners were often the best way to glean a little knowledge about a place. My mother was proving to be particularly adept at extracting interesting local information and gossip. There was no doubt she was loving the whole Coastin' experience; and not just the walking. She laughed when I was scolded by the owner of one guesthouse for having contracted Parkinson's and as a result "being a major concern to your poor mother". The lady had turned to Mum at this point and confided, "I have problems with my boy too." I left them to compare notes. Mother to mother. They chatted for some time.

"What is wrong with her son?" I asked Mum after her chat.

"I hardly like to tell you." She was smiling.

"Why, what?"

"Well, her son wants to become her daughter."

"Oh God... how awful for her."

"Which one?"

"The mother... and him...her...all of them."

I tried to be open-minded about the similarities from the mother's perspective, but never really got beyond the first fundamental hurdle.

Both mothers had sons who, through no fault of their own, were having their physical capabilities and appearances altered. And in both cases, this had probably been due to some mix-up at the gene factory before birth.

I can see now that there are similarities between the two cases. I can. Initially though, I found it difficult to appreciate any link at all. It all seemed a bit tenuous to me. After all, I had Parkinson's disease. He wanted to have a sex change!

The beginning of the Teesdale Way into the centre of Middlesbrough must be one of the grimmest starts to a long-distance walking track in existence. Grim though it was, there was something vaguely Wizard of Oz-esque about the experience. Dorothy and her chums had a Yellow Brick Road, whereas my companions and I had a blue pipe marked with the word "effluent". Dorothy's quest was to find a wizard who could convey her back to Kansas. We were after the Middlesbrough Transporter Bridge to convey us across to Hartlepool. Both Dorothy's scarecrow and I wanted new brains... and so on.

Lyndsey had come up again for a few days. Since her exams had finished, she had had more time to devote to Coastin'. I was pleased that she seemed to be enthusiastic about it. I was even more pleased that she seemed to continue to be enthusiastic about me, despite the fact that I was, quite literally, walking away from her. It was still early days for us and I was realistic enough to accept that Coastin' was bound to take its toll on our relationship. I wondered how long it would be before distances became too far for a weekend visit and when my selfish obsession with Coastin' would become sufficiently irritating to be an issue. Like a typical male, I did not analyse it too much; failing to recognise what a good team we were and how reliant on her I had become.

But it wasn't just Lyndsey who had come to support me this weekend. The other friends who joined us (amongst them, Q) had certainly gone beyond the call of duty; using up their precious spare time to escort me on a narrow path sandwiched between a major arterial road and a network of industrial train tracks.

We tried to make the best of it: taking pleasure in the vivid colours of polluted puddles, in the dazzling network of pipes and the stark symmetry of the pylons. But these jokes wore thin after about seven miles.

Conversation was difficult as we marched in single file, never straying from the warmth of our blue pipe. The time was spent gazing at huge shapes on the horizon, which belched vast plumes of noxious gas into a clear blue sky.

At last, the impressive structure of the Transporter Bridge came into view, but almost immediately, it was eclipsed by an even more impressive sight. My friend, Mr Beef, he of the hamburger on the first day, was walking towards us.

It was good to see him – even if he had mysteriously turned up on the wrong weekend. He had thought he was coming to attend a party in Newcastle that was arranged to take place a week later. Why had he come to Middlesbrough then?

Mr Beef looked sheepish.

FROM TEES TO KNEES
15 MILES
JUNE

## CHAPTER 11

I first met Mr Beef in St Andrews, Scotland, where he had been at university with Mule. At first, he was shy about knowing everything. He would not be confrontational with his knowledge in any way. His understated, gentle and tactful manner was quite charming. It didn't last long. Pretty soon Mr Beef, realising he had found someone who quite enjoyed listening to his inexhaustible appetite for facts, was duly regurgitating them at every opportunity.

And yet not all of his facts are totally accurate. Two years ago, Mr Beef informed me that the quack of a duck does not echo. For two years I imparted this little gem of uselessness whenever the occasion would allow it. Now he informs me that this is in fact not the case. He tells me a government grant was awarded to establish the scientific truth behind the statement. The study found that indeed a quack does echo.

But with most things he is unerringly accurate. Mr Beef can recite pi to 100 numbers. He knows the Highway Code by heart. I have no doubt he is fluent in several long-extinct languages.

If Mr Beef was gravy, he would be made with cream, brandy and a fine beef stock. It would not be drizzled, but poured like a custard, overflowing randomly in uneven dollops, adding substance and texture to the most boring of meals.

Today was never going to be boring. Lyndsey had a soft spot for Mr Beef. The first time she met him was the first time she came round to my flat, on our second date.

We had been to the theatre. I thought this would be quite a classy thing to do, but Mr Beef, who was my flatmate at the time, would shatter the illusion as only he could. After the show Lyndsey had come back to my flat and we sneaked into the living room so as not to wake the slumbering Beef.

The scene was set. Romance was in the air. I put the kettle on and Lyndsey kindly decided to put a few things in the dishwasher. She opened the door to the machine and as she pulled out the bottom tray, she let out a small yelp. Stretched over the entire bottom compartment was a pair of unfeasibly large boxer shorts. At this moment Mr Beef stumbled into the room unannounced.

"Beef…" I said. "I mean, what the hell?"

But Mr Beef was defiant. "The washing machine is broken. It's lateral thinking, Izee," he said almost triumphantly.

"But Beef, they are your dirty boxer shorts – in the dishwasher."

At which point Mr Beef gingerly picked his underpants out of the machine, held them up to the window and said with satisfaction, "Yeah, but – well actually, they're clean now."

The Fleming family whose B&B I had stayed at in Habrough had travelled up for a day's Coastin', and with Lyndsey and Mr Beef in tow, we were able to cross the River Tees thanks to the Transporter Bridge still being open on a Sunday. Today's walk was not nearly as bad as I had predicted, and once we reached Cowpen Beauly Country Park, there was some reasonably pleasant scenery to be enjoyed.

A couple of days previously, I had received a copy of an e-mail sent to the Parkinson's Disease Society by the head ranger of Cowpen Beauly Country Park which stated the following: "I understand from a visiting member of the public that Mr Isaacs will be passing through Cowpen Beauly Country Park this weekend. We very much regret that owing to the fact that it is a bank holiday weekend, none of the toilets will be open during his visit. We wish we had been given greater notice of his arrival whereupon we could have laid on extra staff."

Whilst it was extremely kind of the head ranger to write such a letter, even I had to query whether my presence in Cowpen Beauly Country Park warranted the laying on of staff to man the toilets. How many extra staff would he have employed for such a purpose, I wondered?

I warned the group of the lack of open WC facilities in Cowpen Beauly and everyone took appropriate precautions against being "caught short". As it happened, I was actually rather glad that no one had been forced to give up their bank holiday. I wouldn't have needed to use the facilities anyway during the hour or so that we took to pass through. It would have been terribly embarrassing after all that effort for me not to grace the Park toilets with a visit.

The strange thing was that despite all the fun we had with this story, we realised afterwards that we had not actually caught sight of any WC facilities in the Park anyway. It was a pity really. I had been quite expecting some sort of splendid Victorian stone pavilion outside of which I could have had a photograph taken entitled, "Tom not going to the toilet in Cowpen Beauly Country Park".

It was another hot day and Mr Beef had smothered himself in a white grease in an attempt to keep the sun's rays from his "sensitive English rose" complexion. Régine Fleming and the girls took an instant liking to the scent of the sun-tan lotion and Beef wondered whether he had, by chance, stumbled across a new weapon to add to his girl-pulling armoury.

"I can't smell anything," I remarked.

"That's because you're not a girl!" Mr Beef spat back.

In view of recent similarities drawn at the B&B on the Cleveland Way, I actually felt rather relieved at this news. But then, on turning round to check everyone was together, I found to my surprise that a group of teenage girls seemed to be following us.

"You see!" beamed Mr Beef.

Perhaps there was something about his sun-tan lotion.

We climbed up narrow lanes towards Hart, where Ken Fleming had left his car. I took a last lingering look at the Tees Valley and could just make out the hazy shape of the Transporter Bridge. Next stop Tyneside, and from there it was really not that far to Scotland.

On entering the pub in Hart, we were welcomed exuberantly by a group of well-lubricated regulars. Between them they established that we were on a walk in aid of Parkinson's disease, and whilst collecting the drinks, I fell into conversation with one of them.

It became clear fairly quickly that he was having considerable difficulty in focusing on anything beyond his beer, but he seemed determined to find out more.

"So who's got Parkinson's disease to make you want to walk such a long way?"

"I have," I replied, looking him straight in the eye.

I felt a bit sorry for him. He had not been expecting this response and he just sat there looking totally perplexed. The pregnant pause continued for some time, so I helped him out of his predicament by laughing, slapping him on the arm and saying, "It's OK, I'm still able to walk around the coast of Britain, so it can't be that bad."

I had been too open with him and he took this as carte blanche to regale me with a lecture on how awful it would be to have Parkinson's at my age. I suspect he thought he was being sympathetic. But then it got worse.

"I knew a bloke who had Parkinson's who was 65 and he died two years later," he said. "That was bloody awful. We reckoned he was unlucky, but to get the problem at your age, well it's …" He couldn't find the word to express how awful it was.

"It's really not that bad," I found myself saying, "you do not die of Parkinson's. It is not life-threatening."

But in his drunken stupor, my friend, whose name was Matt (later to be named DiploMatt), had not heard me properly. His response was one of the most surprising I have encountered.

"Oh, I'm really sorry, mate. You must feel awful. I mean, basically, you're completely f***ed." This was sympathy I could probably do without.

An even drunker man came to join in our conversation. He had been told about what I was doing and was laughing hysterically.

"You mean to say that this bloke," he looked around for encouragement, "is going to walk around the coast of Britain. With those legs! I have never heard anything so funny in all m'life. Can I come with you?"

While the man was chortling, DiploMatt, who knew I had Parkinson's and genuinely thought he was a diplomat, made feeble attempts to shut his friend up without me seeing. Having failed, he turned to me.

"Sorry about old 'Knacked-Knees'," said DiploMatt diplomatically, "he doesn't mean any harm. He's got his own problems. His knees are f***ed."

It was all becoming totally excruciating. I was completely unconcerned about old Knacked-Knees, although I did think it was a bit rich for him to take the mickey out of my legs. However, I was not really in the mood for hearing how appalling it would be to have Parkinson's at my age. I already knew that. Most of all, I just wanted to go back to talk to my friends, who were sitting at the table waiting for me to return from the bar with the drinks. I left them both, with Knacked-Knees still guffawing and DiploMatt informing the barmaid about the horrific illness with which I was afflicted.

"Poor bloke is f***ed," I heard him whisper as I left.

There was a pleasant ten minutes spent chatting at our table before Knacked-Knees stumbled over to wish us all luck. "I'm gonna come with ya!" he said, laughing hysterically, and promptly fell out of the door of the pub and thumped against the wall outside.

DiploMatt, who was supposed to be leaving in the same taxi as Knacked-Knees, arrived at the table and surprised everyone by asking to be sent a sponsor form. As Lyndsey and I rustled around in bags trying to find one, DiploMatt continued, "Yeah, my wife is into all this charity s**t." He paused to study his audience and found it to his liking. Turning to me he said, "You've got some good lookin' birds, like, with you on this walk. You don't mind if I talk to them do you – after all, you're not going to be around much longer."

The silence was deafening. No one could quite believe what he had said. The Flemings, Lyndsey, even Mr Beef looked stunned.

I burst out laughing. Everyone looked relieved. I don't think they had ever heard anyone being quite so tactless. Come to think of it, nor had I.

We heard the honk of the taxi's horn outside. Knacked-Knees was becoming impatient. DiploMatt apologised profusely for having to leave. He thought he had been a hit.

The Flemings left us and Lyndsey, Mr Beef and I continued to Blackhall Rocks and Blackhall Colliery, which to all intents and purposes were just one long featureless street. Neither felt nearly as welcoming as the pub in Hart.

As if in recognition of the change in our surroundings, storm clouds gathered and it started raining heavily. Mr Beef had forgotten his waterproofs, and in their place, he had purchased a roll of black bin liners in the hope that they would offer some protection. He busied himself trying to fashion the plastic into some sort of coat.

Lyndsey and I gave each other concerned looks; we were not sure how we felt about walking the streets of a place hit badly by the demise of the coal-mining industry with a man who was dressed like the lead singer of a 1980s punk rock band. We kept our distance.

Dunbar
15th June

Berwick-upon-Tweed

Holy Island

Castle
Bamburgh

Dunstanburg

Northumberland

Newcastle
5th June
Sunderland
Blackhall Colliery
Hartlepool

## CHAPTER 12

"Aaaagh, my leg!" I screamed in a whisper. It was three o'clock in the morning and, stumbling in the darkness, I had just bumped into my bed, banging my leg badly at the exact point where I had broken my tibia two years previously. The plate and six pins which had been removed last year had been kept as trophies to the injury on my mantelpiece at home.

I did not give full voice to my agony because we were staying with Neil and Heather, two friends from Newcastle. I slept fitfully afterwards and when it came to getting up, the pain was sufficient for me to have some serious concerns about the future of the walk. I waved goodbye to Lyndsey as she got in a taxi to go to the station and then home. Once she was out of sight, I went to see if Mr Beef was ready for the day's walk.

"I'm not coming," came the grumpy response.

"OK," I said. "Why?"

"You've done me in, Izee, it's going to rain, and I've no more plastic bags to wear."

I couldn't argue with his logic. Pehaps I didn't want to, as I recalled the image of the bulging bin liner that had walked through Blackhall Rocks last night. A horn sounded outside, indicating a taxi had now arrived for me.

"Blackhall Colliery please," I said, climbing in.

"But that's Pit Yakker country!" said the taxi driver, as if I was asking him to take me into Apache territory.

"I'll take my chances," I replied spiritedly, but not really knowing what on earth he was on about. My mind was on other things this morning, like how on earth such a huge man had managed to squeeze himself into a Ford Focus.

I mused that maybe he had been forced to become a taxi driver because once in the car he had been unable to extricate himself again. I had always thought that if I could get to Newcastle, I would probably be able to finish the entire walk. I was now so close to achieving this, and yet the leg was putting me in slight danger of getting stuck in "Pit Yakker country". I voiced my concern to the rolls of fat at the back of the neck of the taxi driver in the front seat.

"At least you made it past the Moongkey 'Angers and the Smog Monsters."

"The who?"

"The Smoggies of Teesside and the Moongkey 'Angers of Hartlepool..." He proceeded to tell me the legend of how during the Napoleonic Wars, a French ship had been wrecked just off the coast of Hartlepool, the only survivor being a monkey in a French sailor's uniform. Having never seen a Frenchman before, they put the poor beast on trial, found him guilty of spying and sentenced him to death by hanging. "... and then they oong the moongkey!" said the voice from in front of the neck which was jigging up and down like a concertina. I wondered whether the monkey's neck had done the same. Poor thing.

"Are there any other dangers I should know about for my walk today?"

"Too reet there are, pal," he said, clearly finding it difficult to hide his excitement at the question. "If you make it past the Pit Yakkers, yer'll affto contend with the Mackems of Sunderland and the Sand Dancers of South Shields."

My mind boggled at the thought of all this proud parochialism within such a small area of the north-east. But as we neared Blackhall Colliery, "the neck" seemed to soften its views towards Yakkerdom: "I 'aven't been doon 'ere, like, for years." He reflected. "The co-ust round 'ere is tip-top like."

"Where are you from originally then?"

"Doon't tell anyone like, but I'm a Pit Yakker meself..."

My knee did play up that day and I hobbled past Yakkers, Mackems and on to the Sand Dancers of South Shields, where I took another taxi back to Neil and Heather's.

"To Newcastle please."

"What you want to go there for? It's full of Geordies like."

* * *

There was no fog on the Tyne to be mine when I crossed on the ferry from South Shields to North Shields. It did not stop me singing the song immortalised by Paul "Gazza" Gascoigne in his heyday as a Newcastle United player. Football is big in the north-east. There was an element of truth in the statement that I had given to BBC Radio Newcastle, that I supported Newcastle United. Certainly I felt as though I could hold a reasonably informed discussion about their progress in the latter stages of the season.

"... with Shearer and Solero up front, I think we have one of the best strike forces in the country," I stated confidently. Mispronouncing the popular Peruvian striker Nolberto Solano's name was bad enough; but replacing it with a word that made him a popular iced lolly with a soft fondant vanilla ice cream filling would not do much to promote my cause in the massed ranks of the "Toon Army". Extraordinarily, I seemed to get away with the mistake. My official entry into Newcastle upon Tyne was to be tomorrow, when I was to be welcomed by Steve Cram (world record holder over one mile and athletics commentator). In the meantime my objective was to cover as many miles as possible. I knew that beyond Newbiggin-on-Sea there were many Northumbrian treasures to be enjoyed. The castles at Warkworth, Dunstonburgh and Bamburgh; my first ever visit to the Holy Isle, Lindisfarne; the promise of beautiful sandy bays, clear waters and fantastic rocky outcrops; all were enticing me to keep up the pace and reach the most northern extremities of England. The incessant rain helped my progress and, despite the increasing pain in my leg, there seemed no point in lingering at Tynemouth or Whitley Bay. I reached Blythe at 8 p.m. It was dusk, and in the failing light I recognised a familiar sensation in the back of my neck. For the first time on the trip, a sort of sixth sense made me alert to the presence of an unidentified malice in the air. Something told me that I did not want be walking around Blythe for much longer and I was pleased to see Neil's trusty red Volvo tooting at me and flashing its lights before real darkness came. As I rose from Neil's sofa later that night, my right leg gave way from underneath me and I winced with pain.

"That doesn't look too good." Neil was down-playing the moment with feigned lightheartedness. I had been stupid to walk so far today. I just hoped that I had not done myself irreparable damage which might impinge on my chances of completing Coastin'.

Fortunately, the next two days of my schedule were comparatively "low-intensity" and I was hopeful that 48 hours would be sufficient time for my injury to heal. The leg sponsors, Ryder Architects, had organised a reception for me on the Quayside. Among the guests was Steve Cram, whose duty it was to shake my hand as, symbolically at least, I crossed over from Gateshead on Newcastle's Millennium Bridge. But Steve Cram was not the sort to just come for a handshake and then leave. Instead, he entered wholeheartedly into the spirit of the occasion (even after being on the receiving end of some verbal abuse for being a Mackem and a Sunderland supporter), and undertook a series of television and radio interviews on behalf of Coastin' as well as attending the post-handshake party. Aside from the importance I had attributed to Newcastle from a morale perspective, it was also somewhere I had spent a lot of time working in my surveying days, and the fact that there were many familiar faces in the crowd who had come to support me also made me feel fantastic at having reached the city.

Back on the road, I was pleased initially with the progress my leg seemed to have made after two days' rest and, fresh after my Newcastle experience, and with Blythe now behind me, my spirits were high. Newcastle had also provided a much-needed injection of a sense of the purpose of the walk. It was too easy to be preoccupied with my own personal pride in physically undertaking the walk, instead of focusing on the thing that really mattered – Parkinson's. I felt as if the Geordies had nudged me back into line a little bit, whilst at the same time being characteristically enthusiastic and generous in their support.

After five miles on the motorway-like A198, I was still in reasonably good fettle and was looking forward to finally reaching Newbiggin-on-Sea, which I anticipated would be the start line for some fantastic walking. While I was entertaining such happy thoughts, I did not see the small group of three youths who were messing around to my left. As I walked past them, a fourth youth stepped out from behind a wall and hurled a large bucket of water. As the water arced towards me, I lengthened my stride fractionally and arched my back so that it splattered harmlessly on the pavement behind me. I glared at the backs of the youths as they ran off, laughing hysterically. Oh to be Bruce Lee at a time like this. To be able to run after my assailants, unafraid, and then to subject them to a battering they would never forget. In my years of watching martial arts movies, the only skill of Bruce Lee that I had truly honed to perfection was the strange chicken-like noises he emitted while in the throes of kicking the hell out of his enemies. I decided that chicken noises alone would not be appropriate in the current situation.

Slightly shocked by the incident, I found myself flinching when, five minutes later, an old lady thrust a £10 note in front of my nose.

"I just drove past you a mile or so back and I'd seen you on the telly. I wanted to come back and give you this."

The gratitude I displayed to this lady may have been a little over the top, but my faith in the fellowship of mankind had been on a bit of a rollercoaster ride this morning. I was directed by the lady through a large residential estate as a "short cut" which I did not really want to take, but felt obliged to do so after her generosity. Hiking with a large rucksack in areas of densely populated suburbia is amusing for everyone except the hiker. You can almost be certain that everyone who sees you is saying or thinking the very thing that you think they are saying or thinking – "What a plonker!"

Druridge Bay lived up to expectations; a jewel after a fair amount of north-east drudgery. There had been a few times on this journey when I had felt truly exhilarated by Coastin'. Walking on this flat sandy beach in a stiff breeze with relentless white breakers rolling in to shore was one such moment. Druridge Bay is magnificent and empty. A few years back they were thinking of putting a nuclear power plant there. Thank goodness they came to their senses. For my journey up to Lindisfarne, I was joined by Davey Ads and his wife, Sally. Davey had calmed down considerably since I had shared a flat with him in London seven years previously; so much so that many of his friends now referred to him as "New Ads". Sally, his wife, who is regarded by everyone as the best thing that ever happened to her husband, would every now and then cajole "Old Ads" to reappear.

It was a shame. I had been so looking forward to this section of the coastline. The scenery was everything I expected. The castles were all beautifully positioned, majestic and indomitable; as castles should be. The beaches seemed remote and wild; they were wonderful. It was the weather that failed us. Newbiggin-on-Sea proved to be just an aperitif; the rest of Northumberland poured a lot more than buckets over us. I was very glad of the company for the next few days, even if the conversations were stilted and muffled from within the confines of voluminous wet-weather gear.

Just beyond Craster (kipper capital), we were suddenly delivered a break in the clouds and for a few moments the haunting ruins of Dunstonburgh Castle stood emblazoned in a golden light on the horizon like something out of Arthurian legend. As the clouds enveloped the scene in gloom again, we saw a man approaching us with a large piece of string tied around his neck, at the end of which was a key the size of a large soup ladle. He cast a sympathetic eye over our dejected and drenched forms and, thinking we were on some fanatical pilgrimage, made an offer from the sheer kindness of his heart:

"I'm afraid I've just locked the castle, but I'll let you in if you want to have a quick look."

We had to decline his extremely gracious offer. We were bound for Beadnell and any delay would allow the cold moisture of the day to penetrate the protective layers of both our clothing and our minds and would dampen our resolve to reach today's destination.

After a long and tiring day we demanded a lot from the pub that we ate in that night, and it duly delivered. We were all hungry beyond words and we did not have to wait long for our three mixed grills with chips. When the plates were delivered to our table, they were piled so high with food that they seemed to defy gravity. The chips looked superb: big, chunky and crisp.

"Is there any ketchup?" I asked Ads.

"Only sachets." He threw three of them over and I grimaced. My hatred of extracting the contents of tomato ketchup sachets began long before my Parkinson's symptoms rendered the whole process totally impossible. The chip to sachet ratio just made no sense to me and for a meal of this size, I reckoned the sachet count would be well into the teens.

"I'm going to adopt a three-tier phased assault," I announced to my companions. "Three sachets at a time at four-minute intervals."

Ads smirked and I realised it might have been a mistake to publicise my intentions. When he saw me wrestling with the first sachet, he started laughing. When it did open and squirted over my fingers, he guffawed. When I applied pressure to the sachet and it exploded out of the unopened rear end and splattered all over my freshly washed shirt, he went purple with hysteria. And when, finally, a single pathetic blob of ketchup flopped lamely onto my plate, he passed out under the table. I mopped up the red sauce with one chip. "I'm not going to have any more ketchup," I said grumpily.

* * *

At Seahouses I clocked up my 750th mile without realising it. The miles were beginning to come and go without my really stopping to think how far I had actually come. It had been the major towns I had reached or the major rivers I had crossed which gave me a sense of destination and achiev-ement. So far, these had been reaching my family's flat in Thorpeness; crossing the Humber Bridge into Hull; and, more recently, reaching

Newcastle upon Tyne. At each of these destinations I had given myself a psychological pat on the back. I was making progress.

The other noticeable indicator of progress which made me pause for reflection was the change in accents. For many miles I would travel without detecting any real shift in intonation or inflection. Then suddenly, I would overhear someone say something in a completely new brogue which would, for me, define my onward passage around the country and at the same time bring me a warm, glowing feeling when I considered the amount of coast I had covered. In television terms, I had come from EastEnders, through Farming Today, All Creatures Great and Small and Auf Wiedersehen Pet: serious changes in accents; and yet when walking, these permutations of the same language were not always discernible.

Here at Seahouses, they certainly were discernible. I happened to tune into a conversation being held between three fishermen sitting propping up the harbour wall and realised that I couldn't understand a single word they were saying. There was no pause for breath or break between words at all. In fact, each sentence just sounded like one very long syllable. Here there was no accent change, but more a completely new method of speaking. As I reflected on the significance of this we rounded a corner and something of even greater importance to the walk entered my field of vision: Scotland!

One of the most pleasing aspects of a coastal walk is climbing to the top of a headland or, as in this case, rounding a promontory to see the next piece of the coast unfurl before your eyes. The coastal scenery that revealed itself beyond Seahouses was the most memorable yet. The view was majestic; bathed in a rich orange sunshine which had been distinctly lacking in the past few weeks. A sweep of pristine sands provided a stunning foreground to Bamburgh Castle, which sat proudly and commandingly above the dunes with splendid indifference to the rigours of time. Beyond Bamburgh was Lindisfarne: the Holy Isle, with its ruined abbey and castle perched on a rocky outcrop acting like a gateway to the Scottish hills, which formed the backdrop. It was tantalisingly close, but for the time being I was content with sharing some of the best coastal scenery in England on a beautiful summer's day with two close friends. What could be finer?

While I was having one of my "special" moments, my two close friends were studying ducks. The significance of the ducks was lost on me, but to be fair, I think the importance of my "view" did nothing to particularly excite them either.

* * *

My leg had not completely recovered from the bed incident back in Newcastle, and now there was a new horror. A blister was causing me some discomfort and this was not helped by an unavoidable section of walking along the A1, followed by a good hour of walking through fields of hayfever-inducing grasses. All ailments were forgotten though as I reached Holy Island and marched across the causeway at low tide. In a perfect purple sunset, I sat and contemplated the road ahead. Tomorrow I would reach Berwick-upon-Tweed, and beyond that was Scotland, where I would remain for three and a half months. Scotland would signal a slowing down of the fund-raising efforts, largely due to the holiday season and the fact that I would be walking through more isolated areas. This would be a time when I could relax a bit more and enjoy the walk for walking's sake; where publicity and sponsorship demands would be less pivotal to everyday life. I was selfishly looking forward to that.

I took a day off in Berwick-upon-Tweed and scurried around within its impressive and totally underrated fortified walls. I was in search of birthday presents for Lyndsey, who was coming to visit me later on that day... with her parents. I was apprehensive, to say the least, about meeting Lyndsey's parents for a meal that evening. What would they be thinking? Here was a man with Parkinson's who was off gallivanting around the country for a year and yet also seemed to be making advances to their daughter. I would not have felt particularly chuffed about it, had I been them. Mad questions started running through my head – like what I would say if Lyndsey's father took me to one side and asked me my intentions towards his daughter. "This could be a disaster," I thought to myself. After all, it was quite possible I might suffer a sudden attack of the trembles, in which case it could all be over before the starters. I imagined what Mr Taylor might be like: probably huge, dour, strictly Presbyterian with a big nose, whisky-reddened cheeks and a crippling handshake. In fact, he was of medium build, thoroughly amenable. It did not take long for me to relax in their company and I started regaling them with stories of the walk, amongst which was the Newbiggin-on-Sea episode.

"I wish I had been Bruce Lee at that moment," I said.

"I prefer Steven Seagal," said Mrs Taylor.

I spluttered on my Thai green curry. "Sorry?"

Steven Seagal happened to be my favourite action hero, specialising in films displaying his individual brand of far-fetched martial arts which he practises without compromise, seemingly without effort and without being troubled by his opponents, regardless of number.

"I like Steven Seagal," she repeated.

"Oh yes, what's that one where he is the chef?" said Mr Taylor.

"Under Siege," I said, trancelike, and unable quite to believe my ears.

"He has just brought a new one out. It's called Belly of the Beast," went on Mrs Taylor enthusiastically.

My girlfriend's parents like Steven Seagal movies. All my earlier concerns seemed as if they were a lifetime ago.

I had conspired with my B&B owner in Berwick to ensure that Lyndsey's birthday was special. I had orchestrated an absurd treasure hunt around the room for her to find various presents and this was followed by a champagne breakfast with classical music. Unfortunately, having put on this show, the romance of the moment was curtailed when I began a show of a different kind – a freak show. Lyndsey had never seen me shaking so badly and I didn't want her to see me like that. She reacted with typical humour: "This is my birthday! But you still have to steal the attention away!" Nevertheless, she was visibly shaken at the sight of me so visibly shaking.

I had an appointment at the Scottish border at 12:30 p.m. and it soon became apparent that this was not going to be achievable. There seemed to be some complication with my pills this morning, such that I made a mental note not to have champagne for breakfast every morning. I seemed to be having problems positioning my legs in the right place for comfortable walking. On my left side, instead of heel toe, heel toe, the outside of my left foot seemed to hit the ground first, followed by the toes and then the heel.

It had been arranged for a young piper called Murray to announce my entry into Scotland. Murray was in the car when Joyce, the organiser, picked me and Lyndsey up on the A1 and drove us to the border. Before we reached the lay-by on the border, my medication kicked out and I began shaking again. I felt like a complete fraud, almost as if I had driven the whole way and not just the last few miles.

Heaving myself out of the car, I managed to join Murray on an epic journey of ten yards across the border I had not yet reached. While Murray played the bagpipes, I hobbled beside him with hands that were flapping around so much as to look as if I was accompanying him on the castanets. As we passed a parked BMW, the man inside and on the phone scowled at us before winding up his window to block out the din. I didn't really care about this. I didn't really care about the shaking. I didn't even care that I had not yet reached the border. For a moment, as the upbeat drone of "Scotland the Brave" filled the air, I didn't care about anything. I just felt fantastic.

Earlier that morning, Moxy and Elaine, two friends who had travelled up from London, had arrived as requested in Berwick-upon-Tweed at 9 a.m. ready to start walking. By 1:30 p.m. on that same day we had covered a distance of a mere two miles. When my shaking finally stopped and we reconvened at the supermarket just outside Berwick where we had left them, Moxy had a wide grin on his face. "It's quite easy, this walking lark, isn't it?"

The recrossing of the border an hour or so later was as rewarding as the first effort. Lyndsey, Moxy and Elaine provided rapturous applause and more champagne was popped. I savoured the moment. Elaine was on home territory, having been born, bred and buttered in the area. For the next day and a half a map was barely needed, and she pointed out various things of interest along the way. Bit by bit, we were able to piece together a picture of what the area was all about and what it was like for Elaine growing up here. At a railed-off section of sea wall in Eyemouth known as The Bantry, Elaine explained how this had been the location where school disputes had been settled out of the school grounds. "Reet then, al mit yoo five o'clock doon The Bantry!" she recited, looking threatening. Lyndsey copied the accent and the look. Moxy and I felt slightly scared of our respective Celtic girlfriends.

By the time we reached the delightful village of St Abbs and realised that the only eating establishment was a mile up the hill at the Haven Hotel, we were in serious danger that they would stop serving before we got there. With Moxy and Elaine staying elsewhere, we summoned up our final reserves of energy and ran up the hill. We burst through the doors of the hotel, puffing and panting. We had already decided that Lyndsey should do the talking.

"Can we have some food?" The choice of words revealed our desperation. As did the slightly psychotic expression that Lyndsey was sporting.

"Sorry, we stopped serving at 9 p.m."

At this point, Lyndsey lost the plot completely, and pointing at me, said, "But he's just walked all the way from London!"

"And it's her birthday," I piped up.

It worked. The kitchen staff relented and we were given two huge slap-up suppers.

"They're on the house," the proprietor of the hotel said, smiling happily.

For thirteen of the last fourteen days there had been a prolonged spell of rain at some point during the day. The 22 miles from St Abbs to Dunbar did nothing to change my bad run of luck, except for the fact that Moxy had had to borrow some wet weather gear and it was lurid orange with purple lining. It made him look like a lobster. It was extraordinary how much entertainment we squeezed out of this fact alone.

Lyndsey and I had some time alone from Dunbar to North Berwick. It was the first time we had really had any chance to reflect. Lyndsey had walked a long way with me since her exams had finished and we had spent a lot of time in other people's company. I loved the fact that she was so easygoing and did not seem to dislike anyone. By the same token, it was clear to me that all my friends thought she was fantastic. We were getting on famously and from my perspective further analysis might have spoilt the good times we were having together. So instead of saying these things as we walked through the John Muir country park, I just thought them, and in so doing joined the other millions of men around the world who have been similarly foolish.

I was even more foolish to enter a field full of bullocks near the Tyningham Estate. We were about halfway across when they started showing an interest in us and became quite frisky. I was aware that there are many deaths every year caused by stampeding cows, and for a few horrid moments thought we might become two more cow statistics. But Ewan the Stick came to the rescue and, raised above my head in the style of a great sorcerer, stopped the bullocks in their tracks. Lyndsey was impressed with this. I didn't let it show, but at the time, I was frightened out of my wits. At Tantallon Castle we met up with Davey Ads and Sally again and discovered, much to our dismay, that they spend most of their holidays learning about the birdlife of East Lothian. While Lyndsey and I enjoyed our first views of the Firth of Forth and across to the Fife coastline, Ads and Sally were focusing on a large rock out at sea, the summit of which was white as if it had been snowing.

"That's Bass Rock," Sally informed us.

"It appears white on top because 21,000 pairs of gannets reside there," Davey Ads continued. Lyndsey and I had to admit that this was vaguely interesting. Of significantly more interest to me, though, was the fact that we had now reached golfing country. At Muirfield they were preparing for the British Open, but we also walked along the fabulous links courses of North Berwick, Gullane and Craigielaw.

Ahead of us was Edinburgh.

CHAPTER 13

"Would you like a bread roll, sir?" The waiter was young, spotty and anxious to please.

"No thank you. I cannot eat anything with wheat in it." Shazzer, who had come up from London, also declined. We were having supper in our hotel. Lyndsey had gone to meet friends in Glasgow.

Our starters came, and while we were waiting for the main course, the waiter approached us again.

"Would you like a bread roll, sir?"

"Er… no, thank you. You see I can't eat anything made of wheat. I have an allergy."

Shazzer was giggling.

The chocolate ice cream for pudding took slightly longer to arrive than it should have done. The waiter approached us and apologised for the delay. Shazzer and I could hardly contain ourselves. He looked down at my empty side plate. He seemed confused by the lack of crumbs. We willed him to ask the question. Go on, one more time…

"Would you like a bread roll while you're waiting, sir?"

"YES!" I thought.

"No, thank you," I said.

I blurted the words out quickly in the hope that he would leave to enable us to laugh without hurting his feelings.

Friends came and went at an alarming rate around Edinburgh, but it was just Lyndsey and I who left Scotland's capital city bound for Fife.

To avoid a long and unsightly detour, we had been given permission by

Lady Rosebery to walk through the Dalmeny Estate. It was pretty much all that was left between us and the Forth Road Bridge. Puffed up with self-importance, we marched through the signposts marked "Private" and then sauntered through the immaculate manicured grounds. We were trying to make ourselves look conspicuous in the hope that we would be apprehended by a member of the Estate officialdom and be able to say, "We are here under the express permission of Lady Rosebery." No one batted an eyelid at us.

Having passed the main house, we followed the estate road to a beach where we were greeted by a superb view of the bold architecture of the Forth Rail Bridge. About an hour later, we were standing on the road bridge in the sunshine staring through the fiery red structure of the other side of the bridge to the Fife coastline, which extended invitingly; angling slowly northwards.

At every other major bridge I had crossed, there had been large groups of well-wishers. London, Hull and Newcastle had all provided big welcoming committees and media attention. The only thing waiting for me at the end of the Forth Road Bridge was a large black cloud and Lyndsey's parents, who would take her to Glasgow. I waved forlornly at her as she was swept away in the back of the Volvo. I would not see her again until I reached Wick. I suddenly felt very alone. I had said goodbye to Lyndsey on numerous occasions recently, but not after such a prolonged spell of being with her. It seemed more momentous and I missed her almost immediately.

The "Scotland the Brave" ring-tone on my phone rang. I pressed the green button.

"Hello."

"'Tis R.B. Catlow who speaks, with your Aunt Judith..." The word "'Tis" would have sufficed. My uncle Richard was the only person to announce himself in such a way and I had never known my aunt and godmother, Judy, not to be with him. I smiled when I heard the voice at the other end of the mobile phone. The two of them had supported me on two occasions on my other walk from John O'Groats to Land's End and this was their second outing on Coastin', having visited me in Lincolnshire already.

"... establishing contact in order to indicate proximity to their itinerant nephew and godson. Please provide your precise co-ordinates."

While I fumbled with my map and my words, R.B. Catlow had devised his own method of deciphering our respective locations.

"There is a large dockyard on the south side of the Firth. Give me your approximate distance and bearing to the coastline and we can use Pythagoras' theorem to deduce the distance we are apart."

I humoured my uncle with the statistics he required, but by this time I had identified from the map that I was only 20 minutes from Dalgety Bay, where they were parked.

"I think you are three miles and about an hour away." My uncle was adamant.

My uncle Richard wore a familiar expression of faint amusement when I turned up 45 minutes later, having run most of the way there, and yet he was not gloating in any way. It is an expression never far from his face. I often think my uncle despaired of the world long ago and now, having retired from trying to change it, he observes it, using its absurdities as a source of endless entertainment. It is perhaps not surprising that he has become an after-dinner speaker of some repute.

We chatted for some time about my route, both past and future. Neither my uncle nor my aunt have travelled widely abroad, but I was constantly astonished by their knowledge of the British mainland.

"See you in Wales," said my uncle, suddenly getting in the car without warning and bringing an end to our meeting in typically abrupt fashion.

The Fife Coastal Path to St Andrews is 81 miles of superb, varied walking. Helped by some decent weather at last, I progressed steadily, sometimes alone, sometimes with friends from Edinburgh. I passed the pretty fishing villages scattered along the northern shores of the Firth of Forth. My rest in Edinburgh seemed to have revived me and I was back on song. My leg was no longer hurting, the blister which had plagued me for the few days in the Borders seemed to have vanished and I was really enjoying myself.

One of my visitors on the walk between St Andrews and Aberdeen was Dr Kevin Lessey, a friend with whom I compete on subjects such as who has the most competitive nature. Kevin, known as "Doc", had turned up wearing a ridiculous wide-brimmed Antipodean hat, earning him an extension to his nickname. He became "Docadile Dundee"; it was particularly appropriate given where we were in the country.

Doc's obsessional desire to ford the River North Esk, instead of taking a minuscule detour to the bridge inland, was strange. To my dismay he did eventually succeed in this quest, but the fact that he had done so clad only in his ridiculous hat and a pair of boxer shorts emblazoned with the slogan "Hot Stuff" was sufficient ammunition for my being able to cancel out any sense of achievement he might have felt.

The next river to cross was Bervie Water in Inverbervie. It was here I passed the 1,000-mile barrier and Docadile Dundee pulled the rug from beneath my feet. Instead of rubbishing the entire walk, as I suspected he might, he and his wife Sue produced a home-made banner congratulating me on successfully reaching this milestone. It was the last thing they did before they left, and the gesture left me in the uncomfortable position of feeling some fondness for my sporting adversary.

I had enjoyed a spell of reasonably decent weather since Edinburgh, but the day I walked 21 miles from Stonehaven to Aberdeen was among the most miserable I would experience. It rained the entire day; from start to finish. I had arranged to meet Malcolm Bruce MP, who had gone to some lengths to help promote my walk, both in Westminster and in his constituency through which I was now walking. He joined me in a small pub in Portlethen Village. I tried to persuade him that it was daft for him to get soaked needlessly, but he was adamant, and full credit to him for that. Eventually it was his calf-height footwear which let him down. After two miles of walking I couldn't help but notice that the Right Honourable Member's lurid yellow wellies had reached their full capacity and were now overflowing with water. No comment was made on either side.

The coastline from Aberdeen all the way up to Fraserburgh is characterised by long sandy beaches with magnificent dunes. There are castle ruins at Slains; superb lighthouses at Boddam and Rattray Head; wonderful golf courses at Newburgh, Cruden Bay and Inverallochy; dramatic cliffs and hidden bays near Bullers of Buchan. I suppose these places are a long way from anywhere, but given the natural beauty of this stretch and the facilities available, I was amazed there were not more people around. Apart from an unsightly firebreathing gas terminal which stood unashamedly on an otherwise perfect stretch of sand between Peterhead and Fraserburgh, this north-eastern outpost of Britain's shoreline was unspoilt and a joy to walk along.

I had been told a lot of things about Colin before I met him in Cruden Bay. I had been told that he had been a double blue at Oxford University; that he had gone on to play football for Oxford City and after that he had gone into coaching squash and golf at international level. I had been told that Colin was a great motivator and communicator, and in this knowledge I had been greatly looking forward to meeting him.

When Colin walked into the room I was immediately struck by his blue eyes, which sparkled with wit and intelligence – because tragically these were all that was left of the man. I had not seen anyone with such bad symptoms of Parkinson's since the patient whom I had seen waiting outside just after my diagnosis. Colin's dyskinesia tossed his body around like a small boat in a storm. He simply couldn't remain still and I felt an overpowering urge to put my hands on him so that he could feel the relative calm that I felt.

I was with Colin for a good hour and it was a trial for both of us. Although Colin was still able physically to perform most of the things he needed to perform, he couldn't do so without an extravagant, almost flamboyant movement which seemed to emanate from deep within him. Communication was the principal problem though. Colin could barely speak and when he ate, he dribbled incessantly. But there was still the odd moment when he was totally lucid and made perfect sense; giving me a few small clues as to the man that Colin used to be.

I suppose it was easy for me; I knew something of Colin's history and knew that in his head he was still the same man. I understood enough to be able to treat him with the respect and dignity that he deserved. By doing this, I managed to battle on with our meeting and his eyes continued to sparkle. At the end of the meal, however, the waitress arrived and stared condescendingly at the scene of devastation around Colin's plate. Bending towards his ear she shouted, "Ooh dear, poppet, we've made a bit of a mess here, haven't we?"

Colin did not reply. He just looked at me. The twinkle in his eyes had disappeared.

After Colin had gone, I felt frustrated by our meeting. Frustrated because I felt I had not got to know him, but most of all, frustrated at his own frustration at being a great communicator, unable to communicate. Nevertheless, Colin had succeeded in his other great skill; he had motivated me. I did not want to suffer the frustrations of such an existence. No one should have to be incarcerated within their own body in such a way. This had to stop. I felt a surge of angry energy course through me and I felt like setting off for tomorrow's walk there and then.

From Fraserburgh to Inverness the coastline changes yet again. The fishing villages of Pennan, Crovie and Gardenstown made me wonder about the ones I had enjoyed on the Fife coast. They now seemed contrived and almost suburban in comparison to these. The understated appeal of these places came from their determination not to be anything other than small fishing villages. Despite the fact that many people have moved here from wealthier parts of Scotland, the area retains a refreshing mix of strong local and traditional values and tolerance of outsiders. Apparently, the accent changes about five or six times in the 20 or so miles between Fraserburgh and Macduff and the graveyards are filled with generations of Macleans and Macleods, almost to the exclusion of any other names.

Despite playing a leading role in the cult film Local Hero, I did not think that fame had cost Pennan any of its charm. Having established that the village hotel was full, I wandered back and forth between the seafront and the line of fishermen's cottages in a quest to find the elusive Mrs Maclean who owned the local B&B. I eventually found her at the local village fete in the local village hall; only to find that the local village B&B was also full.

I went back to the hotel and ordered a lime and soda, which cost me £2.25. I was beginning to think that perhaps Pennan was losing its charm. This had to be the most expensive lime soda in the world. Feeling disenchanted, I downed the drink too quickly and walked out. To all intents and purposes, I was stuck. My luggage was being delivered by a kind girl I had met in Peterhead and a friend was coming to meet me here tonight too. Even if I managed to contact both of them with a change of location, where would I go? There was nowhere within easy walking distance that would have alternative accommodation.

Just as I was about to despair, a man sitting in a group round a table full of drinks caught my eye: "Are y'looking for somewi t'stee?"

"Yes…"

"If y'go knock on number 11 and say that Alan sent you, m'Dad'll let y'stee."

My friend Peter Hayward arrived later that evening and we were put up free of charge in our own self-contained annexe belonging to Alan's Dad. We were treated to wine and snacks on the harbour while a neighbour struck up on the accordion and sang sea shanties. Afterwards the harbour master regaled us with stories of the area in an accent which I found quite difficult to understand. After about five minutes, Pete nudged me and in his best Bedfordshire brogue asked:

"What language is 'e speakin'?"

"English," I replied instinctively.

"'E's 'avin a laugh if 'e thinks that's English."

Pete is another friend whom I met while we had both been travelling in

Australia. I was most fortunate that he had been studying to be an osteopath and had agreed to spend two months of his summer holiday to walk with me. Apart from enjoying his excellent company, this would also allow me to walk the most remote coastal areas of Britain without the worry of becoming stranded by a severe bout of Parkies alone and miles from help.

I had only known Wild Rover for five years, but in that time we had walked many miles together. His intention this time, however, was to accompany me right round to Fort William, a distance of over 700 miles. He had bought a new rucksack specifically for this purpose. Emblazoned on the back of it were the words "Wild Rover", and they seemed particularly suitable. It would become his alias for the rest of the time we walked together.

Wild Rover is one of those people who you think you've got to know until you get to know him. At first meeting, you might mistake him as being aloof, enigmatic, perhaps a touch blase; a man of cool independence, a "Wild Rover". The truth is that he is solid, reliable and as unfailingly loyal a friend as you would care to have.

And yet he retains a mysterious side, a hidden something. This, coupled with his boyish good looks, makes him seemingly irresistible to women. It drives me mad!

I pride myself on dealing with the fairer sex. They are a complex bunch. Yet the efforts that we males make to be charming, witty and courteous often go unappreciated. Why is it that the quieter, more unyielding and less fathomable men are the ones who melt the girls' hearts? How can their indifference be misinterpreted as hidden depths, time after time? I feel it's one of life's great injustices how these philanderers need make no effort; they just sit there smouldering silently, and in so doing win the admiration and affections of many a foolish maiden.

Wild Rover is one of these. It's not his fault. I did wonder though whether Wild Rover's charms would be an asset to the Parkinson's cause or whether they might deflect attention away. Fortunately, these were remote areas in which we were travelling.

As a team we were likely to win hearts one way or the other.

*Mr Beef could still show a turn of speed over 75 yards.*

FROM RELAY TO MORAY
JULY

CHAPTER 14

In his day, Mr Beef had been an athlete of some distinction. According to one source, Beef had been a true speed merchant, taking only 11.2 seconds to be victorious as the Dorset under-18 100-metre champion. It was rumoured that as the gun went, the ice-cream van was seen to be pulling away from the school grounds where the event was taking place. It is, of course, unlikely that Mr Beef will ever attain such velocity on foot again. Even now though, he proudly claims that he could complete 75 metres in the same time and here he could simply arch his back in order to see off the final quarter of the race.

It was owing to his former athletic prowess, together with his job at UK Sport, that Mr Beef decided that he would orchestrate Coastin's involvement in the Queen's Jubilee baton relay for the Commonwealth Games.

As with the Olympics, a relay involving competing nations was underway. In this instance, it was not a torch but a baton that was being carried throughout the Commonwealth and would end up in Manchester, where the Games were taking place. The baton contained a message from the Queen, which would be read out at the opening ceremony. It was also equipped with a red light that flashed on and off in time with the bearer's heart rate.

Mr Beef's circular e-mail ensured my involvement in the relay. It was in response to this that many of my friends had written in to the organisers, suggesting that I was a suitable candidate for baton carrying. I was delighted when I received the official correspondence confirming that I had been selected. The only trouble with the event for me was that all the baton carriers had to run their respective legs in their home regions. There were to be no special dispensations for me, but there was never any question that I would miss out on the honour of the occasion. I had left the Wild Rover in Inverness for two days and flown down to London to play my part in the relay.

On the plane down, a lady sitting across the aisle saw me shaking out of the corner of her eye. "My husband's a nervous flier too."

"Actually, I'm not nervous. I've got Parkinson's." It was strange; that seemed to me to be a better reason to shake than the fear of flying.

"This is the captain," came a voice over the tannoy. "We're expecting some turbulence on this flight, so please keep your seatbelts fastened at all times."

"They must know about my being on the flight." I looked ruefully at my friend across the aisle. She smiled thinly, unsure what reaction to give: whether to laugh or look sympathetic.

Aeroplanes are breeding grounds for Parkinson's experiences. Previously, during a bout of shaking on the way to the US, a stewardess had literally run over to my seat, convinced I was having an epileptic fit. "Are you OK?" she asked instinctively.

"Yes I'm fine," I replied. "How are you?" She had clearly not expected any answer at all and she stood back and studied my face with suspicion. And then realising that I was still completely compos mentis, she had just held my shaking arms and asked, almost in desperation, "What do I do?"

"Nothing," I answered smiling, "just don't ask me to land the plane."

Of course nowadays there are even more problems for Parkinson's visitors to the US. I am always careful that my hand does not slip on the green visa waiver form, for fear of accidentally ticking the box that declares you as someone who has been convicted of Nazi war crimes and/or genocide. On the form, this is found just below "Do you have a physical disability?" I have often wondered whether the proximity of the two questions implies there is a link; that mass murder is supposed to be a natural progression from a state of disability.

Worse still are the conditions of entry, which now require both photographs and fingerprints to be taken at customs. To the Parkinsonian this represents a chance to display your symptoms in a high-profile public place. The poor non-US citizen behind me in the customs queue has to wait for about 15 minutes while the always 'charming' official and I battle to establish something more definitive by which to recognise me than a smudged paw print and a man with about six heads.

It's a nerve wracking experience.

Back on the flight down to London, I was beginning to think that this whole expedition was madness; all this way just to run for about 500 yards. Having had the thought, I immediately changed my mind again and decided it was a fabulous thing to be doing for that very reason. Besides, as I stared out of the left-hand side of the plane on a clear summer's day, there was something immensely satisfying about looking down from on high; floating back easily over the ground I had covered by foot in the comfort of a reclining seat.

I was chuffed with the number of friends and family who had turned out to watch me discharge my baton-carrying duties. I was not so enamoured, however, of the idea of donning a shiny Cadbury's chocolate running outfit. Cadburys, being the principal sponsors of the baton relay, had decided their corporate colours would be appropriate to the occasion. The garments looked quite striking and at first I was optimistic that the overall effect would be reasonably impressive as, in my mind's eye, I glided effortlessly through the streets of London like an Ethiopian middle-distance runner.

Looking in the mirror in the Gents in a pub in Kingston upon Thames, having just changed, I realised my appearance was far from impressive and actually alarmingly close to that of a family-sized bar of Dairy Milk.

Everyone laughed as I walked out of the Gents.

I noticed Mr Beef was already tucking into a free snack-sized bar of Dairy Milk. "You look like a snack-sized bar of Dairy Milk," he said. His eyes flicked from the chocolate bar to me and then back again as if he was having difficulty knowing which one was me. I made a mental note to put on a bit of weight so that next time I dressed up as a chocolate bar, I would be perceived by others as I perceived myself and given family-sized bar status.

Fortunately, it was not long before I boarded a Cadbury's bus full of other similarly wrapped people. There was a real cross-section of Dairy Milk bar imitations going on. These ranged from Dairy Milk miniatures and snack-sized bars right up to an enormous man who looked just like a bumper Easter egg special.

The Cadbury's bus dropped all the relay runners at their allocated positions and I found myself waiting by a lamp-post adjacent to an underpass near the main ring road around Kingston-upon-Thames. "This is a cracking spot," I thought.

Much sooner than I anticipated, a cavalcade of police motorcycles came into view. Behind them were two men, one of whom was carrying aloft something that looked reminiscent of a vacuum cleaner without a head. The other man was of extremely athletic build and looked very similar to someone you would expect to see in an Olympic 100-metres final: Linford Christie, or Carl Lewis. He was clearly the pacemaker.

Before I knew it, the vacuum cleaner had been thrust into my hand, and remembering to grasp the base of the baton to ensure its flashing red light monitored my pulse rate, I set off jogging.

"Are you ready?" asked my pace-setter, who I decided looked and sounded more like a Linford Christie than a Carl Lewis. I was surprised at this question, as I had thought we were already away.

"Er…" I stammered, "Yes!" I stated boldly. But before I had uttered the word, Linford Christie was off and at least ten yards ahead of me already. I lunged after him, anxious not to make myself look a fool in front of my supporters. I impressed myself with the speed at which I caught him. Clearly all the walking had been of some benefit. But upon seeing me at his shoulder, Linford kicked again and accelerated up a long and quite steep hill. By this time, there was no need to show off as all of the support that had accumulated around the starting lamp-post was 50 yards behind me.

I had two choices: either I could slow down in protest at my pacemaker's absurd speed, or I could attempt to catch him up and in so doing probably kill myself. In a moment of pure clarity of thought, I decided that the pacemaker must know exactly how fast the Queen's Jubilee baton needed to be conveyed to the Manchester Commonwealth Games in order for it to reach the event on time.

There was nothing for it. For Queen and country I was going to have to catch up with this Dairy Milk-wrapped Linford Christie look-alike!

Tightening my grip around the vacuum cleaner, which was by now flashing red fast enough to be almost stroboscopic, I gave chase once again. Thankfully, at this particular juncture, there were not too many onlookers. It must have been quite a spectacle to see the controlled, rhythmic glide of the pacemaker and me tearing up the hill behind him, all arms, legs and vacuum cleaners. To my delight I did manage to draw level with Linford again.

"Are you OK?" he asked calmly.

"Yes," I spluttered. It was a lie.

As we rounded a corner I strategically hugged the bend in order to steal the advantage over my pacemaker, who by now I considered nothing less than an opponent. My legs felt heavy, I gasped for air and the baton felt as if it was made of lead.

Out of a roadside pub staggered an inebriated and very angry man. As he spilled his pint all over the pavement he shouted at us with an intensity which was almost savage, "Get a f**kin' move on!" It was not so much the language used, but more the ferocity with which the remark was uttered that threw me. Linford and I were not doing any harm to anyone. We were just a couple of blokes dressed as chocolate bars carrying a flashing Hoover handle around Kingston. How could that enrage anyone so much?

Besides, as far as I was concerned I was getting a f**kin' move on. I was going as fast as my f**kin' legs would carry me. Linford and I both laughed at the unprovoked outburst by Mr Inebriate. After all, I could scarcely feel threatened by his antics. I had a dangerous weapon in my right hand, a highly muscular 6 foot 4 athlete to my left, and I was surrounded by 15 police motorcycles and a Cadbury's chocolate bus within which nestled the most enormous man alive, dressed as an Easter egg.

Just when I thought my legs were going to give up on me and I would have to give Linford the baton to carry the rest of the way, a new crowd of people came into sight, waving their Parkinson's Disease Society banners and cheering me on. The new rush of adrenalin that this provided rejuvenated me and enabled me both to maintain my pace and to continue to hold the baton proudly aloft. I noticed it was no longer flashing; it just maintained a steady single beam of light. I wondered what that meant.

To my delight, the next Dairy Milk bar to carry the baton was just ahead and I stumbled towards him, intuitively knowing that every one-hundredth of a second counted. As I approached the next relay runner I stretched out my arm towards him urgently, willing him to make haste with the message from the Queen that lay within the protective outer casing of the Jubilee baton. But as I was making my final lunge for my own personal finishing line, the next relay runner plucked the relay baton out of my aching, extended paw and just stood there waiting for his picture to be taken with Linford. As I sank to the ground in the dizzy haze of total and utter exhaustion, I was convinced I saw Linford and his new colleague stroll casually past me up the road; they seemed to be chatting idly about the weather. The Queen's Jubilee baton hung limply by the man's side and flashed on…off… on…off…

None of this spoiled the pride of the moment. The fact that I put myself through some considerable pain during my relay leg somehow made it seem more real and more worthy of the congratulatory remarks that I received afterwards. Of course what I had actually done was to display some ridiculously frenzied running over a distance of a mere 400 metres whilst holding a vacuum cleaner in the air. And I had flown all the way down from Inverness to do this.

It was idiotic to feel such pride when my whole involvement in the event was so comical. I suppose to me it was the nearest I would ever get to carrying the Olympic torch; something which, to me, was the very essence of sport.

After I had relinquished the baton, a big group of us wandered back to the pub. I noticed that Dad made a special point of coming to chat with me as we walked. Under normal circumstances, he would probably have left me to talk with other friends who were there. It was good to have a proper catch-up chat with him. With his heart problem precluding him from walking, this would be a year when we would have very little face-to-face contact. When we came to say goodbye, I looked at him and realised that he looked paler and older. For no apparent reason, my stomach suddenly tensed as if I had fallen from the branch of a tree. I ignored the sensation, smiled, waved and set off back to London for the evening's entertainment.

On the way up to London, I wondered about Dad again. He had been suffering with a heart condition for many years. Twelve years back he had undergone a quadruple bypass. All things considered, he had been pretty good since then. But throughout his life he had always adopted a laissez-faire attitude to his health, much to his family's annoyance. It required a respected medical physician threatening imminent cardiac arrest to persuade him that his eating, smoking, drinking and physical activities had to be altered in any way. Not that he did any of these to excess. It was more that he was a "one more won't hurt" sort of person, and for this, we would constantly berate him.

Sunday lunch was the only time when I was growing up that the family would be all together. It was an event when, being the youngest, I would remain quiet and simply observe. The number of times I saw the whole of a Sunday afternoon destroyed because my brother felt that Dad had too much salt on his plate beggars belief. These situations were impossible to diffuse. I achieved it only once – by accident – when my father, peering over a small mountain of salt on his plate, had rounded on me: "Take your forearms off the table," he had said.

I had been confused by this, and as the great salt debate raged on, I considered Dad's instruction carefully. During a rare lull in the histrionics, I had voiced my concern: "But Dad, I haven't got four arms!"

The thunder in his salt-obsessed face suddenly dissipated and he laughed until tears streamed from his eyes. My brother – ever the practical one – said, "At least that's one way of ridding your body of some of the salt." But whereas "blaming Dad" was once a bit of a minefield, nowadays the activity was pursued with good humour on all sides. While Dad was still reasonably dynamic as a City lawyer, this dynamism would now rarely travel back home with him. Dad would be quite happy for us all to revel in his eccentricities and domestic ineptitude. He knew, after all, that when it came to matters of importance, we would all turn to him for advice, in the knowledge that our respect for him would prevail regardless of his salt intake.

Recently Dad had been exhibiting the common traits of clumsiness and absent-mindedness which are the scourge of ageing males the world over. Many succumb to the annoyance and anger they induce. Not Dad. He just thought it was funny. I smiled when I remembered how last summer he had carefully set himself up on a deckchair downwind and away from the rest of us and there, armed with an array of newspapers and legal documents, he had lit an enormous Havana cigar and puffed great plumes into the air. For a moment, he had looked the epitome of contentment and set for an afternoon of browsing, smoking and peaceful slumber.

But then: "CRASH!"

The next thing we knew he was sitting on the ground, astride the crumpled deckchair, with his reading glasses perched skew whiff at the end of his nose and papers everywhere. There was a silent pause. We waited to see if he was hurt. Then the cigar appeared, and with considerable panache he took another huge puff. A grin slowly formed on his face; his shoulders shook up and down and he laughed for ages; silently, hysterically, glorying in his own misfortune. And there he remained, enjoying his considerable discomfort enough to wait until all the family had witnessed his indignity, and until the final bit of humour had been extracted from the situation.

In the last year or so, though, his health had fluctuated quite seriously and at certain times of the day he would be unable to walk more than a hundred yards at a stretch without suffering pains in his chest. Oddly, 18 holes of golf never seemed too much of a problem. It seemed that being able to stop for a little while, as he played his next shot, prevented the game from being too uncomfortable for him.

Even three years ago, when I was walking from John O'Groats to Land's End, he had struggled to walk more than a mile with me. Unlike Mum, Dad was not bothered by this lack of walking just for the sake of it. I remembered he had been much happier careering around the Welsh borders in his absurdly voluminous Jaguar (the Aston Martin being long since gone). He had been totally oblivious to all other road users. As the local traffic scattered before him, he ploughed on along narrow lanes in a compelling display of unabashed opulence. But Dad was not showing off. His thoughts and gaze had wandered far away from the pristine beauty of Powys and were not focused on anything much at all. He was just content in his own space to roll his lavishly specified personal tank from A to B. Here he was free from outside interference; a Field Marshal of the highway for whom all, except combine harvester drivers, would seemingly make way. And in his wake… there would be absolute chaos.

# SHAKE WELL BEFORE USE
(to the tune of "Your Always a Woman to me" by Billy Joel)

*To the fridge in the morning, I reach for my juice*
*There's a sign on the top says "Shake well before use"*
*But I don't need instructions, I have expertise*
*Completely superfluous message with Parkies disease*

*My shaving blade waves like a pair of maracas*
*It's a bit like the Texas chainsaw bathroom massacre*
*And my electric toothbrush has no batteries*
*But I don't need power cause I've got the Parkies disease*

*Oh Mr P he's polite*
*Shook my hand on first sight*
*All those long years ago*
*Oh I don't want to offend*
*Could I just recommend*
*P'raps it's time to let go*

*But danger lurks everywhere when I am trembly*
*Like that time at a charity auction in Wembley*
*And I paid a fortune to see the Krankies*
*Live at the town hall on a day trip to Stockton on Tees*

*And today on the BBC news a reporter*
*Said Holland had vanished 'neath six feet of water*
*They don't know what caused it but it could well be me*
*Last Thursday shook badly when swimming at Clacton-on-Sea*

*So now that's enough and I really must go*
*But thank you for reading this verse and my tales of such woe*

CHAPTER 15

The Wild Rover was clearly bored when I returned to Inverness. He had spent two days on his own and was anxious to get going again. I was too, but at the moment the contents of my pack were strewn randomly around the room.

"You should be an artist."

"There is a certain futility about the juxtaposition of the pairs of socks," I replied, examining my handiwork.

Wild Rover sat and stared at my efforts to collect my gear together and then, using no method other than force, to stuff it unceremoniously into my bag.

"You're incredible," he said. "I've never seen anything like it. Don't you have any kind of system?"

"Yes. My system is that I don't have one." I tried to sound proud, but the truth was that my lack of self-organisation annoyed me as much as anyone else. It seemed to have got worse since having Parkinson's.

It had taken me a day to get back from London to where I had left off. We walked past Cullen, over the Spey River and on beyond Lossiemouth. From here the view opened up before us. As the Moray Firth narrowed and the Black Isle became visible, we turned our gaze northwards and the remainder of Britain's eastern coastline stretched away from us. Even from here, it seemed like a prodigious distance. It always amazes me how much land is left beyond Inverness. The distance from this most northern city in the country to John O'Groats is the same distance on foot as from central London to central Nottingham.

Beyond Burghead's unsightly maltings plant, a narrow and grimy strip of beach presented itself. Despite the fact that since Aberdeen I had covered miles and miles of glorious empty sand, there were more people squashed into the next 400 metres than all the other miles put together. I have no idea why this was. The beach continued all the way to Findhorn, which sits at the bottleneck of Findhorn Bay. I had a small wager with Wild Rover that we would be able to cross "the neck" over to the Culbin Forest and not have to make the arduous journey inland to Forres. Wild Rover was only a few days in to his journey and had not yet developed my newfound faith in mankind's spirit of generosity. The information I gleaned from the local sailing club that evening was that I needed to track down someone called Simon Patterson.

The next morning, Wild Rover seemed in a buoyant mood.

"Without this Simon Patterson fella, we're going nowhere except down the B9011 to Forres."

We went into a shop which sold boating equipment. "We're trying to get a ride across to the Culbin Forest, and we've been told that Simon Patterson might take us. Have you any idea where he might be?"

"I don't know where he is because I have no idea who he is..." came the response, to which Wild Rover stood grinning, "... but I'll take you across the estuary, no problem at all."

Ten minutes later, Wild Rover looked on disbelievingly as the outboard motor was launched into the bay for no other reason than to take us across to the other side.

Rather than follow a B road all the way into Inverness, we decided to take a more attractive route following the River Nairn upstream to Cawdor, home of Macbeth. Before doing this we went into the Tourist Information Centre (TIC), and here we stood in a queue and watched in awe at the effortless charm of the man behind the counter.

TIC Man had slicked-back hair and those intellectual half-glasses, which he perched on the end of his nose so that he could glance above them furtively to deliver "come hither" stares to any browsing ladies who caught his eye. He glided from one customer to the next, imparting his oily wealth of knowledge on matters of the far north.

We watched him as he deftly gave short shrift to Helmut the German man requesting information on the Battle of Culloden, only to move on to the voluptuous Ulrika from Norway, with whom he spent a full 15 minutes even though she just wanted a visitor guide for the Northern Highlands.

"The Northern Highland Visitor Guide? Certainly, Madam. And what sort of information are you specifically after?" he said smarmily.

"I just look for what to do in the area," replied Ulrika.

"And what sort of things do you like doing?" came the predictable response with James Bond-like inflection, complete with raised eyebrow.

"I want to see castles," said Ulrika.

"Castles?" oozed TIC Man in mock surprise. "Ah well, you've come to the right place…" and then he launched into a silky monologue which had been honed to perfection through the years; the facts, figures and elaborate descriptions and superlatives flowed creamily from his mouth.

TIC Man tried and failed to book restaurants and accommodation for Ulrika. If he had had his way he would have booked up their whole future life together; hand in hand running through the Highland heather, visiting castle after castle. Ulrika had the sense to leave.

"Can I have a copy of the accommodation guide for the Highlands?" I asked TIC Man.

"Yes. Here you are," he said, handing me the brochure.

\* \* \*

Once again, my health had taken a turn for the worse. As we walked through the battlefield of Culloden, I looked and felt the part. Things did not improve beyond Inverness either, and having made it onto the Black Isle, I began to become seriously concerned about my speed. Just beyond Fortrose, we joined a fabulous shoreline path giving us expansive views over the Firth and across to Fort George. In the water two dolphins bobbed up and down with poise and grace. I couldn't go any further. I sank to the ground where I was and slept. I don't think I had ever felt so exhausted in my life. The dolphins had been the final straw; the fluid movement of their bodies, the minute amounts of energy they employed to move made a mockery of my own situation. I had been battling so hard that morning just to put one foot in front of the other.

Waking up slowly, but still in semi-sleep, I began thinking about how difficult this walk was for me. It was hard to assess it really. I seemed only to be able to live in the present. When things were going badly, like now, I wondered how on earth I had got this far. I tried to pick a scenic viewpoint every time my symptoms forced me to stop, and from here I would look at the coast behind me with a sense of amazement. And then I would look at the way ahead, often with a feeling of inadequacy at the task which was still before me. Could I really achieve this daft challenge I had set myself? For at times like these, it really did seem like the most ridiculous stunt to have chosen to do.

By the same token, there were times when I was walking well that my symptoms seemed to disappear from the radar altogether. The thought repeated itself in my head. There was probably no other time in the past five years that I would have thought that. Coastin' was good for me and however difficult it was at times, the good moments which I had almost every day seemed to allow me to forget all the horrendous times of shaking, rigidity and dyskinesia. Looking out into the Moray Firth, I inwardly thanked whoever it was that had given me a goldfish-like memory.

My phone was ringing non-stop at the moment. There seemed to be a hive of activity back with Q at base camp. On the website, hundreds of people had left messages of support. I looked at the new entries every day and they motivated me like nothing else. In Cromarty, I had stopped to talk by a bench upon which Wild Rover was sitting waiting. After about ten minutes I realised that our ferry to Nigg was approaching the slipway about 400 yards off. I wondered why Wild Rover had not started walking towards it. At this point, Wild Rover did get up off the bench and turned towards me, revealing a face that bore no resemblance to Wild Rover whatsoever. It was a complete stranger. Apologising to Q and hanging up the phone, I sprinted towards the slipway and arrived just in time... to see the boat pulling away. Wild Rover was standing grinning at me, slightly bemused. "Well, that's one we've missed."

I realised that, in my panic, I had left my map behind. It was probably back near the bench. Retracing my steps, there was no sign of the map, so I kept going, eventually finding it a good half-mile back up the hill. Cursing whoever it was that had given me a goldfish-like memory, I began worrying about missing the next ferry too. I started running back, confident that after my superb performance with the Jubilee baton relay, my fitness and speed would ensure that the second boat would not be missed. I covered the ground at a prodigious rate, and I was aware that people were standing watching me; probably in awe. I powered the last 200 yards and reached the slipway, this time only missing the boat by a few seconds.

Wild Rover was still standing there. This time he was not grinning.

"You're useless, Isaacs." He stormed off.

We were three and a half hours late reaching Nigg. Wild Rover recovered his humour quite quickly, and at my expense. The day had been a test of patience for him, and one of perseverance for me. We both passed with flying colours.

Will Cook joined us in Balintore. After the atrocious weather he had experienced in Norfolk, he had come prepared. His array of equipment was inventive, although a little unconventional. The polythene bags in which he inserted each foot so that they were sandwiched between boot and sock and spilt over his boots and down to the ground made pretty good makeshift gaiters. Sadly, they also made him look just like a shire horse.

The Firth of Dornoch looked dramatic as a huge black cloud homed in on our approach. As we crossed the bridge an elderly walker was coming the other way.

"I'm walking from John O'Groats to Land's End." He seemed delighted when we asked him numerous questions about his trip. It didn't seem appropriate to steal his thunder and when he asked us where we were heading for, we responded that today we were just making for Dornoch.

We were well underneath the storm cloud before the taps were turned on us. We had been beginning to wonder whether we might get away with it altogether. But no such luck, and by the time we reached our B&B we were cold, wet, hungry and thoroughly miserable.

\* \* \*

The weather was very much better the following day as we marched alongside the hallowed turf of Royal Dornoch Golf Club. To me, this golf club was even more sacred than St Andrews. Ever since I could remember, my father had been coming here with his cronies for a week in October. Every year he would return home with superb jumpers as presents, which were always two sizes too small, regardless of the recipient. He would also come back sporting a tan, the result, he said, of being outdoors in an unseasonal autumn heatwave, but most likely equally attributable to the amount of whisky consumed within seven days.

Wild Rover had a slightly confused look on his face as we passed a few of the cavernous pot bunkers scattered along the immaculate fairways.

"How on earth are you meant to hit the ball out of one of those things?"

While Will gave Wild Rover a short lesson on how to chop across the ball with an open stance and high follow-through (a shot that he could only play in his dreams), I had a mental picture in my head of Dad trying desperately to do the same thing. I always knew I would win the hole if Dad went in a bunker. It was a mental block; an inability to relax, and it affected him every time. It would usually be after the ball had rolled back to his feet for the third successive time that he would turn to me and see the look of exasperation on my face. And then his shoulders would rock up and down and he would laugh, joyous in his misery before trying again. Invariably, having relaxed a little, on the next attempt he would get out.

Then I remembered how ill he had looked in Kingston and began to wonder whether he was OK. Once again, I dismissed the thought. Right now he was sure to be in his usual Saturday position; reclined, relaxed and distant on his Parker Knoll chair. And yet the transition from that soporific state to which so many hard-working, old-age-approaching males are prone was always very quick to change when guests arrived. I smiled when I remembered how quick it had been on the day I had walked into the room followed by three sleek, bronzed young ladies. Dad had leapt to his feet. The company had encouraged a sprightlier leap than usual, but as was customary, Dad had effected his transformation into effusive host within seconds.

After offering the girls, who were Australian travelling companions, an array of soft drinks, he then inspected his watch before delivering one of his favourite lines: "Or something stronger perhaps?"

In my early teens, I had always been rather proud of the fact that Dad had made the same offer to any of my friends who came round to visit. Even if he did not treat me as an adult when we were alone, he never let me down in front of friends.

"What a lovely man your father is," my friends had remarked later.

My father was good with people. He was good at solving problems, principally because he was a good listener and had a sense of what was right and fair. Most of the people he advised knew and respected his take on things. I counted myself as one of these.

Dad always seemed undaunted by life. Despite his father dying when he was a teenager, and his brother when he was still a young man, these tragedies had hardened him, making him determined, proud and emotionally streetwise. The only time I had experienced a softer side to my father was when Stuart, a golfing chum and business associate, had passed away. In Stuart Hollander's death, I realised Dad had lost someone whom he not only respected and cared about, but who was also the same as him and a part of him. Perhaps Stuart dying had given Dad a sense of his own mortality.

I remembered him saying to me through glassy eyes, "I really liked Stuart."

I suppose it was that he had displayed a gentler side; a more fallible Dad that he had not revealed to me before. I had felt embarrassed and awkward, seeing the totally unexpected display of emotion. And yet at the same time, I wanted to take his hurt away and tell him everything was OK. The moment had left an impression. Whilst feeling sad for my father, I was happy that he had shared such a personal moment with me.

I tuned back in to Will, who was still talking utter drivel about bunkers.

"Do you have any other questions?" Will asked.

"Yes. As matter-of-fact, I do," came the response. "How much further will Tom's right foot travel than his left foot on his journey around Britain?"

Half an hour of peace and quiet ensued while Will went into his head to work out the calculation to this excellent question. By the time we reached the placid shores of Loch Fleet, he gave us his answer: "Twelve inches."

"What?"

"Twelve inches."

We laughed. This had to be more rubbish. But Will was adamant.

"I have assumed a two-inch gap between your feet and not allowed for the curvature of the earth. The equation is simple: $2\pi r$, where "r" equals two inches."

Two days later, Wild Rover and I rang Will up at his office in London.

"We agree with you," we said. It had taken us that long to work it out.

* * *

We had reached Brora, where I was pleased to reacquaint myself with Mick and Kath at Ar Dachaidh B&B. Mick is barrel-shaped, bearded and benevolent with a "nothing bothers me" attitude and a toothy grin which transforms his whole demeanour from vaguely scary to super-softy.

Kath meanwhile is small, fiercely proud and terrific fun as long as she likes you. I had stayed there twice previously and on each occasion, Kath, a Lancastrian thoroughbred, had sent me away with the words, "... and bloody don't come back again."

I should have known better than to mention how pleased I was to see these two no-nonsense northerners again.

"Oh shut up, you'll make me vomit!" was all I got for my trouble.

I liked Kath. She was like one of those chocolates you sometimes get after a dinner party: brittle and bitter on the outside, but with a surprisingly soft fondant centre. I would enjoy being brought down a peg or two by her.

In the end, Kath had plenty of opportunity to tear me off a strip; we ended up staying there for three days while I recovered from a flu-like bug I had caught from somewhere. Wild Rover himself had injured an ankle by falling down a rabbit hole way back on his second day near Lossiemouth. We both needed to recuperate. Kath, meanwhile, tended to our washing and returned it beautifully pressed and folded with the comment: "I am not a bloody Chinese laundry and you have long outstayed your welcome."

We left Ar Dachaidh on 24th July, and as Mick pulled out of the driveway and drove us back to Golspie in his bright yellow 2CV jalopy, we heard a voice shout after us, "... and don't bloody come back again!"

Once past the fairytale towers of Dunrobin Castle, we were able to follow the coast for much of the way to Helmsdale. I had a strange feeling we were being watched as we went; not as you might expect, from the land, but from somewhere on our right. We were being watched from the sea. I turned to find about ten pairs of eyes looking at us with considerable curiosity. All we could see were their grey, round heads, whiskers and brown eyes, which followed us as we walked out of sight.

The A9, with its constant and fast-moving stream of traffic, was becoming tiresome and we were pleased to finally branch off the road and on to the A99 at Latheron. But the change was only temporarily uplifting, as the road was equally busy and did not provide us with any of the views of the coastline which we were now beginning to crave again.

We were now closing in on Wick, the last town before reaching the north coast and perhaps most famous for being the most northerly reference point on the BBC weather map. At Thrumster, we saw a man with a beard approaching us. As we had not seen many solo walkers, we began wondering what sort of a walk he was on and why he was doing it.

"Charity walker from John O'Groats," said Wild Rover.

"No. No backpack. The local eccentric, I reckon; does this walk every day."

"Looks fairly normal to me. Perhaps he's a twitcher."

"They don't usually look normal. I think he's a geologist. He looks like a geologist."

As he drew nearer we became more and more curious, particularly because he was staring at us as hard as we were staring at him.

"Is one of you Tom Isaacs?" he asked to our complete astonishment.

"Who on earth is this?", we thought.

"Yes. I am." I shook his hand cautiously.

"My name is David, and your Auntie Susan's husband Richard is my cousin."

At that precise moment a car pulled up behind us, sandwiching us between it and my new quasi-relative. A lady got out and announced herself as David's wife Rena. "You're surrounded by family," Wild Rover announced with a smile.

I didn't really know what to say, do or feel. It was all too much to take in. I had a lot of questions I wanted to ask.

"You've probably got a few questions." David's mind-reading capabilities were slightly disturbing. "Why don't you come for dinner?"

"Yes, do come," said Rena.

After we agreed to their offer, they seemed satisfied and departed just as quickly as they had come.

It seemed just a bit too good to be true: the apparently chance meeting; the immediate arrival of Rena; the mind reading. Something strange was afoot here. I voiced my concern to Wild Rover. "Perhaps we are the dinner."

Despite feeling a bit like Hansel and Gretel as we plunged deeper and deeper into the Wick suburbia, we thought we could remember our way back to our B&B without the need for breadcrumbs. In any case, as it turned out, David and Rena treated us both like prodigal sons returning from war. And yet Wild Rover could only claim to be the friend of Rena's once-removed cousin's cousin by marriage – i.e. me. It was easier to refer to them as Uncle Dave and Auntie Rena – and so they became.

When you see where Wick is on the map of Britain, you would expect it to be utterly bleak and windswept, and home to more polar bears than humans. The truth is that it is not really inhospitable in any respect. The welcome we received in Wick was second to none. Apart from Uncle Dave and Auntie Rena, we were also entertained by Robert and Annette.

Robert and I shared two illnesses: Parkinson's and optimism. Robert's particular brand of PD meant that he had huge difficulty with his posture and gait. When he stopped, he had great trouble in getting going again and Annette would have to put her foot in front of his leg, giving him a target to step over. This is one of those bizarre quirks of the illness. To a lesser extent, I had the same problem myself, finding it a real effort to make my legs lift high enough to ascend a small incline, but having absolutely no difficulty in climbing steps where the target is more tangible.

Despite the walk back to Robert's house being a fairly stop–start affair, the emphasis was taken off this by the free-flowing conversation.

"We are not going too fast for you, are we?" Robert said with an ironic sideways glance.

After meeting Robert, I thought about the difference between him and me and Colin from north of Aberdeen. I thought about our respective communicative skills. I had heard Bear Grylls say on Radio 4, "When you lose your movement, you lose your expression." He had been referring to the time when he had broken his back before going on to be the youngest person to climb Mount Everest. The word "expression" here, I thought, was used to mean the way you portray yourself. The words are so true. Except of course, with Parkinson's, you actually do lose your facial expression.

Sometimes I feel a bit like a grandfather clock; only able to move by degrees. Every movement is forced, mechanical – cogwheel rigidity.

A Parkinson's disease study was undertaken by the University of Southampton. A man with Parkinson's was asked to press a buzzer every time he thought he smiled during a set period. He was filmed whilst doing the test, and when they reviewed the video recording, it was clear the man had smiled a couple of times. The buzzer had sounded over fifty times.

It is known as a Parkinson's mask. Most people will have experienced talking to someone with a Parkinson's mask, but often without knowing it. They fail to recognise that this strangely uncharismatic person to whom they are speaking is actually trying their hardest to make their face move; to respond and react to the emotional nuances of the conversation.

Without the ability to express emotions, the features of someone with the condition tend to be crease-free, as if the skin is peeled off and ironed every night. The eyes stare. They are seemingly fixed in the middle distance.

My schizophrenia is not one of the mind. It is one of the body. I am able to compare both the Jekyll and the Hyde of my movement daily. When my body becomes Mr Hyde, I lose much of my control. Every single action, from raising a glass to raising an eyebrow, requires immense effort and concentration.

But which is more important, the glass or the eyebrow? At first glance, the answer seems obvious. One is a way of providing yourself with the essential ingredient for life. The other is a seemingly superfluous action, only really required by James Bond actors to express understated surprise. But I would argue it is the eyebrow which is more crucial. You can be fed water by others, but no one can communicate your feelings other than yourself.

Colin had been able to walk and move his arms, and had generally sound mobility. Despite this, his face wore the mask and he had lost much of his ability to speak. Robert, meanwhile, couldn't do anything of his own accord. His symptoms were so bad that he was totally reliant on Annette, who did practically everything for him. Yet this man had the full use of his face and he could speak clearly.

Having spent some time with both of them, I pondered which one I would rather be. There was absolutely no doubt. In the short time I had spent with Robert, he had shown me who he was: a man of considerable spirit and humour, and I came away with a healthy respect for him. Colin, on the other hand had initially given me no sense of the man inside the body. All I could feel was pity. I realised that although I had sympathy for Robert's symptoms, I did not pity him, and the difference between pity and sympathy if you're on the receiving end is vast. The two are separated by what I think must be the most crucial of all human qualities: dignity.

I realised that at all costs, I must be able to communicate and that whatever happened with my Parkinson's, that had to be the priority.

Our final day in Wick was a good one. I was happy because Lyndsey had come up again for a few days. Wild Rover was happy because he found out he had passed his Year 1 osteopathy exams. But it wasn't just us in a good mood. There was a carnival atmosphere in the whole region. People were either going to the Halkirk Highland Games or were preparing for the Wick Gala Procession that evening. We were going to both.

At the Highland Games we were the guests of the Clan Gunn. Lyndsey, who was a MacDonald, had been impressed by this, and I began to see why, as we were introduced to a number of chieftains, lairds and all manner of Celtic dignitaries. One of these, in particular, caught my attention. He was a colossus of a man in full highland regalia. Several shocks of bright orange hair sprang out of his Tam O'Shanter like Brillo pads and I estimated he was at least 7 feet high and 5½ feet wide. I was so in awe of the man, I never did catch his name, but it was something like Laird Jocky McDougal Tavish Sinclair of Caithness. As I held out my hand to shake his, I realised that my arm looked like a bicycle spoke compared to his, which was made out of the trunks of mature baobab trees.

"Pleased to meet you," I ventured a little timidly.

"Yes, jolly pleased to meet you too!" he replied.

My mouth gaped open and I stood in wide-eyed disbelief at this modern-day Celtic Goliath. I had no doubt from just looking at this colossus that he had been brought up on a diet of porridge for breakfast, haggis for lunch and Englishman for tea. Nevertheless, the voice, which I had been expecting to be low, rasping, gravelly and used only when an action would not suffice, was in fact piercing, gaudy, plummy and hyperactive. Had I been asked to identify him from this alone, I would surely have guessed that he had been brought up on classics, rugger and Bollinger from somewhere within the Eton–Ascot–Henley triangle.

Bunty Gunn, the wife of the head of Clan Gunn, Commander Iain Gunn, was on a mission to raise money for Coastin' at the games. With a mixture of brazenness and stealth, depending on the victim, she emptied the pockets of every living creature circulating the games arena, and she did so at a rate of £6.45 per minute. I worked out that if Bunty Gunn continued with me for the rest of Coastin', I would raise about £2.5 million.

We left Wick the next day knowing we were leaving somewhere really quite special. We were John O'Groats-bound.

The weather was not behaving for our final day on the east coast. Just beyond Nybster I received a phone call from Robert.

"What's the weather like?" he asked, despite only being about ten miles away.

"Terrible. It's absolutely pouring."

"I don't believe it," he said with some sincerity. "It's the first bad day we've had in four years." The timing of his dry humour was immaculate.

Taking a right towards Skirza, we followed a track up to a boggy plateau. Despite the uneasy terrain and our tiredness, we enjoyed a fun half-hour watching each other as we made fools of ourselves. The trouble was that with each stride we couldn't be sure whether our feet would bounce off springy heather, propelling us high into the air, or whether we would sink waist deep in a mire of liquefied peat.

Eventually, we arrived at John O'Groats, where so many people finish their "great journeys" from Land's End with such excitement, only to plummet into a deep sense of anti-climax brought about by the sheer desolation of the place. I always think there should be a sign there that says simply, "So what now?", because whether you've arrived by foot, wheel or pogo stick, these words must be uttered by more people here than anywhere else in the world.

There were no such thoughts or words for us when we walked into the car park to find that Robert and Annette had arranged a reception party for us. We were applauded into their midst and swallowed whole into the feel-good factor. In the pub, Robert struggled to his feet. "Today," he said, "we welcome Tom, Lyndsey and the Wild Rover to sunny Caithness." The rain hammered harder on the window outside as if in response to the insult. "'Tis God's country," he continued. The windows rattled. "And, in view of Tom's struggle to build awareness and raise funds for Parkinson's, I would like to pronounce him an 'honorary Scotsman.'"

I went a bit gooey-eyed at this. I knew there is nothing a Scotsman values higher than his nationality and it meant a lot coming from him.

"Wasn't that nice?" I said to Lyndsey afterwards.

"Och, yer'll allwees be sleetly posh and Inglish tae me," she replied in broad Glaswegian.

"I'm awfully sorry, I don't understand a word you are saying." It was in my best public-schoolboy accent. We smiled at each other.

"Do yer no?" she said. "Well yer'll ne'er be a Scotsman then."

"Why can't you speak like that Laird Jocky McDougal Tavish Sinclair? He seemed like a frightfully nice chap."

Our banter was getting more feisty. I liked that.

The official "turning left" ceremony took place before breakfast the next day. Lyndsey, Wild Rover and I walked the two miles out to Duncansby Head. I walked north to the lighthouse where I stood at the corner. Straight ahead of me was nothing but sea, but to my left the north coast lay in wait for my footsteps. It was by far the shortest of the four sides of the country and it would only take a week to reach Cape Wrath. The west coast which followed would take me six months to complete. It was the end of another chapter and, as with all the others before it, it ended too quickly. The Coastin' lifestyle was extraordinary in as much as it was so transitory. People popped into my world and then popped out again and only two of them followed me as I turned on my heels and headed west.

FROM DUNCANSBY TO DURNESS
112 MILES
JULY-AUGUST

CHAPTER 16

Fifteen or so miles west of Duncansby Head lies Dunnet Head, the northernmost tip of mainland Britain. We had taken a detour of ten miles in order to be able to say that "we'd Dunnet", but a sea mist rolled in just at the wrong moment. In Scotland they call this mist "a haar". But there was nothing "Aha!" about it. We couldn't see a thing. What should have been a relatively easy day, walking to Thurso, turned out to be quite tough for me.

Once again my medication was failing me. Instead of the normal smooth transition from one dose to the next, it became a torrid struggle in which I was barely able to walk.

I stopped by the side of the road. Lyndsey stayed with me while Wild Rover continued the last few miles to Thurso.

"Sometimes this is really hard," I said to her.

"The whole thing is hard. You're amazing," she said. "I don't know how you keep going."

I sat back against a large boulder and closed my eyes. I thought about Lyndsey and how two days ago she had brought me back down to size after the welcome at John O'Groats, and yet now here she was picking me up when I was feeling low. It was her who was "amazing". I should have told her this there and then, but I didn't. I wish I had. She was leaving in the morning again. Time seemed so short with her and she was becoming such an important ingredient to both my progress and my state of mind.

The hills were rising up in front of us. Caithness is lovely, but its neighbour is stunning. No sooner had we passed the sign welcoming us back to Sutherland than the terrain became more rugged, the people fewer and the midges more resourceful.

The walk from Melvich to Bettyhill was spoilt by another thick sea mist which at times seemed to come tantalisingly close to lifting, but never did. We had already heard Highlanders talking of their homeland as God's country. We might have believed them had we been able to see it. We felt that Satan had certainly dipped his oar in too. He sent "the midges".

Having been propelled to the brink of insanity before by these horrendous swarming beasties, this time I came prepared. I had arrived in Scotland armed with repellents, head nets, blowtorch and bazooka, all of which were readily accessible to be drawn from their respective holsters at the merest hint of a U.F.F.O. (Unfeasibly Fierce Flying Object). I was armed and ready for action. But on my first night in the country, I was reminded of another deterrent which, whilst apparently effective, failed miserably in terms of being an acceptable addition to my "Action Man" style set of beast-busting accessories. Usually, I would have been concerned that my silky textured, Avon Skin-so-Soft Woodland Fresh moisturising spray might, if found on my person, call my masculinity into question. It was a minuscule sacrifice if the stuff worked.

"Yer'll nay geh across the River Naver," warned the landlady at the B&B. "Yer'll geh caut wi' the tide and yer'd be fools to try it." There is something about a broad Scottish accent which always laces any type of warning with a sense of impending doom.

Wild Rover and I were looking for a bit of adventure though, and made a considered decision to be foolish.

The River Naver may have looked easy to ford from up on Bettyhill, but now we were down at its edge, we could see why Betty had stayed up there. The water was running quite fast and we could tell by its colour and flow that it was a little deeper than we had at first anticipated.

Our attempt at crossing failed miserably; too dangerous. We turned away, admitting defeat, and opted to follow the road round. Our hopes of reaching Tongue early were dashed, but at least we were still in one piece.

I pictured the look of disdain that would have been on the face of Docadile Dundee had he been here. His voice rang loud in my ears like a ghost of forded rivers past: "Bottling out of the river are you?"

We tried again. This time, the voice of Betty Hill rang loud in my ears. "Yer doomed. Doomed."

We made easy passage to a mid-river island and for a while I stood pensively working out the best route across the second channel. As I was doing this, Wild Rover experienced a rush of blood to the head. "Sod it!" he exclaimed and with this he plunged, chest high, into the rapidly moving current. It may well have been a touch foolhardy, but 30 seconds later he was scrambling up the far bank, triumphant.

It was not so easy for me. My balance is not what it used to be and Wild Rover had to come back to carry my pack across above his head. I suffered a few scary moments when the River Naver threatened to whisk me off downstream, but eventually I too clambered up the other side unscathed.

"Thanks, mate," I said.

Wild Rover and I were on a high. Our camaraderie was never better than immediately after we had tested ourselves against some natural obstacle and overcome it. We consulted the map again to revel in the amount of time we had saved by making the crossing. It was considerable, but if the truth be known, our satisfaction was actually not associated with this at all. For me, it was more that I had overcome my Parkinson's to make it across and for Wild Rover it was the fact that he had been able to help me overcome it.

Wild Rover was someone who felt he was only helping when he was actually making some physical effort of his own in order to do so. What he perhaps failed to appreciate on this walk, was how much help he was by just being there.

Carrying our wet boots, we padded across Torrisdale Bay's untouched sands. The beauty of the beach seemed to muffle the rush of adrenalin and allowed us to drift into a state of satisfying, silent reflection.

At the far end of Torrisdale Bay, the River Borgie also had to be crossed. It was a totally different proposition to the Naver and Wild Rover ploughed straight through its gushing shallows without breaking stride. I did the same, reached halfway across and froze.

It can sometimes be that quick. One moment I am a fully functional human being, the next, almost totally incapacitated.

My brain is like a battlefield. I only have a few of my original dopamine footsoldiers left, so every day I call for reinforcements by popping a pill. Normally there is a pretty slow withdrawal of the reinforcements as the Parkinson's "braintroopers" take the upper hand. Today there had been no contest; the reinforcements had exited the battle zone in panic.

Meanwhile, back in the middle of the river, panic was pretty much what I was feeling too. My balance was suddenly non-existent. I clung on to Ewan, my stick, for support as if it was my only lifeline and I made my way, inch by inch, across the slippery rocks at the bottom of the stream. My journey time to the centre of the river had been about three seconds. The second half of the trip probably took sixty times as long.

Up to this point, I had never experienced anything which had displayed the difference between my "on" and "off" periods so clearly, so keenly.

It did not spoil the day. And after a short spell when the only sound was the squelch of our wet boots on the tarmac, we went off-piste.

The heather had an almost downy texture as we strode out over an ever more rugged landscape. The ghostly veil of a sea mist lifted in a strengthening breeze and we were gifted with spectacular views. Hugging the cliff line, which seemed to plummet ever more dramatically into a cauldron of surf and spray below, we made our way round into the Kyle of Tongue.

* * *

It was not that Coastin' was getting any easier. In fact, if anything the periods when I was feeling good were now fewer than those when I was suffering some sort of physical or mental fatigue. It wasn't the fact that the daily challenge was insufficient either, I still found enormous fulfilment in achieving my daily goal of 15 to 25 miles. There were two other principal explanations for attempting a 30-mile day from Tongue to Durness. The first was that there was no reasonably priced accommodation available between the two places. The second was that when people asked, "What was your longest day?" I would be able to respond, "Thirty miles."

It would be a challenge. I had never attempted 30 miles in a day, even in the prime of health, and the prospect filled me with both excitement and trepidation.

This may seem over-dramatic, but walking filled my existence at this time. 4,500 miles was too big, too unwieldy to grasp as a concept or a goal. Instead, I set myself smaller challenges: reaching milestones; fording rivers; or scaling mountains. It would be good to put a tick in the box next to the words "30-mile day".

I slept appallingly, fitfully ducking in and out of dreams where I collapsed at 28 miles, lost my boots, lost my water, lost my way.

Wild Rover had to help me pack, make breakfast and fill my water bottle. I was useless. To complete 30 miles successfully without plying myself with drugs all day, I had decided to make an attempt at starting without taking any at all. The idea was that with his superior strength, speed and greater connectivity between brain and body, Wild Rover would give me a two-hour head start today. Meanwhile he would sort out luggage logistics and attempt to avoid the attentions of the B&B owner, who had grown rather fond of him.

At 7.15 a.m., I tottered, old man-like, down the road. The hill down to the causeway provided momentum so that my legs fell into place thanks to the force of gravity rather than through any express command from me. Once on the flat, my feet scuffed the ground with every half-hearted step. My right arm was stiff, redundant, a dead weight. Like a broken pendulum it hung from my shoulder, resolutely still, oblivious to my forward motion. My left arm battled chaotically with my stick, which was punting me onwards, my only ally to progress. At this rate I would not have been surprised if Wild Rover had caught me up at the end of the causeway across the Kyle of Tongue, not 2 ½ miles from where I had started.

Once again this morning, there was a thick cloud of sea mist, and it cast a dank, oppressive, but rather dramatic atmosphere over the Kyle of Tongue. It matched my mood. It was always a shock to me how bad I was in the mornings without the benefit of drugs. It was awful knowing that this was the real me. This was what Tom Isaacs had become without medication in his bloodstream. It was a particularly sobering thought in this morning's gloom and with 28 miles still to go.

I worked out that if I continued at my current speed, I would arrive in Durness just after midnight. I stopped to let another car go past. I did not want anyone to see me walking this badly for fear that they might stop and offer me a lift. I had honed my technique for doing this to perfection over the past few months. Upon hearing a vehicle from either direction, I would stop walking and pretend to admire the view, whether it was of the finest mountains in Scotland or the most hideous industrial chimneys of Teesside.

On this occasion, I remained stationary after the car had gone. The all-too-familiar tremor began moments later, first in my right and then in my left hand. When I clenched my fist, it subsided.

As a sort of sadistic experiment, I then held both my arms out at right angles to my body, with my fingers outstretched. Once again, for a moment everything was still, but a few seconds later the whirring began and my hands flapped. I continued to hold them outstretched until the movement intensified. For some inexplicable reason, I urged my arms on, and it didn't take a great deal of coaxing before both were gyrating in unison and with frightening velocity.

In this bleak moment, I was once again rescued by a moment of irrational optimism. Okay, so it looked as if I would be unable to walk the 30 miles today, but with my arms whirring like a hummingbird, flying to Durness might be an option. Dumbo, the flying elephant, had big ears – I had flapping arms.

My mood instantly changed. The thought of flying to Durness above the sea mist and the midges provided the mental lift that was required. As is so often the case with me, when the psychological battle is won, so the physical side of things improves. My arms started swinging a little bit more and my Parkinson's shuffle became a more confident purposeful stride. I pondered how much of this infuriating disease was controlled by mental state as opposed to more scientific neurological factors. Maybe the power of positive thought could defeat the illness on its own.

It was a long climb out of the Kyle of Tongue. As I gained height, the visibility barometer registered "end of nose", but at least stopping to admire the views would not delay me further.

I eventually stopped to pop some pills and was immediately ambushed by a huge gang of midge bandits. They were out for blood. And they got it.

It was an attack orchestrated with stealth and precision. They had clearly waited until I stopped to take my pills before deciding to engulf me. It was my moment of greatest weakness. There was only one thing in my armoury that would save me: my dual-function, pump-action, spread-so-thin, skin-so-soft. It was not as readily available as I would have liked.

Parkinson's and panic is not a happy cocktail. As I struggled to release my dermatologically enhancing beauty product from my rucksack, the midges gorged themselves on my flesh. There was only one other option, and it involved assuming the guise of a headless chicken. Sprinting up the road waving my arms and stick about my head, I managed to temporarily halt the rampant orgy of voracious feasting. I examined my wounds. It had been a rout. Hope is nine miles from Tongue. The inappropriately named hamlet was not even a third of the way there and I had taken over four hours to reach it. In the time it took me to climb up the far side of the cavernous Hope valley, the sea mist finally lifted and the wonderful views revealed themselves from behind the curtain. Looking back I could see a white speck on the horizon, moving at vast speed: Wild Rover was closing in.

He caught me up at 15 miles, having walked at an average of over 4 mph. By this time my body had acclimatised to my over-ambitious drugless start to the morning and I was striding out with no doubt that the 30-mile day would be completed.

Rounding the far end of Loch Eriboll, of which we had to complete three sides, the mighty Ben Hope came into view, towering high above its valley. At 3,039 feet (927 metres), it is the northernmost of the Monroes (mountains in Scotland over 3000 feet). The scale of the sea loch and the mountain belittled the rest of the scene. The yawning expanse of Loch Eriboll, where the land had once been, and the monolithic bulk of Ben Hope seemed strangely linked; as if the shapes had been cut and pasted.

It was strange: miles 20 to 30 were the easiest of the day. I was not sure where the new lease of life came from; maybe it was the realisation that I would finish the day and the 30-mile barrier would be broken. At mile 27, I was a bit put out that, despite my energy resurgence, a man driving in the opposite direction to us wound down his window, asking if we would like a lift to Durness.

"I saw you struggling back there and thought I would come back and see if you wanted a lift."

The kindness of the offer; the fact that he had gone to the bother of turning round on a narrow road to see if I needed help, did not dawn on me at first. All I could think of was the word he used: "struggling".

Struggling? I wasn't struggling. I felt unreasonably angry at the suggestion. "I'm not struggling," I said, "I'm just limping a bit."

Having eventually thanked the man profusely, we continued on our way. We waved happily at him as he passed us yet again a few minutes later, but under my breath I was still muttering, "Struggling indeed." I wondered what I did look like trudging along after 27 miles. I detested the thought that I might look needy even when I did not feel it.

My spirits were revived as the sign for Durness came into view. It was 7 p.m.; 12 hours after I had set off.

Two cyclists passed us and shouted across, "We saw you in Tongue this morning. How far have you walked today?"

"30 miles!" We both blurted out. What a satisfactory way to end the day.

Cape Wrath

Durness
3rd August

Tongue

FROM NORTH COAST
TO WEST COAST
31 MILES
AUGUST

CHAPTER 17

Cape Wrath is the most northwesterly point of the country. Not many people go there. From the very beginning, it had been a hugely important goal for me. Now I was so tantalisingly close, it felt like the Promised Land.

In terms of Coastin', its significance was there for all to see. As the crow flies, I would be at my furthest point from London when I stood at Cape Wrath. Everything after it would feel as if I was on the inbound journey. I would be walking home.

Cape Wrath would also bring the first view of the west coast of Britain; my companion for the next 2,180 miles, all the way to Land's End.

But it was more than just the physical location of this last outpost of the British mainland that made my sense of anticipation so great. I had read several accounts by other long-distance coastal walkers, all of whom had been profoundly affected by its splendour and by their sense of achievement in reaching it. I was intrigued by this, and in my head Cape Wrath had become by far my most eagerly awaited stretch of coastal walking of the entire year. For me, the north-west tip of Britain was the biggest milestone of Coastin', save for the finish line; and that seemed too far away to even contemplate. With my perception of this place being based largely on hearsay, now that I was within 15 miles of Cape Wrath I began to realise what an enormous disappointment it might turn out to be. Anything short of "magnificent" and I would feel cheated.

A 30-mile day sandwiched between two restless nights was making me volatile, in terms of both mood and Parkinson's. Doubt in my ability to complete the next two days made me wonder whether we should take a rest day. In mileage terms, the walk round to Cape Wrath and on to Kinlochbervie on the west coast did not seem too taxing, but the terrain would be tough and we would need to carry sufficient food and water for two days.

I realised that it would be sensible to postpone the expedition by a day. I needed time to recuperate. The timing of this decision was, however, not so sensible – we had just pulled away from the quay at Keoldale on the little boat bound for the Cape Wrath peninsula.

Despite my concerns, things still looked pretty good. Alison, a friend from Edinburgh whom I had first met on the boat in Sydney harbour just after my diagnosis, had arrived from Edinburgh and as usual had given both Wild Rover and me a shot in the arm of her concentrated enthusiasm. She and the Wild Rover knew each other quite well, having been flung together on a trip up Kilimanjaro which I had organised but couldn't go thanks to some idiot on a football field who broke my leg. It's a wonder people don't call me "Lucky".

"I can't believe I'm up here," Alison said. "It's so fabulous to be doing this bit of the walk with you boys." But I couldn't match her enthusiasm. I just felt so tired. I almost felt resentful of Alison's enthusiasm. I wanted to be having as nice a time as she was, but for some reason, this morning I was just not enjoying myself.

The small passenger ferry from Keoldale provided a simple method of getting across the Kyle of Durness without a substantial inland detour. The journey was only a few minutes long and it was shared with a small group of day trippers who, at the far side, would be taken by minibus to the Cape Wrath lighthouse. I felt eyes on our backs as the three of us slung on our rucksacks, conspicuously ignored the waiting transport and marched away purposefully up the track, glorying in our self-sufficiency.

The feeling did not last long. The single-track road steepened and there was silence as we suddenly became aware of the weight of our packs. Pride restored temporary bounce to our steps when we heard the minibus rattling up behind us, but once it had disappeared out of sight ahead, we stopped to catch our breath overlooking Durness from on high.

We stared out to the magnificent dunes of Faraid Head whilst below us the swirling sandbanks of the Kyle of Durness shimmered in the sunlight and looked vaguely reminiscent of the vanilla element of a tub of raspberry ripple ice cream. I took a swig of warm water. It was a rather sad substitute.

I fell silent as we walked, and as Wild Rover and Alison chatted animatedly, I felt dejected, purely out of envy of their good mood.

Having turned our back on the Kyle and wound our way through rugged and barren terrain, we eventually turned right down a track. It was here that all thoughts of weariness and possible wrong decisions disintegrated when a truly momentous scene slowly unravelled as we walked the final half-mile down to Kearvaig Beach. The sun's rays were now deeper in colour, casting an auburn glow and adding definition, texture and shadow to an already spell-binding view. The warm blanket of sand gave way to crystal clear surf, relentlessly rolling in between sheer cliffs on either side. It may seem over-dramatic to say it, but my first sight of Kearvaig Beach will be forever etched in my memory. I doubted whether the sight which opened out before me could ever be matched. My sullen mood disintegrated instantly and was replaced with a deep-felt sense of awe. This was it. In the future, when people asked me what was my favourite place on the coastline of Britain, it would surely be here.

There was only one thing to do. I ran headlong into the sea. I regretted it. It was bloody cold! I forced myself not to run headlong out again and having waded in up to my waist, I stood with my arms folded, gazing out to sea in quiet contemplation. As I did so, a bald black head popped out of the sea and seemed to peruse me with its large brown eyes. I stood motionless, wondering whether the seal would come any closer. But it disappeared and I didn't see it again.

After a frenzied splash in the clear blue waters, I was forced back to the beach, owing to both the icy cold of the water and a rather large jellyfish which glided with deadly grace just inches from my right shoulder.

There were a few other people on the beach now but all of them seemed to be immersed in their own thoughts, wandering randomly in their own quiet quarter of the vast expanse of sand. There was something about this place that made us all want our own company and space.

The bothy at Kearvaig represented man's sole intervention in a Celtic masterpiece. A Scottish bothy is a very basic hut or shelter traditionally used by farm workers, but more recently used by walkers and climbers. It stood high on the dunes above the beach and we were glad of it for one reason. It provided a fortification, a barrier against a midge ambush. As the sunlight faded, the midges became totally unbearable and we were all forced to retreat into the sanctuary of the bothy.

Determined not to miss any hint of a sunset, Alison and I clad ourselves in full battle regalia: head nets, gloves, socks wrapped around long trousers – we were ready to face the enemy and went out onto the beach to face the onslaught. After making it through a ferocious wave of attack during our passage through the sawgrass, we found that they were not so organised once their line was broken. The beach was really not too bad and I went back to fetch Wild Rover, so that he did not miss what was going to be a memorable scene.

The sand was bathed gold by the last rays of the sun which burnt deepest red before falling into a black sea.

By the time the sun finally dipped beneath the horizon and darkness set on Kearvaig Beach, the midges had re-gathered themselves into feeding frenzy formation. We hurriedly retired to the bothy, happy in the knowledge that we had squeezed as much pleasure out of this idyllic little section of the north Scottish coastline as we possibly could.

We did not anticipate the early morning raid. The midges penetrated the bothy's defences before 5 a.m. I wasn't ready for them. My head net and the "skin-so-soft" were not immediately accessible and I paid the price. I took a bad hit.

Alison and Wild Rover managed to sleep on, but I took the opportunity to get up and enjoy Kearvaig Beach all for myself.

Having donned my suit of armour, I climbed up the steep-sided slope which framed the bay to the east until I reached a wonderful promontory where I sat atop sheer cliffs to watch the sun rising. Once again, it would have been perfect had it not been for the vast battalion of midges whose one purpose in life was to spoil every treasured moment of coastal paradise. In a rare moment when my head was not filled with thoughts of escaping tiny winged predators, I witnessed the first orange rays of sunlight on Cape Wrath itself.

By this afternoon I would be walking down the west coast. I felt elated at the thought and at the view. Unfortunately, these few moments of reflection cost me dearly. My head net was built to tackle flies in the Australian outback, not the minute midge. They had crawled through the holes and were now attacking my eyes.

Suddenly my patience with midges was at an end and I shouted a stream of obscenities at them. I started to try to run away from them. I was out of control. The midges had consumed my senses and left me with only an instinct to run back to the relative safety of the bothy. On reflection, this was probably an extremely dangerous moment. It was a precarious path between the cliff and the fence demarcating MoD land.

Unless you have experienced midges at their worst, it is difficult to describe how infuriating they are. They prey on the mind as much as the skin. If anyone ever had cause to interrogate me, it would be very simple: lock me in a room with 50,000 midges and I would, within minutes, be singing like a canary.

By the time I arrived back at Kearvaig I had calmed down and had hatched a plan to extract revenge on these most evil of insects.

Finding a particularly midge-infested corner of the beach just short of the incoming surf, I took off my clothes as quickly as I possibly could. I waded knee-deep into the sea and, ensuring that my skin was covered in a thick layer of biting creatures, I immersed myself fully in the icy cold water, uttering the words, "Die, midges!" as I did so.

The satisfaction of committing mass murder was short-lived and as I continued my morning dip I felt rather ashamed at my anger towards one of nature's more successful wee beasties. But this shame did not last long either as, when I emerged from the sea, I was immediately bombarded by the angry relatives of my victims who were eager to wreak revenge by eating me. This had not been part of my plan, and perhaps the punishment was a fair one.

I joined Alison and Wild Rover for breakfast, after which we clambered out of Kearvaig via an attractive river valley. Once back on the main track we paused to take a last lingering look at one of the most memorable spots I had ever visited.

We could have followed the road all the way to the Cape Wrath lighthouse, but instead chose a route along the cliffs, which was infinitely more rewarding. Once the radiation levels of the sun's rays became too much for our midge friends, we enjoyed a wonderful hour on an outcrop above Cape Wrath itself.

We sat in silence. Everything felt suddenly very unimportant. Almost overwhelmingly so. I could quite see how others had been moved to tears.

I turned to look towards the east, looking back at the impressive line of the north coast, which seemed to be shrouded in a blue haze. How was Coastin' doing...? Well, I was a third of the way there and I was on schedule. There was also over £140,000 in the charity pot and lots of publicity. It was all going very well indeed.

But what about me? How was I doing? I gave myself a quick inward analysis and found to my astonishment that I had never felt better.

"Hey, hang on a minute!" I found myself thinking, you have Parkinson's disease, it is currently incurable and your symptoms are going to get worse. What is more you are absolutely exhausted from overdoing the walking in the past few days. I thought back to DiploMatt, the drunken man in the pub near Middlesbrough who had uttered those immortal words, "You are f***ed."

But DiploMatt was wrong. At that precise moment I had never felt better in my life. I felt fulfilled.

It dawned on me that fulfilment has nothing to do with success, wealth or reward, nor health for that matter. Fulfilment was about making the most of my capabilities and concentrating on the things that seemed important to me. Coastin' was giving me an outdoor life, a goal, a course and a life-enriching experience. It was all I wanted. As long as I could move and communicate, I could always have that.

My spirits soared still further and I sank back on the soft tufty grass without a hint of tension in my body.

I stared down the west coast and imagined the shape of the crinkly line between sea and land extending all the way down to England, Wales and eventually to the West Country. It would take me six months to reach Land's End.

My gaze then fell back upon Cape Wrath itself. It did not look very angry today. The word actually comes from the Norse word "vrast", meaning "turning point". It was a far more appropriate definition for today. I felt as if I was turning a corner, and not just in terms of reaching the west coast. Perhaps, at Cape Wrath, I had truly found the answer to my Parkinson's. Perhaps out of its remorseless campaign to ruin my life, I had seen a way to find not just acceptance, but even fulfilment. Perhaps, instead of fighting Parkinson's, I could use its energy and redirect it to really positive effect. Perhaps the rest of my life could be lived not despite Parkinson's, but because of it.

I could have stayed in that spot all day, but we still had a lot of difficult mileage to cover and we headed down to the lighthouse so that Alison could watch Wild Rover and me perform a flamboyant "turning left" ceremony.

Thanks to some friendly lighthouse maintenance men, we were able to replenish our dwindling water supplies and I was able to recharge my camera battery. I was pleased there was not a choice between the two, as I fear I may well have chosen to risk total dehydration rather than miss capturing the images of this wonderful place for posterity.

Having learned a little bit about lighthouses, we went and admired the puffins at the point of Cape Wrath and I wished Davey Ads and Sally were there to see them. Then I thought of all the other people who had walked some of the Coastin' trail with me. I wished I had the power to transport all of them to be with me at that moment to witness this place. It would have at least gone some way to paying back all of the support and generosity that I had been experiencing.

It was a case of tearing ourselves away from Cape Wrath, but we timed it perfectly so that as we walked out of the gates of the lighthouse, the first tourist bus arrived. It was still only 10 a.m.

The seven miles to Sandwood Bay were some of the most outstandingly beautiful miles I had ever walked. But it was tough love. Bit by bit, the sun was sapping energy from our already sleep-starved bodies. The incessant climb and then descent of 200-metre hills meant that we were more conscious of the ache of lactic acid in our limbs than the rush of endorphins to our heads. The excessive heat and uneven terrain had conspired with each other so that after four hours of purposeful and determined walking, we had only reached a deserted little beach just shy of Sandwood Bay.

With the terrain being so rough, it was not possible or even practical for us to walk together. Every now and then we would shout to each other, "There's a loose rock here!" or "Mind this hole!" but we were all pretty much in our own thoughts for all of this period, spread out over the vast landscape. We had to pick our ways carefully, but we also had the good sense to stop every now and then to soak it all up.

When we regrouped at Sandwood Bay, I was totally oblivious to the fact that the other two were not quite as content as I was.

"I fell over," said Alison.

"So did I," said Wild Rover. His tone was more ominous that Alison's and he looked morose. "And these bloody midges," he went on. "We're not stopping, are we?"

"I think we should," I said.

"I need a rest," Alison agreed.

"And I need food," I added.

"Yeah, but these midges… And I'm worried if I stop now I might not make it at all. I fell on my knee and it feels like it might seize up if I stop."

I looked at Alison. There was a bit of tension here and I was keen to knock it on the head quickly. "Sorry mate, I think we must stop. But your pack is heavier than ours. Either share it out or carry on by yourself. We'll be OK."

"Are you sure you'll be OK?" he asked.

"Yes," I said, glancing quickly at Alison. She remained silent.

For once, I had the sense that today might have been a bridge too far for Wild Rover. The combination of injury, heat, midges, weight of pack and physical and mental fatigue had driven him to take a course of action that he certainly would not normally have considered. Leaving Alison and me with lunch, he departed on his own. We watched as he set off up the side of yet another cliff. His face was set in a dark, yet determined grimace. It was clear that the threat of the unthinkable was weighing heavily on him: he was unsure whether he would or could complete the day's walk.

It was strange. With the departure of Wild Rover the day had gone slightly sour. I was not angry with him but I sensed that Alison was struggling after her fall slightly more than she was letting on. There was still a long way to go, and in the circumstances, it would have been more sensible for us all to stick together. At the time of his departure, though, I could see no real downside to his leaving us other than missing his company. I have no doubt that he felt the same way. But now he was gone and the realisation of the level of our fatigue hit home, the rest of the day seemed as if it might require a labour of Herculean proportions if it were to be successfully completed.

Both in an attempt to rid myself of the new concerns and to escape the close attention of the midges, I went for another swim. This also gave me the distinction of having swum on the north and the west coasts of Britain on the same day. I doubted whether I would brave the south coast waters in the winter to complete the set.

Refreshed and exhilarated, I returned to the rock on the beach on which Alison was eating a worryingly small amount of lunch. I, meanwhile, gorged myself on the familiar family-sized bar of Galaxy, which had melted in its wrapper. It was gooey and messy, but wow it was good.

Realising that we couldn't put off the inevitable forever (although I was making a pretty good stab at it), Alison and I hauled ourselves up the sizeable cliff over to Sandwood Bay proper. By the time we had reached it, my brain had decided that enough was enough and that it would not accept any more dopamine packages from my medication messenger service.

There is something called the blood–brain barrier which does not allow much to penetrate the brain from the bloodstream. The pills I take, called "L-dopa", are mixed with something called "carbidopa" so that more of it is delivered through the barrier: a bit like a Trojan horse.

When I am tired or ill or dehydrated or anything other than feeling healthy, my blood–brain barrier does not like it and battens down the hatches. When this happens – which is more often than not – my Parkinson's manifests itself in the most unpleasant form. At its worst it could reduce me to Day Five shaking behind the wall-type symptoms. Today it was not yet quite as bad as that but my mobility became severely impaired and it took the gloss off walking along one of the finest beaches of the entire British Isles.

The heat of the day was over by the time we reached the most welcome tarmac, but the damage had already been done.

"I'm going to have to stop. I'll cadge a lift off someone," she said. A few minutes later I was waving furiously at Alison in the back of a car bound for Kinlochbervie. I was trying to convey a happiness I was not feeling.

And then there was one…

I was convinced my drugs would eventually kick in, but they never did. For the past two hours my concern had been for Alison's welfare – she is fit but she had not benefited from the 1,500 miles of walking that I had done prior to this day. With Alison gone, I only had myself to look after and as I started the lonely four-mile limp to our B&B, I suddenly realised that the day had taken its toll on me as well. I knew I could get a resurgence of energy from taking some further medication, but to my horror I found that my water had run out. I sat on a rock and contemplated my predicament. It did not take long.

To all intents and purposes I was stuck. Here were the problems:

My pride would not allow me to hitch a lift as I did not want anyone to witness or worry about the horrendous shakes that I was experiencing.

I couldn't knock on anyone's door and ask for water for the same reason.

There was no signal on my mobile phone to ring Wild Rover and ask him to come and pick me up in Alison's car.

I could barely walk anywhere due to the ineffectiveness of my last dose of drugs and an increasingly painful right foot caused by too much walking with wet feet.

Some motorcyclists stopped near me, "Are you OK?" they asked.

"Yes, I'm fine." I smiled sweetly and tried to look surprised. I cursed my stubbornness after they had gone. Why could I never admit defeat?

To be fair, I think all common sense had left me by this stage. It did not even occur to me that I had now been walking for nigh on 13 hours in a fierce sun and that it might actually be better for my health to just call it a day, explain the situation to the next people I saw and surrender myself to their care. Instead, I plodded on for about an hour and a half, covering a distance of only two miles in that time. Why O2 decided to put a signal on a hill near the remote outpost of Kinlochbervie I shall never know, but the sight of two bars on my telephone as I neared the village sent waves of joy and relief through my aching body. I sank to the ground by the side of the road and made the call.

"Hello Wild Rover, did you make it?"

"Yes, just. I'm sorry I left you. Alison is here. Where are you?" Wild Rover had a good economy with words – in that one short piece of exchange he had allayed three of my fears. I called him to action and, as ever in a crisis, he excelled. I don't think anyone could have got to me quicker in that situation.

He found me slumped on the ground where I had made the phone call. I was unable to take another step. When Alison's green VW Golf came over the hill towards me with Wild Rover at the wheel I felt relief through every vein in my body.

After showering and medicating, I felt decidedly better and the three of us reconvened to swap horror stories over supper at 9 p.m.

"I was an idiot leaving you," said Wild Rover.

"I was an idiot not taking a hat," said Alison.

"I was an idiot having fish tonight," I said, "there are too many bones."

"You're an idiot for trying to finish the walk," said Wild Rover.

"That is also true," I said smiling. We were all smiling, united in idiocy.

Day 118 had been undoubtedly the longest and the toughest day so far. It had also been the first day that I had been unable to complete in its entirety. Just before I closed my eyes that night, I thought about the day that I had just experienced. Anger at not having completed it? Physical and mental exhaustion at the difficulty of it? Trepidation at the thought of future similar experiences? None of these entered my mind. Instead, my thoughts were filled with how wonderful the entire Cape Wrath experience had been. Day 118 represented some of the best walking I had ever done and I doubted whether it would be matched by anything else I would see on my Coastin' journey.

The knowledge that I still had all of the west coast of Scotland still to come made it all the more fantastic.

I fell asleep with a smile on my face.

Atlantic
Ocean

Kinlochbervie

Lochinver
10th August

Ullapool

Gairloch

Applecross
21st August

## CHAPTER 18

I did not wake up with a smile on my face. I was experiencing hot and cold flushes. I was ill.

I struggled down to breakfast and found Alison with her sunglasses on. This would not normally be worthy of note, but it was unlike her to wear them in darkened corners of rooms.

Alison was not smiling either. The contrast of her blonde hair against the blackness of her sunglasses and mood gave a slightly dangerous edge to her presence this morning. I spoke before I had thought what I was going to say: "You look like a trained assassin."

I immediately wished I had not said this. Breakfast was a tense affair. Alison had contracted an eye infection overnight.

We had all wilted in yesterday's heat, and although now rehydrated, recovery was slow. Wild Rover was faring the best of us, but all our moods were heavy and gravity seemed to be exerting a considerably greater influence on our facial features than was normal.

I sloped off to my room for a bit of sleep while Alison and Wild Rover paid a visit to the optician.

The telephone rang.

"Will you be checking out soon?" I was shaking so much I was hitting my ear with the phone.

"Er, actually, I was wondering whether I could have a bit longer if possible." There was no way I could pack up and get out of the room on my own. I had no control over my hands.

The phone rang again.

"I am afraid you will have to check out now. Mrs Veitch says she has guests arriving any minute and the room must be cleaned."

This was a predicament I could have done without this morning. I wondered if I could appeal to Mrs Veitch's better side. I rang her and told her the situation.

"I have Parkinson's," I said. "Can I just have a little longer as I am not physically capable of packing my clothes at the moment?"

There was a pause at the other end before Mrs Veitch responded with cold, Germanic intransigence.

"Vee need zee room now. You vill vacate by 1100 hours or I vill be forced to charge you zee extra day." At this point she hung up the phone.

I was absolutely gobsmacked. There was an evil force at work here. I was dealing with the "Vicked Veitch of Kinlochbervie".

I considered my options. Should I stay where I was, defiant, and have a stand-off with the woman when it came to pay? Or should I attempt to shove everything into the corridor and hope that she would pass by and see the state I was in?

I chose the corridor. After all, I was spreading awareness of Parkinson's, and when you're dealing with a Vicked Veitch, the only satisfactory means of achieving this is to ensnare her in guilt. I didn't want to do it, in fact I hated the fact that I would have to use my Parkinson's to prove a point. But I was in a bad mood and I felt the circumstances warranted it.

I still felt ill, and even putting everything in the corridor seemed to require immense effort. When a member of staff came to clean the room and saw me, she was horrified and rushed to my assistance.

"I don't think Mrs Veitch realised how difficult this would be for you," she said.

"Well, I did tell her."

"I'm so sorry."

"It's not your fault."

When I reflected on it later a little more objectively, I realised the problem stemmed from a lack of understanding about Parkinson's. Mrs Veitch had seen me at breakfast and had probably been oblivious to the fact that there was anything wrong with me. How could she have possibly understood or believed that 15 minutes later, full neurological system meltdown would have occurred, resulting in my metamorphosis into a human blancmange?

To this day the Vicked Veitch is oblivious to her wrongdoing. I suspect the room cleaner was too frightened to tell her of my plight and I was too ill and too immobile to go and find her for myself. I ended up sitting in the corridor for an hour, waiting for the new guests who did not arrive. The Vicked Veitch of Kinlochbervie probably remains ignorant of the nature of Parkinson's.

The rest of the day was spent in another bed in another B&B. I was only well enough to get up for supper, which was eaten in a restaurant overlooking Loch Inchard. And everything would have been perfect had it not been served by a deathly pale waitress with bloodshot eyes.

"Do you think she's ill because she's been eating the food here?" I asked. But no one heard me above the wave of deeply productive coughing from inside the kitchen.

Alison laughed, "She's got the bubonic plague."

"She reminds me of that bird in The Exorcist," said Wild Rover, delicate as ever. The food when it came seemed fine, but much of the rest of the evening was spent trying to establish whether the waitress's tongue really was green.

The walking from Kinlochbervie down to Lochinver over the next three days was principally along roads. That is not to say it was disappointing. Like a good book, the scenery was captivating and ever-changing. We were all blissfully happy marching from one spectacular view to the next.

Having passed through Foindle and Foinhaven, we reached Tarbet, which marked my 1,500th mile. One-third of the way there. As if in celebration, we climbed onto a plateau overlooking Handa Island. The gathering gloom did not detract from the dramatic coastal scenery. The path that threaded its way through a myriad of small lakes to Scourie was unforgettable.

Scourie Lodge was an old hunting lodge owned by the Duke of Sutherland. It is now owned by Penny and Gerry and as a guest house I cannot praise it too highly. If you're after cuisine, hospitality, affordability and a magnificent garden in which grow the most northerly palm trees in the world; Scourie Lodge is the only place that will fit the bill.

Similarly, if you want to be chastised mercilessly because your walking boots emit certain pungent aromas, Penny's mother will not fail you. She had a point. I would need my third pair of boots soon. Pair two was fast becoming a public nuisance.

There was no other option but to walk on the main road from Scourie to the bridge at Kylestrome. Here we were able to look down admiringly at the beauty of Loch Acairn Bhain and its two dramatic spurs, which plunge deep into the mountains of the Glendhu Forest. It is at the end of one of these spurs, Loch Glencoul, that the highest waterfall in Britain can be found. We crossed the bridge to Kylesku and just beyond Unapool turned right on to the B869. It is an insult to name this particular road by its number – it's rather like calling a Ferrari simply "a car". The B869 has to be one of Britain's most scenic roads to drive, cycle or walk on.

For a while we walked in the shadow of Quinag, a dark, almost menacing lump of rock which rises sheer out of the ground; its height and character seemingly unconnected with anything else surrounding it.

Later on, we veered off the road onto the springy turf and heather-strewn clifftops towards the Point of Stoer. At the point itself, we sat facing north and looked back at the section of west coast that we had all completed. To our right, banks of lilac heather formed the foreground to a sea that lapped half-heartedly against impenetrable cliffs. In the distance, as the glare of the day softened to the orange of evening, the isolated rock faces of Quinag, Suilven, Canisp, Cul Mor and the Coigach range reflected the warmth of the sinking sun. Their form and colouring would not have looked out of place in the Australian outback. All these mountains are ancient; they originally formed part of the Appalachian ranges, now far away in the USA.

The scene made for an almost impossibly magnificent view. Photographs were taken, but nothing and no one could have captured the place or the moment.

Reluctantly we left the Point of Stoer. Alison and I were in buoyant mood and started to sing. She taught me the words to the "Wild Rover":

> I've been a wild rover for many's the year,
> And I've spent all me money on whiskey and beer
> But now I'm returning with gold in great store
> And I never will play the Wild Rover no more!
>
> Chorus:
> And it's no, nay, never
> No, nay, never no more
> Will I play the Wild Rover,
> No never no more.
>
> I went to an alehouse I used to frequent,

I told the landlady my money was spent.
I asked her for credit, she answered me nay,
"Such a custom as yours I can have any day."

I brought from me pocket ten sovereigns bright,
And the landlady's eyes opened wide with delight.
She said: "I have whiskeys and wines of the best,
And the words that you told me were only in jest."

Chorus

I'll go home to my parents, confess what I've done
And I'll ask them to pardon their prodigal son,
And when they've caressed me, as oft times before
I never will play the Wild Rover no more

Chorus

Having learnt the words, I delivered a flawless rendition to our very own Wild Rover. He seemed unimpressed. I wondered whether I would return "with gold in great store".

The thought prompted me to phone Q. "We're up to £156,000," she said, "it's fantastic! Well done!"

"Well done you," I replied. "You're raising the money, I'm just walking." But Q wasn't having any of this and put the phone down on me, saying, "Don't be ridiculous."

Alison left us at Lochinver, while Wild Rover and I settled in to a B&B just outside the town. Here the landlady was extremely kind to us, and this was before we found out that her husband had Parkinson's and before she found out what I was doing. This having been established, we really did get the red carpet treatment.

Vicked Veitch excepted, the hospitality in the northern reaches of Scotland is exceptional. A case in point occurred the following day as we travelled along an incredibly remote footpath near Ardroe. Here there was just a smattering of crofts, most of them redundant or used as holiday retreats for closet hermits from the City. But outside one such building was an elderly lady tending her small garden plot.

"Hello," we said happily, but aware that as two thirty-something males, she might feel threatened or worried by our presence.

But we need not have been concerned, as within minutes she had invited us in for tea and "no" simply didn't seem to be an option. Perhaps she too had been taken in by the seemingly endless charms of Wild Rover's facial features. I was fairly certain that in her time she too had been a bit of a "looker".

Her name was Elma and her house was filled with bits and pieces accumulated over the seven or eight decades of her life. On first impressions it appeared as though there were very few modern amenities in her home. Her husband had died of cancer some years earlier, but she looked in good fettle and was obviously able to eke out an existence here.

And yet gradually I began to realise that Elma was not simply eking; she was thriving in this isolated quarter of the country. When we came to sign the Visitors Book, we found it bursting with the names of travellers from all over the world, all of whom had stopped to have tea with Elma.

The collecting tin for cancer research was conspicuously positioned on a table in the room. We duly donated and this was reciprocated.

"Is there any way I can keep in contact with your walk?" she added.

"I can get updates sent to you," I replied tentatively, unsure whether the postman would, or indeed could, reach such a place.

"Is there not a website? I find everything so much more efficient on the Internet."

I stole a glance at Wild Rover. He was smiling. Elma was smiling too.

All this time I had been sitting next to a huge old wireless and as we got up to leave, I scanned the room to see if she had a television. There did not seem to be anything to prove she had electricity, let alone a TV. But then my eyes came to rest on the telephone. It had fax capabilities. I began wondering whether Elma worked for MI6.

A year after the walk, I went back to visit, and there she was in her garden.

"Hello Tom," she said enthusiastically. It was as if I was an old friend. "How's Wild Rover?" she asked as she put the kettle on to boil.

From Lochinver, it was a 24-mile hike to Achiltibuie following the coast road. The place is famed for its smokeries and its views across Badentarbert Bay to the picturesque Summer Isles. Having sampled the smoked fish, we retired to the B&B and stared out of a huge panoramic window as the sun went down. We doubted whether any B&B in the country had a better view.

Unsurprisingly, the B&B was full to bursting, so we slept in a large caravan in the driveway. It was here Wild Rover learnt a very valuable lesson: never sleep in the same caravan as someone with Parkinson's. My night shakes apparently sent Wild Rover into dreams about sleeping in one of those high-oscillation industrial sieves.

We struck out for Ullapool, where we would have another day off. We were looking forward to Ullapool. It sounded nice.

From the end of the road at Culnacraig, there is a makeshift path which hangs on for dear life to the sides of Ben Mor Coigach. The mountain plunges fast into the sea here. It is steep and dangerous for someone who has lost some sense of balance. The only alternative was to walk back to Achiltibuie and round to the other side of the Coigach range. That would mean the loss of our day off. We struggled on, but it was slow going. This was the most testing walking I had done.

It became so hairy that for a while turning back seemed the only option. But on closer inspection of the map, we realised that we had made it past the most severe buttresses of the mountain, and we followed a small stream upwards so that we were now climbing rather than traversing. This was easier, and when we sat atop Beannan Beage at 1,300 ft (396 metres) and feasted on lunch and a 360-degree view, we realised what a good decision and what a satisfying day it had been.

I was determined not to become too blasé about the scenery in this area. This had happened to me before when I had travelled for long periods through other regions of outstanding beauty. But in Scotland, blasé does not even enter your head. The scenery changes so rapidly down the west coast that it feels like a new country each day. Wild Rover and I were quite literally coastin' at the moment. We were in control; we were fit and we were happy. A more satisfying existence I couldn't imagine. Every day we were setting ourselves a target; a task to measure up to. Come the evenings we had the satisfaction of knowing that we had achieved the day's goal. I wondered whether I would feel this good for the rest of the trip. I desperately hoped so. But something told me that I would not.

Ullapool was ugly. We were disappointed. It has a lovely name. It has such a spectacular position nestled on the shores of Loch Broom. And yet it is undeniably a horrid place.

We had been in the wilderness for a while now and we were unshaven and dishevelled. We felt slightly savage as we approached civilisation. But Ullapool was heaving with tourists, tacky souvenirs and impersonal guest houses. Civilisation?

For the past two weeks I had not had to think very much about the charitable side of Coastin'. We were deep into holiday season and until Ullapool, there was nowhere "local" to get publicity. It felt as if I was on holiday too. But whilst in Ullapool, I needed to focus back on the reason for it all. I needed to make phone calls and arrangements for the route ahead. While I was doing this, Wild Rover went to see what interest could be found in the town.

I was beginning to get concerned that I was having too nice a time and that I should be doing more to promote Coastin'. It was all too easy to forget the cause in this glorious corner of the country. Even my health was allowing me to forget it every now and then. To all intents and purposes there was nothing to do up here other than to grind out the miles; to get the job done. But somehow that didn't seem enough, I always felt as if I should be trying to do more. I felt guilty about having too enjoyable a time.

And if I felt like this, what about Wild Rover? He had not come just for the walk. He had come to help, but other than to ensure I got from A to B, there was not much else he could do. I think this made him feel superfluous at times and perhaps sometimes he wondered why he was there at all. He was, after all, paying for everything himself, and yet he was completely beholden to my goals, my rules and my life. This took its toll more often than not during days off. While I always had tons to do – emails to answer or speeches to write – Wild Rover was left mooching, hoping for a spark of interest to ignite his enthusiasm. I doubted he would find much in Ullapool.

But he came back looking more animated than I had seen him for some time. "What did you find?" I asked, intrigued.

"It's the supermarket…" he panted. "Quick, come and see!"

"What is it? What about the supermarket?"

"No time. Must go now," he gasped. "Galaxy. Family-sized. On special."

I overtook him at the entrance to the car park.

The 22 bars of chocolate that we bought soon became 19. Feeling rather sick, I asked Wild Rover what else he had found in Ullapool.

"Oh," he said, "I went to the Ullapool exhibition on Nepalese culture." I began wondering how interesting this visit had been and eventually curiosity got the better of me.

"Was it interesting?" I asked.

"No," said Wild Rover, "it was bloody useless!"

Wild Rover was similarly scathing about his lasagne that night. After one mouthful he pushed the plate away in disgust. When the waitress came round to collect the plates she asked a bit of a daft question:

"Was everything all right, sir?"

"No," he said as pleasantly as he could muster, "actually it was inedible."

But the waitress was defiant. "Why was it inedible?" she counter-attacked.

Wild Rover slowly raised his gaze at the impertinence of the question. He suddenly looked every inch the chef he was (and still is). Looking her straight in the eyes he said, "It was dry, cold and the pasta has turned to a paste." The waitress had met her match. She retreated and then returned.

"You will not be charged for the meal."

Just as we were about to leave, another waitress, a French girl, approached us in a manner which could only mean one thing. We had been vaguely aware of her hips swaying back and forth and the waft of cheap perfume somewhere to our right all evening. But now she stood leaning forward with her hands on our table.

"Somesing sweet?" she enquired in a manner that bordered on the obscene.

Wild Rover and I stared at each other in disbelief and fumbled for words in the air: "Er…n-n-no thank you." She turned on her heels almost angrily; she clearly realised that we doubted her ability to offer anything sweet. We left the restaurant (if that is what it was) and yet another disappointed member of the Wild Rover fan club.

The Alltnaharrie Hotel used to be a Michelin-rated restaurant, and most of its customers were delivered by ferry across the Broom. The hotel was closed and deserted, but fortunately for us, the ferry was still operating. Once across, we laboured up a steep hill and over to Dundonnell at the foot of Little Loch Broom. We had equipment and provisions for two to three days. We were on an expedition to Poolewe.

To be true to the coast, we should have followed the A832 around the shores of Little Loch Broom to Gruinard Bay and then Loch Ewe. But we were playing hooky. We wanted a bit of drama. We headed for the Fisherfield Forest.

When the torrential downpour came, we felt rather clever. Not only were we going to Poolewe via a far more exciting route, but when we reached the first of the many forests on the map, we would have the uncommon luxury of having the shelter of trees.

But for what seemed like ages, we could see no trees at all. I inspected the map. Various forests were clearly marked: Dundonnell, Strathnasheallag, Letterewe and Fisherfield. But there was no dark green colouring to signify even a small sapling. In fact that area was worryingly brown in colour on the map due to the contour lines being so closely packed together. I raised my eyes to look at the three-dimensional map. Not a tree to be seen for miles; only large rocks, many of which were mountains.

"What the hell is going on here?!" This was clearly some kind of bizarre Scottish joke. I have since even looked the word up in the dictionary: forest – a large area covered in trees. I suppose they got half of it right.

Despite the unfulfilled promise of a majestic pine forest in which to walk; despite the rain, which battered both Gore-Tex and our senses; there was something immensely satisfying about driving onwards through the elements that morning. I was warm, I was not in any danger and the experience appealed to my competitive nature and sense of bravado.

The rain had stopped by the afternoon and we were treated to some breathtaking scenery. This was the biggest range of mountains we had yet encountered. They were, as mountains should be, steep-sided, craggy and massive.

Eventually, the path swept down from a high plateau, giving us our first view of Fionn Loch and the little bothy at Carnmore where we would spend the night. As we neared the bothy it became obvious that it was more akin to a hut. Closer still, it was more of a rickety old barn and by the time we were inside it was little more than a shack. It was dramatically awful.

There was no one in the shack except Malcolm and Barry. These were the names we gave to the sheep skulls that hung proudly on the wall at one end. Malcolm was more substantial than Barry; he had one and a half horns. Barry meanwhile only had half a face. We couldn't decide whether they were there to ward off evil spirits or to attract them. We were glad when it got dark quite quickly so that we could no longer see them staring at us.

At about 3 a.m., I was awoken by Wild Rover telling me to "go away".

"I'm nowhere near you!" I argued.

"I'm not talking to you," he said. "I'm talking to a rat. It is trying to get into my mouth." He had woken to find a large rodent right in front of his nose.

The shack seemed suddenly to be filled with the sound of scurrying. We had had the sense to hang our provisions from the rafters. I fell back to sleep with my mouth shut. Tightly shut.

There was an almost uncanny stillness and silence about the following morning. A sense of total solitude. We left the rat-shack and walked a lot of the day spaced about 200 metres apart. It was that sort of place; where conversation is superfluous.

Fionn Loch had barely a ripple. Its shallows feigned depth by reflecting the height of the surrounding peaks. The cloud cover seemed to give an almost sepia effect to the landscape, and the distant mountains and their summits were interconnected on the horizon like a child's drawing.

As we progressed seawards, the landscape became flatter where the glacier had spilled out of the tightly packed valley. When I saw a large area of woodland, I knew we were out of the forest.

The imminence of the arrival of Mr Beef to these northern reaches of the country was concerning me on three counts:

He was not in the peak of physical fitness.

Wild Rover and he did not see eye to eye on anything whatsoever.

Given 1 and 2, how on earth could I make his visit and his support of my walk an enjoyable experience for all of us?

The first encounter between Mr Beef and Wild Rover had ended in a most unfortunate misunderstanding. Since then all contact between the two had been avoided.

In an attempt to bury the hatchet, Mr Beef had elected to come and walk with me at a time when he knew Wild Rover would also be there. But who would bury the hatchet in whom?

In a straightforward duel by hatchet, the odds were probably stacked in Wild Rover's favour. Although Mr Beef could probably bury his hatchet deeper blow for blow, I suspected Wild Rover might be a little too nimble for him and that his stamina and speed might win the day.

And it was only fair that Mr Beef should lose the contest. It was, after all, he who had tried to catch Wild Rover's attention at a drinks party, but had forgotten his name. This, in itself, was forgivable as they had only had one conversation, in which the subject matter had been place of birth. Wild Rover had been born in Poole, which was of particular interest to Mr Beef as he too had been reared there. Unfortunately, he did not make this fact absolutely clear.

A couple of hours later, after Mr Beef had consumed enough beer to fill Poole harbour, he became afflicted with a common ailment: Alcohol Excess

Induced Overconfident Euphoria – or "AEIOU Syndrome".

The result of all this was that instead of politely establishing Wild Rover's name from somebody else, he shouted across the room, "Oi... Poole-boy!"

Wild Rover had taken offence. Justifiably so. It was written all over his face in the embarrassing silence that followed.

Mr Beef later apologised, but in doing so, slapped Wild Rover a little too hard on the back. Had there been a handy hatchet, it might have been buried there and then; but now it was down to me to keep these two fools from murdering one another. I didn't stand a chance. Fate would take its course.

It should be said that Wild Rover seemed far less concerned about Mr Beef's arrival than I was. In fact, he laughed at my exasperation when I received a phone call from my ex-flatmate telling me that he was currently stuck in Inverness.

It was always pointless being irritated by Mr Beef's tendency to be organisationally challenged. "I'm so hopeless," he said on the phone.

There is a queue of people who find Mr Beef's unaccountable inertia in doing things for himself frustrating. Mr Beef himself is at the front of this queue. And yet when it comes to doing things for other people, he would gladly go well out of his way and subject himself to considerable pain on their behalf. His "walking holiday" would become testimony to this fact.

At 10.30 p.m., Mr Beef reached Achnasheen, 30 miles from our meeting point at Gairloch. We sent a taxi to pick him up. It was long after midnight when he finally arrived.

"Sorry, Izee," he said.

The walk from Poolewe out to the youth hostel at Rubha Reidh was quite boggy in places and my late night had contributed to a predictably unpleasant Parkies morning. Uncle Dave, my newfound relative from Wick, had come to join us and had brought with him a bona fide nephew who was up visiting him from Manchester on a fishing trip. We met up with them near the end of the peninsula where the contrasting colours of the green carpet of grass on the cliffs, the pristine gold beaches, the turquoise sea and the scarlet red of Mr Beef's face made for a memorable scene.

That night, the five of us gathered in a bar. As the conversation flowed easily, I thought about the assembled group of people. It was extraordinary that a retired biology teacher from Wick, a professional cellist from Manchester, a student osteopath born in Poole and Mr Beef should all be together drinking in a bar in Gairloch. Coastin' had brought this diverse posse together in this remote location. I felt rather proud of that.

It was just the three of us the following day. Wild Rover and I were in good fettle and the 20 miles per day that we were currently averaging was not going to assist Mr Beef in a smooth transition from desk job to walking god. He had managed to avoid 9 of yesterday's 24 miles by hitching a ride with Uncle Dave. But today's 16 miles to Craig Youth Hostel would have to be walked in full.

It was more spectacular walking, but the final stretch was technically difficult for tired limbs and the midges were beginning to be a nuisance again. By the time we neared Craig, Mr Beef was quite angry: angry at insects; angry at the state of the path; angry at his level of fitness and angry because we were not quite there yet. When we did eventually arrive, there seemed to be lots of people around.

We found the warden. "Sorry, we're full. There's a party of twenty-four Dutch walkers with us today."

Mr Beef's response to this was surprising. He sank to his knees and reached up with hands clasped above his head. "Please let us stay," he pleaded, as if she had the power to grant him the miracle of accommodation.

"Well, I was going to say," continued the warden, "you can have my room if you want. It's up in the loft."

"You are an angel," said Mr Beef, and for the first time that day, he smiled.

If the previous day had been a tough walk, then the 22 miles from Craig right round Loch Torridon to Shieldaig would be ten times harder. It was a day that became a slow torture for Mr Beef. It was as much a lack of comprehension as the physical exhaustion which disturbed him so much. He simply couldn't empathise with reasons for not taking the most direct route, and swore there was nothing to be gained by the unbelievably spectacular detour around the large rocky promontory which marks the end of Loch Torridon and the beginning of Upper Loch Torridon. From his perspective, it only served up a cocktail of outrageously steep climbs, exposure to blistering heat and a view that gave an insight into the totally ridiculous distance still to be covered that day.

After 2 ½ days of walking together, I was relieved to see that Mr Beef and Wild Rover seemed to be getting on well. They were, at least, now communicating. I think Wild Rover was particularly impressed by the effort Mr Beef was putting into his walking. There was no denying it, Beef was throwing himself 120% into Coastin'.

He looked absolutely knackered.

The walking was continuously stunning. There seemed to be more greenery and more trees around Loch Torridon, and yet above, the mountains loomed high and impenetrable as ever.

We stopped at a shop in Torridon itself, where Mr Beef downed two litres of Diet Coke at the rate of one litre per minute. The name of the village seemed quite apt to Mr Beef. Soon afterwards I saw him eyeing a small child's chopper bicycle which lay on the ground outside the shop.

"No, Mr Beef," I said firmly.

"I wasn't going to take it." He sulked. When I looked at the frame of Mr Beef and compared it to the feeble frame of the chopper bicycle, I rather wished he had taken it so that I could capture the moment on my camera.

Meanwhile Mr Beef toiled on.

About a mile outside Torridon, we passed Torridon Mountain Rescue Centre. "Excellent!" exclaimed Mr Beef.

"It's not a shop. I don't think you can just walk in."

Quite justifiably, Mr Beef was no longer paying any attention to me and was already striding purposefully towards the building in an attempt to be rescued. I wondered whether they had ever had a customer who had walked in off the street before.

He came out with a big smile on his face.

"They said they can't rescue me because I am not on a mountain, but there's a bus to Shieldaig in five minutes."

What he had neglected to tell us was that this bus was the school bus. Five minutes later, we watched a large, sweaty, exhausted man with his rucksack slump defeated on the seat of a bus. Beside him, two small boys with caps on their heads were staring at him with complete astonishment. But Mr Beef didn't care. He was no longer walking.

By the time Wild Rover and I arrived in Shieldaig, Mr Beef had rehydrated sufficiently and was starting the process of dehydration again as he threw all his concentration and energies into the consumption of his first beer of the evening.

The B&B in which we were booked was a bit off the beaten track and so we decided to eat in.

"Mutton and kidney stew tonight," our landlady announced proudly, as if this news would have us salivating with hunger. There was a stony silence after she left the room.

"It will probably be fine," I said. My experiences of food in B&Bs around the coast so far had been good, almost without exception. I fully expected to be pleasantly surprised by the meal that sounded so awful.

Suffice it to say, I was not prepared for the steaming casserole dish that was set before us and sent our senses into collective seizure. The question of "how she made it" was not one which would tax any of us too hard. There is only one method of boiling assorted fragments of gristle in water and only one result. It was now sitting on the table in front of us, inciting a bitter struggle between our hunger and our taste buds.

Of course, we were all far too polite to say anything, and I even found the words, "Looks great!" erupting out of some deep chasm of my subconscious.

After our landlady left the room, we stared at the abomination in front of us. Eventually our famished bodies took control and had us all ladling out the slop onto our plates. Neither Mr Beef nor Wild Rover had ever come across such an awful meal. In a series of increasingly exasperated exchanges they worked each other up to a point at which they were both frothing at the mouth like a couple of oversized cappuccinos. And the ranting went on and on. It continued long after the casserole dish had gone, into the night, and then again the next day as they wallowed in culinary disbelief.

"I could make a better meal out of my mother's donkey," said Wild Rover, "…and he died three years ago."

"That meal was just unashamedly awful," agreed Mr Beef. "A total debacle."

At some stage during all this I realised that although the stew, in all its hideous glory, had failed miserably as a meal, it had actually succeeded at something else which was, to me, far more important. I had forgotten that both Mr Beef and Wild Rover were gastronomes. Both were qualified cordon bleu food snobs, and in their incredulity at the state of their dinner, they had found a common subject. They were united in their revulsion. Friendship had germinated out of a mutton and kidney stew.

\* \* \*

Applecross is a very special place indeed. The walk from Shieldaig took us on a path from which at its highest point it was just a short hop to the summit of Croic bheinn. Wild Rover and I went up to check out the view, to find that the only problem was of knowing which section of the 360-degree panorama to concentrate on. We could see the previous day's entire walk to the foot of Upper Loch Torridon where Mr Beef had caught the school bus. Beyond, magnificent mountains faded hazy blue into a far-off horizon. In the other direction, across a sunlit and shimmering sea, lay the Isle of Skye with its own impressive range of peaks: the Cuillins.

We returned to the path to find that a bull had wandered to within charging range of Mr Beef. Our concern was short-lived; Mr Beef was too exhausted to charge and the bull was safe enough. Both were just happy to graze and ignore each other as bovines tend to do.

Accommodation in Applecross was scarce, relative to the number of visitors. We did have a tent with us, but there was not enough room for all three of us. We decided to mull it over with a drink at the Applecross Inn. We were served drinks by the owner, Caroline, who was interested in our story.

"You can stay as my guests free of charge tonight," she offered.

Having thanked her profusely, we went out to enjoy the sunshine and the view before the Applecross Midge Squadron launched its dusk offensive.

A man with a huge glass was going round collecting money for something.

"You should do that." But Wild Rover's suggestion was not a serious one; we would all have felt awkward collecting money from people during their leisure time.

The man came nearer with the glass. He had collected a lot of money already. He approached us and handed me my own Coastin' card.

"Good afternoon," he said. "We are holding a raffle for a gentleman who is staying with us at the Inn tonight, who is walking 4,500 miles right round the coast of Britain in aid of Parkinson's…"

"Sounds like a complete loser to me," said Mr Beef.

"It's me. I mean, I am the bloke who's walking," I said. "This is amazing."

Later that night, I presented a bottle of whisky and a Coastin' T-shirt to the winner. The Applecross Inn had collected £126.

Applecross was too good to leave after only one night. We checked into a B&B which had some space further down the track in Camusteel. We elected to have a day to do whatever we wanted to do. It was perhaps not surprising then that Wild Rover went roving wild. Mr Beef went to the Applecross Inn with a newspaper and I, well I went for a long walk.

There was an unusual tranquillity to Applecross. Trancelike, I wandered south towards Toscaig, reflecting on everything and nothing. I was in one of those few areas in the world that seemed replete in its natural beauty.

Nothing seemed out of place. Staring out across the becalmed Inner Sound, I realised that my mood matched the scene before me. That probably happens a lot in Applecross.

Going for a 13-mile walk on my day off didn't seem like an odd thing to do at all. The rhythm of walking had become almost a relaxation for me and the desire to explore new places burned stronger in me now, more than ever before. I ate my lunch at the southern tip of the Applecross peninsula looking into the jaws of Loch Carron and over towards Plockton, which we would reach in three days.

Upon my return to the B&B in Camusteel, I was met at the door by the owner, who was beside herself with worry. "Thank goodness you're back," she said. "You'd been so long gone, I thought something terrible had happened."

I was both touched and slightly irritated by this. When I left, I had said I was going for a walk. I suppose "a walk" means different things to different people. But I suspected her concern was fuelled by another phenomenon of which I had had some experience on several other occasions on the walk. Local people who knew what I was doing felt a strange sense of responsibility for my welfare whilst I was on their patch. However remote their connection to me, everyone wanted to ensure I made it through their region without mishap. This spirit of generosity had stood me in good stead so far, but sometimes, particularly when there was a handover from one community to the next, I felt a bit like an Olympic torch.

Mr Beef was next back to the B&B. He looked jubilant – and bigger. "The food at the Applecross Inn is just fabulous," he said.

"*Is* just fabulous? Do you mean to say there is some left? How much did you eat?"

"I had two three-course meals and four pints of Guinness." He looked proud of his achievement.

I thought he was joking. He was not.

No sooner had Mr Beef disappeared for a late-afternoon nap, than the Wild Rover walked in. I could tell he was not happy and had something to say to me.

"I'm sorry," he began. "I'm going to leave Coastin'. I'm going to go back with Mr Beef."

"OK," I said. "Why?"

"Lots of reasons really. I am not enjoying it any more. You've got people to help you now. You don't need me, it's expensive and you're always on the phone and, well, it just really winds me up."

Wild Rover's honesty did not upset me. He had talked to me about the telephone annoyance before; there was nothing I could really do about that, or the expense – that was just how it was. What I had not realised was that the only reason he had really come at all was to support me through the wild coastal areas of Scotland. Perhaps stupidly I had thought that he was also here for his own enjoyment.

"But if you quit now, you won't do what you set out to achieve," I responded.

"What's that?"

"To reach Fort William. To walk 750 miles. If you finish now, you will always feel you didn't finish."

The concept that he might be here to achieve something for himself seemed to make an impact on Wild Rover. This was clearly a selfish perspective, which had not even dawned on him.

I tried to talk him round. "How about if I only make phone calls when you are out of earshot?" I suggested.

I desperately wanted him to walk to Fort William with me; not for myself, even though I would certainly miss him, but because I wanted him to do something for himself; in particular to see Knoydart – a glorious stretch of wilderness still to come. but Wild Rover's mind was made up.

"I'm sorry" he said.

We looked at each other for a moment before the awkward silence was punctured by the inelegant arrival of Mr Beef. He looked even larger than normal having come fresh from his spree at the pub. He seemed to be having a problem focussing and squinted at me as I told him the news.

Despite his apparent state of excess-induced lethargy, Mr Beef's response was remarkably decisive and was delivered with the gravitas of a High Court judge: "Don't be so bloody stupid. You must finish it."

He sauntered out of the room, but his words remained.

My first thought when Mr Beef called Wild Rover "stupid" was to hide any sharp implements in the vicinity. But three days of walking together had made a vast difference. Wild Rover had taken Mr Beef's words squarely on the chin.

I was not surprised when Wild Rover changed his mind at the pub later that night. Once he had realised that he was actually achieving something significant himself, he had to finish his walk almost as much

Wild Rover in contemplation
at Kearvaig

Happy at Cape Wrath

View of the North Coast
from Cape Wrath

Looking back towards Torridon from near Shieldaig

The midges liked Mr Beef.
The feeling was not mutual

Mr Beef has enough of both me
and the walk

Knoydart

Loch Leven

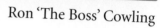

Ron 'The Boss' Cowling

On the way down
from Scarfell Pike

Eric the Pheasant

Emlyn Jones

Buttermere, the Lake District

Lancastrians

Mule in Wales

The Mersey at Birkenhead

Towards Liverpool Docks from Wallasey

Overlooking
Llandudno Bay
and Great Orme

Jocky Noah on the
LLeyn Penninsula

The Talking Sheep

On Snowdon

Ramblings with Clare Balding

The Headless Brothers of Llanrhystud

With heads on

Near Cardigan and the start of the Pembrokeshire Coast path

Precision and Danger
Signs in Wales

Mum in
England,
Wales and
Scotland

as I had to finish mine.

"You won't regret it," I said.

Mr Beef didn't say anything. He just slapped Wild Rover on the back, a little too hard…

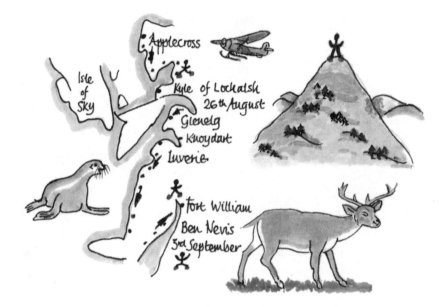

CHAPTER 19

I tried hard not to look for, or expect, any kind of generosity. I certainly was not outwardly asking for donations and did not carry a collecting tin around with me. I felt there was something cheap and demeaning about brazenly advertising for contributions to the cause. Besides, I was concerned that if I wandered around shaking a collecting tin, I might be reported to the Charities Commission. Rattling a charity box is strictly prohibited in this country. It has been deemed unnecessarily aggressive soliciting for money. Since first finding out about this, I have always wanted to be arrested for over-vigorous charity collecting, just for the joy of being able to say in court: "But Your Honour, I can't help but shake my tin!"

But that was for another occasion. On Coastin', funds were being pledged on sponsorship forms, or donated on the website or by post. In fact, by any means other than a collecting tin.

And yet, despite this, I was frequently given a £10 note at breakfast or a free night's accommodation. I was amazed when a B&B did not charge me for my room. This, after all, was their livelihood. And invariably it was the smaller, more modest establishments that were the most generous. I found this embarrassing – but then again, any reduction in expenditure ultimately meant more money raised.

Without fail, it was in the towns and cities that there was less enthusiasm and interest displayed in Coastin'. Travelling through the Highlands of Scotland, where the logistical problems of moving luggage and finding accommodation should have been at their most difficult, actually they couldn't have been much easier. Since we had first reached the region, only a few inhabitants of Thurso, Ullapool and, of course, Kinlochbervie had not rallied to help us. Through a combination of amazingly hospitable B&B owners, friendly postmen and various others, the luggage made 23 journeys between Inverness and Fort William, the cost of which came to precisely £0.00.

Two days after leaving Applecross, we found ourselves on a relatively busy A road on the south shore of Loch Carron, bound for Stromeferry. After all the fantastic walking of late, traipsing in single file along hard tarmac with cars whooshing past reminded me that not all of this walk was fun.

Now someone was beeping their horn at us. The window was wound down, and someone was shouting and waving at us.

"I've got your luggage!" he said.

"Thanks!" we called back as the car disappeared over a hill.

We had never met the man in the car. All we knew was that he was the brother-in-law of the owner of the Applecross Inn and that he was making the 25-mile round trip from Lochcarron especially to deliver our extra luggage.

And yet, this was not particularly abnormal. There was a sense of community in the Highlands – everyone helped everyone else. Although we were outsiders, we were currently riding high on a Mexican wave of support down the west Scottish coastline. Help was not asked for – it was just given, instinctively and unconditionally.

Ten minutes further down the road and we were being beeped again; this time the car pulled over. It was the warden from the youth hostel at Craig on her way home to Essex. Several more occupants of cars sounded their horns or waved furiously at us that day. It felt good. Despite the first stretch of unfulfilling Coastin' for over a month, we seem to be being spurred on by people who knew what we were doing.

The owners of the B&B in Achmore near Stromeferry continued the run of incredible hospitality. Gerald and Margaret Arscott typed a little note about Coastin' and circulated it to all their guests asking them if they would be prepared to contribute. They all did so most generously, but what pleased me more was the fact that Gerald and Margaret had made the effort. They had been sufficiently impressed with the venture to act upon it (Gerald even walked with us the following day). They might well tell a few people about Coastin' and Parkinson's after we had gone. These types of experiences at B&Bs were immensely satisfying.

In fact, I was finding the whole process of meeting complete strangers a wonderfully rewarding aspect of my daily routine. In my previous life it was rare to meet and spend quality time with new people. At home, meeting strangers consisted largely of small talk; people talking just for the sake of it. On Coastin', the characters I was meeting could at the very least offer an insight into the local area. By the same token, these new people seemed to be interested in what I was undertaking. There was a sense of a fair exchange of information and mutual appreciation. These were good ingredients for the walk recipe.

Mr Beef left us at Stromeferry. In a week, he had transformed himself from a lumbering T-bone into an exquisite tournedos. He was leaner, more versatile and no doubt a tad tastier to the ladies. Despite his constant complaining, his totally stubborn attitude and the fact that he had clearly not enjoyed his walking holiday one little bit, I was sad that he was leaving. Nevertheless, as his immediate replacement was Lyndsey, I did not mourn for very long.

It was great to see her again. Her beaming smile as she got off the train made me realise how much I had missed her. This was her eighth visit and it suddenly dawned on me around this time that Lyndsey was not coming so much to support me for Coastin' but to support me for "us".

She was giving so much. I found out later she had even taken out a loan in order to fund trips to see me. And yet, I was still not giving her much back in return; not because I didn't want to, but because I was obsessed – obsessed with raising funds and awareness, walking and finishing.

I spoke to Lyndsey every day when she was not with me, but never did she put any pressure on me. Her total understanding of the importance of this year to me; her uncanny intuition in knowing what I was thinking before I realised it myself; her total command of the situation combined with her ability to make me think that I had control – all of these things made everything so easy for me. It was every man's dream to find a girl like this.

There no longer seemed to be any question of losing her. By now, we were a robust team; confident in each other's feelings and just enjoying the walking, rather than looking too far ahead.

And then she poisoned me.

We had reached the Kyle of Lochalsh. She had found a fantastic organic tea room with all sorts of goodies on display.

"I am going to bring you a surprise," she said.

A few minutes later, she arrived with a huge slice of chocolate cake. It looked magnificent. But with my wheat and gluten allergy precluding any such treats, I wondered where my surprise was.

"It's gluten-free," she said. "It said on the cake label, and the man behind the counter confirmed it." She knew I would want double confirmation of this fact. The repercussions were sufficiently unpleasant to want to make absolutely sure.

I was delighted with my present, and having taken one last look at the plateful shining back up at me, I scoffed it.

I was up all night. Being violently sick at any time is horrible. Being violently sick when you've got Parkinson's, you're stuck in a rather dodgy B&B and you're in the middle of a 4,500-mile walk, is worse.

In the morning, while I remained in bed, unable to walk for the day, Lyndsey stormed back to the organic tea room. I have no doubt her Glaswegian accent became more pronounced as she launched a scathing attack on the proprietors.

She had calmed down a bit by the time she came back. The man behind the counter yesterday had been new. The labels on the cakes had accidentally been switched. These things happen. It was pointless to kick up a fuss. I did feel they could have made a small donation though!

I remained in bed all that day, barely eating a thing. Wild Rover and Lyndsey went to visit Eilean Donan Castle. I felt annoyed to have missed that.

Using a corner of the Isle of Skye as a stepping stone, we walked from Kyle of Lochalsh over to Kylerhea where we caught the ferry over to Glenelg. The day's walk was only about 12 miles and it allowed me to regain my strength.

There was a good pub in Glenelg with a good reputation. The food was excellent. The owner was a muscular young Scotsman who was a bit too good-looking to be likeable. He was the sort who wore a kilt because he knew he looked great in it. There were a lot of middle-aged ladies clucking around him.

When three slightly scruffy characters walked into his pub, he rather looked down his nose at them. That was actually the only thing he did wrong. But I was tired, grumpy and one of the slightly scruffy characters. Much to my companions' amusement, I spent the rest of the evening using this be-skirted man as an object on which to vent my ill humour.

It was 28th August. As we set out for the day's walk, I noticed that there was quite a nip in the air and a splash of yellow paint had tinged the tips of some of the leaves which I was convinced had been fully green the day before.

From Glenelg, we could walk to the end of the road at Arnisdale along the shores of the Sound of Sleat. On the way we saw the owner of the pub. He was still in his kilt and had just launched himself off in a rowing boat. He was still playing the part of a rugged Highlander, and if I am honest, he was doing it a bit too well for it not to be true.

I am not sure why he riled me so much. He just did. Anyway, I derived enormous pleasure from waving cheerily at him. This meant he had to ship one oar and wave back, which, in turn, meant that the boat skewed off course.

"Hah, not so clever now, are we?"

The word "Knoydart" is supposed to originate from Viking times (derived from "Knut's Fjord"). If said in an English accent, it conjures up an image of somewhere small and insignificant; a forgotten, inhospitable tract of land in some remote outpost of Scotland where no one would ever dream of going. And on the map, that is precisely what it is.

Say the same word as if you were a burly Highlander, with a sporran full of haggis, and a head full of Robbie Burns poetry, and suddenly, the place takes on a more menacing profile.

Two years earlier, in Knoydart, I had conducted an experiment involving not taking any medication for 24 hours. Quite why I chose one of the last wildernesses in the country as a venue, I am not entirely sure. After 22 hours I was pleased with how well I had coped and I had managed to get myself about seven miles away from the campsite without serious mishap. Then suddenly my legs packed up as if they had run out of petrol; I was unable to take another step forward. Had I not had my medication with me, it is possible that I might well have "died from wait".

Although the experiment did not feature on the list of "sensible things I have done," it did serve one useful purpose, which after the event I incorporated into my own Scottish verse, so I would never forget:

> From thence to this where'er I tread,
> 'Tis must that I dost feed m' head
> I'll ne'er oot wi' no pot o'pill
> Ne'er more me stuck 'pon blasted hill.

I have never allowed myself to freeze since. The realisation that I was now completely powered by drugs, that I couldn't walk anywhere without them, upset me quite deeply initially. It made me feel a bit like a machine; completely useless when the gas tank was empty. The only resolution to this was to keep the fuel line constantly monitored and to keep moving. Keeping moving would ensure nothing would rust.

I was looking forward to showing Knoydart to Lyndsey. It is such a stunning place whatever the weather, and I wanted her to see it. Besides, as she hails from fiercely proud Glaswegian stock, she was the only one of us able to do justice to the word.

Wild Rover was in a dark mood on the day we began the 15-mile walk from the tea house beyond Arnisdale at Corran to the bothy at Ambraigh in the heart of Knoydart. Even though he had stacked his pack with most of the heavy items, he set off at an alarming rate up the first of six steep mountain passes that he and I would encounter over the next five days. Lyndsey would depart after two days by boat from Inverie via Mallaig. We were very remote now and we all enjoyed the sensation.

As Lyndsey and I toiled behind, I wondered why he felt the need to punish himself quite so much. For him, fulfilment was hard won on this walk. I was pleased he had stayed on beyond Applecross and was also quietly confident that Knoydart could offer whatever he was looking for. Knoydart was made for Wild Rovers. I was also pleased that he and I would be "roughing it" from here to Fort William. Until we reached the top of our sixth pass at the head of Glenfinnan, the only village we would see would be Inverie, which is only accessible on foot or by boat. With four days' worth of provisions on our backs and the prospect of three consecutive nights in bothies, today felt like a more intrepid kind of expedition.

By the time we reached Kinloch Hourn, where a solitary road from Invergarry comes to a dramatic dead end at the shores of Loch Hourn, we were muddy and soaked from alternating patterns of bog, rain and river crossings. Our tiredness was sufficient to warrant our spending the afternoon on wishing away the final seven miles to Barrisdale Bay. But the only thing of real significance as we walked was Knoydart itself and our fatigue seemed to be overhauled by the sheer invigoration of walking along the shores of Loch Hourn.

Of the sea lochs that I know, Loch Hourn is my favourite. The mountains rise very steeply from its banks and yet, despite its vast scale, there is a sense of the clandestine about it, as if it is hiding or guarding something.

We seemed to be dwarfed by the enormity of the place. Little humps that we could see on our path in the distance would turn out to be mighty ridges and we seemed to make very slight progress. Today Knoydart was at its dramatic best. Big white clouds hurled themselves overhead, and in the gaps between them, sunlight coursed down, flooding the valley with wave after wave of vibrant colour. And then just as quickly, the heather, grass, sea loch, Skye and mountains would all return to a dull grey as another cloud swept by.

Staring up Loch Hourn there was murkier, more menacing-looking weather brewing; but it did not seem to be coming our way. Out of the gloom, a solitary tall ship chugged gently towards us bound for Kinloch Hourn for who knows what purpose.

Of course the other reason for not wishing away the final few hours was the fact that we were staying in a bothy. It was difficult to generate quite the same sense of destination and level of enthusiasm for somewhere without showers, carpets, beds or a kettle.

We never did find out the real name of the man in the bothy, but we called him Simon; Simon Coe. He welcomed us warmly, almost as if the bothy belonged to him. "How long have you been here?" I asked.

"On and off for about two weeks." He seemed a bit nervous about imparting this information and for a while he fidgeted and avoided eye contact. It was as if he didn't want anyone to know he was there.

Simon Coe looked more like a Wild Rover than Wild Rover. He was unkempt, unshaven and wore a permanent bemused expression that suggested he was totally mystified with the world. His eyes were constantly shooting around the room as if he had been searching all day for his hair, which was so wayward it might as well have been in the next valley.

When he found out what I was doing and why, his whole bearing seemed to intensify and he started fidgeting again before deciding to volunteer a noteworthy section of his own curriculum vitae: "I used to be psychopathic."

He seemed relieved to have got the words out and was now searching our faces to see how we would react. But our expressions revealed nothing. We maintained an air of total indifference and calm. Seemingly satisfied, he continued chatting to us about his experience of the turmoil within himself.

Meanwhile, we were experiencing inner turmoil of our own. Although we had successfully retained our composed appearances, this was purely a by-product of our being paralysed with fear. In the sentence "I used to be psychopathic", the words "used to" seemed to hold no value at all. And underneath our frozen outer shells, there was pandemonium as we weighed up our predicament. Later we found out that we all came to the same answer – we were in the middle of the so-called "last wilderness of the UK" and about to spend the night in a hut with a psychopath who was trying to cover his tracks. Our life expectancy had suddenly been reduced.

But he chatted on and on and gradually we began to feel less concerned about being marooned with a "Si Coe". I had not realised that psychosis is in many respects the antithesis of Parkinson's, often characterised by an excess of dopaminergic activity in the brain. Wild Rover offered to conduct an experiment in cell transplantation with the help of a Swiss Army knife. Lyndsey and I rather wished he had not mentioned the word "knife".

By the end of the evening, we felt comfortable enough to go to sleep without keeping a running watch through the night, but I think we all woke up relieved that in the absence of shower facilities at the bothy, Si had not taken it upon himself to provide a bloodbath.

Of course, the following day as we laboured up the pass of Mam Barrisdale, we were able to joke about it: "I'm going to see Si's brother, Glen, in about a week."

"What on earth are you on about?"

"Si Coe's brother, Glen… Glen Coe."

"Never mind his brother Glen, just make sure you don't bump into his sister Tess at the supermarket."

"Why, what's wrong with her?"

"She's not called Si Coe's sis for nothing."

You had to be there. At the time it was quite hysterical.

"You two are not at all funny," piped in Lyndsey, but she was laughing as she said it.

Walking through Knoydart gave me a real sense of defying my illness. The combination of both gradient and length made Mam Barrisdale the hardest climb of the walk so far. I imagined the hill represented my Parkinson's and that a cure was at the top. The mental picture spurred me on and I found I had reserves of energy that I didn't know existed. The rush of endorphins I experienced when I reached the top put me on a high for the remainder of the day. I waited for the others to catch up.

"How come you went so fast up there?" asked Wild Rover. "Have you forgotten about your neurological disorder?"

"It was because of it, that I went so fast."

Wild Rover looked confused at my cryptic response but decided not to ask any more questions.

In Inverie that evening, I met someone who made my effort to climb up a mountain seem positively feeble. Lynn Martin was sitting next to me in the pub. She seemed to be fascinated with Coastin' and enthusiastically quizzed me on my motives and progress so far. It was some time before I established her amazing story.

In 1978, Lynn had been involved in a car accident which left her with her pelvis shunted to one side and tilted forwards. It was broken in seven places. Her right leg had been driven through the socket and was broken above the knee. She also had internal injuries, a head injury and was given only a 50:50 chance of survival. When she did survive, she was told that she would never be able to walk again without sticks. It was at this point that Lynn decided that she would start climbing mountains. It took her two years to recover full fitness, whereupon she trained in mountain leadership and rock climbing. I discovered that she had spent the past 18 years taking young people to the mountains to walk and climb.

I felt inspired by her story. She had an indomitable spirit about her which undermined the very foundations of hopelessness. It was infectious, and I felt energized in her company.

Inverie is pretty much just one street which stares out at the narrow entrance to Loch Nevis as if constantly hoping for visitors. A friend of mine, Lee, joined us in Inverie and Lyndsey went home. Although I would see her again soon, I realised that every time she left Coastin' I felt that little bit sadder at her departure and looked forward to her next visit more than the last time. These thoughts were particularly prevalent when, on his first night, Lee distinguished himself with his familiar "sleeping warthog with blocked nose in small cave" impersonation. The next morning, when I told him that I had actually slept better the previous night in the company of a self-confessed psychopath, he seemed very pleased with himself.

It took two days to walk from Inverie to Glenfinnan and the route we took was empty of all human life. It struck me that this was the last really remote section of Coastin' that I would undertake. After these two days, I would always be within a few hours' walk of help. I had mixed feelings about this. I was dismayed at the thought that the "best bit" was, to all intents and purposes, over, but also relieved that even with the prospect of colder weather, and no Wild Rover for company and support beyond Fort William, I still looked in good shape to complete the rest of my journey on schedule and in a reasonable state of health.

The deer-hunting season had begun in Glenfinnan. It had been my intention to walk to Fort William via a valley called Cona Glen, but the thought of being shot and then having my head mounted in the dining room of some Scottish laird did not appeal. Besides, my head might be of interest to medical science. It would be such a waste if it were used purely for decorative purposes. Fortunately, the whole thing was academic really because we walked along the road on the southern side of Loch Eil and caught a ferry across to the largest town we had encountered since Inverness.

Fort William seemed hurried and impersonal. Here, Highland hospitality is replaced by Grampian greed. As the principal gateway to the mountains and hub of all activities for locals of the Western Highlands, Fort William tries to be all things to all people and actually fails at being anything to anyone.

In my UK all-comers list of unpleasant guest house owners, Fort William is the only town represented twice in the top ten: by both Mrs Jones and Mad Jim the Bigot.

Although Mad Jim the Bigot occupies the top spot in the list, there is not much to say about him other than the fact that he managed to combine his deeply unpleasant personality with his deeply unpleasant house to facilitate a quite horrendous B&B experience.

Admittedly, at first, it was quite enjoyable listening to the absurd prejudices of a man totally obsessed with his own nationality. But there comes a point when you can take no more. There comes a point when you wonder how polite you can be to someone who seems to believe that unless you are Scottish, Gaelic-speaking and Presbyterian, you actually have little right to exist at all.

Mrs Jones's appearance on the list, however, can be attributed to a more mundane kind of inhospitality.

I first met her on my walk from John O'Groats to Land's End and immediately deduced that she was a little over-glamorous for the Fort William bed-and-breakfast scene. Everything in her world was uncluttered, disciplined and manicured and when I arrived, dripping on her spotless doormat, she stared at me disapprovingly over her pince-nez. I thought for a second she was going to shut the door in my face. I might have felt some sympathy for her, but this was Fort William – a place where people come to walk in the rain.

From then on it was a battle. I was not allowed to use her tumble drier, I had to use the bathroom at a certain time and only in the morning. I even noticed that the time for my breakfast was different to that of the other guests, presumably so I would not be seen.

I had no intention of staying longer than I had to, but due to my clothes still being wet I ended up leaving ten minutes after check-out time. Mrs Jones made it perfectly clear to me when I left that this total disregard for the rules of the house had ruined her day. I was so furious with her general attitude towards walkers that I have been recommending the place to anyone looking a bit wet or muddy ever since. They would, after all, be better off there than with Mad Jim the Bigot.

Several friends came and went during my four-day spell in Fort William. Most important though was the departure of Wild Rover. There was no doubt that I would have struggled to complete the 800 miles from Pennan to here without him. I was so glad to have been able to share some of the most wonderful walking with a friend. I would miss his company. His last act was to climb Ben Nevis with me, a fitting finale for a Wild Rover and for another phase of Coastin' to draw to a close.

Climbing the highest mountain in each country, Scotland, England and Wales, seemed like an obvious thing to do when I had been planning Coastin'. Firstly, none of them involved any climbing whatsoever; secondly, they were all within a day's walk from the coast; and finally, and most important of all, I love walking up mountains.

Ben Nevis was a short walk from the flat which a group of us were renting for a few days. Self-catering was the only way to avoid another Fort William hospitality experience. Four of us made the four-hour trip up the mountain. As I felt the familiar pull on the muscles in my legs as they strained to keep a steady momentum up the one in five slope, I wondered why I was enjoying the sensation? It didn't really stand to reason. Could my happiness be attributed totally to endorphin activity or was there something masochistic in me? I couldn't think of any other pain I enjoyed. So why did walking, and more particularly walking up hills, always give me a quick fix of euphoria? I continued to ponder this.

The top of Ben Nevis was cold and exposed, and I realised with it being early September that this was something to which I would have to become accustomed. I remembered that my brother had camped out up here one

New Year's Eve in temperatures of minus 20 degrees. It had been after midnight when he and a couple of friends, having wrapped themselves in every layer of clothing they possessed, saw a man staggering towards them clad only in a T-shirt and a kilt.

"Thank God," the man said, collapsing in front of them, "have yoo boys got any whisky?"

My brother and his friends rushed to the man's aid, covering him in coats and sleeping bags in an attempt to prevent hypothermia. But the man had looked confused.

"Dinny bother with that."

"Are you all right then?"

"Noo, I'm nut all rit. Mi whisky ran oot at two an' a haf thoosan' fit and I canny celebrate hogminny up here wi'oot it!"

They stoked the inebriated man up with single malt and then shoved him in a tent for fear either that he might attempt the journey down again or that he might get too close to their gas stove and be lit up like a Christmas pudding. He remained there until first light, at which time he heaved himself out of the tent and set off back down the mountain, leaving a legacy of an alcoholic haze and a rancid smell.

There were a lot of people at the top of Ben Nevis. I find this often dilutes the sense of achievement so I took myself away from the crowds and sat alone for a while, pointing northwards. The slope up which we had just climbed looked extremely steep and I watched as others hauled themselves up it, wearing expressions of unbridled misery. The view across the Grampians was hazy from the top of Ben Nevis, but while I was sitting there, other things became clear. I realised that perhaps it was not so much the pain in my legs that made me enjoy the journey up; perhaps it was more the anticipation of feeling as I did now – exhilarated, fulfilled and never more alive.

I was at the highest point in the land, the highest point of my journey. I was in control of everything except my Parkinson's, but I was sure that even that goal would one day be reached and I was beginning to enjoy that journey too.

"Parkinson's is my Everest," I thought and wandered over to join the others.

On the way back down Ben Nevis, I fell behind the others. For some strange reason I seemed to lack surefootedness and became paranoid about twisting an ankle. Standing high up on Ben Nevis, watching my friends zigzagging like skiers down the loose lumps of scree made me curse my loss of balance. This was the very thing I couldn't control. It was typical of Parkinson's to kick me in the teeth just when I had bought some new shinpads.

But the descent of Ben Nevis turned out to be a lot more than just a kick in the teeth. It was here that there was a fundamental shift in the complexion of Coastin'. To the top of Ben Nevis everything had been getting better and better; an upward trend of physical and psychological well-being. From the moment I left the summit, something changed, and Coastin' would never be quite the same. Up to that point, I thought I had control of my walk and of my life, but my personal journey for the year was only just beginning. It was as if my lack of balance as I came down the highest mountain in Britain was a portent for what lay ahead.

## CHAPTER 20

From Fort William a fresh posse of three friends joined me on the West Highland Way. We would follow this path as far as Glen Coe. People coming the other way asked us whether we were walking the entire route to Milngavie. I wasn't sure whether this was because they were genuinely interested or just so they could prove they knew how to pronounce "Milngavie" – Mull-guy. In any case, it was slightly annoying only being able to respond that we were walking only one and a half days of the route. On hearing this, they looked rather proud of their achievement, only to be completely deflated by my walking companions, who revealed the whole Coastin' story. They probably felt the way I might feel just before I bumped into that bastard who was walking right round the world. I really hoped never to meet him. I had avoided speaking to people with really big packs for this very reason.

On our approach to the top of the Devil's Staircase (a steep descent into Glen Coe), Dad rang. I felt self-conscious and embarrassed about being on the phone in an area of stunning scenery, particularly as a large group of walkers were coming from the other direction. I ended up being quite short with him and telling him I had to go. He had clearly wanted to have a bit of a chat and afterwards I felt guilty about not speaking to him for longer.

We stayed in the Kingshouse Hotel that night. It has become famed for not being able to pick up TV because it is so isolated. This, I am convinced, is a clever Scottish ruse, which not only gives them a good line in publicity, but also saves on the cost of televisions in every room.

The walk from Dalness to Oban would only take two days if we could find the bridge across the River Etive. We paced up and down, wasting about an hour before realising it must have been washed away. The only option was to ford the river.

Squelching boots seemed to send my friends into fits of laughter and worried that with 17 miles to go, any more such delays could jeopardise our reaching Taynuilt, I became very annoyed. When it started to pour with rain, the fun stopped and everyone concentrated on the walking. It was then I cheered up. I pondered that the role reversal displayed the very different goals of the people walking. The others wanted to enjoy themselves – it was their holiday after all – whereas I just wanted to get the job done.

I received another phone call from Dad. Once again, he was more chatty than usual, only this time I felt more responsive. We spoke for a good 20 minutes, sparring for information. I was keen to find out how everything was at home and he wanted to know how I was getting on.

We covered a lot of ground. There was an economy with words in all our telephone conversations, because we understood one another. I find with telephones it is sometimes easy to misunderstand the message due to only hearing a voice and not seeing the expression or the body language.

With Dad I did not need that. I knew from the inflection in his voice not only what he meant, but even where he was sitting. He would be in his study, slouched uncomfortably in his purple orthopaedic chair, with a mug of black coffee getting cold in front of him and a pile of papers that had just been "actioned". It was a comfort to know that everything was the same back home. The phone call ended the same as it always did.

"Keep going!" he said encouragingly.

"I will."

Dad's phone call made me feel good and I picked up my stride and my pace to catch the others, who were now some way ahead. I realised that my self-satisfied thoughts earlier of "just wanting to get the job done" was a reflection not so much of my goal but of the mood in which I had been wallowing this morning. My friends' foremost goal on this trip was not to have a nice holiday; it was to support me. How could I have been so ungrateful? Although they were oblivious to my train of thought, I showed them my gratitude when I caught them up. I was annoyed at myself for taking such good friends for granted.

Taking my friends three miles in the wrong direction on the way to Oban the following day was not a particularly good way to continue to strengthen my friendships. The three miles of retracing our steps were annoying and energy sapping. By the time we reached Oban, we were all utterly exhausted, but my earlier failure with the map was forgotten when we checked into a lovely B&B overlooking the island of Kerrera and the Firth of Lorn.

The following day was another day off and I was annoyed by the interruption of my "Scotland the Brave" ring-tone resonating from my bedroom. "Who is ringing me at this ungodly hour of the morning?" I wondered.

It was Mum. She was due to fly up to Scotland later that day to do some walking with me. I had not seen her or Dad since the baton carrying in June.

"Dad is having terrible heart pains. He's OK, but I am taking him to hospital."

"Is he OK?" I asked urgently. I needed to hear it again.

"Yes, he's fine," came the response. "He was out 'jollying' with all his cronies last night after 18 holes of golf, if you please." She was irritated that Dad had, once again, failed to be sensible.

I felt relieved. Her annoyance was a measure of the seriousness of Dad's condition. Perhaps it really wasn't too bad. Dad had had these pains before, and when he recovered, we would all good-humouredly tease him about preventing Mum from leaving in an attempt to avoid certain daily chores. Dad would be only too pleased to play his role in this family charade.

As I was supposed to be having a day off, Greg and Kath, the owners of Rahoy Lodge, where we were staying, ordered me to relax in their hammock. The midges did not appear and I was left alone rocking gently back and forth on a glorious early September day. Greg brought me a bunch of grapes and a glass of chilled white wine. My worries about Dad subsided. He would be OK. He'd always got through these little scares. Truly content and relaxed, I drifted in and out of sleep. This was it. This was the way life was meant to be. It was a treacherous calm before the most hideous of personal storms.

I was not to feel like this again on the entire journey.

That evening, Mum rang again. Dad was OK, but it had been a heart attack and he had been kept in hospital for an operation. "It is relatively minor surgery really, but not without an element of risk," she said.

The operation was to be on Friday. Friday 13th September. I am not superstitious, but the day did instil in me a sinking feeling. I tried to brush it aside, but it would not go away. "Should I ring to say don't have the operation on that day because it doesn't feel right? No. Don't be ridiculous.

Everything will be fine."

It was a 14-mile day from Oban to Loch Avich. I had to accept that the dramatic scenery of recent weeks was now behind me. The mountains were now hills and the valleys had turned from Us to Vs. Nevertheless, I was perfectly content marching fast through Kilmore and then on to Loch Scammadale and Lochavich House. I was collected from near here by Bridget Oatts, who lived in the area and whose husband had suffered from Parkinson's. Generously, she had offered to escort me all the way back to Oban. I was enjoying my time so much at Rahoy Lodge and had decided to stay there for as long as I possibly could.

CHAPTER 21

Greg and his dog, Fleabag, decided to join me. He parked his car near the church in Kilmelford. Bridget Oatts was there once again to transport me to the start point on the shores of Loch Avich for the walk to Kilmartin.

It was an absolutely magnificent day. Summer still prevailed over autumn and the Domhain valley through which we were walking was lush and unspoilt. In fact, in places, it was a little too lush, for when we left the road at Lagalochan, Greg, Fleabag and I could be seen splashing about in knee-high swamp. I was embarrassed about leading my visitors through such terrain, but both seemed perfectly happy.

Sheep speckled the valley sides and although Fleabag's natural instincts, being a border collie, were to gather them up, he remained steadfastly by our sides as instructed; content just to eye them enthusiastically. No need for Fleabag to prove his superiority. He knew he was higher up the evolutionary scale than these fluffy white muttonheads. He was a good dog, Fleabag.

As we sat for lunch atop a picturesque mound, I witnessed my all-important quota of sea. It was a fantastic view over to Loch Craignish; not magnificent, like others I had looked out over recently, but one which was rich in texture, warmth and colour; more like a painting.

I reflected on Dad. He would be mid-operation. I suddenly felt sick with worry, almost as if the news that he was in an operating theatre had just reached me. I felt fidgety and irritable at my remoteness from home. I should be there. An hour and a half later, I received a phone call. The signal on my phone kept cutting out the voice of my mother. I frantically tried to find higher ground. It cut out for good. The only thing I had gleaned was that there had been complications. The phone rang again. This time I could hear. Dad was in a stable condition, Mum had seen him. She would be seeing the specialist soon and would give me a full report once she had spoken to him.

I felt stranded. Here I was in the middle of nowhere. I should be at home. The family had always rallied in moments of crisis. At least my brother was there with Mum.

I fell silent and Greg tactfully left me to my thoughts. The next phone call came. Dad had to go into theatre again. This time there was more risk.

"Should I come home?" I asked.

"No," said Mum, "I'll ring if you need to."

The words sounded ominous and seemed to strike a hammer blow within me. I suppose the fact that I might "need" to be at home had not seriously crossed my mind. Previously, I had wanted to be there because there was strength in numbers; we could all take comfort in each other's presence. There was no "need" in this. It was just what we did.

"It sounds bad," I said to Greg, and I told him the last part of the conversation. "I don't know what to do." I felt helpless, miserable and about as far away from my family as I could possibly be.

"Go home," he said. "You must go home now. You can finish this walk any time."

I was so grateful for his calm, firm and definitive advice. I knew he was right. I just needed someone else to confirm that it was the correct decision. At least by going home I was doing something constructive. Being on a charity walk suddenly felt so utterly trivial.

But going home was a lot easier said than done. I rang Bridget Oatts, explained the situation and she said she would be there as quickly as she could. Greg knew the next train from Oban to Glasgow was at 6.10 p.m. If I had any hope of getting back to Hertfordshire tonight, I would have to be on it. We had just over an hour to make it. I knew that the odds were stacked against us.

Greg could and would drive fast when we reached his car, but previously when we had driven the road, we had been stuck behind slow-moving lorries. If that happened again we had no hope. Then there was Bridget Oatts, a really kind lady, but I did worry about her ability to drive fast. I had noticed that on the previous two journeys, she had been wearing driving gloves and I imagined her now slowly pulling them on before carefully checking all her mirrors and slowly, painstakingly turning out of her driveway. Greg and I reached the road at Barbreck House and were now storming up it at a great pace, back in the direction of Kilmelford. We found an appropriate pulling in and turning spot for Bridget. She seemed to take an eternity to arrive and, once again, I thought of her driving gloves. I felt like cursing them. My anxiousness had drained all sense of reasonableness from me. It was probably only a matter of seconds before Bridget arrived. We informed her of the time of the train. She looked at her clock and I could tell from her expression that she didn't think we could make it.

"I am afraid I am not awfully good at driving fast," she said.

My frenetic mood softened at her words. I realised she was doing her best.

As it turned out, her "best" comprised taking her small Peugeot to the very limits of its performance capabilities. Bridget was incredible. She hugged bends, she accelerated hard out of corners, she double-declutched into second gear and overtook the juggernaut on a short straight in the road. She grappled with the steering wheel as if she was in mortal combat with a crocodile. It was ironic that she was able to do this because of her driving gloves. We made it back to Greg's car in Kilmelford and while I sorted out luggage to take with me in the back, he tore off to Oban. The traffic was good to us. We got there in time.

The train journey was terrible. The last hour and a half had been spent in pursuit of one goal: reaching Oban station on time. Now I was on the train and my thoughts fell back to Dad. My brother, Mark, had now taken over the reins of keeping me informed. The last phone call had been in the car when the news had been no more encouraging. Rebecca, his wife, was organising my flight back to Luton. It would be tight, but I should make it.

I was standing at the end of the compartment. I didn't want to be near anyone else. I wanted to be alone. A boy of about eight or nine was running up and down the carriage making a terrible din. I glared at him so that he would not come near, but it did not deter him and he stood and stared back defiantly. I tried to ignore him. He seemed to be taunting me. As my drugs started to kick out, my tremor became apparent. The boy stared at me even more. I wondered if anyone would care if I threw him out of the window. He went away when the phone rang.

It was Mark. "If he survives the next ten minutes he should be OK. But his heart could give out at any moment."

This filled me with hope. Just ten minutes, Dad. Just hang on.

I ran out of signal as we entered the mountainous region north of Loch

Lomond. The train stopped at Crianlarich for ages. I felt the most extraordinary pang stab me in the pit of my stomach. I checked my watch. It was 6.30 p.m., about ten minutes after Mark had last called.

When we left Crianlarich, my phone soon came back in range. I waited for what seemed to be an inevitable phone call.

It didn't come.

Maybe I was wrong. Maybe he was OK. In the past, when I had experienced similarly strong feelings, they had sometimes been wrong.

The phone rang. It was Mum. Dad had died.

* * *

I made it home that night. I barely recall the journey. The shock made me numb. I couldn't take it in. I couldn't think at all.

On the plane, I remember being most concerned about how I looked. I was still caked in mud and sweat from the day's walk. I felt self-conscious about the fact that my boots probably smelt. Nothing made sense.

I read a book of short stories I had bought in the airport; anything to protect me from the grief that would eventually flood out. I had to make it home before that could happen.

The next few days were the worst of my entire life. Nothing would ever be the same again. Hundreds of letters clogged up the letterbox for many days; kind people remembering Dad.

The last time I had seen him had been in Kingston upon Thames at the "baton carrying". I remembered how he had made a special effort to chat to me on the way back to the pub and how I had thought he looked older and paler. And then there was that moment when I had had that strange feeling in the pit of my stomach. I knew what that was now; for a fleeting moment I had wondered whether I would ever see him again. It was almost as if I had experienced a premonition that I had chosen not to believe.

Since then, I had spoken to him a lot on the phone, and four days prior to his operation, we had had a long conversation, a good conversation. He had asked lots of questions: how I was; how the walk was going; what the next few days had in store. At the time, I had not thought anything of it, but in retrospect this phone call had been significantly longer than most others. It was almost as if he suspected something.

My family had become a tightly knit unit. Although we were strong as a pack, the shock of Dad's death made the prospect of "making arrangements" too overwhelming for my brother and me to even contemplate for a couple of days. But in a 20-minute conversation with R. B. Catlow we had been lifted from total despair to a grim realisation of the importance of ensuring a funeral which befitted our father; the sort he would have wanted for himself. The value of our conversation with our Uncle Richard was incalculable. He advised us with a clarity and a frankness which only he could provide. His wisdom and practical experience of the procedure were all conveyed in those 20 minutes and through his words we found a sense of purpose and somewhere else to rest our thoughts.

The funeral was nine days after Dad's death and was as he would have wanted it. The church was absolutely packed. The reception afterwards was a fitting send-off. I suppose that everyone has similar thoughts when they lose a close relative. The hole that is left seems much bigger than you could possibly imagine it would be. In the loss of Dad, I felt as if the bedrock on which I depended, the very ground in which my roots had grown strong and steadfast, had suddenly disappeared and I was left trying to clutch onto something that was no longer there.

Nothing seemed to make sense any more. Coastin' and my Parkinson's, which I had previously thought were so important, now seemed like trivialities; they were just sideshows. What really mattered to me more than anything else was the value I placed on things that I could depend upon. I had lost my life counsellor: a person with whom all things of great importance could be discussed. He had always been there for me and for all his family, the provider and the anchor. But much more than any of this, I had lost Dad, and everything that those three letters stood for.

My sense of fulfilment and worth, which in Cape Wrath had seemed so crucial, now seemed more like luxury. Despite my changing feelings towards the walk and my life, both had to go on. There was never any doubt that I would go back to Coastin'. Dad would have hated me to stop.

Besides, his last ever words to me were ingrained in my head: "Keep going!" My response had been "I will." It was an exchange of words which had been without particular meaning at the time; just a way of ending the conversation. Now these words had taken on new status. It was my duty to finish and, whatever was thrown at me, I would do it not for me, not for Parkinson's, but for Dad.

Coastin' was no longer just a project, it was now more important than that: it was my mission.

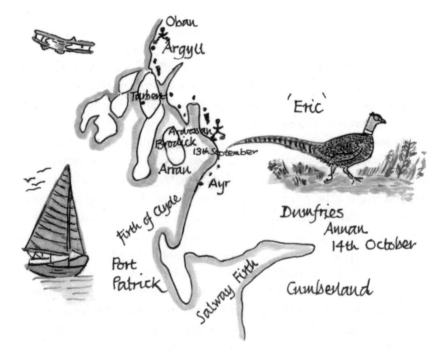

Oban
Argyll
Tarbert
Ardrossan
Brodick
13th September
Arran
Ayr
Firth of Clyde
'Eric'
Dumfries
Annan
14th October
Port
Patrick
Salway Firth
Cumberland

FROM ARGYLL AND ARRAN
TO A CHANGE IN AYR
264 MILES
SEPTEMBER - OCTOBER

C H A P T E R   2 2

Gazing out at that special view across the water and the islands from the first floor of Rahoy Lodge, in Oban, I felt a glimmer of something that I had not experienced for some time. Although I felt cold and hollow inside, the view out of that window felt like the first tentative sip of a nourishing bowl of soup.

I was back Coastin' again. It felt good and yet also strange. Starting again seemed like a final and total acknowledgment to myself that Dad was now gone and that life had to continue. During the past 11 days my motivation for the walk had roller-coastered. From the depths of despair, the like of which I have never experienced, I had with each day clawed my way bit by bit out of an abyss in which nothing really mattered any more.

Fuelled by an overwhelming chorus of encouragement from my family and incredible support from my friends, I had ever so slowly clambered up to a point where my motivation for completing Coastin' would probably never be exceeded. Now there was yet another reason to complete this walk and for the time being it would supersede all other reasons. I knew that my selfishness would dictate that until the memory and pain of Dad's death had subsided, every step would be for him and no one else.

On the journey back up to Oban, I had already decided to resign myself to the fact that Coastin' would, for the foreseeable future, fail to hold the enjoyment it once had. I knew that any moments of sublime scenery would now engender quiet reflection rather than excitement.

Coastin' now had another function. It provided yet another therapy. The healing process had begun.

\* \* \*

It all seemed exactly the same at breakfast in Rahoy Lodge, with Kath serving up the home-cooked treats and Greg coming in later to exchange some good-humoured banter. But it wasn't the same. Whilst I was as chirpy as ever on the outside, there was an underlying hurt. It had been the common denominator for everything, so that the more enjoyment I was having at any particular time, the greater and more poignant the fall back to the memory of Dad.

If ever there had been a time that I needed support and good company on the walk, this was it. I had better than that. I had Lyndsey. She had been incredible for the past fortnight, knowing the right things to say at the right time and when not to say anything, and to just listen. Dad's death had drawn us closer together. And for the first time in my life, I did not feel frightened at the prospect. In fact, I felt bolstered by it.

Now she was with me for ten days and we would walk from Argyll to Arran to Ayr together. I would go through many different emotions during this time and most of them not good. There were times when I wanted to be alone, wanted to walk at a different pace to her, wanted to be bad-tempered. But despite all such extremes of mood, I was incredibly glad of her presence after the funeral. Starting again would have been much more difficult without her.

Greg had absolutely insisted that we should not pay for the night's accommodation and that he would take us wherever we wanted to go. He also supplied us with all manner of tooth-decaying sweets for our journey. We tried to complain but words seemed to fail us. Perhaps we wanted them to.

Greg dropped us at Kilmelford church car park where the tireless Bridget Oatts was waiting yet again to transport us wherever we wanted to go. It was sad saying goodbye to Greg, but I had no doubt that I would see him again.

As I positioned myself in the front seat of Bridget's car once again, and she donned her, by now, familiar driving gloves, I realised that I had developed quite an affection for this kind and totally reliable lady. I had only been in her company for less than two hours in total, and yet in my moment of crisis, Friday 13th September, she had rushed to my rescue. I would be forever grateful. There is absolutely no doubt that beneath the diminutive stature of Bridget Oatts lay a big heart and considerable strength of character.

I was surprised how little it affected me being dropped off at the place where I had heard that Dad's prospects looked bleak. It certainly did not have the same effect on me as Crianlarich where on the train from Oban to

Glasgow I had been consumed with a feeling of dread that my father was no longer living. I had felt the warmth of Lyndsey's hand in mine as we passed through; just a little reminder that she was there if I needed to talk. But the train and I had pushed on back towards Oban in relentless silence.

It was just past noon when Lyndsey and I recommenced Coastin'. By 1.30 p.m. we were hopelessly lost, having followed some random (as it turned out) bits of orange tape through a woodland assuming they would lead us in the right direction. It was all my fault.

"I am totally incompetent," I said, half in anger and half in dejection.

"Look at the fantastic scenery though," came the comforting words of Lyndsey.

She was right, there were marvellous views of open moorland and craggy mountains, but this hardly justified the diversion. The direction we had been walking in for the past 45 minutes had not even been close to being right.

I was glad Lyndsey was with me. Despite our getting lost, she just ploughed on seemingly unaffected and directed absolutely no condemnation at her fool of a boyfriend. I, meanwhile, was furious with my stupidity and promptly led us to another wrong valley.

It was no surprise that we finished the day in the dark and the rain. It had been fantastic weather up here for the past fortnight by all accounts. The weather didn't matter much to me at the moment though. All I wanted was the space in which to walk.

The following day gave me more of the isolation I craved. Even from the map it was clear that the 23-mile walk to Achahoish would be infinitely more remote than walking to Ardroshaig via the Crinan Canal. Coupled with the fact that 23 miles would hopefully scratch a strong itch to really exert myself, the shorter of the two options was discarded.

I was conscious that I was also subjecting Lyndsey to these extra unnecessary miles, but her enthusiasm for the walk never seemed to waiver. She was just happy to be out there walking; distance and direction were immaterial.

Walking 23 miles along a road is wearing both on the soles and on the soul. By the time we reached Achahoish that night, we were shattered. As we neared our destination, it seemed every step we took sent a jolt of pain from the balls of our feet into our shins and up to our hamstrings and lower back. It felt like torture by reflexology.

We had to hitch a lift from Achahoish back to Ardroshaig where Bridget

Oatts had dropped our luggage. It is always a great tribute to a place if it instils in you a sense that thumbing a lift will be no problem whatsoever. The feeling was justified. The second car we saw pulled over.

Despite my prevailing mindset, when I awoke the next morning the prospect of 25 miles did not have me leaping out of bed for the shower. In spite of my best efforts, I succeeded in catching the 7.20 a.m. bus back to Achahoish. Lyndsey, who was now sporting more blisters than she had toes, was going to take the luggage on to Tarbert and meet me later.

Without realising it at the time, I clocked up my 2,000th mile of Coastin' at about the point where I saw a large seal on a rock beyond Ormsary. It was a reflection of how my feelings towards the walk had altered that it took me two days to realise this. Even then it meant nothing. It was as if all the spirit that had got me this far had been sapped out of me. I was now just a walking automaton. Inside there was nothing.

The more I thought about the events of the past two weeks, the faster I walked. Subconsciously, I was pushing myself to the limits in the hope that physical discomfort would outweigh the horror of Dad's death.

Lyndsey joined me with about ten miles remaining. Her happy chatter and enthusiasm raised my spirits, giving me the impetus needed to complete the day. Five miles short of Tarbert, I realised that I had pushed myself too hard. To compound the situation, my drugs kicked out and a pronounced limp revealed itself. For the remainder of the day, my body ignored any messages it was sent. The final two miles were tortuously slow.

There was no shout of "Fore!" as the golf ball ricocheted out of a small clump of trees just a few feet away from us. It would have made a fitting end to the day to be knocked out cold by a golf ball. I raised my hand to wave at the golfers to show I was OK and just limped on. The perpetrator of the near miss looked distinctly worried as he approached his ball and saw me staggering away from the scene.

"I think you hit him, Hamish!" I overheard his companion saying.

I immediately tried to ease Hamish's conscience by waving at him to show that I had not been hit. Unfortunately my Parkinson's would not allow my hand to unclench so that my friendly wave was interpreted as an angry shake of the fist. Hamish responded to this gesture, not with an apology, but with a furious and unintelligible tirade. Parkinson's is a breeding ground for misunderstandings such as this.

The B&B in Tarbert was a welcome sight. I had covered 70 miles in three days and this, combined with the mental and emotional fatigue, conspired to take me to a point close to total exhaustion. I did not even have the strength to go out to eat that night. Instead, I lay on my bed attempting in vain to relax and only managing to toss and turn feverishly before drifting into a disturbed sleep of grinding teeth and unintelligible murmurings.

The following day, similar noises were to be heard escaping from the mouth of the rather grumpy bus driver who reluctantly agreed to transport our luggage to the ferry at Claonaig. It was here that we would cross over to the Isle of Arran, which would be used as a stepping stone across to the Ayrshire coast.

From the west, the Isle of Arran rises steeply out of the sea in a series of interlocking slabs of rock, which meet in almost perfect symmetry at an apex in the centre of the island. The apex is Goat Fell, which at 2,867 feet (874 metres) is the highest peak for over 40 miles in any direction.

I should have been excited at my first sight of Arran, not just because of the view, but also because it signified a change in scenery and the culmination of yet another stage of the walk. But I had never felt gloomier. Despite having started back on the Coastin' trail the most determined man alive, in five days I had punished myself so much that I was now experiencing totally different emotions. In five days, the intensity of my walking and my thinking had reduced me to apathy. "Why was I doing this? What was it all for? Did any of it matter in the least?" For the moment, I couldn't find the answers to any of these questions. I felt so morose, my whole body seemed to be scowling and my face seemed to curve inwards as if it were becoming concave in shape; as if I would never smile again.

As the car ferry chugged across the Kilbrannan Sound, the mountain peaks on Arran were bathed in a dramatic golden light. I tried to puff my chest out and take some big gulps of air in an attempt to blast away the burdens that seemed to be sucking all the energy and motivation out of me. But the recovery was brief. Having reached Lochranza, I sat in stony-faced silence and watched Lyndsey eat her meal in a local hotel that night. My own plateful had been pushed away in disgust and I was wallowing in self-pity. Even Lyndsey's bubbly chatter couldn't remove the thunderous expression from my face. Nor did I even find any humour in the fact that a Japanese man at the bar was slowly working his way through a shot of every variety of whisky known to man. And there was not even the glimmer of a grin to cross my lips when a rather upmarket-sounding English gentleman broke into loud and spontaneous song, having presumably completed the task the Japanese man was attempting.

I am not a big one for getting things off my chest. A good therapy for me that night would have been to shout and scream or to punch the drunk at the bar, who by that time would not have noticed anyway. But instead, I let it fester inside me and I became reclusive, self-absorbed, horrible.

"I'm sorry. I'm really sorry," I said to Lyndsey. "There's absolutely nothing you can do to cheer me up tonight. I'm just in an awful mood."

"That's OK," she said softly. The same words and intonation that were used when I told her I had Parkinson's.

I smiled at her weakly. I already felt a little bit better. She was giving so much. Everyone was giving to me.

Outside the clamour of the hotel it was a perfect evening. At any other time, it would have been the ideal opportunity to sit on the shoreline and listen to the haunting horn-like bellows of the rutting stags that drifted down the valleys in the relative safety of darkness. But on this particular night, all I could think about were my own misfortunes. These were some of my lowest moments of Coastin'.

Above anything else I needed sleep; but nothing was going my way at the moment. At 2 a.m. I was awoken by some raucous behaviour going on outside. Still semi-conscious, I wondered whether the Japanese man and the Englishman had joined forces and were either now performing some strange, whisky-induced wailing or were involved in a highly competitive game of synchronised vomiting. But there were too many voices. It had to be a stag night in order for there to be so much noise.

Lying awake listening to the testosterone-fuelled baying going on outside, I felt sick. I wondered how long I could go on like this. How long before my resolve to make up lost time would snap? It was ironic to feel sick at a stag night at which I was not even present. They were making some pretty strange noises out there. And then it dawned on me. This was no ordinary stag night. This was the original version... with real stags!

Leaving Lochranza the next morning, I knew that I did not have long before my drugs would kick out, because there was a tingling sensation in the back of my neck, and a sense of slight unease in the pit of my stomach. Then the first sign would be in the tips of my fingers before gradually the tingling would become a dramatic tremor of epileptic proportions. I found the only way to stop it would be to go into a sort of semi-conscious state of total relaxation; like a temporary hibernation. Today though, I felt I had to keep moving because if I stopped, I was not sure whether I would have either the physical momentum or the mental motivation to get going again. As I shambled up the mountain pass towards Laggan, I felt my rate of progress dwindle as my limp was exacerbated by my failing medication. After half an hour of battling up the hill, the Parkinson's gremlins finally overpowered me and I slumped to the ground.

"Stop fighting it and just relax for half an hour." Lyndsey looked concerned, which meant that I must have looked pretty bad.

I must have been asleep for no more than five minutes, but when I regained consciousness it was as if I had undergone a complete metamorphosis. Just five minutes of sleep had once again not only restored my ability to move in a co-ordinated and controlled manner, but had also somehow revitalised my energy levels and sense of purpose.

The improvement was nothing short of miraculous and made me wonder whether my Parkinson's might be cured if this component in my brain that brought about such a change by a little sleep could just be identified.

Bolstered by such a radical improvement in my health, Lyndsey and I enjoyed the walk along springy cliff-top turf to Laggan and on to Sannox. The sombreness of recent days seemed suddenly to be blown away by the bracing sea wind.

But having reached Sannox our buoyant moods were immediately subjected to a serious test. We should perhaps have anticipated the worst when we arrived in the car park to find three sets of toilets: one marked "Gentlemen"; another marked "Ladies"; and the final one (which was in an appalling state of repair) with the word "Invalids" emblazoned on it. I took a picture of this wonderful relic of political incorrectness and wondered how on earth it had survived into the 21st century. I realised how lucky I am to have Parkinson's in a modern era when the word "invalid" had been invalidated; perhaps the only word in the English language to commit suicide. Personally, I don't care what anyone calls me. It's not important unless it affects the way they communicate with me. I am always astonished when people get so het up about words. There is a strong lobby group in support of the idea that "Parkinson's disease" should simply be called "Parkinson's." The word "disease" apparently suggests that the illness might be contagious.

"Who cares?" is what I say; let's devote our energies to curing Parkinson's, instead of semantics.

Lyndsey and I entered the small cafe close to the car park jauntily. All that was needed was a bread roll in which Lyndsey would put a few rashers of bacon left over from breakfast. Having queued for some time, we arrived at the counter and saw a huge dish stacked full with buttered rolls – exactly what was needed.

"I'll have one of those bread rolls please," said Lyndsey.

"What would you like in it?" The man behind the counter was surly and I noticed his face was concave like mine had been the day before.

"Can I have the roll with nothing in it please?"

"No."

"I'm sorry?"

"No, you can't have a roll with nothing in it. What filling would you like?"

"But I don't want a filling."

"Well, you can't have a bread roll then."

It was at this stage that I felt the urge to enter the discussion. It was a mistake.

"How much do you want for a bread roll on its own then?" Perhaps I came across like some sort of bread roll tycoon who thought he could buy his way into any bread roll negotiations, or perhaps it was just my English accent. Either way Mr Bread Roll was clearly enraged by my presumption that I would be able to purchase one of his coveted buttered rolls "at a price".

"We do not sell bread rolls on their own," said Mr Bread Roll definitively.

And that was that.

I looked around at the queue behind in the hope of securing moral support from the other customers. To my astonishment, there was an air of impatience and even a sense that Lyndsey's initial request had been positively impudent.

With the bread roll man now already serving the next customer, we were forced to slope out of the cafe without even so much as a crumb for all our efforts. We were unsure whether to be furious or to descend into fits of giggles; so we remained dumbfounded.

"What is it about you Scottish and your bread rolls?" I said to Lyndsey. In Edinburgh, they couldn't stop giving you bread rolls and here in the west, they were clearly a great delicacy.

The idea had been to meet Lyndsey's brother-in-law, Roddy, at the "Saddle" of Goat Fell, the highest peak on the Isle of Arran, and then, having successfully "bagged" it, to trundle down into Brodick. Just as we commenced our march up Glen Sannox, there was a bleep on my phone. It was a message from Roddy.

"I'm at the Saddle. Cloud cover is at 500. Do not come up Glen Sannox. There is too steep a climb up to the Saddle on slippery rocks. Not worth going up Goat Fell as can't see a thing anyway. Repeat, do not come up Glen Sannox."

Normally, when faced with someone telling me not to do something, I have a tendency to do it anyway. But I decided that anyone who used the phrase "Cloud cover at 500" would probably know what they were talking about. I was also slightly in awe of his staccato, minimalist approach to communicating on answering machines. The mere fact that not a single word was wasted gave the message enormous credibility. Even though I had never met Roddy and very badly wanted to scale Goat Fell, I was tempted to heed his advice. Besides, if a goat fell then so could I.

"What does Roddy do?"

"He's a policeman." This fact made the decision a lot easier. We made an immediate about turn and resigned ourselves to the long road walk around the coast to Brodick. It was here we eventually met up with Roddy, who proceeded to single-handedly convey our entire luggage (and his own) as a pedestrian passenger on the ferry to Ardrossan. He seemed completely indifferent to the enormity of this task.

The following morning we left Arran bound for the Ayrshire coast ourselves. It was 30th September. Back in Melvich on the north coast of Scotland at the beginning of August, I had thought that leaving the Isle of Arran would signify the end of many things: the end of summer; the end of the mountains; the end of there being no people around; but most of all I had assumed that reaching Ayrshire would mean that I had completed "the best bit" – the best coastal scenery that Great Britain had to offer. Little did I realise at the time that the ferry journey from Brodick to Ardrossan would actually represent the end of "the worst bit" for me. I no longer felt a desire to punish myself so much. It would be a slow process, but the full force of Dad's death was beginning to wane as I entered a gentler, less extreme period of recovery.

Stepping out onto the tarmac from the ferry heralded a rude awakening. Ardrossan, as its name suggests, is not the most picturesque of places. Not since Kirkcaldy on the Fife coastline had I passed through such an unwelcoming town.

But there was no use whingeing about it. I had had my fair share of memorable moments. It was time to press onwards. It was time to put our heads down and just walk. We set about our task in earnest and with purposeful stride Lyndsey and I swept through the likes of Saltcoats and Stevenston without really pausing for breath.

For the preceding three months in Scotland, I had felt a welcome guest. It now seemed that people were no longer pleased to see us and we registered in people's minds as "strangers with rucksacks", and not "people to be greeted and spoken to". It was noticeable that passers-by now avoided any kind of eye contact with us. It struck me how much more pleasant an environment it is when there is mutual acknowledgment between passers-by. There is something quite fulfilling and life-enriching about a warm hello from someone whom you have never met before, but whose path just happens to cross with your own.

I realised that the past few months we had been travelling through areas of outstanding beauty reserved largely for people to enjoy in their leisure time. Now we were walking through places where the harsh reality of life was only too apparent. These were areas where the buildings, the streets and even the people seemed to evoke a sense of decay.

The presence of the River Garnoch and its estuary had made a circuitous journey inland necessary so as to get back to the coast at Irvine Bay. Upon our arrival at the seashore again, I could scarcely believe my eyes. A bridge. A nice spanking new shiny bridge had been built right at the estuary of the river and was not on the map. Had we known about this, we would have had a pleasant beach stroll from Ardrossan instead of toiling through decaying industrial zones.

"Never mind, you'll know for next time." Lyndsey's attempts to soothe failed to appease me.

And so it was that having been really rather pleased with our progress, I was now distinctly displeased. Had we known of the existence of the bridge we could easily have been in Troon by now. As it was, Troon was still a good two hours away.

The walk round the bay was a pleasant one along wide, open sands. It made me see the funny side of the new Garnoch Estuary Bridge. So many times previously on the walk I had been relying on a bridge shown on a map only to find that on the ground it did not exist. Now it was the other way around and I realised that this was far worse!

We were tired by the time we reached Troon but ploughed on after lunch along the beach. I found myself biting my fist as we passed golf course after glorious golf course; every one of them immaculate and steeped in golfing history.

Ayrshire is an odd place: a paradox in terms of scenery, architecture and wealth. One minute you can be walking through run-down housing estates or seedy threatening dockyards overflowing with pollution and a sense of malevolence; the next you can find yourself walking alongside the pristine velvety fairways of Troon or Turnberry where fat Americans in Rupert the Bear trousers unfurl great wads of banknotes for distribution to wily old caddies with creased leathery faces. It seemed whatever the walking environment through which we were passing, Lyndsey and I were inappropriately dressed, and we hurried on until exhaustion took its hold in Prestwick.

Although I had still not been feeling myself for the past few days, the next couple of nights improved things - they were to be spent free of charge in the lap of luxury. The first night was a stay at the Montgreenan House Hotel where the bedroom was so big that not even my exploding rucksack made an impact on the floor space. We had been given the Honeymoon Suite. The four-poster bed was a room in itself, the bath the size of an olympic swimming pool; Lyndsey spent hours in there, and when she came out, wrapped snugly in a thick towelling robe, she seemed to be glowing.

"Relaxed?" I asked.

"Not really," she said, "I've just done a hundred lengths!"

The following day we found ourselves at the even more prestigious Turnberry Hotel. We felt self-conscious as we tramped through the immaculate grounds looking like a couple of destitute backpackers and caked in mud from head to toe. When we came face to face with the doorman, we were surprised that he welcomed us with a warm smile and directed us to the check-in desk. Here we stood dripping on the pristine marble floor. Our appearance was of no consequence to the staff at the Turnberry Hotel; we could have been visiting ambassadors by the way we were checked in and shown to our sumptuous suite.

After we had cleaned ourselves up, we were able to retrace our steps to reception by following the incriminating trail of mud we had left on the way up.

The luxury of staying at two first-class hotels in a row certainly did my mental state no harm. Since returning to Coastin', I had continued to grind myself down so that, physically, I was in pretty poor shape. Mentally, however, I was considerably better; the despair was slowly melting and there was a time and space for fond memories amidst all the wretchedness.

The walk from Prestwick to Ayr docks was equivalent to walking out of Buckingham Palace and down the Mall and suddenly finding yourself propelled by some trickery to the midst of the roughest part of the East End. We both immediately felt threatened, as if we were being watched. Our pace quickened and our gaze became fixed on the road ahead.

Ayr is an odd place. At first glance, it appears to be almost well-to-do, with its period buildings and bustling high street with all the normal multiple retailers. But lurking beneath the surface there is a darker side, one common with other towns on the west coast of southern Scotland. Unemployment is rife here, as are all the problems that come with it.

We sped on down to the beach and upon reaching the estuary to the River Doun, we curved in upstream for a mile or so and found the famous bridge "Brig o' Doun", where in Robert Burns's poem Tam-O-Shanter's horse only just made it across to avoid being caught by a terrible witch.

Culzean brought clear blue skies and a walk around to the castle that provided the best scenery we had experienced for days. I felt my fitness return and for the first time for what seemed like ages I was Coastin' once again rather than simply walking off the horror of losing Dad. And yet every day there were little reminders of him not being there. Every time my Mum rang me, I half expected the "clunk" of the other phone being picked up when Dad realised that she was talking to me.

If there were constant reminders for me, all the way out here on the west coast of Scotland, I could only imagine how unbearable it must be for the rest of my family who would have had many more things to spark memories of Dad and ignite the terrible cycle of thoughts surrounding the events of the past month. In a sense, I was dreading going home again, which I would have to do for the interment of Dad's ashes, as somehow his death would be more real there.

The gardens of Culzean Castle were stunning and we paused to admire them before continuing on a little cliff path through lovely woodland. Here there were superb views back over the coastline of Ayrshire and that well-known huge slab of granite protruding like an upended ice-cream cone straight out of the depths of the Irish Sea. The lonely, sheer-sided form of Ailsa Craig is a glorious sight when it is visible. It is said in these parts that when you can see Ailsa Craig it is about to rain and when you can't see Ailsa Craig it is already raining. "Nonsense!" I snorted.

It was just beyond Turnberry that the storm came in from the west. I had not been prepared for the speed of it. Without warning, the skies suddenly turned very dark, the clouds billowed and thunder cracked. The heavens opened and the teeming rain was upon me as I frantically battled with protective garments. The problem with my high-tech equipment was that though highly specified in terms of breathability, water resistance and durability, all of this came to nought if you didn't get the blooming stuff on in time.

The storm only lasted five minutes. It had taken me four minutes to get suitably dressed. The aftermath was spectacular and despite being drenched I basked in the glorious after-storm sunshine complete with dramatic rainbow. I decided that this was my favourite time to walk; in the wake of a storm when everything seemed fresh, new and sparkling as if it had all just been through a car wash.

Lyndsey went home at Girvan. Her support, encouragement and enthusiasm since starting Coastin' again had guided me to a point where I could begin to enjoy parts of the walk once more. Over the past two weeks Coastin' had become more like Rollercoastin', due to the massive swings in my physical and emotional state. I thought how odd it was that during this most terrible of times for me, there was undoubtedly a strengthening of the feelings that Lyndsey and I had for one another. She had been there for me through this ordeal every step of the way as if she had been part of the family. I smiled at the train of thought. Was this the beginning of a sense of commitment? I had never had one of those before.

Alone, I set off on the A77, which hugs the coast from Girvan. There is little option for the coastal walker but to follow it to Lendalfoot and then on to Ballantrae. Rather like a schoolboy avoiding cracks in the pavement, I became quite determined in my attempts not to walk along the main road. If there was a path, beach or field as an alternative, even if the route was a far more protracted way of reaching the same destination, I would take it.

At Ballantrae, I cut inland and followed tracks and minor roads over exposed barren moorland to the Lochinch Estate, from where I struck out west towards Portpatrick.

Portpatrick is nestled between cliffs west of Stranraer and occupies a position on the map at the centre left of "The Rhins", which is that vast fishtail-like peninsula stuck out at the western extremity of Dumfries and Galloway.

Exploring Portpatrick's harbour was a very pleasant experience, even though there was an icy cold wind coming off the Irish Sea that cut right through me. It was a reminder that winter was drawing ever closer. The town has a colourful jumble of well-maintained period buildings cosily assembled round a stone dock from which, on a clear day, Ireland is visible.

Portpatrick marks the start of the Southern Upland Way from the west. It seemed a lifetime ago that I had walked the final section of this 212-mile footpath on the east coast to Cockburnspath – and I suppose, in one sense, it was exactly that.

I pulled my coat tightly around me, more in protection against further soul-searching than against the cold. The cliff path from Portpatrick to Blackhead lighthouse on a blustery but clear day soon stirred my blood into an enthusiastic froth. I realised how much I had missed the soaring cliffs and the waves that crashed against them, and I felt energised by the gusts of wind that buffeted my face almost playfully.

The lighthouse was impressive. In immaculate white, it stood proud and exposed. It seemed indomitable, indifferent to the constant battering from the elements. It was here I turned inland and realised I would not be this far west again until I reached the Lleyn peninsula in Wales.

Once past the sweep of Killantringan Bay, the Southern Upland Way followed minor roads and tracks almost all the way to Chlenry. Strange place and house names leapt out at me as I walked, such as Knock and Maze, Knockquhassen, Meikle Mark and Spout Wells.

It was just beyond Ochtrelure that I was joined by a fellow-traveller whom I later named Eric. Eric looked a bit shoddy and he seemed to glare, unblinking, with a manic look in his eye. But when he approached and started walking down the lane with me, he seemed friendly enough and I had no reason to doubt his good intentions. After all, I had never been befriended by a pheasant before.

It was an extraordinary feeling walking down a road side by side with a pheasant. When I stopped, Eric stopped; and when I turned to the brightly coloured bird and asked him what he thought he was doing, he just stared back at me with his big bulbous eyes. It was a little unnerving. And yet when

I set off again, he followed; three or four steps to my one. I have video evidence to prove it.

For half a mile this went on and I was beginning to wonder whether Eric might be joining me for the remainder of Coastin'. It would certainly be good publicity: one man and his pheasant walking around Britain in the hope of curing Parkinson's disease. I even began worrying that he might steal my thunder. I could see the headlines now, "Eric the Pheasant says Parkinson's is a fowl disease"; "Eric arrives at the Millennium Bridge in triumph"; "'I didn't fly any of it,' says Eric".

But just as I was beginning to think that it would actually be quite fun to have a pheasant to accompany me on my journey, Eric shot ahead in the road in front of me, blocking my way. I stopped in my tracks and wondered what was going to happen next.

I had not anticipated that one of the biggest dangers to my life on Coastin' would be a pheasant; but when Eric launched his attack on me, all beak, wings and claws, I saw my life flash before me. It was the shock of it that made his assault so effective. One moment he had been Eric, the pleasant pheasant, joining me for a bit of a stroll. The next he was trying to kill me.

I pushed Eric away easily enough, and for a moment he sprawled on the tarmac. I seized the opportunity to try to sidestep past him. But Eric was quicker than a roadrunner and stronger than an ostrich. Hissing, spitting and splaying his wings, Eric launched himself at me for a second time. Once again, I batted him off and then for a moment there was silence as we stood in the middle of the road facing one another; two beasts locked in mortal combat.

It was at that moment that I received a phone call. It was Q. Keeping my eyes fixed firmly on the winged predator, I started speaking.

"Hello Q. I am glad you rang. I am currently being attacked by a pheasant. Any ideas?"

All I could hear was snorting and giggles at the other end. What's the use of having a Q if she hasn't got a pheasant-defence mechanism? And her laughing was really not helping one little bit. I hung up. Apologised to Eric for the intrusion and returned to the heat of battle.

Then I remembered that I did have a gadget: my walking stick, which I had not been using today. I reached behind me to the straps of my rucksack and unsheathed Ewan. He glistened black in the sunlight.

"Aahh, not so brave now then, are we?"

I really said this. It was quite gutsy.

I saw Eric take two steps backwards. He was retreating... no, he was taking a run-up.

For a third time Eric came at me, but on this occasion I was ready. Eric received a large prod from Ewan and was knocked sideways, leaving a gap through which I ran. And believe you me, I ran. Behind me I heard the furious beating of wings and I knew that Eric was in hot pursuit. I turned to face him with Ewan drawn in front of me. Eric stopped and the psychotic look in his eyes softened. He was beaten. He knew it. The duel of Ochtrelure was over.

Slipping Ewan back into his holster, I swaggered off into the setting sun wondering if anyone would believe what had just happened. I could scarcely believe it myself.

* * *

I met Alistair Smidgeon-Peacock in the driveway of his farmhouse B&B. This was not his real name, but it is not far off!

"Ah, you must be Isaacs."

"Tom," I replied, holding out my hand and then wincing whilst it was squashed like a tomato somewhere within the confines of his enormous military grip.

Smidgeon-Peacock was hugely welcoming to me and ever so slightly patronising. He found out pretty quickly what I was doing and immediately launched into a monologue about his own charity which he had set up for war veterans. I asked him why he had chosen this particular cause, to which he replied: "We all do what we can, don't we? My view is that he (pointing upwards) is watching us all the time and therefore we must do our very best."

It was not quite the answer I was expecting, but I was nevertheless highly impressed by his constant references to God, even if he was a touch on the sanctimonious side.

Smidgeon-Peacock recommended the local pub for a meal and kindly picked me up afterwards.

"The food was fantastic in there," I enthused.

"Really?" he replied with genuine surprise, "thought the place was dreadful last time I went – steak like old shoe leather."

"Thanks for recommending the place then..." I thought.

"I tell you, it will be quite some bloody feat when you finish this here walk of yours," continued Smidgeon-Peacock.

"Quite some bloody 'feet' is about right; you should see my blisters." It was a tried and tested joke. It usually got a smirk at the most, but on this occasion, I seemed to have struck gold. Smidgeon-Peacock could barely control himself with laughter. In fact, he guffawed so loudly we nearly swerved off the road into an early bloodbath which was unlikely to be restricted to my feet.

I couldn't decide whether I liked Smidgeon-Peacock or not. I noticed that he avoided talking about my Parkinson's. I don't think he could quite get his head round why I was so open about it. I reflected that if he had the illness he would have kept it secret for as long as possible: considering it a weakness; a flaw in his character. I had noticed similar traits in others of that age group. Once again, I realised how in many ways I was lucky to be part of a generation in which illness and disability no longer meant you had to go to the toilets marked "Invalids".

The accommodation at the Smidgeon-Peacock farmhouse was traditional. It was one of those places where the basins are the size of baths, and the baths are the size of small battleships. In my room, my bed was huge and so bowed in the middle that it reminded me of the bed belonging to the father bear in Goldilocks. When I got into it, I found myself rolling down and down into its warm but murky depths and enveloped by layer upon layer of sheets, blankets, electric blankets, eiderdowns and bed covers. In fact, so heavy and so warm and so deep was the bed, it was as if Father Bear himself was lying on top of me. I went to sleep worrying that with my usual lack of mobility in the morning, I might have to call for help to release me from this horrific fairy tale.

I did manage to prise myself free in the morning and proceeded to drink a litre of water with my first pill of the day to rehydrate myself after all the effort. I padded along to the communal bathroom only to find that the door did not have a lock. I had planned to run the bath and to swim a few lengths of it prior to breakfast, but having wrestled with the enormous stopcock to release a dribble of hot water, I gave up. The combination of the fact that the bath would probably not have filled before the end of time, and the fact that even if it did someone was bound to walk in at either the precise moment of entrance to or exit from the bath, made me consider my other options. I returned to my room and had my bath in my basin instead.

When I left Smidgeon Peacock, he gave me a slap on the back and for a moment looked quite choked and emotional. "Good luck and God be with you."

I couldn't bring myself to say "God be with you as well" back at him. I suspected that he was pretty confident that God was already very much with him. He was a strange mixture and reminded me of a swashbuckling hero from a Wilbur Smith book on the Boer War. Half religious zealot, half terribly British gent and perhaps a smidgin peacock.

\* \* \*

Much of the walk through Dumfries and Galloway was spent on old military roads and dismantled railway lines. I had originally planned to follow the coast more closely, but being way behind schedule, I decided to adopt a straighter line heading through Newton Stewart, Creetown, Gatehouse of Fleet and Dumfries.

It was an unremarkable section of the walk. The weather was fairly miserable, which precluded too much hanging about anywhere. I decided that the best policy was simply to get on with the walking. I did this exceptionally well but it was more than balanced by an uncanny habit of choosing paths that were impossible to follow, didn't exist or led into impenetrable jungle. For three days in a row I finished walking in the dark. If ever there was a time when I felt lonely on Coastin', this was it. But the word "lonely" never actually entered my head on the entire journey.

Q visited for a few days. She had been amazing since Dad died. It was a huge comfort to me to know that all the commitments which had been made on the strength of my original itinerary had been reorganised and that I did not have to concern myself with ensuring that I did not let anyone down. With help from the Parkinson's Disease Society, Q had sorted out everything without any fuss at all. We chatted while we walked and made plans for the second half of Coastin'.

It was difficult to believe that I was only halfway. I seemed to have been walking for ever. Any day now when I was not getting up and walking seemed decidedly odd. I thought the second half of the journey would probably feel quicker – it certainly had done on John O'Groats to Land's End. But this time it would actually have to *be* quicker. By the time Q took me back down to London for the interment of my father's ashes, and taking into account planned days off for Christmas, a wedding in Thailand, and a few other essential events, I only had 150 days to complete a further 2,275 miles.

Just over 15 miles per day was certainly achievable in the summer, but was it really achievable during the dark winter months, and could I really go without any "extra" days off? I felt quite sick at the thought of not making it back to London in time and decided to invest in a large head-torch so I could partake of some clandestine night walking.

Despite the pressure of time, I was pleased to be going back home to see my family again, even if it was just for one day. There had been a sense of guilt when I had first returned to Coastin' at the end of September. It felt a bit as if I was running away from the responsibility of it all; deserting them for my own selfish ends. But I also knew that they and Dad would have wanted me to continue. Besides, the family were tough in a crisis and my brother was infinitely more capable than me at sorting out Dad's affairs.

While I was back and staying at my family home in Hertfordshire, I discovered that a sum of £8,000 had been donated instead of flowers at Dad's funeral. It was an extraordinary amount of money and testimony to his popularity.

The words inscribed on the plate where Dad's ashes were interred were "Counsellor, Gentleman, Friend". It summed him up. We huddled round the little plot in the cemetery staring at the words and Dad's name above them. All I could think of was that Dad would have so hated being dead. He was too alive to be dead. And this little nameplate and his ashes beneath it really meant nothing to me. Dad was gone. There was nothing left of him.

I could see the rest of my family felt the same. This place would hold no special memory of Dad, because flowers, graves and death had nothing to do with him when he had been alive. The brief ceremony did serve an important purpose for all of us though: it was way of saying a final goodbye.

Gretna Green
Carlisle
Scafell Pike 24th october
Lake District
Seatoller
Grange-over-Sands
Morecambe Bay
Lancaster
Blackpool
Preston
Mersey
Liverpool 6th November
the Wirral
FAIR GROUND
POPCORN

CHAPTER 23

I looked forward to getting back to England for lots of reasons, but one of the things I was most looking forward to was that I would be back in the realm of the "public footpath". The right to roam in Scotland is only good in so far as "roaming" is physically possible. To move between two points on foot without interference or obstruction by barbed wire, peat bog, motorised vehicles, wild beasties and, of course, large men in skirts shooting at you because they think you're a wild beastie, would be joyous.

It was inevitable, I suppose, that before I crossed the border, Scotland had one final trick up its sleeve.

Mum had joined me on Coastin' for about ten days. We all hoped that a bit of sea air and exercise would do her no end of good. We left Annan and took a coastal path along from Battlehill right on the edge of the Solway Firth. On the map the path was shown very clearly and it looked an ideal way to progress almost all the way to Gretna. I had learned a long time ago that the old Chinese saying, "All paths lead somewhere", did not apply in Scotland, but you still don't expect a route which has clearly been well trodden to suddenly disappear before your eyes.

What lay ahead of us seemed to be impenetrable. There was a tiny gap which was lined with thorns, creepers, thistles and nettles. I winced at the thought of having to go through the gap, especially as there was no guarantee of there being any daylight on the other side. I might well have done it on my own, as I was feeling strong, but I was concerned about Mum.

"We had better turn back."

"Really?" she responded.

"There is no way through."

Mum looked at me.

"We can't go back," she said, and with these words she marched headlong into the tentacles of the prickly jungle that lay ahead.

"Follow me!" she ordered, without bothering to see if I was.

I did not see her for a good fifteen minutes after this, but I knew she was near because every now and then there would be a loud yelp and then a little chuckle When I eventually broke into the clear she was sitting triumphantly on a wall administering plasters to various parts of her body. She was caked in mud and blood, and seemed to be wearing a blackberry bush. I limped half-heartedly towards her.

"Wasn't that tremendous?" she said.

For a moment I questioned her sanity, but then I recognised something in her manner. Her determination, her stubbornness were my own. It was the same way that I had felt when starting back on Coastin' after dad's death – a grim determination to prevail.

There was more of this type of walking to come, so that we only covered just over 2 miles in three hours. The route was a disaster, no one in their right mind would have persevered with it; but this mother and son were united in their resolve and in their tenacity. Our success in forging a path through the most difficult terrain that the Solway Firth could throw at us was completely irrational but utterly satisfying.

* * *

The border with England lies just past Gretna and follows the line of the River Sark. It seemed like an appropriate place to celebrate the halfway point. This involved considerable jumping up and down and punching the air. I was not sure what else I could do. The actions didn't really matter. It was just a great feeling to have made it this far, to have walked the entire coastline of Scotland. Having Mum there to witness it after everything that had happened made it all the sweeter.

After all my excited ranting about footpaths, there wasn't one to be seen to take me across the River Esk. This made entering the north-west corner of England on foot a dangerous affair. It involved tiptoeing along the inside of the crash barrier of the A74, a road where the life expectancy for the average walker is estimated at 22 minutes. I did it in 18 just to be sure.

My return to England put me back in familiar territory. Walking in places which were familiar to me, even though I was only halfway, actually made me feel like I was almost on the home straight. It was ridiculous really with five and a half months still to go. After all, there was still the north-west and south-west corners of England, the whole of the south coast and Kent to be walked. Oh yes. And Wales.

Having received a good send-off from a Parkinson's Disease Society group in Carlisle, Mum and I set off to cover the flat lands of northern Cumbria as quickly as possible. For a while we followed the course of Hadrian's Wall on the strange straight road which ran between Burgh by Sands and Drumburgh. After this, it was a case of grinding out mile after mile of long quiet roads and fields, many of which gave us pleasant views back over the Solway Firth, where we had forged a way through the jungles of southern Scotland. Having been so relieved by the fact that I was now back in the realm of the public footpath, I was unimpressed with some of the signposts for the Cambrian coastal way, which literally had us going round in circles for a while. On one occasion we climbed over a fence and ended up walking through someone's back garden. There was nothing for it but to be absolutely blatant about it. A young man was mowing the lawn and seemed completely nonplussed by our appearance.

"Sorry, we're lost!" I shouted at him over the noise of the mower.

"You're in my parents' back garden!" he shouted back, smiling, before stopping the machine.

"I would take you through the kitchen," he said, "but you're a bit, well, muddy." Instead he led us to a gate from where he pointed to his driveway and the public highway beyond.

"You obviously get this all the time," I said.

"As a matter of fact, you're the first to be found actually in the garden."

"Oh – sorry!"

I was on my own by the time I reached Newton Arlosh. Accommodation was scarce in this area and Mum had gone off in her car to the metropolis of Silloth in the hope of finding a B&B.

On the whole, my Parkinson's had withstood recent setbacks incredibly well. In fact, I noticed that there had been no particular deterioration in my health over the summer months' walking. I knew from previous years that the winter seemed to make it worse and I was concerned how it might affect me over the coming months.

Masking the shaking hands and the limp was often possible by shoving my hands in my pockets and remaining still. This is precisely what I tried to do when, upon walking down a quiet farm lane, I was confronted by a sizeable herd of dairy cows who were being directed by a farmer into the next field. Being cows, they were not in any particular hurry. Having waited for some considerable time, I found that I couldn't keep myself still and felt myself commence some fairly high-intensity wobbling.

As the farmer followed the last cows through a gate he regarded me with suspicion and only nodded a greeting.

"Hello," I said loudly. I wanted him to hear, to understand that I was a man of "good vibrations" and not some waggling weirdo.

"Are you all right?" he asked, as clearly I was in some difficulty.

"Yes, I'm fine. I have Parkinson's and I'm often waiting for my pills to work. But I'm being picked up in a moment anyway."

"Where are you trying to get to?"

I gave him my 15-second version of what I was doing.

"Good Lord, that's some feat," he said.

"Some feet is about right!"

He stared me for a moment as if he was waiting for the punchline. When nothing came, he went rushing off and leapt into the driving seat of a large tractor. Pulling out a small metal box, he emptied the contents into his hand and returned.

"Sorry, this is all I have at the moment." He put two pound coins into my hand. It was episodes such as this that made Coastin' the most rewarding experience – it was the spontaneous acts of generosity from complete strangers that reinforced my motivation. They gave me a very real sense of worth; a reason for it all. And yet there was also something sad about these moments too. In a perfect world, I would have liked to sit down and get to know this farmer; to find out the story behind the £2 gift. I had learnt along the way that there was so often a story. It was frustrating to have been on the receiving end of such kindness and then to just walk away.

Two minutes later, Mum passed the farm in search of me. She was driving slowly to ensure she did not miss any turns. The farmer and his wife had apparently seen the slow-moving vehicle and came rushing out of the farmhouse.

"Are you the lady with the incredibly brave son?"

Mum swelled with pride. It was a fantastic thing for her to hear in light of everything.

I was just about to be savaged by a large dog when Mum eventually picked me up. Having got into the car and marked on the map where to start from the next day, I noticed the place was called Raby.

"I think you picked me up just in time."

I was beginning to realise that my walking was actually not the most relaxing pastime for my mother so soon after Dad's death. Naturally, she worried when she saw me limping and shaking. The fact that she had rescued me just seconds before I had been torn to shreds by a rabid dog probably hadn't helped either. Certainly the walking had not come quite as smoothly as I had wanted, but I couldn't decide whether this was just normal or whether the problems I encountered seemed magnified because Mum was there. She was certainly not herself, although probably I would have been more concerned if she had been. She seemed as if she wasn't quite there; as if the real Mum was sorting itself out inside and would eventually reappear on the surface. I was pleased she seemed to be pulling her life together. She just needed time. We all did. I just wished I could avoid some of the dramas that were unfurling almost routinely every day.

When we entered a field full of bullocks, I heard the rumble as they started lumbering towards us, but I was confident we had enough time to make it to the gate at the far side.

"I think we had better start jogging," I said calmly. But I said it too calmly and Mum reacted slowly.

"Come on!" I said, a little more anxiously this time.

"What? Why?" she said.

I looked at Mum and then I looked at the flared nostril of the lead bullock. There was no time for explanations; that bullock wanted a couple of new trampolines.

"RUN!" I shouted, in some anguish. After all, I would have to be the last one over the fence and I hadn't come all this way to be run over by a bullock.

Puffing on the non-bullock side of the fence, I was concerned that my panic would have sparked a bad reaction in Mum. But once again, she just laughed. As long as it was her life and not mine that was being threatened there was no problem. I began wondering, if it had been a closer call with the bullocks, whether we would have stood at the fence and had a stand-up row about who should go over the fence first.

It had never been my intention to walk all the way down the Cumbrian coast. I just couldn't see the point in it. As long as I adhered to the rule of seeing the sea every day, I could afford quite extravagant forays into the Lake District proper. Even on the map there was no competition. The coastal route would have taken me through places such as Maryport, Distington, Workington, Rottington and Nethertown. Compare these names with my alternative route which would mean that I would travel through such mouthwatering places as Buttermere, Loweswater, Gatesgarth, Seathwaite and Cockley Beck. It would be just daft to miss out on these delights.

After the relative solitude and lack of media attention in Coastin' down the west coast of Scotland, every day in Cumbria there seemed to be something extra, other than the walk, going on. The local Parkinson's groups seemed particularly active here. Some came out in force just to cheer me on. Others came out to walk with us. The presence of these kind people helped me to reaffirm my motives for the walk and bit by bit I was recovering my perspective.

One Parkinson's sufferer in this region stood out head and shoulders above the others. In fact, it was difficult to think of anyone whose enthusiasm for Coastin' surpassed that of Ron "The Boss" Cowling.

Up to now, news of Ron's activities had been reaching me through the Parkinson's Disease Society, but having reached Silloth and started down the coast of West Cumbria I started wondering what the man would be like. He seemed to have been on the case from the very beginning and despite having quite advanced Parkinson's had left no stone unturned in pursuit of support for Coastin'.

My "Scotland the Brave" ring tone began its familiar bleeping. "I must get that changed," I thought, answering the call.

I couldn't understand a great deal of what was being said to me, but it was clear that it was Ron. Ron was someone else whose Parkinson's had affected his speech. His words ran into one another, becoming blurred and indistinct, but as soon as I spoke to him I recognised that Ron had the ability to communicate through sheer force of personality; through drive and enthusiasm for life.

Ron had decided to pay me a visit early so as to welcome me to Cowling country. He arrived in a big 4x4 Landcruiser, out of which appeared wives, daughters, grandchildren and pets. I would later discover that this was about the minimum entourage that Ron would have around him at any one time.

Eventually, the front offside door opened and, with some difficulty, Ron levered himself out of the car and attempted to summon up the momentum to set himself in motion. Once moving, he marched easily over towards me. I could see he had that familiar twinkle in his eye that I was beginning to become accustomed to from such people. He extended his hand towards me like a benevolent Mafia boss and I hope he will forgive me when I say that even with his Cumberland brogue, he sounded a bit like Marlon Brando.

He welcomed me enthusiastically. He didn't need to say much, because in my mind I had already imagined his opening gambit: "Welcome to my country. This is my family. Look around you. These are my people. If you want anything, you only have to ask."

Both Ron and his family walked with me for a little while and then they left. It dawned on me afterwards that the round trip from their home at the southern end of the Lake District was probably about 140 miles. I began to realise that nothing was going to be too much trouble for Ron "The Boss" Cowling and family.

Cutting inland from Allonby, the hills of the Lake District soon rose up before us and it wasn't long before Mum and I reached the Vale of Lorton. The autumn colours were in their prime now and higher up on the mountains there were even the first signs of winter. A thin layer of white, like a light dusting of icing sugar, had swept across the hilltops above the deep browns and terracotta of the trees. It was like being surrounded by huge chocolate fudge cakes. It was close to perfection.

By contrast, my health was going through a purple patch. But quite apart from these strange aubergine-coloured blotches that seemed to be slowly creeping up my ankles, I was in better fettle than I had been since the north-west Highlands. Fortunately, this coincided with my having to take on two very tough days.

Walking down the western shore of Crummock Water with Mum in gloriously random weather conditions was a terrific experience. Mum was leaving to go back home the next day and at last we had stumbled across some wonderful scenery for her to enjoy. At times, during the sunny periods, the vibrant burnt yellows and reds adorning the mountains around Buttermere made us just stop and stare. At Gatesgarth, Mum and I made a plan that we would meet up again at Seatoller Fell car park. Meanwhile, I had an ambitious idea to follow a ridge stretching between three peaks and down to Seatoller Fell at the top of the Honister Pass.

"If the weather's bad, I'll come back down and walk up the road. Whatever happens though I will meet you at Seatoller."

My mother was always incredibly helpful whenever she came to visit. Having a car available made the whole process of walking so much more flexible. There was no accommodation at Seatoller Fell, and yet I was able to finish my day there and come back the following morning.

I shudder to think of the number of car parks in which Mum has awaited my arrival whilst supporting me in long-distance walking challenges. She would expect me to be late. Despite my best intentions, I always seem to underestimate the time it will take to get anywhere. When it started growing dark at Seatoller Fell car park, however, Mum started to despair. As far as she was concerned, there was no way I would have turned back. The weather did not look too awful and, in any case, I never turned back. I should have been at the car park by now, and therefore I must be either stuck or lost up there.

Sick with worry, Mum had gone into the Slate Quarry Shop in the car park and had asked what she should do.

"My son is up on that mountain and it is getting dark."

The man in the shop started to shake his head and look up towards the gathering gloom on the mountain.

"It looks pretty rough up there. It's been snowing all afternoon. Which track was he on?"

"I've got the maps in the car on which he showed me where he was going." My mother turned to go and fetch them.

"Pretty soon it will be too dark to find him. I think we might need to consider calling for a search party," said the man encouragingly.

In the circumstances, this was not a particularly helpful statement. It was at this point, at any other time, that my mother would have remembered my final comment to her – in bad weather, I would walk up the road. But this was just over a month after Dad had died. It was not surprising that Mum assumed the worst.

As Mum left the shop in search of the map, her heart was pounding and her eyes filled with tears. "This simply cannot be happening," she thought in despair. It was at this moment that I arrived at the car park, a little puffed and red-faced, but without any concept of the latest high drama. "Hello!" I said cheerily. But I only had to take one look at my mother's face to realise what had happened. Her relief flooded out.

The fact was that I had been forced to turn back by the weather. At the top of the first mountain, Hay Stacks, a blizzard had come in from the north and visibility was down to about 25 yards. I had decided that the right thing to do for everyone was to turn back. Ironically, it was through being sensible that I had contrived to do the very thing I was trying hard not to do: to worry Mum.

We could have done with a quiet evening that night, but we had been asked to attend a meal with the local Parkinson's group. I felt tired and guilty and not very talkative. Someone had announced that I had come 2,350 miles to be with them that night. It rolled off his tongue as if I had driven it.

2,350 miles. They couldn't have any idea what it had been like. How could they?

A lady came up to me. "Did he say 2,350 miles?" I nodded grimly. "And you walked all that way?" Perhaps I was wrong. Perhaps they did understand. "Well, that must have taken you very nearly a week," she said. I could scarcely believe my ears.

I paused, trying to choose my words carefully. "Actually it's even longer than that."

"Oooh, is it?" she said admiringly. "And when will you be going back to work?"

"Probably next year some time."

"Yes, quite right, dear. Have some time off."

I had not thought about the subject of work for some time. On the north-west coast of Scotland I had been having too much fun to worry about going back to work, and in the last month, it had obviously been very low down on the list of things to think about. The mere mention of returning to an office upon my return to London pulled me up short. But right at that moment was not the place or the time to make decisions or even consider future plans. The matter was filed away in the "pending" section of my brain (along with cure, and being on time). I would need to think about my future when I had more time and space.

People tended to have preconceptions when I mentioned that my friend Emlyn Jones was coming to walk with me. The name Emlyn Jones conjures up an image of a steam-engine driver on the Ffestiniog Railway; or a footballer who plays right half for Wrexham; or an impressive tenor in a male voice choir from "the valleys". You might also expect that, though British, he might possibly speak a wonderful "other" language which bore no resemblance to English at all.

None of the above has anything to do with Emlyn, except maybe for the language part. He's a quantity surveyor from Newcastle. He speaks Geordie fluently; it is his only language.

You would think that my journey from Seatoller Fell to Seatoller to Seathwaite and then across mountains to another Seathwaite might incorporate, at some stage, a view of the sea. But this was by no means certain. In my quest for some fantastic walking, I had by now come quite a long way inland and today was my biggest gamble as far as seeing the sea was concerned. I was relying on the weather.

Today also brought my attempt at the second of my three mountains. Sca Fell Pike at 3,205 feet (977 metres) is the highest mountain in England, and yet it is shorter in stature than Ben Nevis at 4,406 feet (1,343 metres) and Snowdon at 3,560 feet (1,085 metres). I had chosen my company carefully for today, opting for someone who I knew had years of experience of walking in the Lakeland Fells. Emlyn had years and years of experience. In fact, it was said in surveying circles that he was as old as the mountains themselves.

In addition to Emlyn, Ron "The Boss" Cowling, through whose county I was still walking, had organised an attachment of army regulars to ensure my safe passage over the mountains. The fact that I had two guides for the day, when I actually felt rather indignant at the thought of needing any, contributed to the prospect of the day ahead being reduced to a battle of egos when it came to the map reading. To minimise this likelihood, I had asked Emlyn to work out the route. This he duly did using charts, compass and quill pen. The only problem I could foresee would be when the army recruits produced their assessment of the "right" way having used state-of-the-art global positioning satellite technology and digital cadastral surveys.

As it was, the army recruits did not show up at Seathwaite at the appointed time anyway. I was slightly annoyed by this and felt particularly sorry for Ron, who had spent so long organising for them to come with me. I couldn't wait. I was meeting Emlyn halfway up Sca Fell Pike; he having started his climb from the Great Langdale valley.

It was a pristine day and, in a sense, I was glad to have this time to myself, partly to reflect on the day before, but also to enjoy the views of the Lake District at its best.

Emlyn had a big cheesy grin on his face when we met just below Esk Hause. A mountain rendezvous above the snowline given my current form would surely be a recipe for disaster. But for once, everything went smoothly, and if Emlyn's grin was mild cheddar, mine would have been Gorgonzola.

From Esk Hause, it was only a mile or two and about 200 yards in altitude to the top of Sca Fell Pike, but the weather had turned and we found ourselves wading through deep snow with ever-decreasing visibility. Had I been on my own at this point, I might well have been forced to turn back, but Emlyn was unperturbed and pressed on confidently.

Four young men appeared out of the mist behind us. They seemed to be jogging. "Oh God, here comes the army," said Emlyn.

I was incredibly lucky. At the peak of Sca Fell Pike, the clouds lifted, providing views from the Solway Firth down to Morecambe Bay. I had been desperately worried about the prospect of not complying with my strict rules and it was ironic that the range of the view from on high probably allowed me to see more sea today than on any other day.

On the long walk back down the other side of the mountain to Cockley Beck, Emlyn's stamina began to waver. It was hardly surprising. Not only was he at least 30 years senior to the army boys, but he had also driven from Newcastle upon Tyne at 4 a.m. that morning and had already walked a much greater distance, having started his ascent from Dungeon Ghyll. Ever so slowly his grin faded and he started looking a bit despondent. As his pace slackened he began falling behind and he started suffering from a pain in his leg. Meanwhile, the soldiers were tearing around everywhere with seemingly boundless energy, so that Emlyn and I felt like a couple of sheep being herded down the mountain. As we reached the top of a pass beneath Bow Fell, Emlyn's fatigue began having an effect on his sense of humour, and with all four army regulars for a moment within earshot, he bellowed, "Will you stop charging around like a pack of bloody labradors!"

Of course, the only purpose this served was to ensure that the labradors pranced around even more. In fact, one of the privates strayed so far ahead that his lance corporal was forced to connect thumb and index finger together and release a most impressive whistle. The private came bounding back and was scolded roundly in front of all of us.

Emlyn stepped gingerly down the steep slopes of Bow Fell. Meanwhile, I decided that I too could be a labrador and started a steady trot down the slope, trying to keep a momentum going to reduce the strain on my knees. I felt I was doing rather well and became conscious of the fact that I was being observed by a couple of the army recruits, who were sitting eating a sandwich. No sooner had I realised I was being watched than I took a nasty tumble, rolled a couple of times and then, extraordinarily, I appeared to be back on my feet again. I seized the opportunity to continue a few more steps to give the impression that the whole thing had been intended in the first place – but of course it looked like nothing of the sort. With only my pride hurt and a slight twinge in my dodgy knee, I realised what a lucky escape I'd had. A stupid fall like that could have jeopardised everything.

The going was easier when we reached Mosedale, and I waited for Emlyn to catch up.

"Where are those bloody labradors?" he said. As far as he was concerned, it was us against them.

"They are going to wait for us at Cockley Beck."

"They should be kept on a leash…" grumbled Emlyn.

By the time we met up at Cockley Beck, the soldiers were tired, I was exhausted and Emlyn was scarcely with us. It was raining and the light was fading fast. With five miles still to go, I had my doubts whether we would make it to Seathwaite that night. In retrospect, I think the only thing that was keeping me going was the fact that I knew Emlyn was in a worse state than me. After about an hour and a half of struggling up the road from Cockley Beck, I inspected the map using my new head torch. Having found the dejected face of Emlyn Jones in the darkness (his cheesy grin now a grimace) I said, pointing at the map, "Not far now."

But Emlyn recoiled in the glare of my torch. "How do you expect me to hear with that thing shining in my eyes!"

I did not answer the question. I couldn't have even if I had wanted to. It dawned on me that the labradors were no longer the object of Emlyn's ill temper. It was me. I was the sole reason he was there after all.

By now, the weather was appalling and we were battling against horizontal sleet as well as the dark and our exhaustion.

A couple of hundred yards further on, a Land Rover arrived picking up two of the recruits, but as we were so close, I was determined to make it to Seathwaite.

"Are you going to get into the Land Rover, Emlyn?" the lance corporal asked kindly.

"No! I will not get in a bloody Land Rover. I am going to finish this thing with Tom."

Emlyn was being a grumpy old sod, but I couldn't help but feel incredibly touched by his commitment to finishing the day with me. His job was to escort me to Seathwaite and by God he did it.

Having reached the hotel at Seathwaite, I left Emlyn grumbling at the bar with the labradors. I dashed upstairs for a very quick shower, thinking that I might need to act as mediator between the warring parties.

Upon my return no more than ten minutes later, it appeared Emlyn had undergone a complete transformation. I found him tucking into his second pint of Guinness, regaling humorous tales to an eager audience of labradors. From Ebenezer Scrooge personified, Emlyn had become Father Christmas with a Geordie accent and a grin the size of a gigantic wedge of Stilton.

Later that evening, Emlyn sidled up to me and said, "Do you know, I would not have missed that day for the world. It was absolutely fantastic. Thank you for giving me a reason for doing it."

Amazingly, Emlyn drove all the way back to Newcastle that night and I did not see him again on Coastin'. The day with Emlyn and the labradors, however, was one of the most memorable of the entire journey.

For the next two days I had even more company in the form of two groups of young cadets who, between them, escorted me as far as Grange-over-Sands. Any time we reached a road of any description, "The Boss" would be there with his entourage and the Land Cruiser.

Ron Cowling had been a Coastin' one-stop shop. He had laid on everything as if it was no trouble at all; he had been the "Legend of the Lakes". In Grange-over-Sands, I approached the Land Cruiser and held out my hand to thank Ron for everything he had done. He took my hand, shook it briefly and with the sort of panache you would expect from this genial godfather said, "It was a pleasure doing business with you."

The next morning when I tried to pay for my accommodation, I was told that it had been taken care of. South Cumbria is Cowling country and in Cowling country, Ron Cowling is "simply the Boss".

\* \* \*

I was on my own again. It was always slightly odd setting off on my own after there had been a flurry of people.

The walk from Grange-over-Sands to Arnside would seem flat and uninspiring after the Lake District. Of course, at low tide it would have been possible to go across the sands here, but only with a guide. As the crow flies, my journey would only have been about a mile, but I was nervous of the sands, even if I'd had a guide. Last time I had been here I was told some terrible stories over breakfast by the B&B owner. I couldn't remember any of these tales; all I could remember was that she kept calling me "chook". The upshot of this breakfast experience was that I would avoid both the sands and the B&B on all future visits.

As a train journey across the estuary was not strictly within the rules, my only other option was to negotiate the River Kent by walking upstream to a bridge and then walking back downstream to Arnside. The round journey was about 16 miles. I couldn't quite believe I had finished the Lake District and was now in Lancashire. I had caught up a few days by cutting in from the coast and not venturing down to Barrow in Furness. I knew I could catch up even more time in Lancashire through making use of its canal system.

Using a combination of the Lancashire Coastal Way and the Lancaster Canal, I was able to make swift progress. The canal felt a bit as if I had got on a walker's motorway and I was concerned that I might be missing some of the sights of the coast. By the time I had reached Preston, however, I had decided that the canal was probably infinitely preferable to the coastal path, whose route beyond Morecambe was attractive enough, but reaching the Blackpool metropolis made me daydream about towpaths again.

Following the course of the River Ribble out of Preston on the Ribble Way allowed me to join up fairly easily with the Leeds and Liverpool Canal just north of Rufford.

I would have enjoyed walking down the coast from Southport to Formby, but once again I elected to move south swiftly for the 30 or so miles left to Liverpool. The towpaths were hypnotic in the same way that Lincolnshire had been. In the absence of the need to map read and with the lack of gradient, my mind began to wander in ever-increasing circles and in stark contrast to the pattern of my walking.

Unlike my life, the canal tow path was free of obstacles and ran in a straight line. As if to confound this theory, I found myself at an important junction near Burscough: left to Leeds and right to Liverpool. I double-checked the sign. It would be so embarrassing to end up in Leeds. Having disproved the "straight line" theory, the Leeds and Liverpool Canal then decided to put obstacles in my way: fishermen. Lots of them. It was obviously some kind of competition. Each one was based about 20 yards from the next so that there was absolutely no scope for any meaningful interaction. All of them seemed cocooned in their own thoughts as, grim-faced, they stared intently into the murky water and battled for supremacy against a tiny fish.

I did not feel like a popular man as I walked down this section of canal. Every single fisherman had to begrudgingly remove the rear sections of his extendable rod to allow me to pass. No one said a word to me. I was distracting them from the matter in hand: staring blankly into a single lane of grey water. I just don't get this pastime.

But however unpopular I was, I knew that I would always be more popular to the fishermen than the canal boaters. In my experience, "bargers" are cheery folk; always ready with a happy wave or a cheeky jibe to the honest rambler. But with the fishermen, it is different. Here there is mutual distrust and bitter acrimony in an endless war for canal supremacy.

I watched as the barge approached. A man in a flat cap was at the helm. He looked to be of a gentle disposition, the sort who could easily have spent a lot of his life immersed in statistics, real ale and boats. And yet as he neared the long line of fishing rods in his path, he assumed a more determined look; became alert and steely eyed. Not a word of greeting came from either direction as the barge slowly ploughed its path. The first in the line of fishermen continued to stare glumly into the water, pretending not to see the boat moving closer and closer to his fishing rods. Then at the critical moment he raised his rod just high enough for the barge to pass underneath, but low enough for the driver to have to duck an infuriating couple of inches. At no point during this stand-off was there any eye contact between fisherman and barger. I enjoyed the theatre of this happening a few times before the barge passed me.

"Hello there." I waved at the man in the barge.

"Well, hi there!" he called back, clearly delighted that someone from the bank was able to talk.

"Lovely day," I said.

"Fantastic. Great to be alive."

"Where are you heading to?"

"Just up to Preston. Got a mooring there."

"Enjoy it."

"Thanks, have a good walk."

The conversation was unremarkable; two people going in opposite directions indulging in small talk. What was slightly surreal about it was the fact that the exchange was held over the top of a long line of fishermen. Who remained totally silent and still while the discussion took place. It was as if two different worlds had collided but had not quite connected.

Just outside Liverpool, I walked past Stanley Dock, a set of abandoned warehouses two miles north of the city centre. I had been involved in buying these buildings on behalf of my former boss. An Italian, he was a flamboyant character and when I had taken him to have a look he had spent no more than five minutes looking around before announcing, "I'll buy it." And sure enough he had. This was the same man who at my interview had infamously announced before I had uttered a word, "When I see you walk through the door I think maybe you're the right man for the job."

He spent his life making decisions on gut instinct and in my year with him he rarely made a mistake in business. As well as a few sharper tricks of the trade, this archetypal property tycoon taught me to run with a hunch.

I remembered quite enjoying the drama of working for him, but I had gone on to be a director of a more conventional property company. In an ever-burgeoning property market, I had achieved some success and it felt good. But it was nothing compared to Coastin'. I wondered if I could go back to that lifestyle after this year; after I had experienced such freedom. Could I go back to a predominantly desk-bound job where my Parkinson's was both a perceived weakness and a real barrier to my working effectively?

If I went back to work in surveying, all I could see ahead was a working life that would go into decline at the same rate as my Parkinson's. But what else was there for me? I couldn't go on walking forever; not now they had made the film Forrest Gump anyway.

For some obscure reason, I had the song, "Fog on the Tyne, it's all mine" in my head as I ferried across the Mersey. I think it may have been because it was a very choppy crossing and the rhythm of the boat pitching better suited this song rather than the more obvious choice.

I was standing on the deck of the ferry gazing back at the liver building when I felt the familiar twitching in my wrist. It would not be long now until I started shaking quite badly. To avoid this public humiliation, I planted my arms down by my side to stop them flapping, realising that in doing so my balance was compromised. To compensate for the lack of arms available, my legs had to move at twice the speed.

I was quite pleased to arrive in Birkenhead. I had had quite enough of entertaining the other passengers with my own version of Riverdance, even if it was a bit more appropriate than "Fog on the Tyne".

I chose the most inconspicuous seat at the ferry terminal, although by now I was pretty used to people staring at me. It happened most days and Coastin' had hardened my sensitivity to "being seen". The only thing to do was to just ignore it and keep shaking.

One of the staff at the terminal, probably in his early 20s, had approached me and asked whether I was OK.

"Yes, I'm fine," I said, hoping that I would not have to expand on this.

"Ehh like, wait a minute, aren't you the guy who's walking round Britain?"

I couldn't hide my smile. Apart from the fact that it was great to be recognised, this was also a reflection on how well Coastin' was doing at the moment in terms of publicity.

Having heard that I was, the man couldn't do enough for me, bringing drinks and food and checking I was OK until I was.

The Wirral would have been an easy stroll had it not been for the fact that upon rounding the corner at New Brighton I was walking into the full force of a Wallasey westerly which threatened to blow me all the way back to Liverpool. It seemed to take forever to reach Hoylake, but having done so I turned my back on Liverpool Bay, happy in the thought that I only had the River Dee to negotiate before I was in Wales.

I had been enjoying the solitude until Mule turned up and ruined everything. Fortunately, he had brought Joey, his wife, and their daughter Nancy. It was fantastic to see them. They had rented a cottage in north-east Wales for a few days, but principally they were there to support me, although Mule did his best to argue otherwise. It was strange seeing my oldest friend with his newborn baby girl. I had never met Nancy before and seeing the three of them as a happy family unit made my thoughts turn away from work and on to Lyndsey for a while.

I entered Wales in pouring rain just beyond Shotwick, feeling that there was too much uncertainty about what the future held beyond Coastin'. It had only been a few years ago that mine and Mule's lives had been going in very similar directions. And yet, although in a sense I wanted what Mule had, there was something else I felt that surprised me. In fact, when the thought first came into my head I decided that it couldn't be true; that it must be the product of my natural instincts to retain a positive frame of mind. But having analysed it again I realised that had I not had Parkinson's disease, then I would not have done Coastin' and, without a doubt, whatever happened from here, Coastin' would be the most wonderful thing I had ever done.

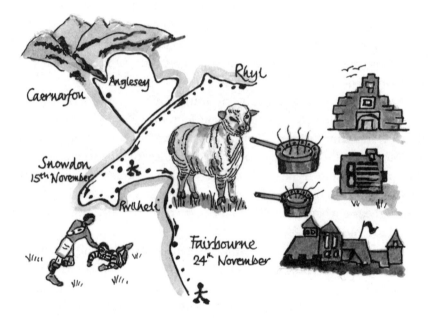

CHAPTER 24

Fortunately, Queensferry and Connah's Quay are not representative of the rest of Wales. They are horrible industrial ports that reminded me of Ardrossan and the worst of Ayrshire. Had I not known this, I might well have charged straight back into England.

I only felt happier by the time I was out beyond Northop Hall, but from here, all the way to Whitford, I had terrible trouble following footpaths. It was as if I was in Scotland again; phantom footpaths luring me into barbed wire traps. All the ingredients for footpath heaven were there: a directional signpost with the words "Public Footpath"; a well-trodden path leading away from it; sometimes even a person coming the other way. But no sooner had I walked 400 yards than everything signifying a pedestrian thoroughfare suddenly disappeared, to be replaced by mocking impenetrables or, even worse, entanglables. It just didn't make sense. I felt as if I should write to the old Chinese master who came up with the phrase "All paths lead somewhere", and ask him to add the following caveat: "… unless you are a Celt".

On one such occasion, I found myself in a field with sufficient barbed wire to stop Steve McQueen on a motorbike. I negotiated the most innocuous of these fences and reached a stony track. This at least gave me a clue as to where I was. The footpath was not far away. As I marched up the track, a minibus was coming in the other direction. Instead of driving past me, it drove at me and then stopped, blocking my path. A surly-looking man got out. He was not pleased to see me.

"Private road this." He oozed malevolence, even if his tone was just unfriendly.

"I'm just trying to follow footpaths and according to this map, there's one just up here on the left."

"You are not following footpaths. This is a private road." His manner was menacing this time. From the expression on his face and the inflection in his words, it was clear that he would have physically stopped me from going up the road if forced. I stared past him at a range of outbuildings in the distance and wondered if he was hiding something.

I shrugged and started walking the other way, thinking that I would sneak back again once he had gone past me. But the minibus did not go past me until I had walked all the way down the track and on to the main road. I was slightly annoyed with myself for giving in so easily, but something told me that it would be wise to do so. The only solace I took out of the episode was that I walked to the main road at the pace of a snail.

If the first few days in Wales had been disappointing, they certainly did not set the tone. Having walked up the west side of the Dee estuary, I had the choice of following the beach to Rhyl or hugging the hillside above the coastal plain which would be longer, but infinitely more scenic. Choosing the latter, I found the starting point of the Offa's Dyke Track on the northern outskirts of Prestatyn. I planned to walk three or four miles of this path, which follows the line of a fourth-century dyke built by the Mercian King Offa and in places still forms the border between England and Wales.

If I had continued a further 173 miles along Offa's Dyke, I would have ended up in Chepstow. The coastal route to Chepstow was over four times that distance.

From Rhyl, where I received a fantastic welcome from the local Parkinson's Group, I joined the North Wales Coastal Path which meant some proper signposts at last. One in particular caught my attention. It informed me that Poelwys Lane was precisely 7/8ths of a mile distant. Precision stuff.

On the outskirts of Colwyn Bay, I passed a man who, on seeing my rucksack, decided he should explain how best to get to the seashore. It was a long explanation as he wanted to give me three alternative routes, and by the time he'd finished, I was getting quite chilly. Thanking him profusely for his trouble, I turned and took a few steps before he then called after me, "Do you like trees?"

"Er... yes," I replied.

"Well, you must go and see the huge tree in Fairy Glen," he enthused and then set about providing me with another set of directions.

Thanking him again, I made to leave, but added: "I suppose if I get lost I can always just keep heading downhill until I reach the sea."

It didn't pay to try to be clever…

"Ooh no, you mustn't do that. If you keep going downhill you'll end up in totally the wrong place." And he explained how this would happen and where I would end up.

By the time he had finished I was totally and utterly confused, so I elected to follow the North Wales Coastal Path signs, as was my original intention. On the way I passed a particularly large tree.

\* \* \*

It was 12th November. I wasn't sure what time it was, but I knew I had woken up too early again. I could hear rain outside the window and wasn't sure whether I felt cold or whether it was just the anticipation of feeling cold. Or, of course, it could have been that I was just shaking.

I summoned up the energy to check my watch. 5.45 a.m. It was too early to take my pills because that would put me out of kilter for the rest of the day. I tried to read a book. I read about three paragraphs but then the book shook too much in my hand. I could no longer see the words. I thought it would have been nice if they had designed the Parkinson's so that the shakes were uniform to all body parts. Maybe it would have been possible to read a book if my head had been nodding at the same rate as my hands. As it was, I was unable to do anything constructive. But it didn't matter. I would lose myself in thought. There was plenty to think about.

Although Coastin' was still giving me enormous satisfaction and there was still nothing I would rather be doing, I also felt it was becoming too much for me. I no longer felt relaxed. I had never really recovered the calm, easy-going state I had achieved in Scotland and I wondered whether I would ever do so.

At the moment, I almost had a sense of claustrophobia. I needed space from everyone so that I could take stock of everything. I felt that while the momentum of Coastin' was still careering in the right direction, I was being left struggling way behind, failing miserably to keep pace with it. It wasn't so much the walk, it was everything on top of the walk: the administration; the logistics of luggage, meeting people and accommodation; the phone calls and my failure to keep the Coastin' website up to date. I felt frustrated by it, but most of all I felt exhausted. I knew that even one day off would be counter-productive. If I had a day off, I would probably become ill. Stopping often made me feel ill. While I was still moving and there was adrenalin in my body, I could keep going.

I was feeling huge pressure on my time. Every day was an uncomfortable juggling exercise trying to keep appointments with reporters, supporters from local Parkinson's branches and people who had come to walk with me. On top of these commitments I had to complete the day's walk, to eat and rest adequately and to allow extra time for the inevitable daily dose of shaking.

When I had been planning Coastin', I had not taken into account the "road show" aspect of the walk and the fact that in order to realise its goals there had to be this element. I knew the number of commitments from now on was only going to increase and that scared me. Somehow a balance had to be struck between the two competing objectives of actually finishing the walk on time, without killing myself, and the charitable goals. The only trouble was that the word "balance" and I did not fit comfortably into the same sentence. Everything in my life (except for my arms) swung violently, first one way and then the other. Even now, I was not coping with my schedule.

Having said that, I would not have had it any other way. Coastin' was meant to be all about spreading awareness and raising money. If other people did not join in and if there were not a few events on the way, then there was little point Coastin'.

I felt better after putting my thoughts into some sort of perspective, and having admitted to myself that I was exhausted, I no longer felt quite so bad.

Despite the horrendous conditions early that morning, the day's walking turned out to be glorious; the best for some considerable time. It was proof of the old wisdom: "Rain before seven, fine by eleven". Inwardly, I thanked those "old wives" for their insight.

From the grassy knoll of Little Ormes Head, I looked forward to the Great Orme; a huge rock promontory which bursts out of the sea like the head of a bloated giant with the twin bays of Llandudno forming the neck.

It was evening by the time I had walked around the Great Orme and stood gaping at the floodlit walls of Conway Castle. It is a magical place and gave me a sense of déjà vu. I realised later that this was because it reminded me of a toy castle which my grandfather had hand-made for me out of wood when I was four. What an enormous amount of work had gone into that gift. I hoped I had made sufficient fuss about it at the time and felt a bit sad that

I could no longer do so. My grandfather had been such an impressive man; brilliant with his hands, whether in his workshop or playing county cricket or golf. I would have liked to have known him longer, but then I suppose I was lucky to know him at all.

I made an especially early start the next morning and spent an hour scurrying around, on and within the fortified walls of Conway. I couldn't understand why more people didn't talk about the place. Of all the towns I had visited so far, I felt Conway was the most attractive and interesting to walk around by quite some way. My uncle would no doubt know a thing or two about Conway and he would be with me later today.

It was still only nine o'clock when I picked up the North Wales Coastal Path again and climbed up Conway Mountain. It had turned into one of those fantastic autumn days. As I gained height and broke through the treeline and into the sunshine, I experienced another Cape Wrath moment. The whole mountain seemed to be ablaze with colour and I was suddenly free of everyone and everything; alone with this incredible 360-degree view which took in Conway Castle, Snowdonia, the Menai Straits, Anglesey, the Great Orme and right back to Liverpool and England.

The moment I stepped over the peak of Conway Mountain, the castle fell out of view and I focused my thoughts and sights on the way ahead. The walk along the ridge overlooking Bangor and Anglesey was stupendous and I took my time soaking up the sun and enjoying an unusual feeling of well-being. Llanfairpwllgwyngyllgogerychwyrndrobwll-llantysiliogogogoch is on Anglesey. It used to have the longest place name in the world until it was overtaken by Tetaumatawhakatangihangakoauatamateaurekaeaturipukap-ihimaungahoronukupokaiwhenuaakitanaraku – a place in New Zealand – and somewhere with about 70 more letters even than that in Thailand.

I was pleased to have the familiar company of my uncle and aunt, who had insisted on treating my mother and me to a few nights in a plush hotel on the north Wales coast. Mum had driven up the previous day and looked far better than she had done in the Lake District. She seemed much more with it, a lot stronger, and certainly more focussed.

In the lobby of the hotel, the owner started quizzing me enthusiastically about the walk. He retrieved one of the old hotel visitor's books which revealed that in 1978, John Merrill, the first person to walk the coastline, had also stayed on his way through. Mr Merrill had scribbled an entry stating the number of miles he had covered to that point and the number of miles he still had to walk. This is something I had refrained from doing all the way round as I thought it was a little bit self-glorifying. At this point, Mrs Hotel arrived and Mr Hotel told her what I was doing.

"That's nice for you," she said, as she cast a disapproving eye on my attire. "Now, shall we get you checked in?"

I thought about her words: "That's nice for you." I supposed it was nice for me but I didn't think she necessarily had the right to say it. Her words had grated and I felt annoyed.

While it was relaxing to have a mother, an uncle and an aunt in the hotel, I was concerned about the following day's walk. If anything went wrong and I did not turn up to a checkpoint on time, I feared that their combined worry would multiply and expand at a rate that you might witness in a nuclear reactor. Not wanting to have a recurrence of the Lake District episode, I allowed plenty of extra time to walk to the lunchtime rendezvous in Llanllechid (chosen because we wondered whether the inhabitants needed to sip water to rehydrate every time they mentioned their address).

It was against the law of averages that my medication should fail me quite so soon that day and in a place where there was no signal on my telephone. As I sat overlooking Anglesey, I remembered I had been told years ago that work expands to fill the time available for its completion. That certainly seemed to be the case today. I also remembered the name of this theory. How ironic! Parkinson's Law. In a similar vein, I thought it was Sod's Law that the grass I was sitting on was so wet.

I started to inspect the map with its array of unpronounceable names. I noticed that the hill on which I was stuck shaking was called Ffridd Ddu and it seemed somehow to capture my sentiments.

I was off like a train as soon as my brain and body had reconnected. I was practically frantic about my lateness and ran much of the way to Llanllechid out of concern for other people's concern about me. But when I arrived, 25 minutes late, I was relieved to find they were happily tucking into sandwiches.

My mother walked the rest of the day with me. My aunt alternated between car and walk. My uncle, meanwhile, rolled sedately in his car through the country lanes with great panache. Every now and then he would appear safely encased within the confines of his salubrious saloon and would waft past; his face as glazed as the windscreen and seemingly indifferent to our frenzied walking efforts.

But R. B. Catlow was not indifferent. On one occasion he parked and partook of 50 yards' worth of Coastin'. Having achieved his goal, he adjourned once more to the comfort of his car; a place more befitting his status and years.

Having left the Catlows for a final push to the foot of Snowdon, it was difficult to see what else could go wrong for my mother and me in our walking exploits. There was, however, to be one final defining moment of the walking element to my mother's visit to North Wales. We had found ourselves unwittingly trapped the wrong side of some dry-stone walling.

"You can easily get through there." My mother was pointing at a minuscule gap between some wire fencing and a stone wall.

I was precisely halfway through the gap when I became stuck. My legs dangled in freedom, but my top half would not budge and remained in captivity. While my loving mother collapsed with laughter, I pondered the most ignominious way of ending Coastin' and concluded that this would make Top Five material.

When my mother finished laughing, she moved a few stones to allow me to squeeze through.

The final half mile into Llanberis was a dramatic and steep miner's track, which had it not been for the high-sided slate walls on either side would have been absolutely terrifying.

Arriving down at the hotel bar that night, I found my uncle and aunt sitting under a life-sized photograph of Mrs Hotel receiving her MBE.

"We thought you would like to sit here," said my uncle, pointing at a chair which he knew full well would be facing the picture. From inside the frame, Mrs Hotel smiled insincerely.

"It's an enormous photograph," I said. "I wonder what she received an MBE for."

"Probably for services to the photo frame industry," R. B. Catlow responded, deadpan.

Over supper that night, Mrs Hotel arrived at the table and told us all about her visit to the Grosvenor House Hotel in London for a recent hotel awards function. It was an extraordinary thing to do given that we were having a pleasant family chat at the time. I noticed that about 15 seconds into her monologue my uncle closed his eyes. They remained closed right through her description of what she had eaten, through to the table decorations and on to the proud moment when she had received her runner-up award. Eventually, she left us alone; at which point R. B. Catlow opened one unashamedly twinkling eye and asked, "Is it over?"

Despite the self-satisfied, egocentric Mrs Hotel, I thoroughly enjoyed my stay at the plush hotel. I signed the visitor's book and remembered the entry of the other walker, John Merrill. Maybe he had a similar experience with Mrs Hotel. Maybe his brag about distance was in response to her total failure to be interested in anyone or anything else.

I signed the visitor's book: "2,700 miles completed, 1,800 miles to go." I am a weak man.

Eight of those 1,800 miles was spent climbing Snowdon the following day. My companions for the ascent were a politician and a journalist, but the experience was not quite as bad as it sounds.

Snowdon did not seem as difficult as Sca Fell Pike and Ben Nevis, but maybe that was because we stopped every 30 yards while the MP explained to the journalist every conceivable peril of climbing the mountain. It was not the most jolly subject to be discussing and it made for pretty slow going, but it was, at least, educational. By the time we reached the summit, I was confident that if I ever wanted to fall off a mountain, I now knew at least a hundred different methods of doing so.

I was also triumphant. Not only had I reached the top of Snowdon having avoided all the hazards (for which reason I shall be voting Plaid Cymru at the next election), but I had also completed the mountain element of my three-part challenge. It felt like a big step towards successfully finishing the whole thing. On the way down I fell silent just thinking about the prospect of finishing. For the first time I allowed myself a glimpse of how that might feel. I decided that it might feel rather good.

Caernarfon Castle seemed to epitomise words such as "bastion" and "stronghold". It is a big elephant of a castle and it stands guard over the southern entrance to the Menai Straits. I had arrived there the day after Snowdon feeling a bit queasy. Standing next to the castle for a photograph made me feel feeble and insignificant, but what came later was far worse.

Since developing Parkinson's, I have found increasingly that any ailment I might contract, such as a cold, cough or flu would not produce their normal symptoms. Instead, everything seemed to manifest itself in the severity of my Parkinson's. Whatever it was that I had picked up in North Wales reduced me to convulsions rather than shakes. It was the worst I had ever experienced. It was unfortunate that my mother was there to witness it but there was nothing that either of us could do about it. And as I lay there looking like something out of a horror film about being possessed, there was nothing that could be said. She knew that I felt helpless about her feeling helpless about my being helpless. These gyrations were not good. Not good at all.

I was a new man the next morning, and a return to Caernarfon inspired the purchase of a CD of Welsh anthems. I took a particular liking to one of these with the title "Sospan Fach". The song starts as a lament but then leaps seamlessly into a rousing chorus of much pomp and pageantry.

"I wonder what the words mean," I said.

"It's about a big saucepan and a little saucepan."

I chuckled when my mother said this. There was absolutely no way that this powerful piece of music, which was like a combination of "Abide With Me" and "Men of Harlech", could possibly be about a couple of saucepans. I resolved to find out what it really meant that evening.

We had been invited to a pub to watch a live band performing. One of the band members had Parkinson's and they were going to collect money on behalf of Coastin'.

I was a bit concerned that the "live band" was going to be a Megadeath tribute group or something similar. My mother did not like Heavy Metal – she was more into Garage – since that's where her car, golf clubs and deep freeze are.

My concerns were allayed when we entered the pub to find some upbeat, foot-tapping Celtic folk music going on. To begin with, there were about four people playing instruments and the rest were sitting listening. But as the evening wore on, the listeners would from time to time reveal a musical instrument of their own from under a table, up a sleeve or behind a beard. By the end of the night it seemed the whole pub was playing some form of music-making device and the atmosphere and sound were such that you couldn't fail to feel uplifted and happy.

In a quiet moment, I asked the lady sitting next to me what the song "Sospan fach" was about.

"It's about two saucepans boiling on a fire."

I couldn't believe it.

* * *

It took two days to reach Morfa Nefyn after Mum had left me in Caernarfon. I was now approaching the extremities of the north coast of

Wales on the Lleyn peninsula; a rugged projection of land characterised by rolling hills, long beaches, steep cliffs and sheep as far as the eye could see.

I was due to be meeting a friend, but between us we had made a mess of the communications. On top of this, I was not entirely sure whether I was in Morfa Nefyn or one of the other villages which seemed to be in the same place. I went into a newsagent, only to find that it was a butcher's shop. There were three distinguishing features of the man who came to the counter: his cauliflower ears, the large machete in his right hand and the blood that was splattered all over his apron. A fourth distinguishing feature appeared when he smiled, revealing the most amazing set of teeth I had ever seen. My eyes suddenly focused on the carcass of a sheep behind him and I quickly took off my woolly hat, in case he made a terrible mistake.

"Um... is this Morfa Nefyn?" I stammered, wondering if it would be sensible to run out of the shop without hearing the answer.

"Bring me that map around your neck and I'll show you where you are." I felt relieved when he put the machete down, but realised too late that by moving to the counter I would then be in range of the teeth.

He pointed to our position on the map. I thanked him and made a move to leave, whereupon he picked up the machete again and wielded it like a musketeer. "In other words, it's that way," he said, finishing his swordwork with a flourish. As I left the shop, a green BMW sped past and then screeched to a halt. It was Jocky Noah.

James "Jocky Noah" Hamilton is an old chum and a legend among men. Apart from sitting next to me in that geography lesson when I had first had the notion to walk round the coast, he had also been the principal contributor to one of my finest sporting moments. In the dying seconds of the final of a seven-a-side tournament in what I knew would be my last game of rugby ever, he dropped a goal to clinch victory. It was a wonderful way to bow out of a sport that had done so little for me over the years. I was hopeless.

Apart from receiving lifelong acclaim from his peers for this one sublime piece of footwork, Jocky is about as loyal a friend as it is possible to have. For me, there is no finer quality than that. But these glowing references extend still further. One of life's most enjoyable experiences can also be attributed to Jocky Noah. There are few better moments in life than to get out of a car which Jocky has been driving... and still be alive. I was lucky enough to have the pleasure on several occasions around the Lleyn peninsula. Sucked back in the passenger seat of his BMW M3 as we torpedoed through minuscule lanes at colossal speed even seemed to cure my shakes. I became totally rigid.

The names of the settlements on the Lleyn peninsula defy linguistic convention. In between Llangwnnadl and Uwchmynydd we passed Rhwngyddwyborth. These words, when written down, look like the sort of things that come out of people's mouths after they have been sitting in a pub drinking vodka and tequila all night. But even if the words did look like the verbal equivalent of someone being violently sick, I was fairly certain that when uttered by a Welsh speaker they would sound as soft and lyrical as the rest of the language.

While I was in Wales I was receiving a daily dose of Welsh from a lady called Blod. Blodwyn Jones was in charge of handling the PR for Coastin' on behalf of Norgine, the pharmaceutical company who were sponsoring the entire Welsh leg of the journey. I enjoyed speaking to Blod. Her voice was always cheerful and encouraging.

"Bore da!" It was all she ever needed to say for me to know it was her, but the conversation would continue in exactly the same way every day for the two months I was in Wales.

"Bore da, Blod."

"Where are you?"

"On a hill near [wherever I was]." I always seemed to be on a hill. I began saying I was on a hill even when I was not.

"You're doing so well. You're brilliant. You're a star."

Perhaps it was not really surprising that I enjoyed speaking to Blod. She managed to make the word "brilliant" sound as if it meant the most fantastic thing in the world. Blod was like having a gin and tonic every day; a little boost to my confidence, motivation and speed.

But Blod was "brilliant" too. She had incredibly good contacts throughout Wales, and being a Welsh speaker, would be able to make even better headway with the press and media than Q, whose English accent would probably be a disadvantage.

Of course, Blod was not the only great encouragement that I had throughout Coastin'. Although it was probably fair to say that I was mildly obsessed with my mobile telephone, it also represented my contact with the outside world. It was without doubt the most important piece of equipment, allowing me to keep in touch with everyone who was important to me, and they, in turn, would keep me focused and in good spirits.

It was particularly noticeable that the first question asked by almost everyone who rang me before the walk started was, "How are you?" Since I had been on the walk, the first question of at least 75% of telephone callers would now be, "Where are you?" I rather liked that. It meant that the walk had managed to dilute the importance of my health. Where I was had become more important.

The most westerly section of the Lleyn is largely National Trust land. With Jocky Noah having some time with his wife and baby, I spent a couple of hours walking beyond Aberdaron to the very tip of the peninsula and gazed down the huge sweep of the Welsh coastline. I felt excited by the next section. There was plenty to look forward to, but in particular I wanted to reach Pembrokeshire. There was a 180-mile coastal path here and I had always wanted to walk it.

Ahead of me was a small island on which there were the ruins of an abbey. I was about to look for the name of the island on the map, but there were a number of sheep close by who reminded me: "Baaaaaaardsey!" they shouted at me.

On my way to Abersoch, I saw a signpost to Llwybr Cyhoeddus. I had been seeing signs to this place since leaving Llandudno. I felt confused, as it was not a place of which I had heard and yet judging by the number of signposts pointing to it, it should have been a vast metropolis.

It dawned on me today. The penny finally dropped. Llwybr Cyhoeddus is Welsh for Public Footpath.

It was already dusk as I started east, padding across the compact sands of the huge beaches either side of Abersoch. In the distance, there was only one other figure on the beach and it seemed to be coming towards me. The swagger was familiar. When I reached him, Jocky Noah and I shook hands warmly as if we had not seen each other for years. Jocky is like that. He is always pleased to see everyone.

"Did you know that I was sitting next to you in a geography lesson when I first had this ridiculous idea about walking around the coast?" I asked him. "You said you would come with me – and here we are actually doing it twenty-odd years later."

Jocky Noah suddenly looked emotional. There seemed to be a glimmer of recognition and I thought I detected powerful feelings rising to the surface. He turned towards me and our eyes met in a moment of profound friendship and total kindredship of spirit.

"Nope. I don't remember that at all," he responded, smirking. The look had been enough for me.

I was keen to keep going that night and continued around the hump of Tir-y-Cwmwd by the road to Llanbedrog. I went into a pub to ask if they knew of a B&B. Even though I had directed the question to the barman, a small crowd of people were propping up the bar, listening intently. They all answered the question at the same time, which made the answer almost indecipherable. I did glean from their enthusiasm that there must be B&Bs available, so I asked where they were. In the ensuing hubbub it gradually became apparent that it really did not matter too much where the B&Bs were, because they were all closed. This would have been sufficient information, but they felt I also ought to know why they were closed. The following information came to light: Dai Lloyd had closed for the winter; Mrs Williams had gone to see her mother in Llandrindod Wells and Mr and Mrs Davies had gone on holiday to South Africa where they would stop at both Johannesburg and Cape Town, and whilst in the latter intended to make a tour of the wine region around Stellenbosch (the same as Barry Hughes from Porthmadog had done two years ago).

Despite spending longer in the pub than I had hoped, the warmth of my reception was refreshing and I knew that had I stayed in there, I would have been made very welcome. By now though, I was tired and in need of a rest. There was only one thing to do. I rang Jocky Noah, who arrived soon after in the green grim reaping machine.

I couldn't be certain, but I think we arrived in Pwllheli before we had left Llanbedrog.

I caught the bus back to Llanbedrog the following day. It was miserable weather and by walking through fields my boots became caked with mud. It was like walking through a thick treacle tart wearing ski boots. It was still raining when I made it back onto the beach and started towards Pwllheli, and I was pleased to receive a phone call. It was Mule's father, Donald.

Unbeknown to me, Donald Cammell had organised a coffee morning for local residents in aid of Coastin' and had decided to ring me while it was on. I was really pleased about this. Nearly eight months into the walk, there were still little surprises like this to boost my morale and keep me in good spirits on otherwise rather miserable days.

I began thinking about my morale and how much the enjoyment of a day's walk hinged upon it. And when I thought about it even more, I realised that actually my whole existence was shaped by it. It was the reason I continued to thrive despite the fact that my health was declining. I suspected that actually both my reserves of courage in my own convictions and my defiance in the face of my condition were limited. I relied heavily on everyone around me to replenish my stocks regularly. Perhaps this was one of the reasons why, in my early days of Parkinson's, it was doing me no good to pretend the illness did not exist. Ignoring PD meant that other people couldn't talk about it with me and I was only able to draw on my own self-belief and confidence in order to maintain a positive attitude. But for me, the source of self-belief and confidence is through interaction with others. I would not have had a chance if I had continued trying to be a martyr.

I was given another big boost in Criccieth where the local school had turned out in force to wish me well on my way. At least I think that's what they were doing. It did occur to me as I walked past the sign which said "You are now leaving Criccieth" with clapping and cheering ringing in my ears that it could just as easily have been that they were rather pleased to see me go.

But the send-off from Criccieth put a spring in my step all the way to Porthmadog. For some of this, the school's headmaster joined me and we talked about rugby. It struck me afterwards that the reason I had enjoyed the conversation so much was that it was a conversation that was not about the walk. It felt like the last time I had had one of those had been at the very tip of the Lleyn Peninsula. And that had been with the "Baaaaardsey" Island sheep.

From Porthmadog the little Ffestiniog Railway runs up to Blaenau Ffestiniog; it is the oldest narrow gauge railway line in the world. A road runs parallel to the railway line, allowing access across the Glaslyn Valley. The toll for this privilege was 5p. There were three people collecting the money. A further causeway across the Vale of Ffestiniog, up which the views were fantastic, advertised a crossing fee of 30p. There was no one collecting on this bridge.

From Ynys, the road was more or less straight to Harlech, but I alternated between it and a soggy path.

I only knew two lines, but it had to be sung: "Men of Harlech march to glory. Victory is hov'ring o'er thee."

It was stirring stuff; a few extra lines would have helped me enjoy the rendition a little more. After a while, I found that I was back singing "Fog on the Tyne".

If Caernarfon Castle is a mammoth, Harlech Castle is a huge lion. It stands high and proud surveying its domain from a dramatic, elevated position. There are few more magnificent castles than Harlech.

It was something to do with the space in which I had to walk today that made me think a bit more deeply about things. With the tide going out, the wet sand reflected everything above it: the sky, the clouds and me. I noticed that the clouds were moving more rapidly than I was. I couldn't keep up with them. I was halfway down Wales now. I felt the walk was going too quickly for me too. It may seem odd to say it, but there didn't seem to be enough time like this to think. Coastin' was everything.

At least this one day had somehow served me up an environment where I could think about all that had happened. I needed a lot more time to work out how the last year would or should affect me. I knew that things that had happened both within and outside of Coastin' would bring fundamental differences to my life, but it was far too early to assess what these would be. I used these precious moments alone to put my mind back into some sort of order in the hope of reaching a stage where I could look forward and not back. I had to make some sense of it all before the gaping post-Coastin' void was upon me.

SOUTH WALES: FROM CLARE BALDING
TO THE COUNTESS OF CARDIFF
496 MILES
NOVEMBER – JANUARY 2003

CHAPTER 25

For the first time on this trip I was starting to realise that there had been a slight deterioration in my symptoms. It was the day the BBC had come to interview me for a half-hour radio programme. It would be, wouldn't it? Parkinson's is like that. It stalks your every emotion; reacts to your environment like a reverse chameleon – becoming visible when you most need it not to be. It was supposed to be an episode of Ramblings. Clare Balding (the presenter) had come to this far-flung part of Wales with her producer and sound engineer to talk to me. I had wanted to start the day's walk at 8.30 a.m. and we had agreed to meet for breakfast at 7.30 a.m.

I had not banked on a terrible night's sleep and was already a bit wobbly at breakfast. I so desperately wanted to give a good interview and to give people a better insight into Parkinson's, but I realised the likelihood of this happening in my ever-worsening state was practically zero. Ramblings was supposed to be a radio programme combining a pleasant walk with interesting discussion. But for the moment, I knew that all the Ramblings team would get out of me this morning would be mumblings and stumblings. And even though this might have given the greatest insight of all, I just couldn't face it. I wanted to portray an upbeat image of the illness.

I asked Clare and the others if they would mind waiting until my next medication started to work. They were more than understanding, but I felt embarrassed. The programme was meant to be called "Walking with a Purpose" and here was I, unable to walk at all, let alone with any purpose.

So everyone waited while I lay quivering impatiently in my room, willing my medication to work.

At 10.40 a.m. I was still quivering. I knew I needed to relax but I just couldn't seem to do it. There was no way I could relax. If my drugs did not kick in soon, the day would be called off. Clare and the BBC would go home and that would probably be the end of it. The shakes suddenly became even more violent. Was this a reaction to my last thought, or was this the beginnings of a "kick in"? A sudden exacerbation of my symptoms was often a sign that things were about to improve.

At 10.42 a.m., the familiar feeling in my limbs and head marked the first signs of regaining control of my body. At these moments, the metamorphosis from Mr Shaky Hands Man to healthy specimen of mankind is extraordinary.

By 10.43 a.m., not only my physical appearance had changed, but my cognitive powers and levels of competence had also improved immeasurably. I felt ready to be interviewed by Clare Balding. I felt ready to walk up a steep hill. I looked forward to both these challenges. Three minutes earlier I couldn't have contemplated any of it.

By 11.10 a.m. we had been walking for 20 minutes. I had been in charge of directions. Having kept the BBC waiting, I was pretty confident that my map-reading skills would not let me down, ensuring no further delay. It was misplaced confidence. For the next 30 minutes, I led the BBC deeper and deeper into a thick forest which covered the foothills of Cadair Idris.

I had started out with the BBC crew so self-assured and composed. But as I took wrong turning after wrong turning, my confidence in my own abilities started to waver. Eventually, feeling stupid, embarrassed and guilty all at the same time, I made a momentous statement.

"We are lost."

The total collapse of my self-esteem in orienteering terms had been captured minute by excruciating minute by the sound recorder. It was not enough that I felt humiliated today by displaying all the leadership qualities of a sheep. It would only be enough when the whole sorry affair was transmitted into hundreds of thousands of people's homes next February on Radio 4. This was not what was planned at all.

Meanwhile, Clare Balding and the crew seemed to be far from upset. Apparently getting lost made good radio. This confirmed my worst fears. At 11.50 a.m. we were rescued by a National Park Ranger. Oh, the shame of it!

By lunchtime, the BBC had decided that they had sufficient footage to make a programme. I felt I had more to say but was not really sure what. I was pleased with the questions Clare had asked. They were direct and dealt with the human side of my condition. She also asked about Dad. I was happy to talk and found it strange that I was prepared to be so open when my words would be listened to by thousands. I think this was because she was good at her job. By the end we were talking as if we had known each other for years – she seemed to understand a lot better than most.

* * *

A friend of my mother's, Gill, has a cottage in Aberdovey. It is a lovely little place and I was booked in there to stay with her for three nights. Mum was once again on hand to lend assistance.

In the absence of a definite boat ride across the River Dovey, there was nothing for it but to strike a path to the first bridge upstream at Machynlleth, where I was greeted by the most glamorous mayor I had yet met. Instead of then heading back to the coast on the main road, I chose to follow a path called Glyndwr's Way south-east towards a place called Staylittle. It did not sound like the sort of place to spend any length of time.

The path is named after Owen Glyndwr, who is regarded as a Welsh hero. Family legend has it that I am a direct descendant of the man. I am proud of my Welsh blood. In fact, fiercely proud. But having studied this Glyndwr chap a little I am not entirely sure that I am all that chuffed that he is one of my ancestors. The path, which supposedly follows a route he took, seems to go round in circles and ends up pretty close to where he started, but unfortunately not close enough for it to have been on purpose. If he was my Great Grandpappy, it would certainly explain the reasons behind my getting lost with Clare Balding. Just beyond the highest point I would reach that day at Foel Fadian (1,850 feet), I veered off Glyndwr's Way. I began to realise why my family used the term "long-lost relative" when referring to Glyndwr – he clearly had no idea where he was going. I, meanwhile, was heading for the River Hengwm, the course of which would lead me to the Nant-y-Moch Reservoir where I had arranged to meet Gill and Mum.

Their journey was nearly as hazardous as mine. The reservoir was miles and miles down an unsurfaced road north of Ponterwyd. The only significant thing about Ponterwyd is that it is situated on the A44 and the only significance of the A44 is that it links a number of insignificant places together in the struggle across the Cambrian Mountains to Aberystwyth. It would be a simple thing, once off the A44, to drive around on tracks and minor roads for decades and not see another soul.

It was desolate scenery for me too, but I was enjoying it. Space seemed so important to my state of mind and health at the moment. Nevertheless I knew I needed to be extra cautious today. In terms of places where I had been on my own, this was the remotest by a long, long way. This was the time when things should have gone wrong. There was enormous scope for everything from a minor hiccup to complete disaster. The chances of anyone being in the right place at the right time were slim. We really had underestimated how empty this area, known as Plynlimon, really was.

Of course, the rendezvous went like clockwork. Mum and Gill might as well have been picking me up from the station. They arrived. I arrived. We drove back to Aberdovey. Why couldn't it always be that simple?

I rejoined the coast at Aberystwyth and started walking along sheep-strewn slopes next to the sea. There would be a lot of this type of walking for the next 40 or so miles to Cardigan where I would join the Pembrokeshire coastal path. In Llanrhystud, a man who was out walking his dog saw my rucksack and asked, "Come far, affyou?"

It was a tough one to answer. The answer was obviously "yes" – but how much more should I reveal? It was raining, and the question could easily lead to a long conversation.

"Yes. I'm walking round the coast."

"'eavens above, you are not that young English lad who's walking the whole bloody lot of it are you?"

Fantastic! I wondered where he had heard about me. The local PDS group? The local paper? Radio? National TV? Celebrity Magazine Weekly?

"How did you know that?"

"I'll tell you how I know that, shall I? I'm a friend of Blodwyn Jones. She's been telling me the story, she has. The whole of Britain is it? That's a long way, that is. Bloody hell, aye, it is. Isn't it?"

The following morning I met the same man again. This time he was walking with his brother and they joined me for a mile or so. Dai and Jeff Morgan were fascinated with the walk.

"What has been your favourite place so far?" asked Dai.

"Aberystwyth is it, Tom?" said Jeff.

"But he hasn't been to Swansea yet."

"Milford Haven is lovely in December." They both laughed with me. I knew that none of these were among the finest towns in Wales.

"Look, let the man speak, would you?"

"Well he's probably fed up answering questions."

"Well, the man can't get a word in edgeways, can he?"

"He doesn't aff to speak if he doesn't want to, does he?"

And so on. At the top of one of the fields through which we were walking was a huge old stone which looked as if at one stage in its history it had been some sort of seat.

"We'll name the seat after you, Tom. Shall we? From now on this will be Tom's seat, shall it? What do you say, Jeff?"

"We'll get it printed on the map. We'll tell everyone. This is Tom's seat, this is. We'll christen it now, shall we?"

"Have a seat then, would you. Yes, have a seat."

I did as I was told and then Dai and Jeff started looking at the way ahead.

"The next bit through that hedge could be a bit tricky, it could. I am not sure you can get through there, can he Jeff?"

"THE MAN HAS WALKED 3,000 MILES, DAI. HE DOESN'T NEED A BLOODY DAFT WELSHMAN LIKE YOU TO TELL HIM WHETHER HE CAN GET THROUGH A BLOODY HEDGE, NOW DOES HE?"

Despite not having said a great deal to the brothers, I had enjoyed their company enormously. Before I left I asked if I could take a picture of them.

I brought the picture up on the digital screen so they could see it. Something had obscured the lens, a thumb or a strap, so that both their heads had been obliterated from the picture.

"Bloody hell, look, we haven't got any heads!"

"That's a bit worrying, that is, Dai."

"There you are, Tom. Put it in your book. You can go and tell everyone you met the headless brothers of Llanrhystud!" And I have.

\* \* \*

There was no coastal path from Aberporth to Cardigan so I took to the minor roads again, one of which told me to beware of low-flying aircraft. I did keep my eyes peeled after this but couldn't see or hear any aircraft in the vicinity. I wondered whether it was just a general health warning like "smoking kills" or "don't drink and drive", but then discarded the idea, deciding that most people would instinctively know to "beware" if an aeroplane was flying straight at them.

Just before reaching Cardigan, I came across another road sign showing the direction to a place called Newcastle Emlyn. I wondered whether my friend Emlyn from Newcastle (he of Sca Fell fame) knew that he had a town named after him. Perhaps his parents had lived near here and told him to go and get a job there, and poor Emlyn had trailed up to the north-east mistakenly, having assumed there had been a comma in the sentence.

I was really looking forward to the Pembrokeshire coast path, which would take me the 180 miles from Cardigan to Amroth Castle beyond Tenby. This would be the first prolonged stretch of way-marked walking since the Fife coastal path. It would certainly be a welcome relief not to have to battle with a map with freezing cold hands and instead just to keep an eye open for the sign of an acorn; the generic symbol for a National Trail in England and Wales.

The path began at St Dogmaels, following the estuary of the River Teifi and gaining height out to the point at Cemaes Head. From here the view opens up and I could see what was in store for the next couple of days. It was extraordinary and wonderful that even after walking all this way, I could get so excited about the prospect of walking a view. This is what happened to me here. Dramatic cliffs adorned a heavily indented stretch of totally unspoiled coastline. The Pembrokeshire coast path was not going to disappoint.

It was a gamble to walk as far as Moylgrove when I had to get back almost to Aberporth that night to meet up with my brother. I was hoping there would be some public transport available. On my arrival in the village, however, it soon became apparent that my predicament was far worse than there just being no buses to ferry me to my night's accommodation. I had simply not bargained for my dilemma. My mobile phone was out of range; it was dark and very cold; I only had £5 in cash on me; the local public phone was not working and pretty soon my medication was going to fail me.

Usually in these situations on Coastin', I had relied on luck to see me through: a ferry, a friend or a fallback plan. But on this occasion there seemed to be no solution and all I could do was just stand there totally helpless, but still strangely confident that something extraordinary would happen any minute.

It did. I caught the eye of a couple who were just going back into their house and seized the opportunity to speak to them.

"Excuse me, I'm trying to get towards Aberporth. The phone is broken and I wonder if I could use yours to call a taxi."

"A taxi will cost you a fortune," the girl responded. "It will have to come all the way out from Cardigan."

"I don't really have any option." There was a pause while the man seemed to be making his mind up about something.

"I'll take you there if you give me £15." I leapt at the offer.

On the journey, the story of what I was doing was revealed and the man (Pete) seemed fascinated. He was even more fascinated when half an hour after leaving Moylgrove we arrived at the hotel where I was supposed to be staying to find that it was boarded up, overgrown and decidedly frightening looking. It turned out that the guide book I had was out of date and the hotel had moved. It took another half-hour to find the new hotel, which was actually beyond Aberporth. Feeling horrendously guilty as I stepped out of Pete's car and having totally ruined his evening, I offered him £30 which I had extracted from a cashpoint on the way.

"I wouldn't dream of it," he said. "I have enjoyed every second. Put the money in the pot." With a wave and smile he took off on his long journey back home and left me standing with my mouth wide open and the three crisp £10 notes flapping both from the tremor in my left hand and a decidedly chilly wind.

My brother had come to walk with me for a day. He and I are very different and yet so alike. In growing up we had both been good at the same things: geography, stubbornness and pride were our fortes. But if I was good at these things, he excelled. In fact, I believe he could have gone on to become a Professor of Stubbornetics. While I am disorganised and absent-minded, Mark is totally the opposite. Whilst my style tends to be a broad-brush approach, Mark is careful, meticulous and likes things well planned.

Throughout most of my childhood, Mark and I took little notice of each other. The seven years between us ensured that to him I was just a pointless encumbrance. When I was born he patiently waited six months before enquiring: "Mummy, when is my brother going to be of any use?"

Despite the distant relationship between my brother and me, he was someone whom I knew would always be first on the scene in a crisis. In recent months, the crisis had been all too apparent and it was Mark who had pulled the family together and given us a platform from which we could start again.

The day I walked the 20 or so miles from Moylgrove to Fishguard with my brother would be the first whole day I had spent alone with him in my entire life. I had stupidly wondered what we would have to talk about. Such concerns were ridiculous. A beautiful day, the awe-inspiring Pembrokeshire coast path and, perhaps most importantly, the discovery that we were both capable of holding an entertaining conversation, meant that we didn't stop talking for most of the way.

From that day to this there has not been an unpleasant word between us. The extraordinary thing was that precisely 12,663 days after I was born, my brother and I found out that we actually liked one another. I was surprised how good this made me feel. What is more, my brother Mark no longer asks our mother when I will become useful. He now directs the question at me.

It's a start.

My Coastin' rules dictated that I could have walked the 32 miles from Cardigan to Tenby in one day. The coastal route, which of course was the whole point of the exercise regardless of the rules, would be 150 miles longer. This fact partly reflects the extent of Pembrokeshire's protrusion into the Irish Sea, but more significantly it is because of the convoluted meanderings of its shoreline, the construction and route of which suggests that it was a joint venture between God and Owen Glyndwr.

It is without question a stupendous path, rich in everything except people; I saw no one other than a few dog walkers and weekenders along its entire length. St Davids, at the south-western tip of Wales, has the smallest cathedral in the country. By virtue of this, it also claims the title of smallest city. It is perfectly proportioned. I remained here for three days walking from St Nicholas to Solva in a series of 15- to 20-mile circuits, each taking in a new section of coast and all of which started and finished at my B&B.

With the golden beaches, island vistas and craggy headlands which surround it, St Davids must win the award as a venue for the definitive city break. It is a city where you really will get a break, being crime-, traffic-, pollution-, people-, and totally stress-, free. The toothless sweep of St Bride's Bay bulldozes deep into the Pembrokeshire landscape from the two rocky peninsulas either side. At the tip of the St David's peninsula, Ramsey Island stands guard, while Skomer and Skokholm Islands are the sentinels that keep watch over the southern entrance to the bay.

On reaching Dale, it is sickening to find the blight of industry on such a beautiful place. Great chimneys belch and huge tankers churn up Milford's once peaceful haven. On a perfect winter's morning before breakfast, I walked the edge of the often ignored peninsula to the south of Dale. St Ann's Head, which lies at the tip of this, looks directly into the mouth of Milford Haven's natural harbour, which graced so many geography textbooks in my youth. After the initial shock, it was a fascinating place to perch and watch the shipping activity.

The path from Dale to Milford Haven is a mixed bag. Whereas before on this path, at the top of each incline, I was rewarded with a far-reaching landscape of deep blue sea, fluffy white clouds and cliffs, here the rewards were a murky estuary, billowing fumes, and the cliffs were now vast metallic constructions used for who-knows-what purpose.

My telephone rang. I had recently changed its tune from the James Bond theme to "The Blue Danube".

"Bore da!"

"Bore da, Blod."

"Where are you?"

"… on a hill."

"You're brilliant. You're a star. What's the weather like?"

"Glorious."

"I saw Jeff and Dai at the weekend in Llanrhystud. They enjoyed talking to you."

"I enjoyed listening."

"They said for me to send regards from the 'Headless Brothers' and wondered whether you got through that hedge." She went on to explain plans for talking to a Milford Haven journalist, attending a reception with the mayor of Pembroke, and further meetings and press calls in Carmarthen, Kidwelly, Llanelli and Swansea.

"I will meet you in Swansea," she said. I was excited at the prospect of meeting Blod. Her effervescent character was infectious and I had come to rely on my daily Blod fix. I had spoken to her every day since I had been in Wales and she was completely committed to the task of awareness for the cause. "You see Tom," she would say, "you've got to tell them the story. I know the story now, you see, I can tell anyone the story in about seven seconds."

I was glad Blod was telling everyone "the story". I wasn't entirely sure what the story was and whether it could or should be told in only seven seconds, but frankly whatever Blod was doing was working, so I just went along with it. About an hour into my day's walk out of Milford Haven my drugs kicked out early leaving me in a shaky and totally useless state. Minutes later it started raining heavily; I needed my waterproofs. But I was too incapacitated to put them on. The only thing to do was to hide in a telephone box, and in here I managed to get my waterproofs on. I took another pill and waited to stop shaking.

A man living above the cafe opposite saw me quivering and thought it was because I was cold. He came down and opened the door of the telephone box

"Hello bach... Look you're freezing cold, boyo. Come in and have a cup of tea and some leeks." (That's what it sounded like anyway.)

"It's OK, I have Parkinson's. I'll be fine in a moment."

He went away and sure enough a few minutes later my drugs kicked in. I stopped shaking. At the same time it stopped raining and I took off my waterproofs in the phone box, revealing my crisp new Coastin' T-shirt.

I pushed open the door of the phone box and strode out like a completely new man. As I did so the man from above the cafe opened his window and shouted across: "Hey, you're like Superman, the way you did that!"

I told a local reporter the story and the next day, the headline read "Superman shakes up Milford Haven".

I was grateful to the people in this area, who were unexpectedly friendly when compared to the town of Milford Haven itself, where the infrastructure and buildings were unwelcoming and poorly maintained. I was also incredibly grateful to whoever built a bridge from Neyland to Pembroke. The alternative would have been a 40-mile circuit via Haverfordwest so as to circumvent the far-reaching tentacles of two wide rivers which flow into Milford Haven.

I liked Pembroke. It was a piece of old Wales before the oil came. The people here were great too and it seemed appropriate that the town's mayor should be a young, portly, jolly-looking fellow. Pembroke Castle is yet another classic fortress and I found myself staring at its thick ramparts reflected in the lake below and wanting to see what was inside its walls. Reluctantly, I turned my back on the place, determined to dispense with the southern shore of Milford Haven as quickly as possible.

From West Angle Bay, it is only a two mile swim to St Ann's Head, where I had been three days ago. I was beginning to get used to these rather frustrating experiences.

It was a pity not to have been able to explore the quite difficult stretch of the coast beyond Rat Island more fully. I was intrigued by interestingly named features on the map such as Sheep Island, Guttle Hole and Black Cave. But I walked this entire stretch in the dark. Not that that would have mattered perhaps for the inspection of Black Cave.

The coast path cuts in to Castle Martin to avoid an artillery range and I rejoined the sea along the most impressive section of the limestone coast on mainland Britain. From the Elegug Stacks to Stackpole Warren there is much to see and a great deal to fall off and into. In my head I could hear my Welsh geography teacher's voice becoming animated and emotional while he explained how these vast columns, chasms and cliffs of his homeland had been forged and then sculpted by natural processes.

Tenby felt English. I think it is something to do with the Georgian and Regency architecture and the name. It is unsurprising that Tenby's name in Welsh, which is Dinbych-y-Pysgod, has not been so readily adopted by either locals or visitors. I am told that those who can pronounce it and say it out loud are often warned about using foul language in a built-up area.

My arrival at Amroth Castle heralded the end of the wonderful Pembrokeshire coast path and almost immediately my route planning became difficult. Through sheer perseverance I hacked my way through to Pendine where, the following morning, I was treated to the most unbelievable sunrise I had ever seen. Ablaze with reds, pinks and oranges, the sky reflected on the seven miles of glistening sand which had been the venue for the land-speed records in the 1920s. Malcolm Campbell's Bluebird was successful several times here, whereas Parry-Thomas in his car, Babs, was killed when he lost control, having been the first person to reach 180 mph.

The only way to avoid the gaping estuary of the Taf and Towy rivers, which meet at Llansteffan, was to steer a course for Carmarthen via St Clears using minor roads. I started wondering in this section whether I might break my own land-speed record. I seemed to be going faster than ever before and was closing in on the 3½ mph barrier. A dank and foggy day down to Kidwelly followed, only to be cheered considerably by my first encounter with Marlene, another of Blod's friends, who was not so taken with the word "brilliant" but did think everything was "marvellous". She was certainly marvellous – one of those no-nonsense, warm, heart-on-her-sleeve sorts of people who you would not want to be on the wrong side of, but of whom it's an absolute joy to be on the right side.

If Coastin' was "brilliant" to Blod, and "marvellous" to Marlene, then the chances were that ex-British Lion and Welsh rugby star Ray Gravell would think it was "really great" at the very least. But Ray, yet another friend of Blod's, who was very kindly putting me up in a local hotel for the night, awarded me with the verbal equivalent of the Grand Slam; Ray Gravell said that Coastin' was a "magnificent enterprise."

Gravell was like a benevolent grizzly bear. He had a big genial Welsh face, moulded by rugby and flushed by the outdoors and beer. It was a face which was smiling even when the mouth was not.

"Do you speak Welsh?" he asked, as if most people in the world did and should.

"I'm afraid not."

"You should learn it," he said. "It's the language of 'eaven."

I had to admit as I followed Ray around the hotel and watched him as he somehow managed to hold three conversations in Welsh and two in English at the same time, there was something of the "'eavenly" about the rhythm and flow of the Welsh over the slightly harsher form and inflection of English. Having said that, the Welsh have a way with speaking anyway. It is as if each word they use is lovingly caressed in the mouth before being uttered. When Ray Gravell said my walk was a "magnificent enterprise" he made the words sound bigger and more important than was normal and it made me feel rather proud.

\* \* \*

It was 21st December. The final three days before Christmas were spent predominantly walking in the rain. I was glad to get through Llanelli and on to the Gower peninsula, where the walking seemed to improve the further west I marched. Just beyond Llanrhidian I was lucky that a break in the weather coincided with an uncomfortable bout of shaking. I sat for an hour and waited for it to pass just outside a fortified house called Weobley Castle. It was not as "weobley" as me.

Despite its reputation, I just couldn't get excited about the Gower peninsula. Maybe it was the weather. Maybe my thoughts were set on getting home for Christmas. It would be a strange one without Dad.

When I reached Rhossili beach, on 23rd December, I did begin to be impressed with the Gower. It was huge and cloaked in a strange blue haze. As surfers came in from the sea at dusk, steam rose from their wetsuits and I felt I had seen the image before; perhaps it was some atmospheric scene in a film. The following day, I walked just 12 miles to Penmaen and went home to Hertfordshire that evening.

Lyndsey came for Christmas. I noticed that my family did not treat her as a guest any more. It was clear they all liked her and she seemed to enjoy the fact that she could relax in everyone's company. Lyndsey could never be anyone other than herself. It's a fine quality. So many people I meet try to be something they are not.

Traditionally, my family goes for a walk on Christmas Day. This year was no exception. The strange thing was, I had never been so keen to go. Despite this, as usual when I stopped Coastin' I fell ill. I was beginning to wonder whether I would have to spend the rest of my life in continuous motion in order to maintain my health. The thought was not altogether abhorrent to me.

On 29th December, a Coastin' posse collected for Coastin' at the rugby fixture in Bath against Harlequins. At half time I wandered onto the pitch with Clare Balding, who had volunteered to help out. We raised £3,000 from the day, which was astonishing. I was still not feeling at all well and did not take too much further part in the day. Instead, I was able to just sit back and observe the activities of my Coastin' friends. They were, every one of them, amazing.

It struck me that Coastin' had sprouted another limb. There was the walk, there was the charity, and now I realised that it had also brought people together who would not otherwise have known each other. Friendships and even romance had blossomed. Lyndsey and I were of course a fine example.

Lyndsey was with me to restart Coastin' on 30th December from Penmaen. The weather matched my state of health: miserable. One and a half hours of exhausting, muddy scrambling due to my poor map reading made me feel even worse.

At Parkmill, a man in a Jaguar rolled down his window and enquired whether we had enjoyed our walk today. Lyndsey immediately embarked on an enthusiastic account of the delights of the journey so far. I wondered whether she had been walking a completely different route from me. Had she really enjoyed the past 90 minutes? "... and when you get to Three Cliffs Bay, it's amazing!" I heard her say. This bit was true. It was stunning. It was the getting there that was the problem.

Once Lyndsey had said all she wanted to say, I sidled up to the man's open window and whispered, "If I were you I would stay in the car. It's terrible out here."

The man smiled and drove off, only to reappear with his wife two minutes later having donned their waterproofs. Clearly, my credibility was dubious. We chatted to the couple and he asked us what we were doing. When I had told him, he reached into his pocket and produced a £50 note. For the umpteenth time on Coastin', I found myself at a loss for words. We had been talking for no more than two minutes.

Buoyed by the man's generosity, my spirits and strength lifted. By the time I reached Southgate, however, I was in serious difficulties.

Parkinson's is erratic, except when something else is wrong. In the same way as happened in north Wales, when my body has to contend with some other ailment or pain, Parkinson's struck with devastating force, giving me an insight as to how my illness might progress. It was a crystal ball that others could see, but I would actually have to be in the thing; living the nightmare.

In the same way as I saw Michael J. Fox as my future self, I now was that person; temporarily suffering symptoms of a future me. Today, for the first time whilst actually walking on Coastin', my Parkinson's reacted to a virus in my body. I thought about what had happened in Wales, when my mother had witnessed something similar. I realised that I was now going *Back to the Future*. The bitter irony of this was sweetened by Lyndsey because when I told her this, she replied, "You look more like you're in *Spin City* to me."

There was inevitability to the fact that the walk to Mumbles Head ranked as the most badly affected by Parkinson's of the entire journey. I tottered as if I had no knee joints and when I came to a hilly section, I would have to jog or else I would have been frozen to the spot. All communication from my head to my limbs had been severed. I was like a car with a loose accelerator cable and worn-out brake pads; revving urgently, idling crazily; everything except moving forward.

I was glad Lyndsey was with me, but wondered what she was thinking. I expected a cure to curtail what would otherwise be an inevitable slide into a future of living constantly in this state, but could Lyndsey believe in it too? It was possible that my future happiness lay in the answer to this question.

"It's only temporary, this," I said to Lyndsey, feeling the need to justify the state I was in.

"I know," she said. It was in that tone; that same accepting tone that I was beginning to recognise so well.

My medication kicked in and the incident was locked away in the dark recesses of my mind; never to see the light until the next time I needed it for comparative purposes only.

Most of the following day was spent in bed, ill, but not before meeting Blod in the shopping centre in Swansea. She was everything I had hoped for:

bright, smiley and hugely charismatic. "Brilliant" in fact. Even though she was quite slight in frame, she had huge presence and reminded me a little bit of a flamboyant flamenco dancer. But no sooner had we been introduced than she was off co-ordinating, organising and telling "the story" in seven seconds to anyone who would listen.

One shopper approached me and asked, "Do you have Parkinson's?"

"Yes."

"I thought so," she said. "You have a smooth face. All people with Parkinson's have a smooth face."

Most people would be only too pleased to be told that they had a smooth face, but I was mortified to think that I was displaying such a quality. I decided it was a little insensitive of the lady (whose husband had Parkinson's) to make such a comment.

For the record, the correct thing to say to anyone who tells you that they have Parkinson's is, "Well, I would never have guessed!" and not the self-congratulatory, "Yes, I thought as much." It is an important thing for anyone with Parkinson's to believe that he or she could pass for someone without a neurological problem, at least at some stage of the day.

The lady was soon forgotten though, when without warning a choir clad in Coastin' T-shirts suddenly lined up on the stairs and sang, "We'll keep a welcome in the hillsides" to me. The wonderful Welsh vocals resonated around the atrium of the shopping centre. I stood there grinning from ear to ear. It was such a special moment. Maybe I was tired, emotional and ill, but I realised when it had finished that my eyes had welled up.

The flu lasted another day and then miraculously disappeared, leaving me fit enough to launch my assault on Cardiff. It seemed sensible to take a wide berth around Port Talbot which just didn't look or sound appealing. We chose a route via the extensive woodland west of Maesteg instead. Crossing back over the M4 to rejoin the coast at Kenfig, we battled along the links of Porthcawl in a strong headwind and having reached the town itself, Lyndsey went home.

The River Ogmore, or Afon Ogwr as they say in Wales, was blocking my path into the Vale of Glamorgan. I had hoped to find a place to cross near its estuary, but it was too wide and too deep. I realised with some despair that I would have to make the hazardous journey up its floodplain to reach the first crossing at Merthyr Mawr. The Ogmore had flooded with all the recent rain, but once my boots were well and truly soaked through, it was actually quite enjoyable splashing around in large puddles and leaping over tributaries. No wonder they call it an "Afon". In the midst of "affing fun", I heard my mobile phone ring.

I reached into my pocket for the machine which had stood me in such good stead for so long and felt its familiar vibrating sensation against my hand. I pulled the phone out as I had so many times before, but in doing so the combination of its vibrations and my wet hands sent it flying high up into the air like a slippery fish. I caught it on its way back down, but then fumbled so that it fell from my grasp again. I made a final desperate lunge and came tantalisingly close to making a dream catch, but instead it only grazed my outstretched fingertips. The telephone fell to the ground and after that there was only one place it was going to end up. Having bounced once, the phone seemed to pirouette perfectly in mid-air before plunging into the Afon Ogmore. Remarkably, owing to its protective cover, it then reappeared out of my reach and floated away downstream still playing "The Blue Danube" as it went. The melody seemed to be mocking me.

There was nothing I could do. It was gone. I thought how much Wild Rover would enjoy the story and decided I would ring to tell him what had happened... DOH!!

It was only now that I didn't have a phone that I realised how attached to it I was. It was my one link with the not-walking world. It was both a comfort and a lifeline; an extraordinary device which allowed me to roam right round the country and still retain contact with everyone I knew. Now the phone had gone roaming itself. In fact, I managed to make an interesting anagram out of Afon Ogmore: "Fone go roam".

Maybe it was because I made more of an effort to talk to people on the route, but after the Great Phone Spilling Incident of Ogmore, I found everyone who walked past me extremely friendly. I am not sure why this surprised me, but I just did not expect such open friendliness so close to Cardiff. People seemed to have time not only to say "hello", but also to have a bit of a chat. The coastline was better than expected too and when I reached Cardiff on 4th January, I already felt well disposed to the place.

The waterfront in Cardiff had changed enormously since I was last there. As part of the Millennium regeneration process, it had been transformed into a chic harbourside community with boutique shops and wide wooden gangways on which to walk.

My official entry into Cardiff was being orchestrated by Blod. All I knew

Dawn at Pendine Sands

Dusk at Rhossili Bay, the Gower Penninsula

Cardiff

Walking at Rhossili

Sunset at Burnham on Sea

Towards Hartland
Quay, North Devon

At Bath RFC with Shazzer,
Silky Smooth and The Fixer

On this spot
– 1st April 1780 –
nothing happened.

Devon

Washing at Port Isaac

Sally and
Berwyn
Thomas at
Port Isaac

'Bit breezy out…' North Cornwall

Beyond St Ives

Lyndsey's body
was a temple

Near Lands End with Lyndsey

Remnants of the tin industry Cornwall

South Cornwall

Rosemullion Head
Near Helford Cornwall

Brighton Beach Huts

The South West Coast Path

Beachy Head

David Jones

Me, Elizabeth and Mike Hurley

The London Marathon team

The final day starts

My family at Tower Bridge

Dad

was that I would be walking from the Welsh Assembly Building to City Hall. What I had not realised was that there would be 40 people walking with me, and press, TV cameras and a reception committee at City Hall.

At the Welsh Assembly, I was given a document in recognition of Coastin' which was signed by 15 assembly members. I was pleased Blod had organised this. One of my missions had been to raise awareness amongst the decision makers.

It was about a half-hour walk to City Hall. A Coastin' cavalcade, bigger even than the group who turned out in Newcastle, were marching with me to Cardiff city centre. On the way, I chatted to a girl called Sharon who worked in the Norgine factory at Hengoed and who, with a friend, had raised £600 at a local pub for Coastin'. She had never met me before and I felt such gratitude towards her for her efforts. She would later raise another £2,000.

Blod caught me up at the front of the procession. "Where are the police?" she said.

"What police?" I asked.

"There are meant to be police to stop the traffic."

I laughed, assuming she was joking.

"No. I'm serious. The chief of police is a friend of mine and we are meant to have a police escort." She got on the phone, looking quite upset.

No more than 60 seconds after she hung up, two police officers arrived and stopped the traffic to let us pass when the occasion required.

"Blod!" I called to her as she retreated back down the cavalcade. "Blod!" I repeated. "You are the Countess of Cardiff."

Blod cackled with laughter. "Brilliant!" she said.

Now our passage was not hindered by cars, we made swift progress to City Hall and, to my amazement, there was a group of about 30 people there too, all in Coastin' livery. At the front of this group was Marlene, who came rushing forward to give me a big hug.

"You're marvellous!" she said. I knew she wouldn't let me down.

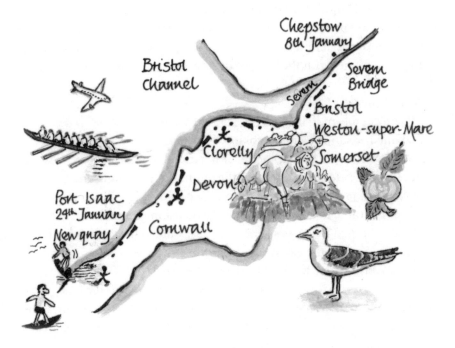

FROM NEWPORT TO NEWQUAY
318 MILES
JANUARY

CHAPTER 26

If the walk into Cardiff had been more scenic and more enjoyable than I had expected, the walk out of it was correspondingly awful. In fact, only Day Two through Dagenham was worse in walking terms than the day from Cardiff to Newport. Pollution of all kinds prevailed in this flat industrial wasteland. Everything about it was unpleasant. While I was having my lunch a white van turned up, emptied its contents of litter and rubbish not 100 yards from where I sat, and then drove off. The practice of fly-tipping is utterly beyond excuse.

Things improved significantly once I reached the Brecon Canal and I was able to cut up and over the River Usk at Caerleon. From Chepstow Hill, I was excited to catch my first glimpse of the Severn Road Bridge. I would need to get my clothes washed to celebrate my re-entry to England and noticed a small village on the map called Undy. It sounded the sort of place that might have washing facilities. It did.

My final day in Wales was the short walk to Chepstow, passing under the M4 road bridge. From here I failed to creep through St Pierre golf club unnoticed. As I laboured across the golf course in full view, I was aware that people were staring at me, but felt that this was not so much because I was a shaky man walking across a golf course with a rucksack, but more because I was not strictly complying with the dress code. And me with my newly washed undies from Undy too.

It was unusual for me to be up and out of my B&B prior to 7 a.m., but this morning I was anxious to be on time for a meeting in England. The border between England and Wales follows the centre point of the River Wye and out into the Severn estuary. This means that most of the Severn Road Bridge is in England, and the first set of 400-foot towers that I approached on the bridge, and the vast span beyond them, made me feel as if I was walking through a gigantic gateway back into my homeland and then, eventually, to the wobbly bridge.

I had walked over the Severn Bridge before, and despite the incessant rumble of cars, it makes for an eerie and lonely walk. But my repatriation did not seem as momentous as the other big event of the morning. This morning, at Severn View service station, I was to meet Steven Gill, the neurosurgeon who had had such success with delivery of a new growth factor called GDNF into the brains of five of his patients. Over the course of two years, these individuals had apparently experienced a resurrection; their functional capabilities being restored almost immeasurably.

I wondered what to expect of this man who had achieved such things. Here was a man who, from my perspective, had almost god-like powers. And yet I knew from my experience of scientists that he was unlikely to be in the least bit god-like. In fact, as I walked across the bridge, I conjured up an image of someone who was tall, thin, balding, bespectacled and actually pretty devoid of any character whatsoever. In doing this I reckoned it would not be possible to be disappointed.

Upon my arrival at the service station, I heard a voice from behind me as I walked through the doors: "Tom?" I turned before saying, "Hello – Mr Gill?"

But then maybe this was not Mr Gill, because the man in front of me had a full head of hair and was now saying his name was "Steve".

"Shall we go and get a coffee?" he said.

As I followed him into the service station, I realised that this was Steven Gill. He seemed too young, too friendly, too... well... normal.

He insisted on buying coffee and we sat down facing one another. I felt myself bursting with questions. I was worried that he would have to leave before he gave me the answers. But Steve Gill seemed relaxed and in no hurry. He baffled me still further by spending the next half-hour wanting to know all about Coastin' and waxing lyrical about my achievements.

Never in a conversation had I been so anxious to move the subject from myself. Having finally done so, we spent an incredibly uplifting hour and a half talking about Parkinson's. I knew by the end of this time that I would never find anyone who I would rather back to find a cure for my illness. Steve was passionate about his work and I could see in his eyes he believed, he truly believed, that given time he could crack Parkinson's. Furthermore, and equally important in a way, here was a scientist with whom I could actually communicate. I found myself understanding much of what he said despite the fact that he had clearly consumed a small medical dictionary for breakfast. When our meeting had finished, I felt positively lightheaded. For the first time, I actually believed it. Previously my talk of a cure had been hope. Now it seemed I could truly believe. I followed the Severn Way, which hugs the banks of the estuary. After the meeting with Steven Gill, I had a spring in my step and practically decided there and then that it was Steve's research into GDNF that was to be the beneficiary of this walk. It was, after all, a treatment that could offer tangible improvements to people's lives within a reasonable timeframe. Suddenly, the money that I was raising, and that others were raising for me, seemed to take on even greater importance.

I swept through Avonmouth, happy that its grim industrial squalor was providing the sort of walking experience that suited my newly lengthened stride and purposeful demeanour. Like Parkinson's, this was an area that needed to be dispensed with quickly and clinically.

Having crossed the River Avon and crossed and re-crossed the M5 motorway about three times near Portbury, I somehow wound my way through a labyrinthine business park to the coast at Portishead.

Before my first visit to Somerset, I had envisaged a place full of leathery-faced farmers chewing on bits of straw, leaning on their combine harvesters and saying "ooh arrrr" a lot. It was terribly disappointing to find that none of these stereotypes existed, and in fact the county is one of the most socially diverse in the country. Unfortunately for me, its best bits are not found on the coast, but in the hills of the Mendips and the Quantocks and in such fascinating places such as Wells, Cheddar and Glastonbury.

Although the stretch of coastal path between Portishead and Clevedon is pleasant, beyond Clevedon a series of inland forays were necessary to negotiate the crossing of rivers such as the Yeo, the Axe, the Brue and the Parrett. The most significant of these was the Parrett where a half-day's detour upstream was required to reach the aptly named Bridgwater, before having to trundle all the way back to the coast to Hinkley Point power station. Bridgwater has a nice name, but given the choice I think I would rather live in the power station.

Happily, I had friends with me for a lot of this little stretch, where the scenery failed to do anything other than reconfirm my lack of attachment to places such as Weston-super-Mare, Burnham on Sea and Watchet. It certainly did not help either that I was going through a period of poor health. On Wain's Hill at the southern end of Clevedon, I spent an uncomfortable two hours avoiding the stares of dogs and slightly more subtle glances from their owners. I may not have been so concerned these days not to be seen, but it was still a miserable experience to be "on show". My thoughts kept returning to my conversation with Steven Gill, and one phase in particular: "What I would give to stop shaking for ever".

The coastal scenery in Somerset is disappointing up to and including Minehead. Nevertheless, its pancake-flat shoreline can provide the most remarkable sunsets and I was fortunate enough to be hypnotised by one of these at Burnham on Sea. Beyond Minehead, however, is a completely different story. Minehead represents the official start of the South West Coast Path, which is without doubt one of Britain's finest treasures. And, like most of Britain's treasures, it is revered by only a few British, quite a lot of Dutch, boatloads of Germans and no French whatsoever. Those people from the UK who rave about the path tend to be those who venture a little further than 200 metres from their car to sample the extraordinary scenery and who challenge themselves with its countless climbs and descents from headland to bay. In fact, in walking the full 630 miles of the path round to Poole in Dorset, as I would be doing, the total height ascended would be nigh on 100,000 feet; over three times the height of Everest. Furthermore, I would encounter 921 stiles and 26,719 steps. Contrary to popular opinion, the South West Coast Path is actually tougher than the Pennine Way insofar as it climbs an average of 148 feet per mile compared to the 127 feet per mile on the Pennine Way. It is also 360 miles longer.

I received a lovely welcome at the western end of Minehead. Representatives from the local Parkinson's Disease Society branch and the local Ramblers group had turned out and applauded as I entered their midst. I pretended to look exhausted, which was in fact a double bluff as I had run the six miles from Watchet that morning for fear of being late. I need not have worried. I was late anyway.

I didn't realise it at the time, but Minehead would herald a change for me and Coastin'. Firstly, there was a change of scenery. The flat Somerset plains dramatically disappear as soon as you are out of sight of Butlin's, which occupies a prominent position on Minehead's seafront. In their place come steep, grassy cliffs which fall away into the sea and hint at the glorious walking ahead.

I also felt better. The shaking that had plagued my walking for the past week inexplicably vanished. Bad shaking took a lot out of me. Apart from the physical discomfort, it also took hours out of my day, which in turn added stress, as I tried to keep up with the Coastin' schedule. It was a vicious circle from which it was extremely difficult to break free. But without my doing anything different, my medication seemed to deliver a far smoother and more effective dose. This happy state of affairs would continue for much of the south-west and was a welcome reprieve in the cold winter months.

Finally, I experienced a slow change in my attitude towards the walk, which developed as I progressed closer and closer to the finishing line. Up to this point the walking had been the single most important aspect of my existence. Every day was a new challenge which had to be faced head on. Even in the aftermath of Dad dying, the walking had been the therapy; the thing to keep my mind and body active in the face of appalling circumstances. But from Minehead onwards the walk would become less and less important. I knew I was going to make it and it was just a case of going through the motions. I had become a walking automaton. You could point me in any direction and I would just keep walking until I reached the destination, happy and yet numb at the same time.

That is not to say that I had lost my enthusiasm for each day or the satisfaction at the end of it, but more that I was indifferent to the mechanics of walking. This enabled me to concentrate more on the charitable aspects of Coastin' as opposed to the physical task of completing it. Walking was now a way of life. It was a text I knew verbatim, and now the extra-curricular activities took precedence. They would provide the icing on the cake; the true goals: awareness, funds and, ultimately, a cure.

The immediate task, however, was to get to Porlock, which was a relatively slow process given my companions for the day. The Ramblers, apart from being an organisation made up of some of the nicest people on the planet, is also one of the most appropriately named institutions in the country. Having adjusted my expectations for the day and discarded the prospect of being at my destination by lunchtime, I relaxed and enjoyed five hours of definitive rambling; that is to say we walked aimlessly and spoke of things of no consequence. It was refreshing to spend the afternoon in such a way after my mad sprint that morning. I was also assured of a relatively relaxing time the following day when Mr Beef joined me again. On a superb day's walk to Lynton, we encountered two old men staring deep into a bank of brambles.

"We are looking for the end of my friend's shooting stick, which has broken orf," came the clipped tones of one of the men – he sounded distinctly ex-army, and if so, was at least a brigadier in rank. We prodded around for a bit making banal guesses as to where the thing might be.

The Brigadier refused to detain us any longer than a few minutes and we set off down the track, only to stumble across the missing piece of equipment in the middle of the track 200 yards from where they were looking. The two men were delighted to have recovered the object.

"I think my friend here owes you two a pint of beer." The Brigadier gave us a wink as if to say, "even though I know you are too young to drink."

Upon our arrival at the appointed hostelry in Lynmouth, the landlady called out from behind the bar, "You look like the two rescuers of the shooting stick belonging to Mr Kipling. There's a free pint each when you want it."

Mr Beef and I were stunned. Not so much by the speed at which the Brigadier and Mr Kipling had got to Lynmouth to order the drinks. Not even by the generosity and friendliness of the people in these parts. We were stunned because we had found someone whose name was Mr Kipling.

Somerset leaves the best of its coast until last. The path wriggles through the trees to Porlock Weir and past the tiny 800-year-old Culbone Church, which nestles in a small hollow, totally hidden and refreshingly unspoilt. And then, finally, Somerset bows out in a blaze of glory when the path takes to the higher ground and provides views back across the estuary to the coast of South Wales, which is clearly visible.

But the scenery does not let up. Once you are in Devon, the 21 or so miles to Combe Martin are some of the finest walking country in Britain. In fact, I defy anyone who is reasonably fit and who thinks walking is boring to hike this section of the coast path and come away unfulfilled. It is not just the views, the cliffs, the valleys, the woods and the challenge; it is the variety of all those elements in such a short distance.

One word of warning though. In Lynton, there is a pub owner who doesn't know the words to Sinatra's "Strangers in the Night" and instead violates the Law of Annoying Noises by singing the tune in a series of "Yompy pompy pom. Da da dee da da. Yompy pompy pom" etc. By the end of the meal I was eyeing my steak knife with terrible thoughts. And for days it stayed with me! Just before Combe Martin, at the top of the hill called Great Hangman, I too could be heard "yompy pompy pomming" just like Sinatra never did. In the end, I felt so offended by myself that I made up my own words to the song:

> Shakers in the night
> Sleep's not improving
> It's an awful plight
> I can't stop moving
> Muscles are so tight
> There's nothing I can do
>
> Brain's motor used to be
> By Aston Martin
> Now it's Zanussi
> And it's on fast spin
> Shake so violently
> The Richter Scale's reached two
>
> Shakers in the night
> We Parkies' people
> We are Shakers in the night
> And yet researchers say
> There's hope now of a cure
> Of that they seem quite sure
> I ask you all for PD's sake
> Let's crack this thing so we don't shake!
>
> If we take up the fight
> Then we'll start winning
> Future looks so bright
> I'll not stop grinning
> When it turns out all right
> For Shakers in the night.

By the time I reached Combe Martin, it had been dark for some time and I was glad of my head-torch. I was booked in to a pub where Lyndsey and her friend Barbra were going to meet me. They had arrived in the bar with their rucksacks on their backs. Barbra, a tall and attractive American, in her typically friendly way, announced her presence with a "Hi there!" – and of course within a few moments the entire pub fell silent; only the odd clink of glass was to be heard. By the time Lyndsey had got through the door with her pack, all eyes were trained on the two new visitors.

Eventually the silence was broken by a soft Devonshire accent: "Don't go out on the moors alone." At this reference to the opening scene of An American Werewolf in London, the entire pub erupted with laughter and Lyndsey and Barbra were welcomed in by the landlord. "Don't worry girls" he said, "Full moon's tomorrow night."

Although the next few days to Braunton were not quite as scenic or as challenging as the previous two, they were equally enjoyable in the company of Lyndsey and Barbra. Things were pretty good. My spirits were high; the weather since Cardiff had been amazingly good, and Q was doing sterling work with the publicity as I walked down towards Land's End. Although I had walked all this before, I had never been down to the West Country at this time of the year. It was equally beautiful in the winter sunshine and, of course, there was hardly anyone around. It came as quite a shock to me that the resorts of Ilfracombe and Woolacombe, which I had only ever seen awash with humanity, were so empty and quiet.

I was religious about keeping as close to the coast as possible right around the south-west peninsula. I was worried that I might not reach my 4,500 mile target by the time I reached London again. Of course, the whole process of measuring the distance walked every day was highly subjective. I was measuring mileage using a wheeled device on a map which would presuppose that all my walking was in a straight line and would take no account of gradient. In all likelihood I had probably already walked 4,500 miles.

From Woolacombe Sands, we walked right to the end of Croyde Hoe to Baggy Point and then all the way out to the tip of Braunton Marsh, which flanks Saunton Sands.

The River Taw's estuary gouges deep into North Devon and the first crossing is at Barnstaple. Here the local news station filmed me walking with the local MP. To my absolute joy, Docadile Dundee appeared while all this was going on. I was correspondingly horrified when the cameraman decided that he wanted Doc to be present in the footage as well. Needless to say, he was only too pleased to oblige.

It was a fleeting visit by Docadile. Having graciously accepted the glory of being filmed for a news bulletin, he walked about another two miles and then left. I asked for the channel to be changed in a pub in Instow because "I think my walk is going to be featured on the local news". The entire pub soon became involved in this excitement and we all stood there waiting for my moment of fame. I soon regretted doing this; having entered the pub rather brazenly, I was forced to slope out in much quieter fashion when there was not even a hint of my story.

I was far less ostentatious that evening in Appledore, and watched the television alone. I did make the news on this occasion. If only Docadile Dundee had been there to see it with me. He had been edited out.

I was so chuffed when two Australian friends, Susan and Desmond, who lived in Hong Kong, said they would come over to sample the "Coastin' experience" – and even more pleased that they had chosen two such superb days on which to join me, both in terms of weather and scenery.

They actually seemed happy enough walking through Westward Ho!, but much of this might well have been due to their enjoyment of the fact that the name of the place had an exclamation mark at the end of it. Once they had extracted every conceivable bit of fun from this and then gone considerably further, I threatened to send them straight back to Hong Kong. From my perspective, the North Devon coastline beyond Westward Ho! was certainly more worthy of an exclamation mark. The stunning mixture of forested slopes, quaint villages and dramatic and exposed geological features makes for some pretty spectacular walking.

There are a number of little fishing villages, and the first of these that we came across was Bucks Mills, which is a little gem set above a historic quay. It is beautifully maintained, and although these days it almost certainly just provides holiday accommodation and second homes, it is easy to fill your head with romanticised images of people eking out an existence here in past times. People either love Clovelly or dislike what they see as its twee phoniness. Not being at all averse to phoniness (having just received my new mobile), I think the place is great. The time to go there is in the winter, when it is relatively empty. In the summer months, you have to take a deep breath and dive into a sea of humanity all clamouring for a piece of the quintessential England it is not.

Clovelly's main street is cobbled and it tumbles down between two rows of impossibly charming cottages. The small and pretty harbour at the foot of the hill is overlooked by the Red Lion Hotel, where we stayed for the night. We had all three enjoyed our experience of Clovelly, but very much regretted our huge breakfast when it came to climbing back up the cobbled street. As we laboured up the cliff, a whistling milkman was coming down with his milk on an adapted tray. "Wheels'd be useless on this 'ill with thase cabbles," he said in an accent which was so North Devonshire it had to be paid for by the Tourist Board.

"That accent wasn't real, was it?" asked Susan.

"I don't know," came my truthful answer.

There was nothing manufactured about the coastline beyond Clovelly. It becomes wilder and steeper, and the views back towards Saunton Sands are wonderful. At Hartland Point, the coast takes a sharp left turn as if in preparation for a change of county. Once the corner is turned, you suddenly realise you are no longer in a chocolate-box world of tea rooms and tourist tat. Quite suddenly, you have ventured into a remote and changing coastal wilderness and the boundaries of your comfort zone need to be pushed out.

It seemed a lot more blustery once we turned south, and I found my balance being affected a little too close to vertical drops onto jagged rocks, which had a reputation for reducing passing boats to matchwood. In fact, such is the formidable reputation of the coastline here, that Hartland Point lighthouse has one of the strongest beams in the country. The fact that our happy chatter had stopped for the moment was not a reflection of dampened enthusiasm. This was rampant, bracing, joy-of-living stuff and we all instinctively knew it would be best enjoyed within our own heads. Besides, the walking required more concentration, more awareness and more absorption of the surroundings.

For a while, I was slightly concerned that we might not make our hotel before dark. This was no place to be hiking blindly, and as if to compound that thought process, a large wave crashed against one of the enormous slabs of rock way beneath me, sending a huge plume of spray high enough for me to reach out and touch. But we reached the hotel in good time. We were windswept, tired and totally fulfilled by our day's walk: it had everything.

After our cushioned existence in Clovelly, the hotel was the accommodation equivalent of the coastal scenery in which it is located. It was spectacular in its inhospitality, and the food made my insides feel as if they had been shipwrecked. At the same time we came away the next morning realising that this was the essence of the place, and that staying there had been an oddly satisfying experience.

Today I was bound for Bude. It didn't seem possible that in one day you could walk from the exhilarating, end-of-the-earth sensation experienced in Hartland to the bucket-and-spade, knotted-handkerchief environment in Bude.

About an hour into the day's walk, we came across a sheep with its head caught in some wire fencing. To make matters worse it was balanced on a tiny promontory, beneath which was a sheer drop. In trying to free itself from the fence, the poor beast had pulled itself back into a position whereby if it pulled any further its legs would disappear beneath it and it would drop off the cliff or, worse still, would be left hanging with its head still in the fence.

We puzzled the conundrum for some time. We couldn't go near the sheep for fear of provoking it to keep pulling; and yet equally, if we left it, it would surely perish soon one way or the other. Eventually, very slowly and carefully, we started pulling the wire fencing away from the cliff edge in the hope that the post which held it there, and which was next to the sheep, would come loose. It all happened in a flash. The post broke free. The sheep panicked, pulled on the fence, and its head came free. For a second it teetered on the brink of oblivion and then, astonishingly, recovered enough balance to make a small jump sideways onto the extra strip of land where the post had once been. From here it was able to leap away to safety.

Relieved and flushed with success, Susan, Desmond and I agreed that this was the perfect time to say our goodbyes. I watched them leave and then turned back south again and started focusing on the rest of the day. I was sad that my friends had gone, but excited at the prospect of reaching Cornwall in the next few hours.

Just before the county line, I entered a small stone bothy that used to belong to Ronald Duncan, the author, who wrote many of his works here overlooking the Atlantic Ocean. Inside, there was a guest book which I flicked through. In keeping with the spirit of the place, many people (particularly Americans) had tried to express their emotions and their innermost thoughts about this idyllic spot in prose and, on occasion, in verse. There were some fantastic contributions in there and I wished I had had a small photocopier with me. Someone had written at the bottom of one page: "I have never read such a load of pretentious old cobblers." This took me by surprise. I had been enjoying the entries. But this observation shed a different light over the musings, and suddenly my stiff English reserve returned and the words seemed to lose their romantic appeal. We are a cynical lot.

Most of the border between Devon and Cornwall follows the route of the River Tamar, whose source is four miles from the north coast and from here wends its way down south to Plymouth. I crossed the border by way of a small wooden bridge across Marshland Water, punching the air as I did so. I would spend 23 days walking about 325 miles in Cornwall, longer than in any other county, and further than driving from London to Penzance or London to Carlisle. I was not at all unhappy about this. Cornwall is a fabulous place to walk. It rivals anywhere in the world as a place to repeatedly put one foot in front of the other.

If my enjoyment was measured in terms of severity of gradient, then I was ecstatic for the rest of the day. By the time I had reached Bude, I had rollercoastered in and out of no less than ten river valleys, all of which were extremely demanding. I was exhausted by the time I reached the town and was glad not to have to go searching for a B&B. The last time I had stayed in Bude, I had accidentally walked into the bathroom while the owner was sitting on the toilet. The image still haunts me today.

Exactly two months prior to this incident, fate dealt me a far happier and more profound encounter: I met Sally Thomas and husband Berwyn. We had ended up in the same B&B in Brora. She had walked most of the way from Land's End to John O'Groats and I had walked the first few days of my journey in the opposite direction. We swapped stories: I was walking for Parkinson's because I had it and she was walking for leukaemia because, tragically, her son Jim had died of it the previous year. We had kept in touch after our chance meeting. For some reason it seemed important to do that.

Now Sally and Berwyn were here in Bude to pick me up and whisk me off to their charming cottage in Port Isaac. I walked with Sally over the next few days and enjoyed her company hugely. There is something about people who have had tragedy in their lives. They seem to understand life a lot better than most. Like others I have met in similar circumstances, Berwyn and Sally are gentle and kind, and ask for nothing. They seem to know what's important.

Port Isaac is much prettier than Bude. It wins on architecture, setting and people, and even sounds like a nicer place to be. This rule of thumb does not always work – there are some towns that cleverly disguise themselves. Great Yarmouth, Pwllheli, Milford Haven and (not forgetting) Bridgwater all sound as though they should be pleasant at the very least, but in fact have very little at all to offer. Conversely, Scarborough, Lizard, Bath and Looe are, based on name alone, places to be avoided at all costs, but in reality are all splendid. Of course the reverse is also true. Dagenham, Ardrossan, Grimsby and Workington sound dreary and are dreary, and Drumnadrochit, Polperro, Berwick upon Tweed and Buttermere are all as good as they sound.

Crackington Haven doesn't actually fall into any of these categories. Granted, it has a name which makes you want to go there and have the "cracking" good time it promises. And on arrival, you might have high hopes about its setting, sandwiched snugly between two big headlands. Yet, when you dig deeper and look around a bit more, you realise that actually Crackington Haven is just a little bit cheap and nasty. Amongst other things, I bought a postcard in Crackington Haven. On the front was a tuxedoed man holding a Cornish pasty and saying, "The name's Pasty, James Pasty. Licence to fill." I looked to see how much I had paid for it and found to my amazement it was £1.50.

Meanwhile, back in London, Q was continuing to provide incredible support for me and seemed to be putting in all the hours that God sent in trying to promote Coastin'. In Cornwall, she received help from the Parkinson's Centre of Excellence run by Doug McMahon and his assistant Alison. A local voice to back up all the work Q was putting in was incredibly useful. We knew from our Welsh experience that the local media tended not to be too enthusiastic when anyone rang up from London with a story, but with Alison's help, we had an incredibly successful run with the Cornish media. I was interviewed by BBC Radio Cornwall three times.

I reached Boscastle before it was washed away. I have not been back there since and hope they have managed to recover some of the charm of the place. The owner of the pub The Cobweb has Parkinson's and on the evening of the day I walked through, Berwyn, Sally and I enjoyed some excellent hospitality and they held a raffle in aid of Coastin'.

It's really not at all far from Boscastle to Tintagel: the birthplace of King Arthur, according to myth, and the cave where he was found by the great sorcerer Merlin. But even if you don't believe in the legend, a relatively recent find of a stone bearing the inscription "Arthnou" suggests there might have been a ruler of that name from the Dark Ages. As in Clovelly, the last time I had been to Tintagel it had been teeming with tourists, but on this occasion there were only three. Despite this, and despite the fact that Tintagel is in a truly wonderful location, the castle itself is still disappointing. There is not much of it left.

The sweep of Port Isaac Bay provides yet another tough but incredibly rewarding walk to the village itself. John Betjeman said of Port Isaac: "It is St Ives without the artists, Polperro without the self-consciousness." Most of the centre consists of a charming hotchpotch of 18th and 19th-century cottages arranged on the incredibly steep, narrow alleyways. One of these, Temple Bar, known as Squeez-ee-belly Alley because it is only 18 inches wide, is on record as the world's narrowest thoroughfare. Port Isaac has been slung together in a totally haphazard manner. There is no order, no planning, no rhyme or reason. These imperfections make Port Isaac almost perfect.

Two dreary and wet days followed, made better only by companions who joined me. The ferry from Rock to Padstow operates right through the winter and this provided quick and easy passage across the Camel River. Padstow is now most famous for its Rick Stein restaurants and the fact that most of London SW6 seems to holiday either here or at nearby Trevose. By the time I reached Trevose Head there was thick fog. A real pea-souper. I was disappointed because from here it is possible to see right back to Hartland Point, and south to Penwith beyond St Ives.

After the fog came the gales. From Trevone to Portreath I was lambasted by severe winds which at times made the walking quite hairy. On a cliff-top just before I reached Watergate Beach, I was walking into such a headwind that I could hardly make any progress at all. As if someone had flicked a switch, the wind then died completely. There was a mysterious silence around me, making me feel uncomfortable and vulnerable.

It was the calm before the storm. When the wall of wind hit me, it knocked me clean off my feet. I swore out loud with the shock and wished I was not quite so near such a large precipice. Having been knocked to the ground, I realised that this was the best place to be and I spread myself as thinly as possible on the ground and waited for the gale to calm down. Initially, even lying there did not feel particularly safe and I jammed my hands and feet and stick into the ground in an attempt to get some resistance. This was my most frightening experience in the post "Eric the pheasant" era of Coastin'.

As I lay there, I gradually became more comfortable and realised that I was not going to be blown back to Bridgwater. And then I felt a strange sensation wash over me. Initially, I didn't have a clue what it was, and then I realised: I had stopped. That didn't mean I had just stopped in the physical sense; it meant that for the first time since I could remember, my body and mind had decided to have a rest, to relax for once.

It is difficult to describe what my thought process on Coastin' was on a day-to-day basis. A lot of people said to me, "How nice to have all that time to think". By that they meant thinking about "big picture" things: life, relationships, work, finances and how to hit a low seven iron from a hanging lie. But it just wasn't like that.

In percentage terms this is my estimate of the time I spent thinking while I walked:

- 50% – not thinking at all as I was walking with someone else or talking on the phone
- 25% – not thinking as I was enjoying the scenery or concentrating on the physical aspect of walking
- 15% – thinking about the walk itself, ways to raise more funds, map reading or thinking about some logistical element of the walk
- 8% – needing to think to walk; at times when my medication was not working, I had to really focus on making my legs move
- 2% – singing or making up songs
- 1% – other stuff e.g. mathematical impossibilities

As I closed in on the finish, time was becoming more and more precious to me. There was so much to do and though Q took a huge amount of pressure off me, I was becoming increasingly stressed and was spending far too much time thinking and worrying about the logistics of the walk than anything else. The situation could only get worse and I wasn't sure I would be able to cope with all of it. Somehow I needed to find more time to do nothing, otherwise I would lose perspective and go Coastin' bonkers. At that moment, I looked at myself lying flat on the ground on top of a cliff near Newquay, and realised that it was probably too late.

When I finally got up and staggered further along the cliff, a man with a great shock of unruly grey hair, which was leaping around on his head like a puppet show, was coming in the other direction. For a moment I thought he might be coming to rescue me, but instead he nodded as he passed and in a soft Cornish accent announced, "Bit breezy out."

FROM NEWQUAY TO POOLE
494 MILES
JANUARY - MARCH 2003

CHAPTER 27

Newquay has become big, brash and ugly. I love it. It reminds me of Australia's Gold Coast, where a similar language is spoken. Suddenly the use of words such as "hey", "yo", "like" and "totally" is increased by a hundredfold. More often than not the words are used together in one sentence such as: "Hey like, yo dude, like totally cool man." But pretty much any combination of the words could be used and mean the same thing.

Out of the water, surfers look and sound peculiar, but get them in the water and suddenly they are graceful and sleek – a bit like dolphins. I always get the sense that beneath their waterproof bodies they are surprisingly intelligent (the surfers, that is – everyone knows dolphins are intelligent).

The beaches from Newquay to St Ives are the best in the country and there is room enough for everyone. Perran Beach and the beaches which provide the curtilage to St Ives Bay are two and six miles long respectively and both provide pristine golden sand and crystal blue water. Newquay to St Ives is a comfortable three-day walk, stopping at Perranporth and Portreath en route. Apart from the few miles around Hayle, the wonderful scenery continues all the way, but each resort or village encountered along this 40-or-so-mile stretch has its own individual micro-culture.

The changing personalities of coastal Britain are fascinating. I couldn't help but overhear a conversation as I was marching up the slipway at Porthtowan. It was between two salty seadogs and a rather plump, rosy-cheeked lady. They were leaning against a boat on the pebbles, two of them gazing wistfully out to sea as if being on land was a bit of an inconvenience, and the other looking as though she had spent as much time behind the stove as she had on the waves.

"So what's your favourite food, Gerald?" asked the round lady.

Gerald took a long draw on his pipe while he considered the question. "I think my absolute favourite 'ud be fish and chips."

The coastal route from St Ives to Penzance is about 40 miles and I don't think anything else matches it in the entire country. It is, quite simply, a coastal work of art and I would happily walk it over and over again. Before you get to St Ives, the north Cornish section of the coastpath is one long panoramic view after another. It is as if everything is being seen through a wide-angle lens. In walking it my thoughts had matched my field of vision in that there were no fixed horizons. Everything in the distance was a blur and didn't need to be considered in detail yet. But beyond St Ives, there were no huge vistas and everything became more focused. More care was required with my walking as the path was now strewn with small rocks. The speed of my progress seemed to correspond to my levels of concentration. I could almost feel the hive of activity going on in my head as the delivery of messages between my eyes and legs battled to keep up with the momentum I was generating. I knew I was risking ankles here, but I was enjoying a rare partnership between mind and body. Like someone walking across a stream on a narrow plank, speed overcame some of the shortcomings of balance.

As the intensity of effort in my walking increased, so I began to notice the details of the landscape; the textures, colours, shapes and sounds. There seemed to be a constant hum as the strengthening breeze caressed the smooth surfaces of the rocks, searching for cracks and hollows.

Cracks and hollows were beginning to open in me in the final push towards Land's End and I too was beginning to moan. The last time I had walked this section, it had been the same. I had been in the final throes of my walk from John O'Groats to Land's End. I had not wanted to finish at all. Its ending spelt uncertainty. When I had arrived at Land's End, I had felt dazed and the entire occasion had been anticlimactic.

Even though it wasn't the end – even though I still had 833 miles to go – I couldn't shrug off the legacy that John O'Groats to Land's End had left me. I had hoped to be as ecstatic as I had been at Cape Wrath; after all, I had now finished the West Coast. Lyndsey and Mum had come down to celebrate with me and the local Parkinson's group was sitting in the Land's End Hotel ready to congratulate me. So why did I feel so miserable?

I suddenly started feeling uncertain about things. Not so much the big issues, but more the smaller ones; the fine print which revolved around my future. Perhaps it was the fact that it was the last major milestone, but I began realising that I needed to confront three fundamental aspects of my life: Lyndsey, dealing with the end of Coastin' and my future. It was as if the change of scenery had changed my priorities. Expansive views had given way to more attention being given to things in close proximity. Now big-picture issues were replaced by matters closer to hand; closer to home. It would be a significant change in attitude, which would shape the remainder of Coastin'.

I felt nothing at Land's End; nothing at all. It was February 3rd. With only two months to go, my sense of impending doom was a little premature. There was still some great walking to be done, but somehow I felt different. All the emphasis would be on the finish now. All the walking would play second fiddle to the increasing time being spent raising awareness. I would have less time on my own. It was going to be a hectic and exhausting time which I would somehow just have to get through. In my head though, the walk, in the sense of the pure simplistic pleasure it was giving me, was over.

Much of the South Coast would become a blur. Days ran into each other and I seemed to be haring around meeting mayors, MPs, Parkinson's branches, reporters. The thrill of being out there on my own fighting the elements and my neurological condition would never be recovered. I knew I had done it – knew I had defied three major problems: my condition, the elements and the horror of Dad's death. I had taken on every obstacle thrown in my path and bulldozed through it. I had done this for lots of reasons, but one of these was selfish. I had done it for myself. The knowledge that the challenge was nigh on complete had given me inner strength and confidence, which no one and nothing could take away from me. But what the hell would I do next?

If, at Land's End, you face away from the hordes of people, the tacky signs and the showy hotel, and gaze instead at the craggy sculpture of the coastline, or out to the distant Isles of Scilly, you can get a sense of the place and the way it must have been. Walk half a mile to Pordenack Point and you will find that it is, in fact, still like that.

There was to be one last fanfare, one last encore before I was enveloped in the fog of the Coastin' finale. Walking from Land's End round to Porthcurno in any weather is wonderful, but after a week and a half of fairly grim weather conditions, it all came right once I had turned left. This segment of the coast is one that is perfect in every respect; the area around

Cape Wrath being the only one to match it. The clifftop walking is easy, the view changes with every stride, the rocks are piled haphazardly and sometimes precariously on top of one another like a gargantuan, unfinished 3-D jigsaw. As the sun was reeled slowly back into the sea and it reached the lowest setting on its automatic dimmer switch, we watched as the shadows of the rocks lengthened, rock on rock.

It was a superb way for my mother to reach the end of her stay in Cornwall and she left the following morning, leaving Lyndsey and me to ourselves. We were both aware of the importance of the next week and a half we would spend together. We had been dancing around the issue of commitment for long enough. Although nothing was said, we instinctively knew that this time spent in Cornwall could spell the end or the beginning. It was the first of the three big questions I had to address and I wanted to get this one right. If I did, then maybe the other two would fall into place.

We had just passed a sign telling us to beware of a blind cat when I first heard the strange noise. It sounded a bit like a cat, but there seemed to be words mixed in amidst the dreadful howling. The perpetrator of the noise was a man wearing headphones striding at great pace towards us. Generosity would have me say that the man was singing, but that seems a bit harsh on the banshees who are only ever said to howl, cry or wail.

David Cotton was undertaking a 6,200-mile walk around the coastline of Britain called Coastwalk (which, after this morning's experience, I renamed Caterwaulk). It was here, close to Tater-du lighthouse, that Coastwalk met Coastin'. We shook hands. We knew we would meet today and yet it was a strange phenomenon nonetheless. He had started out from Edinburgh and was walking clockwise. I was pleased that we had bumped into each other on our respective journeys, although I suppose it was unlikely that we would have missed each other, particularly while we were both following the South West Coast Path.

It was an extraordinary year for coastal walkers. David was raising money for Riding for the Disabled, but there was yet another walker, Graham Harbord, who had set off from Gloucester to raise funds for leukaemia after his wife, Carol, had tragically died the year before. Graham was also walking anticlockwise and would meet David twice en route. It was David who was the first one to realise that we were all pounding the coastline at the same time, and from then on we kept in touch with each other's progress by text; united in coastal camaraderie. And we still are.

We never did see the blind cat.

Having crossed paths with David, Lyndsey and I continued to find an elderly man excitedly recounting something to a group of walkers about a mile further on. It became clear that he was getting animated about the fact that he had just seen a bloke who was walking the entire coastline of Britain.

"Did you see him?"

"Yes."

"It's amazing isn't it?"

I nodded.

"Apparently there is someone else doing it with Parkinson's, and he's in the area too!"

I thought the man was going to have a heart attack when I told him that I was that man. He seemed suddenly short of breath and unable to speak at all, which was perhaps just as well because we were in a hurry to reach Penzance before nightfall.

"I think you made his day!" said Lyndsey.

We moved base camp from a cottage near Land's End to a lovely B&B in the Lizard owned by a radio presenter and his wife, who were hospitality personified. The weather didn't fail me and made for some quite breathtaking walking high above St Michael's Mount and around Mount's Bay. Redundant tin mine buildings punctuated the vivid blue sky and sea with terracotta chimneys. It was the same colour scheme as my London flat. It was strange how that didn't feel very far away any more.

Church Cove and Cadgwith are little gems tucked away on the eastern side of the Lizard. But the truth was, my mind was no longer focusing on my surroundings. Quite suddenly I had found myself transported back into the real world where the future was all-important; where I could no longer live for the moment. Decisions needed to be made, and now was the time to make them. The fact that Lyndsey and I had not actually seen a soul on the path since leaving Penzance, and the weather continued to be uncharacteristically excellent, certainly helped my deliberations.

One thing did seem absolutely certain. In fact, I'm not sure why I had any doubt about the way I would feel about Lyndsey. I think it was probably just the stereotypical male commitment phobia which had made me a bit jittery. Now we were together, on our own, doing what we both enjoyed most, there was not a single doubt in my mind. We were totally happy in each other's company and any question marks either of us had had about this time together were forgotten. I had to admit to myself that perhaps this was it. This was a person with whom I could spend the rest of my life.

The Helford River would be the first of many drowned river valleys preventing me from making eastward progress. I was glad that they would not all entail the same 13-mile detour. Having said that, the empty lanes around Gweek, Constantine and Porth Navas made a more than pleasant change. My perception of the Helford area in February was that the pace of life there couldn't be any slower. There was no traffic on the roads except for an elderly man in a small electric buggy who was on his way back home with some groceries. I felt slightly embarrassed about overtaking him, but he did not seem to mind in the least.

From the shade of the woods surrounding the River Helford, the boats moored on the estuary gleamed in the sunlight. Their masts made the familiar clanking noise in the breeze. This was the heart of sailing country and as I neared Falmouth the boats appeared to increase in size and become more elaborate in design. The ferry from Falmouth to St Mawes was still operational and probably saved me about a week's trek up to Truro and back. We had been given the names of some people to stay with. They were friends of friends of friends. When we arrived at their house to find it was similar in size to Buckingham Palace we were slightly in awe. When we asked them if they sailed and were shown to the back of the house where they had the QE2 parked in the river, awe became envy.

Over the course of the three days spent staying in St Mawes, Lyndsey and I walked the Roseland peninsula in its entirety, having been ferried backwards and forwards by outboard motor to the various starting and finishing points for each day. Once again, the hospitality of strangers had left me lost for words.

I don't think I had ever been quite so sad to see Lyndsey go a few days later in Charlestown, on the outskirts of St Austell. The past two weeks had been the longest time we had ever spent together and it had been an unmitigated success. In Mevagissey, we had spent a long time wondering whether to buy two paintings by the same artist which complemented each other really well. In the end, we had decided to buy one each. This, to me, was an absolute endorsement of how far we had progressed in the time we had spent together. This was new territory for me. It was also an acknowledgment of the fact that one day soon there would come a time when we would live together.

Lyndsey had chosen a good moment to leave. The coast from Carlyon Bay to Polkerris seems to forget completely that it is in Cornwall, and industry and caravans reign supreme. The only thing I could find of interest in the area around St Austell was the fact that, although it is on the south coast, it is actually further north in latitude than St Agnes on the north coast.

Fowey, however, quickly puts a stop to the rot. The town cascades neatly into the river which bears its name and once again saved me a lengthy upstream tramp by providing a ferry across to Polruan. From here I lost myself in my own head, thinking deeply about how to make the most out of the last 60 days. As I had not actually looked at the map once that day, I rather stumbled across Polperro. The fact that I was walking aimlessly along the cliff edge, and suddenly found myself staring down at this almost absurdly pretty fishing village, made it all the more appealing and enjoyable. I spent about an hour there scuttling round its narrow streets, hoping to hear the raucous cries of pirates from one of the dark and smoky inns which I passed. The closest I came were the giggles of some Japanese girls whose boyfriends were taking pictures of them. I consoled myself by walking up the far side of the village while whistling the theme tune to Captain Pugwash.

Twenty-five miles later, having been swept along Whitsand Bay with a fantastic following wind, rounded Rame Head and delved into some of the architectural delights of Kingsand, I reached Cremyll. The ferry ride across to Plymouth was significant on two counts. Firstly, I was back in Devon; secondly, and more important to me at the time, was the fact that I managed to stop whistling the theme tune to Captain Pugwash and instead reverted to my ferry favourite, "Fog on the Tyne".

As if in anger at my leaving after it had treated me so well, Cornwall somehow managed to cook up some black clouds out of a clear blue sky and send them drifting over Plymouth as I landed. It was to be only the beginning – the first of a series of unfortunate incidents in Devon.

As the rain began to crash down, I felt the familiar dissipation of signals from my head to all moving parts of my body. The slide from contentment to misery was quick and I found myself having to hide from the stares of passers-by as I hobbled and wobbled through the streets of Plymouth. It was not an easy place to remain inconspicuous.

When I arrived at an evening's destination in this sort of state, I always waited until my next dose of medication kicked in. This was not because I felt embarrassed about how I looked, but more because of the prolonged pitiful glances I would have to endure and the terrible fuss that people would make. I couldn't blame anyone for these types of reactions; in fact, they were commendable; it was just better if these situations could be avoided. I had used this rule right the way round the coast and there had probably been about 25 occasions where I had been forced to loiter with no intent, other than to stop shaking, for up to an hour. Plymouth was one of these.

My hotel was near The Hoe, where Drake had finished his game of bowls prior to blowing the Spanish Armada to smithereens. It was an unusually smart place for me to be staying, but the hotel was part of a chain that had kindly offered to put me up in various cities while Coastin'. Having settled down to a state where it no longer looked as if I had 30,000 volts running through me, I went in and collected my room key.

"I think my girlfriend brought some luggage."

"We'll have it sent up to you, sir."

It was the usual arrangement. The last person to leave me would take my luggage on a couple of days ahead.

When the porter brought my things up, I immediately noticed that there were items missing from a box: some maps; some CDs; a CD rewriter which I used to back up my computer and a huge bar of chocolate.

"I think there are some things missing."

"That's all there was." But his response was too quick; he had been expecting it. I suspected as soon as the porter spoke that he had something to do with my "lost" items.

I was angry that someone should do this to me. It was an inconvenience I could do without. I wanted to take the porter into a darkened room and shine a table lamp in his eyes, but then at that moment I would have suspected Mother Theresa if she had been carrying my bags. In fact probably even more so. What on earth would Mother Theresa be doing in a hotel in Plymouth carrying my bags anyway. This would have been highly suspicious, particularly as she passed away a few years back.

Fortunately, most of what had gone could be replaced, and I began feeling philosophical about the event. After all, I had been incredibly lucky that I had not been the victim of any other theft or crime up to now.

It was after supper that I rediscovered my rage when I suddenly had a yearning for a bit of chocolate. This was close to provoking a crazed vigilante rampage through the streets of Plymouth in search of anyone with fresh chocolate on their hands. I wanted vengeance... until I found that the hotel actually provided complimentary drinking chocolate in the rooms.

I calmed down after that.

When the hotel manager gave me a cheque to cover my losses, I felt slightly embarrassed. The hotel had been so good to me and yet, equally, I didn't see why I should suffer the loss when my luggage had been put into its care.

Despite meeting a large crowd of Parkinson's supporters and having tea in the mayoral parlour, I was pleased to be walking out of Plymouth the following day. It had not been particularly kind to me.

After the Great Chocolate Robbery of Plymouth, I was comforted to be meeting up with a group of friends who had arrived to support and walk with me over the course of the weekend. At the River Avon we could have waited for low tide to cross over to Bantham, but instead marched up to the bridge at Aveton Gifford.

The Devon scenery resumed normal service for two days from Bantham to Torcross. On my left were deep green undulating hills and woodland. Beneath me, on my right, a churning sea was providing a testing day for an array of colourful sailing boats seemingly going nowhere in particular, but doing it at a great rate. I crossed the Kingsbridge estuary using the ferry at Salcombe, and particularly enjoyed the walk out to Start Point, where, on my own for a few days, I recaptured some of my enthusiasm for walking for walking's sake. This was particularly the case because I was conscious that very soon I would need to start practising my running.

It had been Mr Beef's idea for me to finish Coastin' by doing the London Marathon. Initially I had been dead set against the idea, but having remembered how I felt at the end of John O'Groats to Land's End, I had given it some further thought.

"You can't just walk to the Millennium Bridge and then suddenly stop. It will be an enormous anti-climax," Mr Beef had reasoned before I had even set off.

"I'm not just walking anywhere!" I had protested. "I'm walking 4,500 miles!"

"Izee..." Beef had gone on, "the London Marathon is two days after the day you plan to finish. You would be missing a trick not to do it. People identify with 26 miles of running, they can't possibly relate to walking 4,500 miles. Only you and a few others in the world will know how that feels. The Marathon is a moneyspinner and you should get some publicity out of it. Also, I can guarantee you that at the end of the Marathon you will have had enough exercise. You will be ready to finish."

I had been swayed by these words and had committed myself there and then to the quite extraordinarily stupid venture. Since then, I had managed to persuade 12 friends to run with me as a unit. Lyndsey had also agreed to attempt the 26 miles and even one of my patrons, Vanessa Lawrence, who was director general of the Ordnance Survey, had applied for a place in the ballot. I will never forget the day she rang me when I was in the Lake District to tell me that she had been selected to run. "Disaster," she said. In fact that was all she said.

The upshot of all this was that I needed to start training pretty soon. In Dartmouth I met Dave Birssy, another young Parkinson's sufferer with a "fight it" attitude. He was also going to be doing the Marathon and we spent the day walking from Kingswear to Brixham, chatting about our respective lives and how they had been affected by Parkinson's. Common illness is to friendship what superglue is to adhesives. I found myself talking to Dave about things I would never discuss with people I had known for half a decade, let alone half a day. It was not something I would like to do all the time. I have found introspection to be more prone to depress than to uplift. But talking to Dave was therapeutic, and put things into perspective. There were others out there like me with the same concerns, the same confusion about what the future held.

The South West Coast Path has no other option but to try and make the best of the next 40 or so miles, which passes through the so-called English Riviera. This was exactly what I had been dreading. When I looked at the map for the remainder of my journey, there was very little else I was looking forward to walking. Dorset would be interesting; I had not seen much of the Dorset coast. Perhaps some of the South Downs would also be enjoyable. But sitting at Berry Head, at the tip of the headland in Brixham, all I could see in front of me was urban seaside sprawl. I felt a stab of regret for everything that had gone before. Had I appreciated everything enough? The answer to this was a resounding "Yes!" The problem was I just wanted more of it. I was a natural coastline junkie.

It was, of course, great news that my days were now filling up with extra duties. Whether that would be meeting the local Parkinson's branch, walking with an MP or having a chat with the local radio station, it was all increasing awareness and sponsorship – and the toll on me. I was beginning to run on adrenalin.

I received a telephone call at 8 a.m. on my mobile.

"Hello. Where are you today?"

"Er... who is this?"

"It's me, um, Willie, the man you met when you were putting on your raincoat." I racked my brain and amazingly did recall Willie. I had met him back in Cornwall on one of the many occasions it had started to rain.

"Ah yes, the walker." I wondered how on earth he had got my number, but was not unduly concerned that he had. He had been pleasant enough; quite chatty in fact. There had been nothing particularly odd about him. I remembered he had a pretty sound knowledge of the long-distance footpaths of Britain. I pictured him in my head. He was probably in his mid-60s, grey hair, glasses, a slight stoop, and I recalled that he seemed reluctant to retain eye contact during our conversation.

"Your itinerary on the website says that today you should be in Dartmouth; I just wondered whether that's where you are."

"No. I am actually ahead of schedule and will be walking from Brixham to Babbacombe today."

"Oh." Willie sounded disappointed. "Goodbye." I was left holding the telephone, wondering what had just happened. There were too many questions left unanswered by his phone call, not least why he had called. It was easier just to forget about the incident. Perhaps Willie had been in the Dartmouth area and wanted to walk with me.

Later on I rang the Parkinson's Disease Society's head office to find out if anyone there had given Willie my telephone number. They were terribly upset about the fact that they had. Apparently, Willie had said that he was someone who was going to walk with me. I was still not in the least bit concerned, remembering him well enough to know that he was completely harmless.

"I've got a stalker," I announced with pride to the Parkinson's Disease Society. They did not think this was particularly funny. In fact, I got the impression that they were extremely worried.

There was no sign of Willie for the next few days, but there were lots of people around Torbay, and I started my marathon practice by running most of the way from Babbacombe to Topsham in hideous weather conditions.

It was the most appalling weather on the day from Torquay to Topsham. In fact, it reached my list of top five worst weather days for the year. Will Cook was with me. He had walked for five days of Coastin' in total, and three of these had been on days on the "worst weather" list. This particular day was the stuff of which disaster movies are made: wind and rain, hailstones and huge waves threatened to curtail not just the walk but our lives.

By complete contrast, the four people who joined me for the weekend walking from Topsham would have had no concept of the day before. They were seeing Coastin' through rose-coloured spectacles. Their one and a half days of walking involved only sunshine and scenery. How could they have possibly imagined yesterday's scenes of devastation? For them, my world of walking seemed to be filled only with springy turf, blue oceans and kissing gates.

The last section of Devon did the county justice. I had been left with a slightly stale taste in my mouth after ploughing through the faded and peeling English Riviera, walking from Sidmouth along the cliffs to Branscombe, a site which would later make the world's headlines following the acquisitive activities of hundreds of local beachcombers/scavengers following the wreck of the Napoli cargo ship; but the last part of the Devon coast once again fuelled my appetite for walking. We arrived in Beer. As the saying goes: "When in Rome, do as the Romans do; but when in Beer…"

While my weekend companions stopped to sink a jar or two, I decided I ought to continue my journey in the vain hope of reaching Dorset by nightfall.

I failed miserably. The light was already fading by the time I was walking up Haven Cliff beyond Seaton. I was aware I still had about four miles to go to reach Lyme Regis and wondered if I should try to hitch a lift and come back to this same spot tomorrow. As if he was reading my thoughts, a man walking his dog approached me.

"Not thinking about walking the 'undercliff' at this time are you?"

"Probably not," I replied a bit meekly.

"Best if you walk back to Seaton, I say." He was a little too authoritative for my liking.

"Thanks for the advice."

I decided there and then that I would pay no attention to someone whom in my head I had labelled "the last headmaster in Devon".

I would definitely walk the undercliff, wherever and whatever it was. If necessary I would go out of my way to walk the undercliff. The undercliff would be conquered by me, today, now. I marched off from the scene defiantly, only slowing down when the headmaster was out of sight and when it occurred to me that something called an "undercliff" might not be particularly safe at any time, let alone in pitch darkness. Perhaps I was being a little headstrong.

Nevertheless, the terrain seemed easy enough, the path was easy to follow and I could see nothing remotely dangerous about continuing. In the gathering gloom, I found myself walking deeper and deeper into what seemed to be a tropical rainforest. There were strange animal noises and every now and then my arm or leg would become temporarily tangled up in some of the creeping plant life which seemed to prevail. I felt as if I was in some Tolkien novel, where the trees might suddenly come to life and try to grab me, or some mixed-up beast that was half kangaroo and half sabre-toothed tiger would bound out of the undergrowth and attempt to devour me. But apart from my childish imaginings, the journey to Lyme Regis on what was presumably the undercliff path was totally uneventful, thanks to the strong beam of my head-torch.

Upon my arrival at my B&B, the owner looked perplexed. "You haven't walked the undercliff in the dark, have you?" When I replied that I had, I thought I detected a quick sign of the cross and a glance to the heavens. But I might have been mistaken.

I was disappointed when I found out that by walking the undercliff in the dark, I had effectively missed a totally unspoilt and unique section of the coastline, which was designated a Nature Reserve in 1955 for both its variety and its proliferation of unusual fauna and flora. In retrospect, it was probably also a pretty stupid thing to have attempted in darkness.

I never did find out why I should not walk the undercliff in the dark. I shall have to go back and find out one day.

I couldn't quite place Lyme Regis. It is nice enough, but seems to struggle with identity. Perhaps this is a legacy from the days when the country's well-to-do used to visit it for the sea air. I was left wondering whether it really was genteel or whether it was actually just a little bit shabby. Having said that, there was a good cosmopolitan mix of people and certainly a more youthful population than in the area around Torbay.

Given the fact that not everyone was as long in the tooth as my imaginary sabre-toothed tiger from the undercliff, I thought it was a little harsh to name the area the Jurassic Coast. But actually the phrase is not intended to be a joke at the expense of the inhabitants. It relates to the extraordinary coastline, the geology of which offers an almost complete record of 185 million years of the Earth's history. It has been designated a Natural World Heritage Site for this reason. As I walked along the beach at low tide, there were many people scrabbling around looking for ammonites, fossils and Tyrannosaurus Rex paw prints. There was also metal detecting, Frisbee throwing and a lady collecting driftwood which she intended to fashion into unusual furniture and sell at a vast price. There was much to see all the way to Charmouth.

The path became tougher. Fog cloaked the summit of Golden Cap cliff, and with the coastal path a little too close to the sheer 600-foot drop below, I chose to bypass the domelike structure, opting instead for a lower-altitude route well beneath the heavy shroud of mist. It was a pity because on a clear day the views would have been particularly good from up there.

Walking along the ten miles of Chesil Beach sounds, on the face of it, quite an attractive proposition, until you remember the beach is shingle from start to finish. I was still tempted by the challenge, but a "Danger Area" marked on the map about eight miles along it, next to the words "Rifle Range", made me change my mind. It would have made me really fed up to have trudged four-fifths of the way along the beach, with each step sinking into shingle, if I ended up being shot. So instead, I followed the acorn signs and drifted into Abbotsbury, which is full of "olde worlde" charm, and eventually joins up with the shores of The Fleet; a tranquil lagoon sitting between Chesil Beach and the land towards Weymouth. On the way I passed a grey-haired gentleman with glasses, who avoided eye contact. I couldn't be sure that it was Willie, but I think it was.

Chesil Beach is made of the thinnest threads, attempting to hang on to the errant Portland, which seems to be trying desperately to escape the clutches of the mainland. Man has intervened further here, harnessing the wannabe island with the A354. Initially, I grumbled about the fact that allowing Portland its freedom would have saved me 13 miles. In the end, I very much enjoyed walking around its rocky slopes. At the tip of the peninsula, Portland Bill lighthouse is a big, pristine structure with a bold red stripe across its middle. It seemed to convey the character of the place and its people: hardy, weatherbeaten and proud.

On an absolutely atrocious day, I met the Right Honourable Member of Parliament for Dorset South, Jim Knight, and his dog. Jim and I staggered a good four or five miles together through tempest, gale and swamp, shouting messages to each other in between squalls of wind. He was without doubt the most impressive walker of the MPs who had joined me, and probably the nicest too. I wanted to show him how much I appreciated his turning out for me, and launched a politician-style charm offensive.

"The Lib Dems have been fantastic turning out for me. I think I'll vote Lib Dem at the next election."

But Jim looked crestfallen. "Have any of my Labour colleagues been out walking with you?"

To make matters worse, when Jim eventually turned back, his misguided dog followed me instead of its owner.

I had Durdle Door all to myself, which was unsurprising given the weather conditions. While I was there, though, the sun broke out, bathing the limestone arch in a glorious orange light. I stayed there for some time taking photos, but the combination of wind and my shakes made for disappointing results.

I was tired, wet and hungry by the time I reached Lulworth. I don't think I had ever been so pleased to see Mr Beef, and when he pulled out two wrapped bacon sandwiches for me in the Lulworth Cove car park, I could have hugged him... had my arms been long enough.

A crowd of people turned up for a weekend of walking around the Isle of Purbeck and into Poole Harbour. In quite wild conditions, we climbed cliff after cliff. I was acutely aware that these would be my last real hills of the journey and I would have felt really despondent had friends not been there to keep my spirits up. We rounded Anvil Point, passed through Swanage and into Studland Bay. Even friends were incapable of salvaging my mood on the ferry from the Isle of Purbeck over to Sandbanks at the entrance to Poole Harbour. This marked the end of the magnificent South West Coast Path. No more acorn signposts. I was nearly home.

'The King of Kent'

Southampton
12th March

Bournemouth

Isle of Wight

Portsmouth

Arundel

Brighton

Ham Street

Broadstairs
31st March

Folkestone

Dover

FROM BEEF TO SANDWICH
267 MILES
MARCH

CHAPTER 28

The Beef family dynasty has its seat at Canford Cliffs, and we were able to walk there from the ferry at Sandbanks. Lyndsey, who was also with me at the time, had never experienced a Beef family banquet before. I, meanwhile, had not eaten anything for the past three weeks in preparation for the event. And I did feel as if I was running on empty at that time. I was desperately trying to keep pace with the demands of the walk and all the other activities that were now becoming part of my daily routine. Most days were spent chasing my tail and I became aggravated by my inability to achieve as much as I had hoped. Looking back on it now I can see that it would have been impossible to successfully complete the schedule I was setting myself. Over the course of the next 17 days of walking from East Dorset to East Kent, I walked with a total of 112 different people; I was filmed for TV four times; I prepared and delivered four different speeches; I gave numerous interviews for radio and local newspapers; and on top of all that I was training for the London Marathon. The only person who couldn't see how exhausted I really was, was me. It was only the combined forces of stubbornness, determination and adrenalin that enabled me to keep going. The same combination of forces enabled me to complete everything on my plate at the Beef family banquet. It was not that I did not want to finish the gargantuan feast that was laid before me; it was more the fact that I prided myself on my spatial awareness and, after a cursory inspection, I just couldn't see how the contents of my plate could possibly fit within the body beneath my neck. Nevertheless, somehow I made the maths work.

The Solent Way begins at Milford on Sea and provided an attractive way of reaching Southampton via Beaulieu and a ferry from Hythe. Two of my four speeches were delivered here. The first was to the staff at the Ordnance Survey, who rewarded me by providing all the latest maps for the remainder of my journey. The second was at a dinner organised by Orion Pharma, who had sponsored the leg from Plymouth. I was quite pleased with my performance at this. That was until one of the neurologists attending came up to me afterwards and said, "I met another little man who made a big noise in the US only the other day." It was clearly meant as a compliment, although I couldn't quite see in which part of the sentence the compliment was hidden.

Wild Rover made a welcome return to Coastin' the following day. He would be part of the group who would be running the marathon with me. We jogged along the shores of Southampton Water and turned left up the Meon Valley, chatting about the highlands of Scotland as we went. It was great to have shared that whole experience with someone else who had appreciated it as much as I did. He told me he had fallen for a girl.

"What's her name?" I asked.

"Well – her stage name is Miss High-Leg-Kick."

"She sounds nice."

My sister Caroline and her family joined me for the short walk from Hambledon to Rowlands Castle on the border of West Sussex. A batch of new Coastin' T-shirts in children's sizes had arrived, courtesy of David Jones and Next. There were 12 of us that day parading Coastin' through the Hampshire countryside. This was a good turn-out under any circumstances, but seeing my four nieces, aged 13 months to 10 years, all walking and all decked out in their Coastin' finery, made me glow with pride. I was so pleased they had come to walk with me. I knew Caroline had been aching to do some Coastin', but previously the distance and the sheer logistics had made it impossible. It was certainly of some comfort having a bit of normality around, and also a joy because they did not ask the same questions as everyone else. Instead of the standard "Where's the favourite place you have been?" (Cape Wrath) and "How many pairs of boots have you worn out?" (five), it was "Where was your least favourite place?" (Dagenham) and "How many times your own body weight in chocolate have you eaten on the journey?" (three) and "What was your most frightening moment?" (Eric the Pheasant).

Rather than endure mile after mile of promenade trudging, I decided that I would be far better off following the South Downs Way in Sussex. This would enable me to enjoy the hills to the north of the stretch from Chichester to Newhaven and still have plenty of opportunity to see the sea each day from the path's elevated position. Besides, I had been to Bognor Regis, Littlehampton and Worthing before, and none of them had inspired me sufficiently to revisit them. I did, however, venture seawards for a brief jog through Hove and Brighton before taking to the hills again. I rejoined the South Downs Way just below a place called Loose Bottom, which didn't sound like a very good place to rejoin anything (certainly the contours were showing a lot of relief in the area). Things clearly were not getting any better for whoever did the naming in these parts, because a few miles later I reached Breaky Bottom. At Southease, I thought perhaps the worst was over, and an hour further on still, I was delighted to pass just north of a valley known as Well Bottom.

It was about this time that I gave a speech at a parliamentary reception at the House of Commons. This had been organised by the Parkinson's Disease Society, whose slogan for the year was, "Time to Care". I had gone to the same function a year before, and had talked to a portly MP who had been told about Coastin'.

"How many miles will you be walking each day?" he had asked.

"About 16," I replied.

"That's no great shakes," he responded.

If you analyse it, his reaction to my average daily mileage was a priceless faux pas and I was pleased to be able to recount the tale as part of my presentation. (The MP in question was not there.)

For the rest of my talk I tried quite hard to drive home a strong message and finished my talk by saying the following:

"You are the decision makers and you can make the difference. Let me show you how "U" can make a difference. "Time to Care" for people with Parkinson's, yes, but "U" can eradicate the need to care altogether." With this I had held up a sign saying "Time to Care" and then turned it round to show a sign saying "Time to Cure". The "U" had made the difference. I had been rather pleased with this. The truth was that I thought the "Time to Care" slogan was a little bit weak. When there is real hope of a cure in the next few years, why not shout about it? Momentum is what is needed, and talk of a cure will fuel that momentum. Hope, even if it is false, is better than no hope at all. If, in the 18th century, Dr Samuel Johnson was correct in his belief that "It is worth £1,000 a year to have the habit of looking on the bright side of things", and every person in the country with Parkinson's subscribed to this view, in today's money, we would have £8.4 billion to spend on research every year. It struck me that maybe this was the kind of money and the kind of people-power that might make a difference. Perhaps, if everyone involved with Parkinson's started believing in a cure, and talking about a cure, then perceptions would change and more emphasis would be given to neurological illnesses. But despite all my big talk and optimism, I was disappointed with the evening. I came away from the reception feeling small and insignificant. I had spent many hours working on a speech in the belief that this was my big chance to get my message across to the country's decision makers. After all, if there was a government-commissioned study into whether or not the "quack" of a duck echoes, surely there were funds available to look at a few of the exciting new developments in Parkinson's disease research. But only a few MPs turned up, and although a couple of them came up to me afterwards, I did not get any sense of having penetrated either their heads or their hearts. What use were words to influence people who traded in them as a profession?

I was to have a final day of solitude before I finished the walk. It seemed a long time since I had enjoyed any time to take stock or to reflect. It was lovely walking down from Westdean through Seven Sisters Country Park and I felt a real sense of home-coming when I climbed up Cliff End and inhaled large gulps of sea air. I felt as though I had not enjoyed any coastal scenery since the Isle of Purbeck. Everything after that had been awash with humanity. My re-acquaintance with high cliffs and the sea prompted me to consider the two longest journeys I had ever made. Both had been born out of necessity; both were physically and mentally draining and both had changed the course of my life in fundamental ways. Parkinson's and Coastin' were two competing forces pulling me until I was fully stretched. It was strange to think that, had I not been diagnosed with an incurable and degenerative neurological disorder, I would never have had so many good things in my life. The walk was of course one of these – I simply would never have done such a thing had I not had Parkinson's. And this was not just about scenery and the physical enjoyment it gave me, but also about the people who had been involved, such as Q, Tommy Silk and David Jones. Of course, Parkinson's had also been directly responsible for my meeting Lyndsey, someone with whom I now hoped to spend the rest of my life. But there was something more to it than that and I couldn't put my finger on it; the perennial problem. I fished out a carton of juice from my backpack and pulled the straw out of the polythene wrapper. It was a bit fiddly, but I managed, and inserted it in the hole at the top of the carton. My eyes were drawn to the now familiar words printed there: "Shake well before use".

I remembered how the words had hit me so hard on the day of my diagnosis; how I had felt doomed to a life of shaking and being of little use. I also remembered how, later on, I had laughed at the same words, realising that the instruction was somewhat superfluous given my condition. And now, towards the end of my walk, they meant something different again. Maybe before Parkinson's, I was doing nothing particularly constructive. Could it be that the words I was now looking at were telling me that I had become useful to the world when I had started shaking?

I had not even considered the prospect before, but suddenly I had a vision of my future. Here was a new take on everything. This was something that I could do with my life, not despite Parkinson's, but because of it. It would be a chance to make a difference, however minuscule; to do something positive where my Parkinson's would be a help, not a hindrance. I felt light-headed, and a huge burden seemed to have been lifted from my shoulders.

I thought about the MPs and my disappointment at not being able to make the impact on them that I wanted. Maybe there were other things I could do. I felt, and still feel strongly, that although the cure may ultimately be about money and science, there has to be a momentum to galvanise each of these; to ensure the two are brought together in an effective, co-ordinated manner where commercial forces play second fiddle to progress. This driving force has to come from those affected. The push for the cure will be empowered by public opinion. This is where everyone can help. We can all make a difference. Part of the problem here was that I felt most people with Parkinson's preferred to hide. It is such a visible disease that Parkinson's groups tended to be "think tanks" rather than "movements", yet Michael J. Fox's energy had shown what could be done in the States. We didn't have anything as proactive as his organisation over here. My mind started whizzing as I enjoyed the rollercoaster walk along the Seven Sisters, seven chalk cliffs whose blustery summits seemed to inspire my thought process. It was fantastic to feel enthusiasm coursing through me again. It was another project, something to get my teeth into, which I cared passionately about. As with the early thoughts on Coastin', I didn't know which direction I would go and I knew it would be a long way, but it was something I knew in my heart was right. I would take on Parkinson's, head to head. I might even win.

I did not even realise I had reached Birling Gap and therefore had completed all seven of the "Sisters". I began to concentrate a little more on the scenery. The short cropped springy grass, a real sense of elevation and the view of Beachy Head and the red-and-white-striped Royal Sovereign lighthouse ahead seemed to have woken me from my zombie-like state of the past few weeks. This was seriously good walking.

A grey-haired man was standing gazing out into the English Channel. I had spotted him from a distance. He had been walking towards me down the hill from the top of Beachy Head, but now he was turned almost with his back to me, seemingly transfixed by something out at sea. I followed his gaze and couldn't see anything out of the ordinary. This did not surprise me and I smiled to myself before tapping him on the shoulder.

"Hello, Willie."

Initially, Willie pretended to be surprised at seeing me. But he knew that I knew this was no coincidence. After a brief chat about the weather, Willie made a minor admission: "I'm just spending a few days in Eastbourne," he said. "I wondered whether I might see you on the path somewhere."

I was pleased he had not pretended our meeting was a complete coincidence. It might have made me a little suspicious of him. But Willie was clearly embarrassed by the fact that I was talking to him. He looked agitated and was anxious to get away. I let him go and never saw or heard from him again. In a strange way Willie did me a favour, though. Later on that day, I pondered why Willie had felt the need to come and see me on my walk. OK, perhaps it was a little bit strange to determinedly seek out the location of a man with Parkinson's who is walking along the coast, but I also realised that Coastin' was something that had captured people's imaginations. The concept of my trying to do something about my own condition seemed to have quite a compelling effect. Initially, I had been concerned that as I was both the one fundraising and part of the reason for the fundraising, it might be perceived by some as selfish or even begging. But on Coastin', I had never had any sense of this at all, and in fact, quite the contrary. People recognised that I was trying to raise awareness of a slightly "taboo" illness and also proving to the world (and myself) that Parkinson's sufferers are ordinary people who can do extraordinary things. I was seen as living proof of the need for funds. The reason was right there in front of people, making the cause palpable, and everyone felt part of a team effort to ensure I reached that finishing line.

I had been blown away by all the comments on the message board on the Coastin' website. The amount of encouragement I received in the daily messages of support that I read made such a difference to me. It was clear from a very early stage that Coastin' had struck the right chord and this was something I wanted to bottle and bring out again at a later date. It was a circle of feel-good. If others with Parkinson's could experience such a groundswell of support, they would all come out; would stop being invisible; and something major could be achieved. I thought about the Breast Cancer movement and how their PR had gone from strength to strength. With the help of glamorous celebrities, they had managed to make their cause "mainstream". I wondered whether this would be possible with Parkinson's. Perhaps we could revisit the currently in vogue 60s and 70s, when the word "shake" had been fashionable. Elvis had been "all shook up", the Beatles had asked us to "Shake it up baby now" even before we twisted and shouted, Michael Jackson also told us to "Shake our bodies down to the ground" – and where would Mr Stevens be if he had not been "Shakin"? The problem with making something out of this idea was that most find it difficult to deal with chronically ill people indulging in self-mockery. I suppose it is difficult to know how to react. But it could easily be heroic, and I decided that this should be an idea to motivate all people with Parkinson's. Individual achievements by patients could lead to collective triumph over adversity. I had started the walk motivated by a need to raise funds for research. Now I had nearly finished I realised that my motivation had changed as the walk progressed.

Having been propelled along by the support I had received, by my meeting with Steven Gill and by the amazing success of the venture, I felt more motivated than I had about anything ever before. I would leave the world of property for the time being and concentrate on curing Parkinson's. I would follow my heart, not my head. All my best decisions had been made when I followed this rule. It had been a "head" decision that made me avoid the coastline from Rye to Hythe via Dungeness. When I had been planning the route, I had noticed no less than 19 "Danger Areas" on the map in this section. Once again, I chose the safer option, not wanting to deal with any loose bullets from the firing ranges.

Rye is the first place upstream that the River Rother can be crossed. I left its pretty cobbled streets on a perfect spring morning. It was 27th March. In just two weeks I would be back in London and it would all be over, except of course that the way my mind was currently running, it would be just the beginning. I had chosen to walk along the Royal Military Canal to Hythe via Hamstreet. In fact, this follows the original shoreline from Roman times and made for an easy passage into Kent; my final county. It had been somewhere back in Wales that I had been told by Q that someone called Roger Howard had rung up, saying that he wanted to help "Young Isaacs" in Kent.

"Roger Howard?" I had said. "Are you sure?"

I barely knew Roger Howard. He had gone to the same school as me and was part of the Old Boys' network. It was difficult to pinpoint how old an Old Boy he was, but he was a good 20 years my senior. I knew only two things about Roger, that he was a good golfer and he could kill a man stone dead from 100 feet armed only with his sense of humour. He was one of the archetypal old school tie brigade who had the potential, after a few drinks, to be involved in political incorrectness – yet not quite of an age to be able to get away with it.

From this limited knowledge of the man, I couldn't have expected what materialised. I didn't have any idea that Roger was, to all intents and purposes, the King of Kent. I did not have any concept of the amount of work Roger had put in to my passage through his county until I reached it. He had galvanised Parkinson's branches, schools, TV, radio, newspapers and pharmaceutical companies. All had knelt before him. But his piece de resistance was a wonderful day I spent with him on the day after I had rounded the White Cliffs of Dover and walked into Deal. Passing many of Britain's finest golf courses on my way round the coastline: Muirfield, St Andrews, Carnoustie, Troon, Turnberry, Royal Birkdale, Royal Lytham, Royal Porthcawl and Celtic Manor to name a few, I had gazed longingly at the hallowed turf of each and every one. Only golfers will understand how much I wished I could chase after a little white ball along these fine links courses. There are three such world-class golf courses on a stretch of links beyond Deal; Sandwich, Royal St George's and Prince's. Entry to any one of these courses is extremely difficult and I had resigned myself to another miserable morning of wistful staring. But the King of Kent had organised something special. Not only would we play golf, but we would play all three courses in one day. Obviously we would have no time to play 54 holes, so Roger had arranged that we should only play holes which were going in the same direction as my walk, thus ensuring that I would make reasonable progress out towards the Isle of Thanet peninsula. And so it was that the King of Kent orchestrated perhaps the most remarkable of all Coastin' days.

The 31st of March would see me progress 21 miles from Deal to Broadstairs, be presented with a cheque by Pfizer Pharmaceuticals at their offices near Sandwich, and on the way, play three of the finest golf courses in the country.

"Must see young Isaacs off the premises in style," he said.

He showed no mercy and thrashed me three up with two to play. "You're no better at golf than your father."

"I'm better than him in bunkers," I replied spiritedly.

"That's not saying a great deal, is it, young Isaacs?"

These were the King of Kent's final words to me; and once he had relieved me of the set of clubs he had lent, I set off towards the Isle of Thanet. If Roger Howard was the King of Kent, then Ron Jones was the Thane of Thanet. He was the father of a close friend, and Ron's superb house on the seafront at Broadstairs provided a haven for me for the next two days. It was the calm before the storm that early April would bring. Waking up on my birthday in Broadstairs, I couldn't see any reason to celebrate. I was tired beyond all tiredness, my walk was coming to an end and my enthusiasm, which had been revived in the past few days, seemed to have disappeared completely as if someone had switched out a light. I immersed myself in my own head and all I found there was gloom. At least Lyndsey was here to keep my spirits up.

"Happy birthday!" she said, handing me a large envelope. I opened it, expecting a card of some description, but instead pulled out a picture of a donkey with the words "Donkey Donk Dean" on the front. Confused, I searched in the envelope for further clues, finding a letter which announced, "Congratulations! You are the proud sponsor of Donkey Donk Dean."

It was all too much for me. I had woken that morning feeling utterly miserable. I had already decided that there was going to be nothing to celebrate unless I could get my brain to stop ticking over so I could finally rest; I so desperately needed rest. But now I was the proud owner of a donkey called Donk Dean. I started to laugh.

"You've bought me a donkey!" Lyndsey was unsure whether I was happy or appalled, such was the intensity of my reaction. "My own donkey!" I managed to splutter as my sides split with delight and tears rolled down my face. I felt a huge surge of pent-up emotion and stress erupt out of me as if it just needed an excuse to come to the surface. For the next five minutes I was in a state of complete hysteria, unable to communicate at all, other than to say the words "A donkey!" over and over again.

"That's one of the best presents I've ever had," I eventually told Lyndsey.

Millennium Bridge 11th April · London · Tower Bridge · thames · Southend · Margate · Broadstairs 31st March · the Tower · Gravesend · Gillingham · Rochester

CHAPTER 29

April had finally come. It was a month I had been dreading for some considerable time. Not only did it mean the end of the walk, but it also brought uncertainty again. It brought the post-Coastin' void. Everything for the past eighteen months had been clear; my path quite literally mapped out. There had been a few hiccups on the way; I had got lost a few times, experienced some hostile weather and been attacked by a mad pheasant, but on the whole I had known my direction and what to expect. April brought an end to all that. Then there was the question of my Parkinson's. It had deteriorated over the course of the year and I was not sure if I could, or indeed wanted to, just fall back into a day job. But if I didn't, how would I earn a living? Where would I live? After a year on the coast I now felt irresistibly drawn to the sea. Could I really go back to my Pimlico flat, to the eternal rumble of traffic along the Vauxhall Bridge Road? And if not, what about Lyndsey? She had been incredible, just incredible, all year, but what would happen next? Would she come with me?

What about going back home to Mum – and Dad not being there? There would still be his study, his belongings, his model Aston Martin and Mule's daft cartoon of him playing golf. Would I experience another period of mourning, or would these things now elicit smiles of happy/sad reflection? I knew I was entering a period when I would badly miss his sound, practical advice. I knew everyone would rally round to help, but he would have been there in a unique capacity. I wanted him there as Dad, the person to whom I had always turned for advice. His would have been the best. And he would have so enjoyed all my proposed homecoming celebrations; working the room, schmoozing the ladies, pretending that he had walked a lot of it too. I wished he could see me finish.

But Mum would be there. What a terrible year she had come through – and yet, through her despair and worry, she had still somehow been a tower of strength for all the family. How proud she would be when I finished.

The rain on my back was cold. I wished I had squeezed my waterproof top into the small backpack I used for marathon training. No one was about and it had been a long lonely jog to Herne Bay from Broadstairs. Botany Bay, just up from North Foreland, is a momentous-sounding place. Captain Cook must have been reminded of it in some way when he first landed in Australia. I couldn't see the likeness, but it was significant for me also. It was here I made my last left turn. The home straight.

I had been forced to run to keep myself warm. But as I ran, there seemed to be an endless stream of questions entering my head about what the future held. The silent barrage was disturbed by the "James Bond" theme tune on my mobile phone. It was David Jones ringing me to say he was looking forward to seeing me at the Millennium Bridge next Friday. I was glad he was going to be there. He had been such a boost to me at the beginning.

David's phonecall and some brightening weather prompted happier deliberations. I thought of all the wonderful people I had met during the year. What an extraordinary thing that I was suddenly mixing with the chairman of Next, with politicians, with huge pharmaceutical companies, with sports people and celebrities. In a few days I had been invited to speak at the House of Commons and later in April at Kensington Palace in front of the Duchess of Gloucester. And was it all going to my head? Maybe just a little bit... And then my thoughts drifted to the other people I had met. People who had given so much and asked for nothing in return: the workforce at Harwich, the farmer in Lincolnshire, the Flemings, Uncle Dave and Auntie Rena, David and Kath in Oban, the indefatigable Ron Cowling, the Countess of Cardiff, Steve Gill and Roger, King of Kent. And then there were other people, extraordinary people whose antics sometimes inspired me, sometimes enraged me and often just made me laugh: Darth Vader in his new role as a stinging nettle exterminator, DiploMatt and old Knacked-Knees, Robert in Wick, the Wicked Witch of Kinlochbervie, Lynne Martin, the Headless Brothers of Llanrhystud, the staff at Norgine Pharmaceuticals and Willie the Stalker.

Finally, I thought about my friends. So many of them had contributed so much. It made me emotional just thinking about it.

What a long way Coastin' had come, not just in mileage terms, but also in terms of what it had achieved. The £250,000 fundraising mark would be smashed, of that I was quite certain, and the press coverage and overall awareness of Parkinson's generated had already exceeded even my optimistic expectations. But above all these things it was the ordinary people who had been involved; all those hundreds of people who had taken my walk into their hearts and made it into something far more remarkable than just a bloke walking round the coast. From a personal perspective I would be able to look back at Coastin' with pride. I had turned my life around, by embracing the very thing that was throttling me. As a result, it had loosened its grip slightly, and I had accepted it as part of who I am. There was worse to come I was sure, but for the time being at least I was OK. Mentally, physically, OK.

\* \* \*

The water on my right was looking distinctly murkier than I was used to and seemed to have a depressingly oily veneer. I gazed out as I had done so many times before on the trip, and decided that actually there had not been too many occasions on the journey when the state of pollution of the sea had been bad enough to upset me. I stared at the gently lapping waves in the foreground. There was an unsightly froth, which formed at the extremity of each ripple as it ebbed and flowed. It was strangely reminiscent of beer. My eyes then focused beyond the shoreline to the vast energy of the sea itself and I noticed that, for a change, it was not more water I could see on the horizon. It was land. Essex! I could see Essex. I had come full circle.

From here on, everything I did or thought sparked a memory or emotion. The peaks and troughs of my year were queuing up to welcome me home. Today these feelings seemed to be close to the surface, giving me an almost continuous sense of personal drama and significance. Absurd as it may sound, I looked across the estuary at the fume-belching chimneys of Essex with the same romantic notions as someone who had just walked the Inca Trail and was now staring down at the glory of Macchu Picchu. I had seen these odious carbuncles 51 weeks ago – and now I had walked right round Britain and could see them again. It was a pity, though, that my sense of achievement had to be reflected in these monstrosities. Never mind; I was sure that in the next week or so there would be more appropriate and more poignant landmarks on which I could rely to give me a more prolonged sense of accomplishment. The dismal complexion of the beginning of the Thames Estuary was beginning to have an effect on me. I suddenly felt a strong desire to be on the north-west coast of Scotland where the sea had been a rich blue and every direction had a spectacular view. But now I was in Whitstable Bay, not Scotland. I managed to find some contentment in the fact that I would not have to walk round the Isle of Sheppey, which sits rather unemphatically just north of Sittingbourne and Faversham.

I was going through the motions now. It was just a case of getting back to the Millennium Bridge without mishap. The next few days were spent marching or jogging through increasingly unattractive, urban areas. The Saxon Shore Way, which I was still following, made it all bearable enough, even if it did take me in an extremely circuitous fashion to Rochester where I was able to cross the Medway. The Hoo peninsula was a little more rural and pleasant, but I was not concentrating on it very much. It was as if the valve in my head that controlled how much of my immediate surroundings I was taking in had been slowly tightening ever since I had reached the end of the South West Coast Path at Poole. Although I was still covering 12 to 20 miles per day, the scenery and the walking were not registering in my consciousness in the same way as earlier on in the year. My thoughts were gradually becoming totally preoccupied with the finish.

I turned up the collar of my waterproof jacket, as a chill seemed to infiltrate my outer garments and instantly change my internal thermometer from "comfy" to "decidedly cold". I no longer felt as if I was being buffeted by the elements, but more intimidated by man's influence on these outskirts of London. There was more litter, more foul smells and a sense of degradation and grime.

Three figures were crouched in the shadowy undergrowth to my right. It was growing dark now and it was difficult to see what they were doing. Their faces were hidden and they were all wearing dark hoods. I saw black metal contraptions being screwed together. They looked like some kind of automatic weapons. I felt my heartbeat quicken as I fixed my gaze straight ahead and pretended I had not seen them.

I sensed their malice when they became aware of my presence. They were murmuring something; devising some plan that somehow involved me.

"Let's get him," one of them said, and I heard ever-quickening footsteps behind me. I turned to face my foe. The speed at which this frightening situation had developed was alarming. The long black metal barrel of the silencer was being screwed into place. The telescopic sight-finder was already trained on my head.

"No one would hear me die," I thought to myself. I looked to see if I could see their faces, but they were still hidden from view. Running was pointless, with the size of that sight-finder they could pick me off from 500 yards.

"Are you a twitcher?" one of them asked, imitating the stereotypical voice of a computer nerd (which he clearly thought I was).

My Parkinson's was letting me down again, unless he was referring to how my dead body would be in a few minutes just before rigor mortis set in.

"No," I said as my assailants came closer and fully into view. "No, I'm not," I repeated as it became abundantly clear that I had misinterpreted the situation entirely.

"Do you want to see a rough-legged buzzard?" came the same geeky voice, but from a different mouth.

The gun was a twitcher's telescope. The voices had not been an impression, but their own. Their hoods were bobble hats and thick woollen scarves knitted carefully by their grandmothers.

"No thanks, I'm in a bit of a hurry." They looked crestfallen.

"They're very rare, you know." There was desperation in his voice.

"Sorry." I left them.

I have always been a smooth-legged buzzard sort of person.

* * *

Gravesend. The final map was ceremoniously withdrawn from its compartment in my pack. Of course, it was the same one that I had used on the first day. I spread it out on the breakfast table, staring in disbelief at the two highlighted lines on either side of the Thames, which marked my passage to and from the centre of London. As the river narrowed, so the lines converged until finally joining at Greenwich, at the Cutty Sark. All the other hundred Ordnance Survey maps had been completed and now it had come down to this last one. I didn't voice the significance of this to anyone. It would have been impossible for anyone else to understand, or to respond in a suitably profound manner. The ceremony of the final map was silent to the outside world, but in my head it had huge meaning. Extremes of emotion battled for supremacy. My head felt like a church double-booked for a wedding and a funeral. In the end, I couldn't solve the problem. I did not know whether to be miserable or ecstatic; I just felt numb.

It seemed almost incomprehensible that I was going to make it. Little wonder, therefore, that the notion of walking the coastline of Britain seemed to be one that others couldn't quite grasp. The scale of it, in walking terms, is simply too unusual, too extreme to be fathomable. Even I couldn't really conceptualize it in my head as anything more tangible than "a bloody long way".

This might have been part of the problem for the *Daily Mail* that morning. We had been hoping for a double-page spread to kick-start the publicity for the final few days. There was no mention of Coastin' at all. It was a bad start. My mood became thunderous. But then I took a step back for some long overdue self-analysis. It was sometimes hard for me to totally disregard the fact that I actually quite enjoyed seeing my name in the paper. I knew this was just vanity. I am always most impressed by those who do not enjoy the limelight and think that such people must be really deeply good. Perhaps I was just a bit too surface-level, revelling in my own glory. How much of this morning's disappointment was due to the fact that I wanted a picture of myself in the *Daily Mail* and how much was it because I wanted publicity for Parkinson's? I dug deep to find the answer and found with relief that whilst it was certainly a bit of the first, it was undoubtedly more of the latter. One of the greatest things about Coastin' was that PR for Tom meant PR for Parkinson's. While the walk continued they were one and the same. I heard Q's voice in my head, "You're a media tart."

Having accepted that it was justifiable to be angry, I resumed my thunderous mood. In place of Coastin' they had a feature about a woman who was taking twenty vitamin pills a day and whether it was doing her any good. Surely what I was doing made a better story than this. *Surely.*

Passing under the Queen Elizabeth II Bridge, which supports the M25, was another telling moment. On the way out it had been my first major landmark. I remembered wondering what I would be thinking if I ever made it back under this gigantic structure. And having now made it back there, I was thinking about what I was thinking a year earlier. It was obvious, had I really thought about it. The Darent and Cray were the last rivers to be crossed. Both were successfully negotiated at Dartford. I had seen better rivers. I had also seen better towns. Nevertheless, the news I received in Dartford was better. Elizabeth Hurley's office had been on the phone to Q and it was confirmed – she wanted to walk with me on the last day. This meant we were guaranteed publicity for Parkinson's with my arrival at the Millennium Bridge. This also meant that all my chums would see me with the iconic Miss Hurley. This was good. My bad mood evaporated. I doubt whether anyone had ever before made up a song entitled "My heart soared in Dart-ford". The tune wasn't up to much even if the principal lyric was exceptional.

The riverside path to Greenwich took considerably longer to complete than I had anticipated. The Thames does some extreme meandering here and the tarmac was wearing on the feet. A few close friends, one of whom was Shazzer, had joined me for the final days. I was very glad of their company. I knew they would accept my increasingly mercurial temperament. They were just there and were keen to help in any way they could. Meanwhile, I was caught up in an emotional cocktail. It was not so much the bitter-sweetness of closing in on the finish, though. It was more to do with Q trying to ensure the final day went according to plan. She so wanted it to be successful and special for me, and I so wanted it to reflect the quite unbelievable amount of effort she had put into the year. The phone just kept on ringing. If the others were thinking that I was a slave to my own self-importance, they certainly did not show it. I was aware of the sort of obnoxious image I might be projecting, but I really did feel this was important. I had walked for a year, with one of the two main objectives being to raise the profile of Parkinson's. There would be no better time to achieve this. We had to get it right.

Canary Wharf's mighty towers jolted me into the stark reality of where I was. No more countryside. I had reached Central London, where people rushed everywhere, where passers-by no longer said hello, and where unyielding angular surfaces and the sharp din of City life smothered the soft rounded vitality of Mother Nature. That was how I perceived it. Of course, I would get used to it. I always did. But coming back to London after a long stint away was always suffocating.

I was now beyond Greenwich on the south side of the river and covering the same ground that I had covered a year ago. The circle had been completed. It was now just the small matter of the final mile or so to the Millennium Bridge. There should have been an enormous sense of arrival, of accomplishment, of anticipation. I felt nothing at all. There was still only numbness.

## CHAPTER 30

### EARLY MORNING

The morning had delivered a cool haze above London. It was difficult to predict which way the weather would go. I thought about Dad and inwardly asked him to sort it out. By 10 a.m. the haze had evaporated, and with it went my numbness. The City was now basking under a pristine blue sky. Its brightness was slowly soaking into everyone and everything. People were smiling. London looked fresh.

I had slept terribly. It was inevitable, but it would have been so nice to wake up this morning revitalised. I was in reasonable fettle though. It was a big day and I intended to enjoy it.

As Mum, Lyndsey and I walked over Tower Bridge from the Tower of London, I felt confident the day was going to go well. Q had thought of everything. All we needed now was for people to turn up. The first posse would be assembled on the southern side of the bridge. We would meet them at 10.30 a.m.

### 10.30 A.M. – TOWER BRIDGE

There was not a soul there. Not a soul. I was gripped by a sudden panic. Had I got the wrong time/day/bridge? Had they already set off without me? Was this some kind of a joke?

"Izeee!"

It was the familiar greeting call of Mr Beef and it was most welcome. He stomped Godzilla-like towards me with a broad grin on his face, which, needless to say, was bulging under the strain of a Danish pastry. The arrival of Mr Beef seemed to prompt a flow of people.

"You're BRILLIANT! You're a star. They still talk about you in the valleys!" Countess Blodwyn Jones, all the way from Cardiff, had cued up the words in her head; she knew how much I liked them. The idea that they were still talking about me "in the valleys" was simply preposterous. I loved it.

We were on our way; an unlikely mob comprising family, friends, patrons, photographers and some drummers from Hackney who would provide us with a "jungle beat". It was hoped this would stir up a carnival-like atmosphere as I took my final few steps back to the Millennium Bridge.

## 11 A.M. – HAY'S GALLERIA

I was walking with a huge grin on my face. Gone were any thoughts of no one turning up. There were now fifty to sixty people parading along the south bank of the Thames in a happy throng. The ripple of support that had turned out at Tower Bridge had become a mighty wave by the time we approached Hay's Galleria. This was great. No, this was absolutely fantastic.

An American tourist approached the rapidly building procession. "What's this, some kinda protest?"

"No, it's the end of Tom Isaacs' 4,500-mile walk round the coast of Britain," someone replied.

"Now why would anyone wanna do that?"

"He's raising funds to find a PD cure."

"Jeez, that's a hellava way to walk to try and find one. Where I come from you can get a 'peedeecure' in most places for 30 bucks. But I guess he needs something real special done if he's walked that far."

It was gently explained to him that I was walking because I had Parkinson's, not because I had dry skin on my feet.

On we went. Q had wanted a "Pied Piper" effect. She was getting it. The Hackney drummers continued their rhythmic hypnosis and, trance-like, I followed. People were coming to talk to me now and I have no recollection of what was said or how I responded. My mind had become like a thick Tuscan bean soup; there was not a huge amount of thought in it, but its effect on me was intensely gratifying. It had dawned on me some time ago that although the landscapes I had witnessed on the walk had been unforgettably magnificent, it was the people who had actually made the year's experience so utterly fulfilling. And here they all were, representatives of everyone who had been involved. A triumphant Coastin' procession, snaking along the Thames Path.

At London Bridge Hospital we stopped again to attach ourselves to the GSK (Glaxo) crew, who were the pharmaceutical company sponsoring the day. At this point I turned around. The only thing I could see was an ocean of Coastin' T-shirts. I gulped as I tried to take it all in, but I was all lump and no throat. I was dumbfounded. This was truly amazing: hundreds of people. They had all come to cheer me home.

I caught a few people's eyes. They twinkled back at me, saying "Well done" with their expressions. I beamed back at them all.

11.30 A.M.
– THE GOLDEN HIND, CLINK STREET

The moving throng was ablaze with laughter and chat, and those forever pounding drums. The beat seemed to take on an almost coercive character; calling everyone to arms. With this legion behind me, I would surely be able to defeat Parkinson's. I felt energised to the core. I would always have this day filed in the memory bank. I would ensure it was easily accessible for the rest of my life.

"I understand Liz Hurley is about to join you," said the presenter of Radio 5 Live to whom I was speaking on the phone. I had clean forgotten that bit of excitement still to come. I looked at my watch.

"Yes, she'll be here any minute," I replied.

"Can we hang on until she arrives?" she asked. This sounded as if it could cause problems. What if she turned up late? What if she didn't want to speak to Radio 5 Live? How was I going to be able to embrace her properly on arrival if I had a phone in my hand?

"Actually, I was hoping for a quiet moment alone with her." The presenter took the hint that it was not going to be easy, wished me luck, said I deserved a quiet moment alone with Liz Hurley and signed off.

Moments later, Liz arrived in a white car. I sensed all the lads behind me staring in awe and wonder, whilst all the girls were looking very closely at the quality of her skin; I got the sense they were saying to each other, "What's all the fuss about?"

She looked pretty good to me. Together we set off on the final half-mile to the Millennium Bridge. I led the way, confidently striding out in a manner that said, "OK Elizabeth, I'm the walker around here. Just you leave this to me." I marched off at a great rate, she duly followed and almost immediately we came to a dead end. I had gone the wrong way. She laughed.

I had hoped to be a little more impressive in the first minute of walking with Liz Hurley. The fact that the crowd behind had all followed made the whole thing farcical. This was taking the Pied Piper theme too far. I realised I was in danger of being trapped with Elizabeth Hurley in a human concertina. On another day I might have quite enjoyed this, but for the moment I was feeling red-faced more than red-blooded. Everyone scattered before us as we doubled back. For a moment there was chaos as I tried to rectify my mistake. It was meant to be a slick show; a piece of theatre for the cameras – but the Pied Piper had chosen the wrong route.

I was worried that Liz might throw a showbiz strop and march back to her white car, having deemed the whole thing a shambles. I looked across at her nervously and she gave me a beaming smile. "I can't believe you have walked all that way," she said.

"I am not surprised you can't believe it," I said, "if current form is anything to go by."

She laughed. "That's not what I meant. It's amazing what you have done."

Having recovered the route, we set off at quite a pace. Photographers snapped and snapped; running backwards and crashing into walls, parked cars and people as they went.

Mule's father, Donald Cammell, was now waiting ahead to greet me and filed in alongside us. He did not have the faintest idea who Elizabeth was, so I introduced him. "Donald, this is Elizabeth Hurley. Elizabeth, Donald."

They acknowledged each other. Donald was splendidly none the wiser and chatted away, seemingly oblivious to the increasing numbers of paparazzi homing in. "Good crowd," he said.

"Yes, it's amazing," I replied. But I was desperately trying to think of something that Liz Hurley and Donald Cammell would have in common. One was a Coastin' superstar who was often abroad, lived in one of the most exclusive neighbourhoods in Britain and had made an extra-special effort to be here today. And the other was Liz Hurley. While I was pondering on all this I realised that they were now talking to each other.

"Oh, so you must be Mr Cammell," I heard Elizabeth say. I had forgotten that it was indirectly through Mule that I knew the Hurleys and that Elizabeth was here at all.

"That's right," said Donald.

Behind us followed a pack of younger men dragging their tongues along the ground in Elizabeth's wake, and who would have given their eye teeth to be Donald Cammell at that moment. Donald meanwhile asked me, "Who was that charming young lady?" The irony reflected the sadness of the male species.

I was not prepared for the next bit. Another cordoned-off area was accessed via a small corridor of fencing. As we entered I realised that I was now, undeniably, well and truly out of my depth. A thirty-yard bank of photographers three or four deep were lined up, cameras cocked and ready to shoot. This was a species of paparazzi I was not accustomed to. They were not here for me. They were here for Elizabeth. This was now a different ball game altogether. Tentatively I stepped forward into the arena with my completely unruffled companion.

They were like wolves or hyenas. Celebrity scavengers. It struck me that while I felt intimidated by this pack of men who looked as if they had seen a bit of life, Elizabeth toyed with them. To her they were not wizened wolves, but innocent puppies.

"Liz, this way! Liz, over here! To this camera, Liz! Give him a kiss, Liz." She was calm and graceful. She was a pro. I felt a bit like a hanger-on.

The mother of my friend Sharon was peering over the wall of photographers. They all had digital cameras with foot-long lenses and were baying for Liz. My friend's mother had a tiny instamatic; above the brash shouts of the all-male paparazzi I heard her pipe, "Tom! To this camera!" It was one of those classic moments. There seemed to be a lull in the proceedings while everyone took stock of what had just happened.

"Tom, this way! Over here, Tom! Big smile for me, Tom!" They knew my name now. Sharon's mum had done me proud.

Elizabeth left. She seemed almost sorry to be leaving so soon; as if she had wanted to do more to help. She had been quite charming. But afterwards I was furious that the reporters interviewing me seemed only interested in how I knew Liz Hurley, rather than the fact that I had just walked 4,500 miles. I had been prepared for this, but it did not change how I felt. How they had the gall to stand there and ask me such questions, I'll never know.

## 12.30 P.M. – THE MILLENNIUM BRIDGE

I was led up to the same ex-wobbling bridge from which I had started. I had just begun to wobble slightly myself. There seemed to be well-wishers everywhere. Ron Harvey, who had greeted me into Rhyl in North Wales, and who was also a trustee of the Parkinson's Disease Society, asked if he could come onto the bridge with me. I was touched by this. Of course he could.

Tony Hawks was on the bridge. Chris Steele (TV doctor) was on the bridge. A huge gathering of the Parkinson's Disease Society had come. Faces galore. Now I faced the slight dilemma of where the finishing line was. Should I stop at the top of the ramp on the south side? Should I stop near the middle of the bridge? Or should I go the whole way to the northern end? The decision was made for me. I knew Coastin' was over at the moment when I saw Mum rush out towards me.

"You've made it!" she said, flinging her arms around me. The words were simple and yet heavy with meaning.

We had been through so much since Parkinson's had come into our lives.

But now there were two other faces I needed to see. I turned around and they were there – Lyndsey and Q. I couldn't have done this without the three of them. Four people had crossed that finish line today. I was just the glory boy.

I couldn't hold it all in. This was too much. For the first time that day, I could show what completing this walk really meant to me. It was a fleeting moment of unrestrained emotion; walking across, giving my mother a hug on the Millennium Bridge in London, and falling to pieces.

She was right. We had made it.

THE LONDON MARATHON
APRIL

CHAPTER 31

13TH APRIL 2003

Had enough? Well, I certainly had. But for you, the reader, there is still one final chapter to get through – and I had one final challenge. Count yourself lucky, you have only a few pages to read. I still had 26 miles to run.

Doing the London Marathon, after everything else, was clearly just over-reaching myself. I found that the reaction to this final event was odd. I had often received slightly strange responses from people to what I was doing, especially from those who had witnessed my true symptoms. Usually, when I told them about the 4,500 miles I was walking, I would receive cautious praise. When I mentioned the mountains, people tended to look surprised, even disbelieving. But when I mentioned the marathon, eyes would dart this way and that, as if people were looking for an emergency exit. "Keep away from the nutter!" Lunacy is in no way a good advert for the Parkinson's awareness that I have worked so hard to promote.

There were many endings to Coastin' and every one of them was special in its own right. At the end of the Marathon itself, two days later, I was surrounded by fifteen of my closest friends all following me as a unit, holding aloft an enormous Coastin' banner, which they carried for the entire 26 miles.

There was a time on that morning when I had been convinced I would never complete the last of my three challenges. None of my pills had worked and when I looked in the mirror, I didn't think I had ever seen myself looking so poorly. A text message which said "Go Tommy you're a Titan" made me realise that I had to finish the thing, even if it took me two weeks and I came in after the bloke in the diving-suit.

"I've never seen anything look less titanic than you right now," Lyndsey said, helpfully. After that I staggered up to the starting line and people stared at me in wide wonder: "He can't really be thinking… Yes he is, look. There's the number on his chest."

But as if there was some unnatural force for the good at work, the moment I crossed the starting line, I suddenly stopped shaking and somehow propelled myself through 26 miles to the finishing line some five hours later.

"What fantastic friends I've got." This was the thought with which I completed the London Marathon. I soon became less magnanimous. It suddenly dawned on me that my year was over. I paced around the finishing enclosure for a moment, wrapped up in my own thoughts. I had actually done it. All three challenges. I had done them all.

I knew that in a few hours a deeper, more powerful sentiment which lurked beneath this ecstatic exhaustion would rise to the surface: one of loss. Coastin' was over.

The Parkinson's Disease Society had laid on a little function for all their marathon runners in the Strand Palace Hotel. By the time I had walked there from The Mall, I had stiffened up considerably. A crowd of people were standing at the bottom of the stairs as I arrived with a few of my fellow-runners. As I stepped gingerly off the top stair, I became aware of three things. First, that everyone was applauding; second, that my team-mates had not started walking down the stairs with me, leaving me to soak up the glory alone; and third, that my legs had seized up and I was in agony. The applause quickly became laughter as everyone witnessed a most inelegant and inglorious descent of the stairs; my last Coastin' action. It seemed very fitting.

## FROM POST COASTIN' TO TOASTIN'

### EPILOGUE

Two days before the London Marathon, back on the Millenium Bridge at the end of Coastin', Sir Richard Nichols, Alderman and ex-Lord Mayor of London, was standing in full regalia at the other end of the bridge to welcome me officially back to the City of London. This was only the second time on that day that I had even contemplated the fact that the walk was over. I felt no sense of achievement or finality. In a few dignified sentences, however, Sir Richard had managed to remind me of the magnitude of the walk.

"This is a truly remarkable achievement," he said. "You have done so much this year to raise the profile of Parkinson's, and it is a condition which does not feature prominently in the minds of either the public or decision makers too frequently. Congratulations! It's one hell of an achievement."

It was not so much what he said, but more the way in which he said it. Just for a moment he held my gaze; his controlled, deliberate manner added gravitas to his words. It allowed me to catch my breath, to steady myself, and – just for a second – to feel a deep sense of pride.

On the same evening, there was a party at the Royal College of Nursing in Cavendish Square. I went on stage to thank everyone but was unable to say the words "Mum", "Lyndsey" or "Q" without having to screw my face up in an effort not to become over-emotional. When I came down from the stage, I was amazed to see there was barely a dry eye in the house. Mr Beef came up to me and whacked me on the shoulder. "Great speech, mate," he said. "Those tears were a masterstroke." I smiled. Clearly I hadn't fooled anyone.

Three months later, lethargy was winning me over. It was a hazy summer's day in London. I had arranged to meet Lyndsey on the Millennium Bridge. It would be the first time I had been back there, since the end of Coastin'. For once in my life, I was early! I took my time. No need to adopt the same frantic pace as everyone else around me.

St Paul's Cathedral loomed large on the skyline. Dominant and immovable, it dwarfed everything else with its splendour. Its dome had been a beacon for me not so long ago. Beyond it, the Millennium Bridge would be reaching across the Thames like an extended arm to the Tate Modern. I wondered how it would feel to stand on it again?

Three months ago the bridge had been awash with smiles and laughter. Beaming faces had welcomed me back from 4,500 miles of walking. Now the faces were unfamiliar as they hurried by. All eye contact was avoided and everyone seemed to be focused introspectively. The bridge was bustling, but it felt empty. I was disappointed that it did not seem to recognise me at all.

About midway across, I stopped and planted my forearms on the railing, resting my head on them. I looked at the view to the east and remembered how daunting it had all seemed at the beginning. It was over now.

I had been worried that there would be a huge void in my life post-Coastin'. I had been certain that I would suffer withdrawal symptoms from my nomadic lifestyle, from walking, from the sea, from having a fixed goal every day, from chocolate. But actually none of these had materialised. Far from being a void, my life was taking on a new mantle altogether.

I had decided not to go back to work immediately, but at the same time, I wanted to ensure that my whole life did not become inextricably absorbed by Parkinson's. There had to be a balance so that it did not become all-consuming. For the time being, however, it was as if I had no choice. There did seem to be constructive things I could do. My path was almost being chosen for me.

I was asked by Radio 4 to be involved in a half-hour documentary looking at the status of Parkinson's disease research in this country. The father of the producer of the programme, Lucy Dichmont, had Parkinson's. Together, we went optimistically in search of a cure.

We did not find it.

"We would imagine that, with a fair wind, this treatment could be available for trial in five years." The standard response from the scientists we visited did not excite us. It wasn't good enough. We went to see Steven Gill, the neurosurgeon from Bristol who had met me on the Severn Bridge and welcomed me back to England. It pretty quickly became apparent that his research was more advanced than anyone else's.

The "before" footage in Steven Gill's video was harrowing; the patients displayed a complete inability to convey themselves from a chair to the end of the room and then back again. One after the other they revealed the tortuous symptoms with which Parkinson's disease sufferers can be beset: their bodies gnarled and decrepit; their movements ranging from non-existent to violently flamboyant, but nothing even remotely mid-scale. It made for traumatic viewing.

And then the "after" pictures.

Even sitting in the chair the patients looked different: the shape of their bodies; the honesty of their posture. A miraculous metamorphosis was already quite apparent. Then, one by one, they would get up without difficulty or hindrance. They would stride purposefully across the room and then back to the chair; upright, dignified, normal. They had been resurrected.

I was excited about awarding the Coastin' funds to advancing this breakthrough treatment. The money was still rolling in and it was looking as if the total could well top £350,000. £30,000 extra had been raised by the marathon team alone. To think I had been concerned that we might not reach the £250,000 target!

Afterwards, I realised that the videos of the patients with Parkinson's had not only won me over in terms of awarding funds, but they had also rekindled a new drive within me. At last, here was something tangible to cling on to. Here was a treatment that had not only stopped the progression of Parkinson's in its tracks, but could actually reverse the symptoms. I felt energised by a new sense of purpose, a new crusade. Steven Gill needed funding to carry out further clinical trials to conduct research into a more practical delivery mechanism of this GDNF drug into the brain. Delivery was currently via a rather clumsy and improbable pump device, which was inserted inside the patient's abdomen. The surgery might be cutting-edge, but the pump was a distinctly blunt instrument.

It seemed absurd to me that Steven needed more funding for the trials. It did not take a scientist to know that he was on to something extraordinary. Parkinson's could be reversed. It was there for all to see. I felt exasperated both by private sector greed and by public sector bureaucracy, both of which appeared to stand in the way of real progress. Now, at the time of writing, and despite my unrelenting conviction that the GDNF molecule is both safe and very effective, it still remains unavailable.

Standing on the Millennium Bridge, I stared out over the City of London. The heat of the day was growing more intense. I closed my eyes. Suddenly, I was back in Cape Wrath with its towering cliffs and sense of isolation. A gust of salty air hit my face and I could see the swell of the sea and the white caps glinting in the sunshine. In the distance, the brilliance of Kearvaig Beach's pristine sands seemed almost celestial.

I remembered that wonderful feeling of reaching the West Coast. I had felt invincible then. Everything had felt as it should do. How could I have known that a few weeks later those feelings would be completely destroyed? Dad's death had made both the walls that I had built to deal with Parkinson's and most of my other defences come tumbling down. It would take a long time for them to be fully rebuilt, but I was getting there. However, at that moment, standing on the Millennium Bridge, I realised that there was total helplessness in the loss of a parent or loved one. There is simply nothing you can do.

Parkinson's is a very different matter. I learned this year that it is possible to challenge its ceaseless encroachment. Perhaps one day I would beat it altogether. It is certainly conceivable that some time within the next ten years, I might be able to insert the words "used to" when I say, "I have Parkinson's."

I resumed my thoughts of Cape Wrath and smiled as I reminisced about the happy times spent with my friends, Alison and Wild Rover. In my head, I started singing the song Alison had taught me in honour of the man himself: "Well it's no, nay, never, No nay never, no more…" The words seemed appropriate as I looked back to the South Bank, to where I had walked up onto the bridge that day, to where I had finished Coastin'.

Lyndsey was there smiling at me. I wasn't sure how long she had been there, but she had not interrupted my silent reflections. God, I had been lucky to have her this year. And maybe those final two lines in the song could now also apply to me and the most incredible girl I had ever met. "…Will I play the Wild Rover, No never, no more."

She nestled up close to me. "Come on," she said gently.

The following Spring - I had no idea of the date, but I did know it was Easter Sunday – Lyndsey and I were on top of a hill just inside the border of Scotland. It felt great to be back out walking again. We agreed we should do more of this in the future. The future. What did that hold? One thing was for certain, Lyndsey would be there. I would not let her go now.

When I asked her to marry me, she said "Yes".

Later I discovered it was 11th April 2004 – by coincidence, the anniversary of the start and end of Coastin'.

## THE END

## Appendix

## Coastin' Rules and Statistics:

**RULES**

- To travel anti-clockwise around the coastline of mainland Britain keeping the sea on my right
- To walk an average of 15 miles per day
- To start and finish the walk at the Millennium Bridge in London
- To complete the challenge in precisely one year (April 11th to April 11th)
- To follow a route on 1:50,000 Ordnance Survey Maps all of which must depict the sea somewhere on them it
- To see the sea, a sea loch or tidal river estuary every day
- Estuaries could be crossed by ferry or I had to walk inland to the first available bridge
- To climb the highest peaks in Scotland, England and Wales en route
- To never forget that I was the rule-maker and could therefore change them at will – but I never did

**STATISTICS**

- Maps used – 101
- Most number of miles walked in a day – 30 miles (Tongue to Durness)
- Number of boots worn out – 10 (5 pairs)
- B & B's stayed at – 238
- Number of people who walked with me – 1032
- Favourite Place – Kearvaig, nr Cape Wrath
- Least favourite place – Dagenham
- 2280 miles walked in England, 1490 miles Scotland, 730 miles Wales
- Ate twice my own body weight in chocolate
- Longest Coaster – Wild Rover – 852 miles
- Shortest Coaster – Katie Boxall – 1 step, at one year of age
- Most friendly people – South Wales and Lincolnshire

## COASTIN' ACKNOWLEDGEMENTS

There are so many people to thank. The list could be endless. For anyone I have forgotten; I am sorry.

I have been incredibly lucky to have met so many fantastic people on both my Parkinson's journey and my journey around the coastline of Britain. Without all of your support none of this would have been possible. THANK YOU!

## FOR HELP WITH COASTIN' PROMOTION:

Adrian Teasdale, Alison and Dom, Anna ex-Orion, Anne & Judith Efford, Anne and Tony Baldwin, Atko and Whatshername, Bailey and Claire, Barbra Lewis Green, The Bayer Family, Ben de Haldevang, Big Don Cammell, Big John Mair, "Blodwyn Jones "The Countess of Cardiff", Bob Holness, Boxall Family, Brendan , Bronwyn Boyes, Callum Caldwell, Caroline and Geoff Adams-Spink, Carolyn Bayer, Cheeky and Claire, Chicken Tikka Masala, Christine and Faye at Tarlo Lyons, Claire Felton, Colin Holloway, Colin Ritchie, Coker family, Cook - Will and Kath, Cordelia Hughes, Craig and Hels, Cranny, Dan and Patti Butler, Dan Cornelius, Dave and Jackie Hart, Davey Ads and Sally Snorks, David Peck, Dazzer and Carey, David White, David Wiles, Deirdre O'Brien, Denise Moore, Dennis and Diana Silk, Diana "The Badger" and Charlie Macfarlane, Doc and Sue, Donna Leslie, Dr. Chris Steele, Dr. Jonathan Brotchie, Elizabeth Hurley, Emma and Pat Middleton, Eric Hislop, "Fi, Russell and Charlie", Frank Boundy, Gareth Andrews-Jones, Gary Plumb, Geoff Burnett, Gina and Nev, Guy Murray, Guy Cornelius, Hannah Morgan, Helen Grossman, Helene and Collin Newbury, Henry Davis, Hew and Ann Squirrel, Higgins the Butcher, The Hitchcock Family, Irene and Noel Ashton, The Isaacs Family, Jacko and Nico, Jacqui Williams, James Berlis, James Goff and Ben, James "Sammy" Samuda, James Wilson, Jane Humphreys, Janet "The Hare" Steele, Janet Morgan, Janet Oliver, Jason Mills, Jason and Hazel Purcell, Jemima Warrack, Jeremy Kelly, Jill Pollock and Geoff, Jenny Kpedekpo, Jeremy Smith, Jeremy Stokes, Jimmy Bruce, Jocky Noah and Benny, John and Elizabeth Adams, John and Lorna Kelsey, Jo d'Alton, Jonathan Clarke, Jonny Morris, Jonny Ross, Josephine Cerqua, Julie Lewendon, Karen Bird, Krazy and Sara, Laura (my nurse from Oz), Laura Bach, Lemon Goldfish and

Charlotte, Linda Beaney, Lisa Bradshaw, Liz Cornelius, Lizzie "The Sexy General" Graham, Louise and Mark, Lucy Lunt, Malcolm Grey, Maria and John Slattery, Mark Field M.P., Mark and Louise, Mark Thompson, Martin Dare, Martin Pedler, Bob and Mary Baker, Megan, Beth, Emily and Katie Boxall, Mel Ridge, Michael Hurley, Michael Palin, Michael Rose, Mike Geraint, Mike Hurley, Miles Delap, the Montgomery family, Moxy and Elaine, Mr and Mrs Leck, The Newbury Family, Nick Bonham, Nick Cook, Nick Pearce, Nora Bach, Olly Rayburn, Parker, Pat Hodgson, Paul Lund, Pete Sweet and Sue, Peter Harsant, Peter Murray, Peter Sullivan, Peter Sutton, Phil "but seriously" Collins, Phoenix and Grant, Pippa, Princess Shazzer, Prof. Peter Jenner, Rachel Haynes, Randy, Dr Ray Chaudhuri, Ray Cumbo, Rhino and Stuart, Richard Cawdron, Rob "Ruth" Stevens, Rob Sykes, Robert Freeman, Robert Meadowcroft, Rodger Broad, Ros Gallaghar, Sam Guglani, Schombie and Karen, Scott Evans, Scott Sinclair, Sian Masterton, Silky Smooth, Simon Harris, Stephan Lepakowski, Stephanie Pemberton, Steve Cram, Steve Bleakley, Steve Meridith, Steve Smith, Stevey "Massive" and Helen Redding, Sue Caulton, Sue Myatt, Susan and Desmond Film, Susan Gillies, Swabey Family, Taylor Family, Ted Appleby, The Dumphy Clan, The OMT's, The Squirrel, The Wilcox Family, Thomas and William Isaacs, Tiggy Miller, Tim Geldard, Tom "Sherpa" Willcox and the Landlady, Tony Booth (MTS) Tony and Gill Wright, Tony Harston, Tracey and Simon, Tubs and Alison, Wendels, Wild Rover.

FOR GENEROSITY OF SPIRIT ALONG THE WAY:

All the generous owners of everywhere I stayed on Coastin'.
All the seaside Parkinson's Disease Society branches (and Watford branch).
A special thank you to Vanessa "The Fixer" Lawrence, for her massive contribution to the entire journey.
Also specialthanks to Candi "Gula" Mair for typing up endless diary entries which I dictated on to tape as I walked and to Cooky, Sean, Schombie, Brian Swabey and Liz Cornelius who have not been thanked enough thus far.

Abigail Harvey, Alan and Kate Gorham, Alan Creevy, Alison and Grant Franks, Alison in Cornwall, Ann and Mark Brew, Alun Pugh M.P., Andrew George MP; Annette and Terry Lumby, Ashley Krais, Barbara Ferguson, Barbara Thompson, Barry and Sheila Salter, Basia and Bill,

Bath RFC, Bear Grylls, Bridget Oatts, Bryan Ifans, Bryn Davies, Bunty and Iain Gunn, Caroline in Applecross, Charles Holme, Chris Lines, Colin and Rick Holloway, Colin Ritchie, The Countess of Cardiff, Curly Wurly and Jason, Dai and Jeff Morgan, Dan Hammond, Dan of Burham-on-Crouch, Dave at Findhorn Boat Yard, Dave Birss and Family, David and Anna of the Hope Inn in Tollesbury, David and Vivien Culling, David Barron, David Cotton, Delyth Lloyd, Derek Martin of Malden, Donkey Donk Dean, Donna Lesley, Dr Doug McMahon, Dr. Mike Geraint, Elma MacPherson, Emlyn Jones, Eric Farr, Eric Hislop, Eric the pheasant, Ewan the stick, Finlay Kerr, Fiona Crombie, Gail Rollins, Gerry and Margaret Arscott, Gill Hollander, Gillian Thomas, Graham Harbord, Greg and Kath Surtees and Fleabag, Hamstreet School, Hugh Morgan, Hywel Williams MP, Jan and Ken Murphy, Jim Knight MP, Joan Campbell, John and Hilda Brew, Kath of Kinlochleven, Lady Rosebery, Lynn Martin, Lynne Allard, Maggie and Dennis Ross, Mairi of GJW, Malcom Bruce MP, Marion and Sandy Henderson, Mark Caudwell, Marlene of Kidwelly, Michael and Julia Brotherton, Mick and Kath of Brora, Murray the Piper, Neil and Heather Adamson, Neville Griffin, Norgine staff, Penny Hamilton, Paula and John Cox and family, Penny and Gerry of Scourie Lodge, Pete and wife of Moylgrove, Pete Darroch, Peter and Gillian Miller, Peter Sneddon, Prof. Steven Gill, Public Schools Golfing Society, Ray Chaudhuri, Ray Gravell, Ray Simpson, Rena and David Oliver, Richard and Judy Catlow, Richard and Shally Hunt, Rob Rhodes, Robert Farrell, Robert and Annette of Wick, Roddy Montgomery, Roger Howard "The King of Kent", Ron and Jean Harvey, Ron "Thane of Thanet" Jones, Ron Poole, Ron "The Boss" Cowling and Family, Russell Brown M.P., Sally and Berwyn Thomas, Sally Roberts, Scott Sinclair, Sharon Lewis (Hengoed), Sheila Harvey-George, Sheila Standen, Steve Irskine, Sue Thomas, Terry and Annette Lumby, The Astley-Cooper Family, The Butterworths, The Cammells, The Cobweb Inn, The Flemings, The Harwich International Port Control Centre, The Matthews Family, Will and Libby Duckett, Will and Nicola Cecil, Willy the Stalker, Winston the Landrover.